— TREASURES OF THE SAN JUANS SERIES —

VOLUME II

REYNOLDS'
LAST BEST CHANCE

1875-1916

*True Stories of Grit, Gumption and Gambles that
Transformed America*

BY DON BOOHER

ISBN 979-8-9934766-2-9

Second Edition
Printed in the United States

Cover and Text Design by Laurie Casselberry
Laurie Goralka Design

Cover photo: **Revenue Tunnel, ca 1889.** William Henry Jackson photo of innovative electric motor "burro' entering A.E. Reynolds' highly profitable Virginius/Revenue Tunnel. This accomplishment inspired confidence that similar results could be achieved with Reynolds' Vermont/Ocean Wave Tunnel. *(Courtesy of History Colorado, Denver)*

booherbookorders@gmail.com

VOLUME TWO

Contents

Dedication

Reynolds' Last Best Chance, *like its previously released companion* Fortress San Juans, *could not have been written without the support of my loving wife Lana. Again, thank you for your enduring patience, encouragement, and prayers throughout the research- ing and writing about ordinary people accomplishing extraordinary feats.*

Acknowledgements

In addition to recognition in endnotes and the bibliography, the following contributors to this writing warrant special attention.

Reynolds' Last Best Chance is a factual narrative focused most often on everyday men and women working their way through life as best they could. Their efforts may be extraordinary but largely unnoticed. When noticed, the local newspaper is often the only lasting source of information. Carolyn and Clarence Wright's *Tiny Hinsdale of the Silvery San Juan* is an exception to this observation. The *Lake City Silver World*, *Lake City Times*, *Lake City Phonograph* and *Tiny Hinsdale of the Silvery San Juan* are relied on repeatedly to explain the events and personalities in this book. It is safe to say that this book would lack soul without their contributions. Much gratitude is extended to Grant Houston, the current *Silver World* editor and owner, for making available his archives and vast knowledge of Henson Canyon and Lake City mining legacies. Much gratitude is also extended to the Wright family for permission to include first-hand accounts of conversations and observations only Carolyn and Clarence could provide. In their own words they make the case for why these accounts can be so insightful.

> *Because so many authors with a flair for historical sketches have gone from place to place gathering material, which many of them no doubt thought authentic, and have published articles about different parts of Colorado which are not true, we have decided to write about the true happenings in and about this area, where we, as descendants of the real pioneers, grew up. Our parents came to Lake City in covered wagons, the Wrights in the 70s and the Hunts in the 80s, as will be described in the book. We not only remember the stories they told us, but have their diaries which were written on the way here and after they arrived. We also have the scrapbooks made by both our mothers, containing clippings from the papers as far back as 1876, as well as many of the papers dating from that time.*[1]

With similar gratefulness, boundless thanks are owed P. David and Jan Smith at the Western Reflections Publishing Company. A mentor when privileged to have one is a precious gift to an author. This author was doubly gifted with the interest and counseling of P.David and Jan. In addition to excellent editing and editorial advice, their command of Colorado mining history demonstrated in the wide range of their own writings contributed greatly to the authenticity of *Reynolds' Last Best Chance*. Thank you P. David and Jan!

Similar care and willingness to ensure the narrative is geologically sound was generously provided by Harvey Duchene, a member of the Geological Society of America, the American Association of Petroleum Geologists, the Rocky Mountain Association of Geologists, a Fellow of the Explorers Club, and the National Speleological Society. Harvey is an internationally recognized scientist especially well-versed in the development of San Juans mining and local history. Thank you Harvey!

History Colorado's Stephen H. Hart Research Center archives warrants special recognition. It is another prized resource of original materials, a treasure trove of Albert Eugene (A.E.) Reynolds documents and correspondence. Research Center staff assistance in uncloaking the details of Reynolds' San Juans mining legacy was invaluable and greatly appreciated by this author.

Then there are secondary sources that earn high praise for their mastery of primary information and academic rigor. Lee Scamehorn's biography, *Albert Eugene Reynolds, Colorado's Mining King*, is an incomparable example relied on extensively when discussing Reynolds' character and accomplishments. How could it be otherwise? Not only are other sources lacking, Scamehorn's scholarship excels in every imaginable way. When discussing San Juans geology and mining history, three historical writers and a USGS Bulletin published in 1911 also rise to this standard. Ovando James Hollister published *The Mines of Colorado* in 1867. Self-taught, his treatment of geology and mining practices was equal to the best science of the day, and is still largely supported by the latest research. G. Thomas Ingham, also self-taught and a contemporary of Hollister, provides in *Digging Gold Among the Rockies* a perspective on early western mining developments rarely if ever found in twenty-first century writings. Frank Hall in his four volume *History of the State of Colorado* provides unequaled 1890 eye-witness accounts, always perceptive if not always correct. At the opposite end of the knowledge spectrum, John Duer Irving and Howland Bancroft authored *Geology and Ore Deposits Near Lake City, Colorado*, a classic USGS Bulletin explaining in exquisite scientific detail the geological context for the treasure tale you are about to read.

But perhaps the most insightful contributors deserving special praise are the *Reynolds' Last Best Chance* characters themselves. The incredible courage, sacrifices, and work ethic of the men and women you are about to meet exemplify the generation that settled the San Juans. Without them there would have been neither intriguing treasure hunts nor captivating treasure tales. What you are about to read is more about them than the treasure they sought. They and the clues they pursued explain why the Vermont/Ocean Wave lodes and Reynolds' "ace-in-the-hole" tunnel offered Reynolds' his best chance to make a mine.

Particularly revealing quotations are indented and italicized for emphasis and authenticity. No effort is made to temper their crude edges or censor their offensive tones. The objective is to better convey the culture and highlight the circumstances of those that experienced this adventure. Accompanying author comments, when there are any, are [bracketed].

One final reminder—in the interest of faithfully conveying the nature and vernacular of the era, the language of the characters in this book is preserved at the risk of offending current sensibilities. In some circles "Dago" may be a derogatory term for Italians, but in the early twentieth century it was simply one of many common ethnic slangs. It was derived from the Spanish given name "Diego," which was a very common name in Italy in the 1800s. It also had a nautical origin and referred to Spanish or Portuguese sailors on English or American ships. Its usage dates to the 1830s. Usage gradually broadened to include anyone from southern Europe before narrowing again in the 1870s to refer only to Italians.[2]

Notes—Preface

[1] Wright, Carolyn and Clarence, *Tiny Hinsdale of the Silvery San Juan*, pg. 10.

[2] Source: www.wordorigins.org/homepate.htm. By the same token, no offense is intended by use of terms as common as "White," "Red," "the boys (laborers)," "the girls (soiled doves – pejorative in its own right – of saloon fame)," and the like.

Last Best Chances

"Gold! Gold!," the magpies squawked —
magpie banter sometimes coquettish, magpie banter often mocked,
banter from the journaling class, "Pied Pipers" far from last.
"Go out, claim your fortune, gold elephants you're sure to see.
Go out, your chance for a dandy life is calling thee."

The Forty-Niner crowd was quick to act,
The Pipers declared California gold a proven fact.
"Your last best chance to see the elephant is here!"
Yes, but the paying prospects were gone when I got there.

The Pikes Peak bunch sang a similar song.
"Your last best chance for gold is near," but they were wrong.
I learned treasure was in quartz rock but no one shared where.
I learned silver was too cheap to care.
I learned I could work hard and still come up bare.
I learned Pike's elephant was hard to find
no matter what the Pipers opined.

"Ho, for the San Juans," now I hear.
"Your last best chance for gold," a Piper swears.
"Scrounge up a grubstake, Denver & Rio Grande fare,
Sanderson coaches carry you the rest of the way there.
"The San Juans are surely your last best chance,
plenty of prize elephants at this mountain dance!"

From deep within whispers a weary voice,

"stay home, you'll regret chasing this mountain whim."

Then boldly the Piper pipes in again,

"you'll miss out if you miss the San Juans dance,

mountain dances are where gold elephants abound,

trust I know where gold prospects are found."

My answer to the Piper comes as no surprise —

with my own "Ho, for the San Juans!" my spirits rise.

I'll see the gold elephant, I'll stake a gold mine,

I'll follow the steps of the lord of the dance,

I'll trust the Piper leads me to my last best chance.

Oh, why do I listen to Piper advice,

any better than trusting a roll of the dice?

I'm down to my last shot in the mine tonight,

I'm down to my last pan of beans and rice.

What if the Piper isn't right —

the magpies' gold elephant isn't in sight,

the San Juans aren't a dandy mountain dance,

this claim isn't my last best chance?

— Author —

Preface

Reynolds' Last Best Chance is a rare behind-the-scenes look at the development and workings of a San Juan mine. It also is a treasure tale with clues and maps fueling one man's vision, not of chests brimming with coins and jewels, but of mineral veins enriched with high-grade silver and maybe even gold. A.E. is that man.

A.E. considered the Vermont/Ocean Wave Group one of the most promising mining properties in southwest Colorado, properties worthy of a decades-long search for the mother-lode. Well-acquainted with the district and mining in general, he had good reason to think so. In 1899 he invested most of what was left of his once sizeable fortune and exhausted his once extensive credit-line on a daring plan. Of the scores of his 1890s projects, among the hundreds of so-called elephants in his corral of mining properties, Reynolds' strategy to turn a profit

Albert Eugene Reynolds (1840-1921). Like so many of his generation, he left home at an early age, accomplished extraordinary feats on the frontier, and wagered his last dollar on a San Juan silver mine others considered played-out. *(Frank Hall,* History of Colorado, *Vol. IV.)*

and redeem his reputation depended on successful completion of what came to be known as the Reynolds Tunnel. Patterned after his highly profitable 1888 Revenue Tunnel near Ouray, Colorado, the Reynolds Tunnel would reach 1,500 ft. into the southwestern flank of Uncompahgre Peak, accommodate ore carts, and intersect richer mineral veins and the lower, proven workings of the Vermont and adjacent Ocean Wave lodes.

But *Reynolds' Last Best Chance* is not a biography, nor is it about risky gambles or champions and villains of American industry although there are elements of both. It is in part an adventure, in part a treasure tale, and in part San Juan social commentary. It is an account of an easily underappreciated generation working an easily overlooked mine in an easily underappreciated corner of the American West. San Juan frontier challenges spawned and nurtured profound qualities of character easily discounted in the era of America's explosive territorial expansion and equally explosive industrialization. Sadly, the character of this generation is often ignored. Worse yet, what remnants remain are barely discernable today.

Undertaken in the midst of turbulent times and Reynolds' own financial troubles that would limit his ability to pursue multiple ventures, he considered the Vermont and Ocean Wave properties his best chance to "make a mine." Paydirt was elusive, but clues to its whereabouts were not. The drama entwined in this mystery is what *Reynolds' Last Best Chance* is all about. It is about the vision, character, and work ethic of men like Reynolds, and the generation of young Americans—the "boys" in mining and blue-collar jargon—that unearthed the clues and believed in the treasure. Reynolds also believed in the treasure. He never lost faith it would be found. He also never entertained the possibility that his best chance to make a mine would turn out to be his last. That diagnosis would be left to "Dr. Retrospect."

Reynolds' Last Best Chance picks up where *Fortress San Juans* left off, arguably a tale of numerous centuries-long epic treasure hunts in their own rights. In it we learned that to nineteenth-century gold-seekers the Great Plains and western mountains were formidable foes, and the San Juans Range was a fearsome natural fortress barring access to the treasures it held. Seventeen thousand square miles of remote and unyielding terrain guarded its gold and silver and kept its secrets. If the daunting wilderness did not intimidate adventurers, Native American war parties did. Even so, young America's western expansion, in large part the handi-work of a generation of courageous immigrants pursuing free Oregon home-steads and California and Colorado gold, demonstrated that strength of pioneer character could triumph over unrelenting hardship and constant threat of death. Breaching the San Juans fortress and its inner-most castle-keep (Henson Canyon by another name) would demand the same grit and determination. Mining its treasures would, too.

Not to be underestimated in these developments was the indispensable roles played by two characters central to that narrative, Ute Chief Ouray and San Juans toll road pioneer Otto Mears. Chief Ouray was friend and ally of Colorado Whites when many other Ute Chiefs and the majority of their people were their mortal enemies. Whether out of wisdom or avarice, historians argue for both, on many occasions Ouray came to the aid of emigrant and settler alike. Historian Frank Hall described him as short of stature, long on charm, a wise leader in tune with his times.

He stood about five feet seven inches high, and became quite portly in the latter years. His head was strikingly large, and well-shaped, with regular features, and bearing an expression of great dignity in repose, but lighting up pleasantly in conversation. In his ordinary bearing his manner was courtly and gentle, and he was extremely fond of meeting and conversing with cultivated white men, with whom he was a genial companion, compelling their respect and favor by the broad enlightenment of his views. In his habits he was a model; never using tobacco, abhorring whisky, and only taking a sip of wine when in company of those who were indulging, and then only as a matter of courtesy to them. He never swore nor used obscene or vulgar language, was a firm believer in the Christian religion, and about two years before his death united with the Methodist Church. His name, Ouray, or more properly U-re, was simply a pet name given by his father, and, so far as he knew, had no particular significance. [1]

Ouray along with Kit Carson averted open Ute warfare during the earliest days of White emigration and settlement in the San Luis Valley. Kaneache, Chief of the Muache Utes, initiated hostilities on the Rio Las Animas that prompted a U.S. Army counter attack. Kaneache sought Ouray's help in making war on the Whites. Rebuffing the invitation, Ouray seized Kaneache's runner and sent out loyal messengers to warn the Whites on the Huerfano of the impending attack. Hall salutes the Chief by using this example...

... to illustrate the sterling honesty and the general character of this remarkable chief, the statesman of his nation,

Friends and Partners. Two decades of working with one another for peace and prosperity, Chief Ouray and Otto Mears account in large measure for the rapid settlement of the San Juans. A robust mining industry benefiting from a robust toll road and rail network was a notable feature of their legacy. *(Courtesy of P. David Smith)*

and the only man worthy of that high distinction in the history of that people. Though a warrior of renown, brave to rashness in battle against the natural enemy, he comprehended that the Caucasian had come to stay and to over-spread the land; that resistance would be useless, and only result in the exter-mination of the red men.

The nature of the Ute is much like that of the wild Apache – bloodthirsty and cruel. There have been many occasions when the strong, restraining hand of Ouray has prevented his people from taking the war path in force against the isolated settlers in the mountain regions. In looking back over the past it is a matter for wonder that we escaped with so few murders, depredations and outbreaks, when the causes and opportunities were so numerous. [2]

As for Otto Mears, his friendship with Ouray began early in his deal-ings in Colorado as a trader, and was a critical factor in his ability to underwrite toll roads through Ute lands. Well versed in Ute culture and fluent in the Ute language, he became a U.S. Army translator as well as trusted broker of the 1873 Brunot Agreement.[3] With the Brunot Agreement as a framework for peaceful Ute—White coexistence, and Chief Ouray more or less firmly in control of his people, overcoming the last barrier to an unrestrained assault on Fortress San Juans was at hand. The time for Otto Mears and his network of strategic San Juans toll roads to take their place in history had arrived.

The term "fortress" is a fitting description of the southwest quadrant of Colorado. The San Juans are bordered on all compass-points by towering rock walls and moat-like river canyons. It spans sixty to one hundred miles from the San Luis Valley west to Utah, and as much as one hundred to one hundred and fifty miles from New Mexico north to central Colorado's Uncompahgre Plateau. Headwaters of major western watersheds tumble from its flanks, but none defeat its maze. They flow their separate ways to the Mississippi River, to the Gulf of Mexico, to the Sea of Cortez, and the Pacific. But retracing their courses does not open routes into the inner courts—retracing their courses leads to their headwaters seeping weakly from the flanks of their respective maze walls. Even broad-mouthed canyons carved out of the range by ancestral glaciers all too soon pinch out or turn back upon their own contorted spines.

There are outer defenses, as well. The Rocky Mountain Front Range effec-tively blunts assaults from the eastern Great Plains, seven hundred miles of arid defenses in its own right. Guarding approaches from the south and southwest are the thousand-foot-deep V-shaped, sheer-walled canyons with "entrenched meanders" of the Animas, San Miguel, and Dolores Rivers. Farther northwest Escalante and Dominquez Canyons, equally foreboding, shepherd the moat-like Uncompahgre and Gunnison Rivers to the Colorado River. Its youthful can-yons above and below present-day Grand Junction effectively bar access from the northwest and north. East of its confluence with the Uncompahgre, the northern flank is further protected. The Gunnison roars from its headwaters along the Continental Divide through the 3,000 ft. deep Black Canyon of the Gunnison to Delta, Colorado, completing the Fortress San Juans moat. Ancient trails that do exist offer little relief on any flank, fewer still suitable for a horse and none for a wagon.

Fortresses built by human hands have castle-keeps and gates, prominent and boldly constructed, foreboding even to the invited guest. The San Juan fortress is no exception save for the fact that its castle-keep is a canyon and its gates are passes. Finding what looked like a breach in a San Juan rampart was an occasion of great joy for early Spanish expeditions. "What discoveries must lie on the far side?" they surely wondered. Yet, navigating one breach usually gave way to frustration over the need to ferret out still another breach. The San Juans is a textbook example of defense in depth. Beyond one ridgeline, one range, one bench rises another and another. More ramparts, more snow-capped pickets, more promise of alluring discoveries, but never enough time and never enough provisions to reach the inner courtyards. Had there been more evidence of treasure, or more

TREASURE TALE – THE FIRST CLUE

Like all great adventures, the first clue that there was a Vermont/Ocean Wave treasure tale to tell came to the author unexpectedly. Shortly after acquiring the long-abandoned Vermont claim with the intent of preserving what remained of its weathered miner's cabin, a gift of Lee Scamehorn's biography of Reynolds surfaced. Surprisingly, Reynolds was a notable Colorado entrepreneur and early owner of the Vermont/Ocean Wave Group.

Not surprisingly, Scamehorn's account of Reynolds' life, times, and Vermont/Ocean Wave hunt for high-grade silver ore was captivating. Local newspaper accounts added to the mystique. They also added perspective to the preservation mission—in fact, they nearly replaced it. Scamehorn's narrative and footnotes led to more clues. Reynolds was a meticulous notetaker and record keeper who required his miners to do the same. Much of their correspondence and many reports were faithfully catalogued in Denver's *History Colorado* archives. One look at the *Reynolds Collection* archived there and curiosity about one mining entrepreneur's vision for one of his hundreds of Colorado mines grew into a near-obsession. Learning more about him and especially the heart and soul of "the boys" that worked the mine, their families, their community, and what motivated their labors, became a priority. *Fortress San Juans* became a necessary prequel. Reynolds' last best chance to unearth a treasure became a treasure tale.

days in mild seasons, there may have been more Spanish pluck. Sufficient "pluck" came two centuries later with a few French and English but mostly American mountain men, motivated not by gold but by beaver.

In *Reynolds' Last Best Chance*, we learn that developing the mineral wealth of the San Juans and unearthing the treasure of the Vermont and Ocean Wave lodes would be no less demanding. In the spring of 1875, Henson Canyon arguably was the last vestige of the eastern San Juan region's nearly impregnable wilderness. It was a tortuous watershed rendered nearly impassable by marshes, fallen timber, and avalanche debris. Descending 4,139 vertical feet over nineteen miles from present-day Engineer Pass to present-day Lake City, it was about to become the epicenter of Colorado's San Juans hullabaloo. While this last bastion of the mountain fortress would produce scores of "last chance" mines promising hand-some returns, more often it would send a beggar home. In every instance a mine was a treasure hunt and every hunt had a tale.

Together, *Reynolds' Last Best Chance* and *Fortress San Juans* serve a common purpose. The objective of both is to unmask a kaleidoscope of events and person-alities that help explain how one of the most expansionary periods in American history led to one of the most speculative San Juans mining ventures by one of Colorado's most resourceful nineteenth-century entrepreneurs. The Vermont/Ocean Wave Group was among a handful of the earliest and most productive mining properties in Henson Canyon, but because of a variety of ownership and management issues it had a jaded history. Reynolds saw past that history. His confidence—his "ace-in-the-hole"—was grounded in replicating his successful Revenue Tunnel in nearby Ouray County. Oddly enough, the "stay-behinds" of nearby Lake City, self-proclaimed "Queen of the San Juans" in the depths of a deep recession, no longer blessed with boomtown stature by the 1890s, were con-fident it was their ace-in-the-hole, too.

Notes—Preface

[1] Hall, Frank, *History of the State of Colorado*, Vol. II, pg. 510.

[2] Ibid., pgs. 510-512.

[3] The commonly named "1873 Brunot Treaty" was not a treaty, but rather an "agreement" whereby the Nuche (Ute) would cede mountain lands suitable for mining in exchange for hunting rights and stipends. Treaties were between sovereign nations—by 1871 Native Americans were not considered sovereign. Moreover, a Ute delegation led by Chief Ouray carried the agreement to Washington, D.C. in October 1873, but Congress did not approve it until April 24, 1874. (*Colorado Encyclopedia*)

CHAPTER 1

Treasure Tale

There comes a time in every rightly constructed
boy's life when he has a raging desire to go
somewhere and dig for hidden treasure.
— Mark Twain —
The Adventures of Tom Sawyer

The boys were reassured there was treasure ahead,
but which clue should they follow?
— John E. York —
Reynolds Tunnel

Unlike Reynolds who was well-versed in all matters pertaining to mining, the earliest Henson Canyon prospectors and miners had some practical knowledge of geology but little patience for understanding the science supporting it. That did not seem to matter. When it came to locating promising ore deposits, the prospector's attention was fixed on outcrops and staking his claim before someone else did. Motivated more by the hunt than working a mine, the claim was usually sold as soon as he could locate a usually gullible buyer. Miners and investors, on the other hand, more inclined to study the matter, nevertheless relied on past performance rather than scientific speculation. Instinct or ignorance was more to their liking. Miners pursued veins when they were visible or hunches when they were not. Deeper appreciation for the nature of the dirt [1] they were burrowing into—development work required to reach mineral-rich ground—might also have proven wise. To Reynolds' credit, his success summarized by Lee Scamehorn in labeling him a mining king was the product of a self-taught understanding of geology, the experience of trusted men who actually worked in mines and knew "all dirt was not created equal," his own experience gleaned over decades of hands-on involvement in his mining ventures, and his courageous investment in new technology and innovative approaches to vexing problems. From humble beginnings such as these often spring epic treasure tales.

It is fair to say that A.E. earned his place among Colorado's mining industry icons with the Virginius Mine. Reynolds and a partner purchased the Virginius in 1880 for the kingly sum of $100,000. The Virginius is located about eight miles west of Ouray at over 12,000 ft. in Governor Basin. Nearly impossible to reach once winter weather set in, and inspired by the profitable Sutro Tunnel near Virginia City, Nevada, Reynolds commissioned the Revenue Tunnel in 1888. He also replaced steam power with direct current electricity, illustrated by the "electric mule" about to enter the mine, built a state-of-the-art mill at the mine's mouth, and improved roads between the mill and the nearest railroad in Ouray. The 7,741 foot tunnel, designed to drain upper levels of the Virginius [and adjacent mines] and remove ore 2,000 ft. below the upper workings where snow was less of an issue, was completed in 1893.

The Virginius/Revenue Tunnel generated $300,000 in profit each of the next eight years. By the time the mill burned and mining was suspended in the 1920s, the "Reynolds' calculated risk" had produced over $28 million in silver and gold. The mine is still worked off and on today. [2]

Reynolds' Revenue Tunnel, ca 1889. Innovative use of an electric motor "burro" or "mule" contributed greatly to Virginius/Revenue Tunnel profitability. This legacy inspired confidence that similar results could be achieved with the Reynolds/Vermont Tunnel. *(Courtesy of History Colorado, Denver)*

Although other self-taught *Reynolds' Last Best Chance* characters stand on far different rungs of the social ladder, they play enlightening roles in our treasure tale just the same. A drover working for his next meal by the name of Pike Snowden and a young camp cook on a western lark by the name of W.F.E. Gurley exemplify the ironies and insights provided by their contributions to Henson Canyon culture. As different as men could be, neither of them similar to Reynolds in any meaningful way, Snowden and Gurley became lifelong friends. Snowden lived his life in Henson Canyon and became a mine owner, recluse, and colorful local sage. Gurley returned East to academic pursuits and became an internationally recognized scientist and curator of the University of Chicago's Walker Museum . Snowden claimed and worked the mine Reynolds bought and would develop for two decades through his Vermont/Ocean Wave tunnel. Gurley preserved in his writings the frontier virtues of Snowden in insightful remembrances that enrich us to this day.

Honored by biographer Lee Scamehorn as "Colorado's Mining King," [3] by any name Albert Eugene Reynolds was an ambitious mining magnate well-versed and shrewd when it came to the risks and rewards of treasure hunts. But

ROBBER BARONS

America's post-Civil War industrial revolution had a dark side and its champions were easy prey for public scorn. "Robber Baron" described extraordinarily successful entrepreneurs as unsavory and usually predatory capitalists. Monopolistic practices in order to set and maintain exorbitant prices for goods and services was their stock in trade. Common techniques were acquiring or exerting control over natural resources, corrupting governments, buying out or undermining competitors, and manipulating stock values with the goal of defrauding investors. The *New York Times* first used "Robber Baron" to taint the 1859 business practices of Cornelius Vanderbilt. Quite likely misapplied for political purposes, at best it simplified complex circumstances and even was in some respects true. The term stuck and quickly became fashionable journalism.

In Vanderbilt's case, his shipping enterprise demonstrated that companies hired by political cronies *and* subsidized by tax revenues and enabled to charge high prices could be forced out of business by less-costly competition. Honest competitors needed neither exorbitant prices nor tax subsidies to turn a handsome profit. Rather than praise, Vanderbilt was accused of predatory practices. Countless other nineteenth and early twentieth-century industrialists earned the same treatment. By virtue of his vast mine holdings, A.E. Reynolds fit the "robber baron profile." By virtue of his character, he never had to bear that shame. His great debt rather than great wealth may also have spared him that honor. [4]

he was not ruthless. Yes, his life-long mantra was "buy low, sell high," and "tend to your knitting," but he was not predatory. Despite ranking among men of great wealth and accomplishment—the Vermont/Ocean Wave Group but one 1899 project among his thousands of holdings—he was no robber baron. Nor was he considered one, at least publicly. The likes of John Rockefeller, Andrew Carnegie, Leland Stanford, J.P. Morgan, Henry Ford and Cornelius Vanderbilt, legendary men who epitomized the generation that accounted in many ways for America's industrialization, were not as blessed. Yes, Reynolds swam in the same sea, acquired his fair share of eastern capital from the same deep wells of America's abundance when needed, and commanded a vast network of mining properties that contributed handsomely to Colorado's and the nation's prosperity. But, he escaped being painted by the same caustic brush. Why? Partly because the extent of his holdings was not apparent. He prized his privacy, enhanced considerably by his mountain-West home and his utter disdain for news editors looking for sensationalism. He also did not deserve the scorn. His character belied "robber status," and truth be told, his 1900s net worth after accounting for his debts was more in keeping with a pauper than a baron.

Robber Barons: Common in late nineteenth- and early twentieth-century characterizations of highly successful entrepreneurs, A.E. Reynolds was never considered a member of this maligned club. For good reason. While biographer Scamehorn viewed his mine holdings as kingly, his decades of fair-dealings and philanthropy testified to a life honorably lived. *(Wikipedia)*

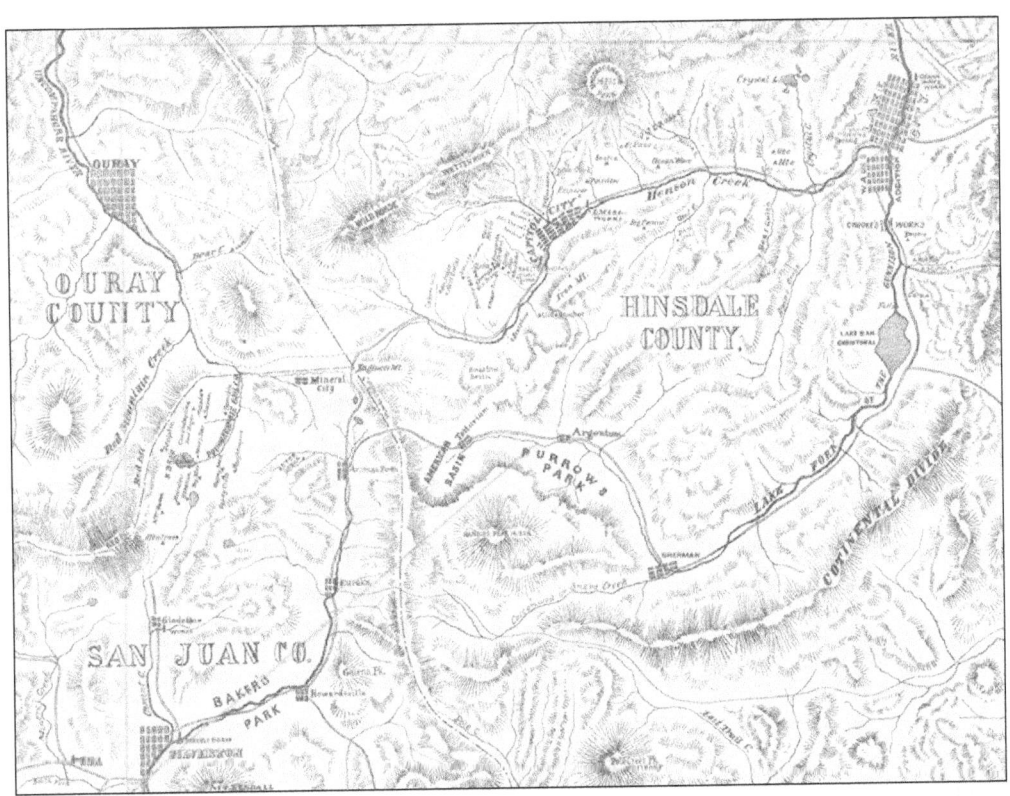

Lake City Region. One of the richer segments of the Colorado mineral belt. Henson Canyon's El Paso Gulch is the epicenter of Reynolds' treasure tale. *(Courtesy of History Colorado-Denver)*

The Vermont/Ocean Wave treasure hunt begins long before Reynolds Tunnel with a vanguard of dreamers huddled around campfires at the mouth of a remote San Juans canyon—Henson Canyon, *Fortress San Juans'* castle-keep. They are America's ragged survivors of the mass migrations, prior treasure hunts, and civil and Native American wars dating back to the 1840s. Unknowingly of course, much less caring, they will lead the 1875 San Juans goldrush, soon to be silver rush. Their assault has been long and painful in coming. The last great gate, Engineer Pass, seemingly the most direct route to the Henson Canyon treasure trove, has been outflanked by Otto Mears' more circuitous but wagon-worthy toll roads that bypass the canyon but not Lake City. [5] The confluence of Henson Creek with the Lake Fork of the Gunnison River, an ideal site for a rest stop, is also an ideal site for a mining camp soon to be a boomtown.

The "San Juans excitement" including Reynolds' hallmark Revenue Tunnel, ebbed and flowed more than once throughout the waning years of the nineteenth century and the early 1900s. [6] So too would the fortunes of the Vermont/Ocean Wave Group. No less raucous when silver discoveries were more common than gold, in the region and in the Vermont and Ocean Wave workings for sure, development would continue despite fleeting successes. Failure for one risk-taker

LAST CHANCE MINES
[AND JUST ABOUT ANYTHING ELSE]

"Last Chance" was a common mine name reflecting frustration over prior failures and recognition that resources were about at an end. (It also was a popular name for saloons, livery stables, general stores, and anything else that struck the owners' fancy and was located at the edge of town.) In A.E.'s case, the Vermont/Ocean Wave project held the greatest promise of all the mines he was developing in the 1890s. He never considered it a "last chance." By gambling standards, his odds for success, always high in the eyes of promoters and the naïve which he was neither, nevertheless seemed high to A.E. He had won and lost fortunes on scores of western mines. The Vermont and Ocean Wave mining properties, improved with a haulage tunnel, in his judgment was his best chance at the time. In hindsight, whether it was his "best" chance can be debated, but without a doubt the untimely arrival of the death angel ensured it was his "last."

would look like an opportunity for another, a bargain "you betcha." No matter. The *Lake City Silver World* would be a faithful booster of good times, and no less adamantly in the worst of times than in the best of times. Would not the arrival of rail service be proof enough that the "Queen of the San Juans" would survive? Would not an idle Vermont or Ocean Wave be tempting enough to pique the interest and attract the investment of a bargain-savvy contrarian like A.E. Reynolds? Would not evidence of rich silver reserves be reason enough for another generation to hunt for more? Would not the trials and tribulations of their hunt make for an engaging treasure tale?

Notes—Chapter One: Treasure Tale

1 "Dirt" was commonly used to describe even solid rock that was considered mine waste. Any material that stood in the way of accessing ore-bearing veins was "dirt." "Muck" that had to be removed from underground workings after blasting was "dirt." Development work, meaning work that was not expected to unearth veins, produced "dirt."

2 Paulson, Don, Ouray County Historical Society Curator, Ouray County *Plaindealer*, February 22, 2013.

3 Scamehorn, Lee, *Albert Eugene Reynolds, Colorado's Mining King*. [Scamehorn's comprehensive treatment of Reynolds' accomplishments and shortcomings is thoroughly documented and a fascinating read. Also see abundant primary sources archived in the History Colorado Library *Reynolds Collection*.]

4 *The New York Times*, February 9, 1859, "Robber Baron (Industrialist)," Wikipedia.

5 Usually referred to as "Otto Mears toll roads," it is important to note that he was responsible for them not as constructor or even superintendent of construction crews, but rather as promoter

and organizer of investors. He was not a wealthy man other than in his ability to attract those who were.

6   Reynolds' mine properties near Ouray and Creede, Colorado, namely the Virginius/Revenue Tunnel and the Commodore, generated sufficient profits to fund his share of other ventures including the Vermont/Ocean Wave tunnel into the early 1900s. Eventually all of his mining ventures felt the effects of the ups and downs of the silver market, including the transition to the gold-standard. [A secondary consequence of the 1899 "Silver Panic" was a more determined search for gold prospects.] The consequence for the Vermont/Ocean Wave project was often suspension of work, late-payments to the workforce, and reassignment of key personnel to and from whichever mine was in the greatest need of supplies or posed the greatest risk of a walkout. That said, like Otto Mears, A.E. was adept at securing other peoples' money.

CHAPTER 2

The Hunt Begins

(March 1875, Base Camp, Mouth of Henson Canyon) The twenty-seven men that winter over do so with little more than their treasure dreams and what their pack animals could carry. The pilgrims include "… myself, father and brother; a few at the Hotchkiss Mine … Pike Snowden and partner up Henson Creek a ways…."

— Eugene Barthoff, 1931. [1]

(Spring 1876, Mile 7, Henson Canyon) I worked, as a miner, on one of the shifts at the Big Casino mine. In going to this job—with the mine superintendent—I plodded along the old Henson Creek trail which was primitive and very tedious owing to the considerable depth of snow, as well as the slides. At that time, due to the zig-zagging of the creek through the walls of the canon, there were sixteen bars and as many footlogs on the trail in the first mile and a half above Lake city.

—W.F.E. Gurley, 1921. [2]

Twenty-seven pilgrims grew into hundreds and then thousands over the course of a year. Prudently bypassed for centuries, brutally rugged Henson Canyon was an ideal natural castle-keep in an ideal natural mountain fortress.[3] Spanish Conquistadors turned back at the outer fortress gates. Fearsome Ute commanded the interior courts, watersheds, and the maze of gulches and canyons that confounded every approach. All that came to an end before the winter 1875 set in. The prospect of gold again emboldened treasure-seekers. The difference this time around—the previous "time-around" being the Pikes Peak or Bust crowd and their 1860-61 overflow into the High Country—the treasure-seekers had some inkling of the southwesterly reach and richness of the Colorado Mineral Belt. More importantly, they could travel most of the way there by railcar, wagon, or coach. More important than that, by the following spring enough provisions would be freighted into booming Lake City—swelling storerooms like a spring tick swells on a fresh host—to keep miners well fed and hard at work wherever a promising quartz outcrop could be found.

The geopolitical and physical barriers separating young America from Henson Canyon treasure had fallen like dominoes, at first slowly but surely in the end. The first dominoes were the most powerful foreign nations on Earth—France, Spain, Britain, and Russia—the superpowers of their day who vied for "Polk's Prize," the western half of what became a two-ocean United States of America. Ally to foreign nations, the wrongly labeled "Great American Desert" took its turn at fending off determined masses from the States seeking boundless fertile lands and promised gold. The "Great Desert" often exacted a painful toll on all who challenged it but did not stem the flow. Ancestral tribes bullied and corralled, harassed, and warred to no avail; but it was no laughing matter to be sure. Even young America at war with itself could only delay a final assault. An industrializing America required the metals abundant in the western mountains, no different than the struggling 1850s American economy required California gold to grow out of a prolonged recession. Aided by immigrant labor and a transcontinental railroad, 1870s opportunists and town-builders found their way to the San Juans.

Mouth of Henson Canyon. Inviting at first glance save for heavy undergrowth, within a mile the canyon narrows and the grade steepens. Henson Creek snakes back and forth across what little canyon floor exists, always turbulent, a raging torrent during spring runoffs. Any trail of any consequence must work its way through gaps in sheer canyon walls to benches and ridgelines less encumbered with centuries of tree-fall. Foot-traffic struggled in the best of conditions, pack-animals even more so, wagons not at all. *(Author's collection)*

The treasure troves securely nestled within the San Juans fortress, uncompromised for centuries, began to fall to restless settlers and prospectors in 1868. Somewhat threatened in earlier times—sovereignty eroded by fragile accommodations whereby the Ute ceded dominance of the High Country but not their valleys—capitulation was assured in the wake of the 1873 Brunot Agreement [4] that opened the southern leg of Colorado's mineral belt and Henson Canyon to exploration. A year later, prospectors overran the castle-keep. The last Ute overlords of the last mountain bastion stood down. At last, treasure only limited by imagination could be unearthed with impunity. All that had stood in the way of a full-throttled assault on the upper Lake Fork of the Gunnison watershed was lack of one good reason to build a wagon-worthy road and supply depot to its doorstep.

Otto Mears' idea of "a good reason" did not take long to mature. Noting the mercantile traffic derived from Animas River Valley silver mines accessed from the south by a tortuous route, Mears the promoter of roads had a better idea.

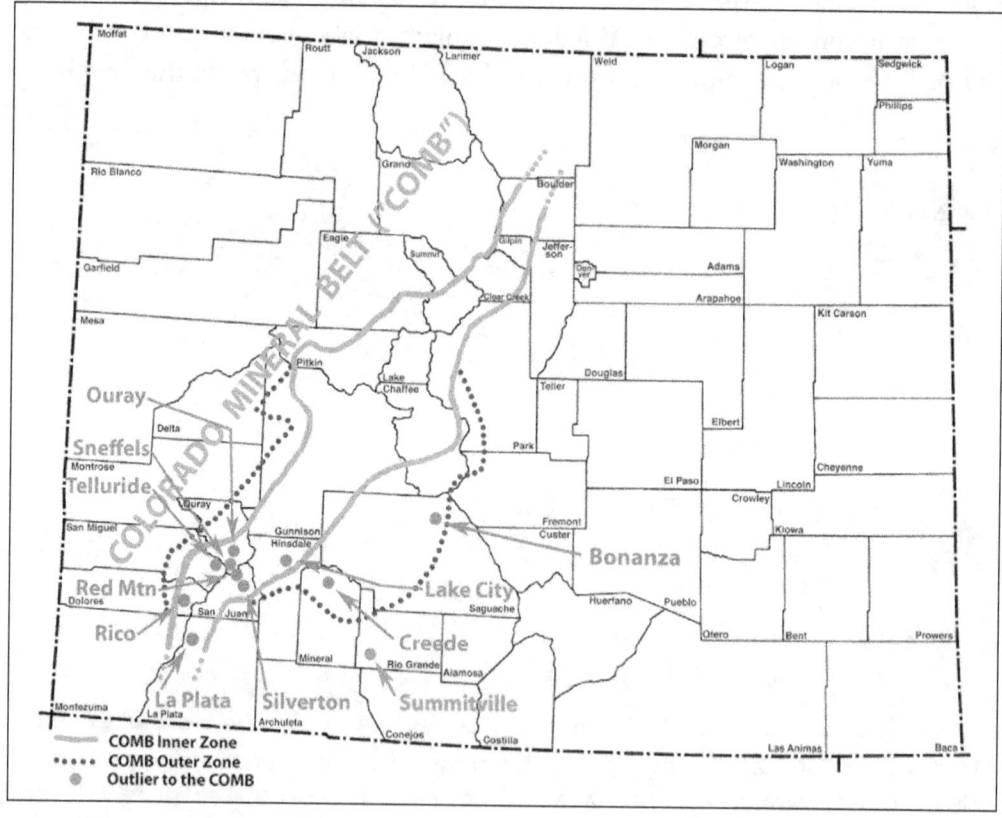

Colorado Mineral Belt. By the end of the 1870s gold and silver deposits throughout the state convincingly confirmed what geologists of the day were discussing. Lake City's Henson Canyon watershed was squarely and wonderfully situated to produce ores of great value. *(Courtesy of Colorado School of Mines Museum of Earth Science, Golden, Colorado)*

With Enos Hotchkiss as trusted road superintendent in charge of the day-to-day operations and other people's money, Mears organized and oversaw not only a better engineered road from the northeast, he also helped establish the town of Saguache to better support it. As for Hotchkiss—who happened to be a veteran of the California gold rush—he knew a thing or two about treasure hunts. In the process of building Mears' road, a toll road of course, from Saguache to the Lake Fork of the Gunnison Valley, he filed a claim on gold discovered along the way. Whether he was the first to spot it, or one of his laborers did as some believe, it matters little. Hotchkiss owned the claim and a very valuable gold mine bore his name. More consequential, seemingly overnight the discovery converted a toll road work camp into Lake City, the requisite supply depot needed to exploit Henson Canyon and the Lake Fork of the Gunnison watersheds. In terms of logistics, it is fair to say that Otto Mears was pivotal in providing the means by which both Henson Canyon and Upper Lake Fork development could avoid Engineer Pass and Cinnamon Pass respectively. Rather than accessing the canyons from the rugged headwaters of Henson Creek and the Upper Lake Fork, far better to access them from the relative comforts of soon-to-be Lake City.[5]

In addition to roadbuilding and establishing trading outposts, Mears' business interests also contributed to the development of Henson Canyon and the Upper Lake Fork by accounting for a large percentage of the commercial activities of both Saguache and Lake City. Helen M. Searcy writes in *Pioneers of the San Juans Country*, "southwestern Colorado owed its development more to Otto Mears' pioneering spirit than to any other man. No history of the State could be written without him as one of the chief actors on the stage of the pioneer and creative period."[6] Perhaps somewhat exaggerated, perhaps not, most will agree Otto Mears' contributions to San Juan development were timely and profound.

Saguache or "Swatch" when Mears spoke of it, was reason enough for this accolade. Lake City embellished the honor. He envisioned "Swatch" as a location where he could create an unrivaled supply depot for growing markets in all directions. Tending westward to the top of Cochetopa Pass was a gulch and ancestral Ute trail soon to become the route of his toll road into the heart of the San Juans. (Mears also built a toll road to Gunnison, later the beginning of the D&RG railroad right-of-way over Marshall Pass.) Considering Ute sensitivities, Saguache was relatively secure. Pressing west into the sacred Ute homeland on Ute ancestral trails was another matter.

Mears foresaw a thriving Saguache where others saw only sagebrush. It was strategically located to supply expanding markets in the upper Animas River Valley provided a road or two was constructed. Rather than the longer and difficult route up the Rio Grande and over Stony Pass, Mears imagined a shorter and less difficult wagon-worthy route along the base of the range, then teased west from Saguache over Los Pinos Pass or Cochetopa Pass, up the Lake Fork of the Gunnison River Valley, and over Cinnamon Pass to newly founded Silverton

Otto Mears (1840-1931). Mears epitomized American exceptionalism. If A.E. Reynolds could be considered a mining king, Otto surely qualified as a toll-road king. *(Wikipedia)*

and other mining camps in Baker's Park. This route had never impressed army surveyors as suitable for wheeled traffic. Mears thought otherwise.

With sufficient capital—someone else's money, of course—and labor, vision, and determination, constructing a toll road was Mears' solution. Just to be sure, he hedged his bet by also investing in developing Saguache, not simply as the eastern terminus of his Saguache and San Juans Toll Road, but also as a self-supporting way station between established New Mexico settlements, bustling Denver, and points east. If he did not succeed in monopolizing business in Saguache and San Juans camps, he would monopolize the best way of getting to them. Mears' concept of development and monopoly was a well-stocked general store; a flour mill; a sawmill; a wheat, oats and potato farm; a cattle ranch; pack trains to and from Denver; and part-interest in a freighting business whenever and wherever wagon-worthy roads led. Where a wagon-worthy road did not lead, Otto was inclined to invest in or construct one and often did. He also knew the value of a supportive local newspaper which he invested in both in Lake City and Saguache. [7]

Early in the development of the San Juans, the presence of Ute was threatening and at times deadly, but the absence of wagon-worthy roads was even more debilitating. Hoofed animal and Ute trails were passable for trappers and traders, but emigrants and miners needed coaches and wagons to keep up with the demand for provisions and equipment. Constructing such roads with little more than picks, shovels, and black powder was low on anyone's priority list. Citizens and city fathers both thought it best to exhaust scarce resources by clawing silver and gold out of the mountains. For what could pass as a wagon road, it seemed that mountain trails needing grading and roiling streams requiring bridges was too great a challenge. Mears thought otherwise on all counts. Where there was a need, there had to be a way. Where there was a way, there had to be money to be made.

Rugged mountains, high passes, wicked gulches, and marsh-burdened drainages demanded investments that only private entrepreneurs could provide. Private investment meant tolls sufficient to recoup costs and compensate for risks. Successful toll road investors were rare. Those who did succeed were generally both shrewd engineers and even shrewder managers of other peoples' money. While not fitting the profile of the "robber baron class" of the day, they earned the same despised reputation. Mears was similarly dishonored. Afterall, to many it did not seem quite right that the back-breaking work it took to mine treasure should be graciously surrendered to a listless attendant at a toll gate or country store.

Compared to surviving on the lawless streets of San Francisco, how daunting a task would building toll roads in Colorado seem to Otto Mears? While the risks were high, so were the prospects of handsome profits. Mining camps and new districts offered bountiful opportunities for merchandising provided there was a way to deliver the goods. The days of hearty traders with backpacks

---

CAPITALIST MEARS

Otto Mears was an unapologetic capitalist. When it came to mercantilism and toll roads, he was unfazed by the level of difficulty, the risk to body and soul, or the cost. In the twentieth century only "Big Government" had the funds—tax dollars—required to build infrastructure. In the nineteenth century, governments were small and often infrastructure was funded by entrepreneurs. Taxes—a tool of the devil—was not an option. Monopolies were viewed similarly, but Mears did not have a problem with the concept of monopolies as long as they were his, nor with criticism that he unscrupulously profited from them.

Mears was orphaned in Kurland (present-day Latvia) at age three. At age nine relatives unable to care for him any longer, shipped him to other relatives in England. Given the grit he exhibited later in life, he may have run away instead. From England, Otto or his relatives somehow found him a way to sail to New York City, where he stayed a year with another relative. In 1851, he was off again to yet another relative in California. This leg of his journey involved another long sea voyage to the Isthmus of Panama, a dugout canoe and horseback ride to the Pacific coast, and another ship to San Francisco. All this adventure by the age of eleven showed every sign of fierce independent, confident, and courageous character. When President Lincoln responded with force to Southern secession, Mears volunteered for service in the Union's western army. In August 1864 he was discharged in Las Cruces, New Mexico, worked odd jobs as he walked to Santa Fe, and went to work managing a clothing shop owned by Elsberg and Amberg. From there he partnered with the Staab brothers and opened a general mercantile in his own name (Mears and Company). In 1865 he relocated his business to Conejos where he went into partnership with Lafayette Head to build a sawmill and grist mill. His business savvy would soon lead him to Saguache and his first toll road.[8]

Toll Gate. What point was there in building a toll road if there was no bottleneck ensuring collection of the toll. The route between Ouray and Silverton was narrow, nearly impassable where Otto made a way for wagons, his toll house, and gate. (*Wikipedia*)

and travois trekking along narrow trails were over. The quantity of provisions, explosives, equipment, and all manner of building materials was too great. Wagons and carriages—railroads as soon as possible—were imperatives. Otto Mears was quick to see a need he could satisfy. He stitched together toll roads and boomtowns, in part financed with his own considerable resources gleaned from his other endeavors, in part with finances from others. Eva (E.F.) Tucker explains:

> It was easy enough to incorporate a toll road company. As Mears himself said, all that a man needed for the right to construct and operate a toll road was to acquire a charter for a five-dollar fee. In the early days, this required a trip to Denver, but later on one could get such a charter from the county. This document awarded the right to operate the road as a toll road for twenty years. No map, layout, or engineering design was needed—a simple statement of the beginning and ending points and perhaps some indication of the general route were the only requirements. [9]

Otto's toll roads were not only the gold-standards of engineering and financial success, they also were an absolute necessity for facilitating High Country hard rock mining and establishing mining camps and settlements capable of supporting them. Before wagon roads, Tucker continues:

...all goods both into and out of an area would have to be hauled by pack trains of burros or mules. In mining areas even the ore would have to be packed out on animals. Before roads were "improved" there was some wagon travel, but it was slow, laborious, and often risky. For example, in a report to the governor, Otto Mears said that the fifty-five miles of mountain trail to the Indian Agency at Los Pinos sometimes took ox-drawn wagons as much as eleven days to make the trip.[10]

As for trails wholly unsuitable for wagons, it was even more obvious to even the dullest trader or miner that survival required a better solution than increasing the size or number of teams.

A mule could carry 250 pounds upgrade and 350 down, whereas the most a burro could manage to carry was an average of 200 pounds. However, a mule had to be fed, but a burro could eke out sustenance on the scraggly grass of the mountain slopes. Mules were irascible and notoriously difficult to control, and they had to be led. Of course the "mule skinner" could ride the lead mule, but burros could only be driven. Burros learned to go in single file only when the trail was too narrow to accommodate them as a herd. When a fork in the road appeared, dogs had to be trained to nip the burros on the side of the wrong trail, turning them toward the desired direction. Burros also did not have to be shod. Horses were used, of course, but they did not have the surety of footing of either mules or burros, essential in these mountains, and horses had thinner skin, making them less useful in packing.[11]

Despite their limitations, wagons never completely replaced pack animals—burros and mules in particular. Underground or on trails between precarious mine portals and passable wagon roads, they served dutifully well into the early 1900s. In these circumstances, the only threats to their full employment were the miners themselves, the occasional tramway built when mineral values justified such an investment, and trucks. Yes, *trucks.* Early in the twentieth-century motorized vehicles accounted for profound societal changes including Western mining.[12]

That said, nineteenth-century wagons made the difference between a paying mine and one that was not. High-grade ore in canvas (burlap if canvas was unavailable or unaffordable) sacks astride burros or mules covered early development costs, but lower grade ores were more common in Henson Canyon mines and required extensive development. Low-grade ores also needed more processing and greater volumes that in turn required more robust wagons and hopefully railroads. Reynolds' San Juan mines needed wagons to get their ores to market— wagons needed wagon-worthy roads that Otto Mears profitably built. Difficult to reach mines needed burros to get ore to the wagons.

The Poncha Pass Wagon Road was Mears' first toll road and ensured the prosperity of both the town of Saguache and himself. In 1870, he constructed this well-designed road between the San Luis and Arkansas River Valleys that linked Denver by way of Saguache to the upper Rio Grande River Valley. Practically speaking, Denver and Santa Fe became sister cities, albeit by way of a bone-jarring 360-mile route. Mears first transportation venture confirmed the worth of his toll road vision and inspired him to tackle routes that were even more ambitious.

Foreseeing a rush of adventurers and camp followers into the heart of the San Juans, Mears signed on Enos Hotchkiss as construction superintendent. In 1874, Hotchkiss began the Saguache and San Juans Toll Road. Anticipating increasing prospector and settler interest in joining their braver brethren farther west in the upper Animas and Uncompahgre River Valleys where new mines were being located, Mears acted. Sensitive to the effects of rushes, including California and the Colorado Front Range, he knew that the slightest "eureka" quickly triggered an avalanche of newcomers that would mean quick dividends for a toll road. Of course, he had no idea road construction would sometimes unearth gold along the way. Through no foresight of their own, some individuals are blessed abundantly despite themselves.

Hotchkiss roadbuilders barely outpaced the rush into the upper Lake Fork of the Gunnison Valley, and Mears did not rest on their accomplishments. Ever wary of his Del Norte competitors, Mears challenged them further by constructing the Antelope Park and Lake City Toll Road from Lake City south to Antelope Park and eventually Del Norte. The Antelope Park and Lake City Toll Road opened to traffic in November 1875. It reduced by one-half the distance travelled between Lake City and Del Norte. The strategic consequences, in short, of Mears' vision was establishing Saguache as the premier supply hub serving Denver to the northeast, the

Burros. Like the contribution of the horse to the Ute, the burro played a strategic role in the ability of San Juan pioneers to travel, mine, and secure all manner of provisions necessary for daily life. Gradually nudged aside by mules and horses pulling wagons, themselves displaced by trucks, burros served faithfully well into the twentieth century. *(Courtesy of P. David Smith)*

central San Juans to the west, the Arkansas River Valley to the northeast, and the upper Rio Grande Valley to the south. The westward, wagon-worthy, generally all-weather (considering that day and age), road connecting Saguache with the upper Lake Fork of the Gunnison River Valley and the upper Animas River Valley was a precondition for the establishment of Lake City. Ironically, the intended Animas River Valley saw few wagons cresting Cinnamon Pass, but Lake City clearly benefited. The opening of a wagon-worthy road south along the upper Rio Grande River to Del Norte and northern New Mexico further underwrote Lake City's self-proclaimed royal (Queen) stature.

Is it not understandable why Otto Mears was credited with playing a central role in the San Juans excitement. There had to be a Saguache supply hub before there was a wagon road west into the heart of the San Juans. There had to be a gold find along the wagon road to transform a Ute seasonal hunting camp at the confluence of the Upper Lake Fork and Henson Creek into the Town of Lake City. There had to be thousands of gold-seekers and camp followers from all points of the compass to transform Lake City into a queen. Likewise, the prospect of gold and a base camp to support ill-prepared mobs that would pursue it had to be satisfied. Preconditions—there always were preconditions.[13]

"City" would not suffice for long. "Queen of the San Juans" was a brash exaggeration, of course, but inevitable. Boosterism at its best, the fact that a settlement of any consequence was in the making was actually an unintended consequence, a by-product of

Ever the Mercantilist. Otto Mears understood the connection between supply depots and toll roads. Each nourished the other. His Saguache emporium along with other thriving businesses supported his toll road to Lake City and beyond. His toll road earned revenues that enabled his Saguache mercantile to be an early Lake City outfitter, and Lake City to support traffic back to Saguache. (Lake City Silver World, July 3, 1875)

the grander enterprise of building a wagon-worthy road to transport vast quantities of provisions and equipment from Saguache to the Silverton region of the upper Animas River Valley and returning with vast quantities of silver-and gold-bearing ores. Thirty miles west of Lake City as the crow flies, on the far side of the 14,000 ft. mountain range scarcely marred by a Ute trail, lay the upper Animas Valley and the future boomtown—clearly a formidable competitor for

LAKE CITY MINING REGION

Lake City straddles the confluence of the Lake Fork of the Gunnison River and Henson Creek, a creek equal in volume with the upper Lake Fork and no doubt deserving of a more prestigious name. More descriptive for both would have been the East and West Forks of the South Fork of the Gunnison River, but as the Platte River watershed demonstrated, those names were too cumbersome to survive.

The name "Lake City" was neither cumbersome nor presumptuous when it came to describing a mining region. John Duer Irving and Howland Bancroft in *Geology and Ore Deposits Near Lake City, Colorado*, justify the honor by explaining that its distinguishing attribute was found wanting in other regional settlements.

> *(The Lake City story) is one of alterations of general depression and of excessive activity which have rendered its existence a little more eventful than that of the neighboring towns in the San Juans Mountains. These alternations have been due to several causes, but chiefly to the extreme richness of a few of the ore bodies discovered and the poverty of the rest. The periodical discoveries of new ore bodies of promising appearance were immediately followed by great inrushes of all sorts of people, whose presence made the country thrive for a time. Similar variant conditions have prevailed to a greater or less extent in almost all mining centers, but in few places in Colorado have they been so pronounced as at Lake City.[14]*

Among the geologist-crowd, both favorable and unfavorable circumstances made Lake City a unique mining district. On the favorable side of the ledger, prospects were squarely embedded in Colorado's recognized mineral belt and boasted several relatively rich gold and silver mines. On the unfavorable side, the region was remote with a preponderance of marginal reserves of low-grade ores. Among the common man, "Lake" made sense—a number of them including Lake San Cristobal surrounded the townsite. Among the booster class, nothing less than "City" would do despite a prolonged war of attrition with "village" stature always looming just over the horizon.

the crown—appropriately named "Silverton" ("silver by the ton"). Almost certain, in the mountains surrounding that alpine valley with its brave village awaited treasure. Otto Mears would provide wagons and coaches a way to exploit it profitably. With the filing of the Hotchkiss gold claim there was even more reason to search for treasure along the way. If the San Juans fortress and castle-keep legacies were not already dead and buried, the combination of toll road and gold would be the last nails in their coffins. A new legacy was beginning, the development of the Lake City mining region, Henson Canyon in particular.[15]

At a minimum, the upper Lake Fork of the Gunnison watershed at the eastern base of the San Juans range, already at an elevation approaching 9,000 ft. at Lake City, needed a stagecoach stop with stables and provisions for travelers. Exhausted passengers could be ignored but fresh draft animals were required before undertaking further ascent. Whether Otto Mears saw Lake City's potential is debatable (although he was quick to invest in it), but he did see on the far side of Cinnamon Pass a booming Silverton worthy of becoming the western terminus of his toll road. As unintended consequences go, a booming Silverton was a precondition for not only the Saguache and San Juans Toll Road, not simply for a Lake City rest stop along the way, but most importantly for the massing of interest and resources required to finally assault the San Juans castle-keep. As matters went, customers willing to pay Otto for the privilege of traveling on his toll road over Cinnamon Pass to Silverton did not materialize. Lake City did.

Silverton, Colorado 1874. A worthy contender for "Queen of the San Juans," Silverton also sat in a rich arm of Colorado's mineral belt. Straddling the death-defying but direct route between Ouray and Durango was a great asset—its elevation and its winters were not. *(Library of Congress)*

That slight change in plans was precondition enough for not one but two toll roads in and out of Lake City mentioned above.

By Frank Hall's standards, he too considered Lake City not only the offshoot of the discovery of gold just south of town, but also the offshoot of relentless boosterism of Lake City's *Silver World*. Boosterism, of course, was never considered fraud in the mining West even when it was fraudulent. Selling overvalued or worthless claims to gullible Easterners, or even neighbors, assumed that the "buyer was aware." In any case, boosterism was daily fare for every hometown newspaper of the day. By most accounts, it was a sacred duty. Fortunately, in the case of Lake City boosters, some claims in the district actually were truthful. *Silver World* editor, H. M. Wood, was as fine a civic booster as money could buy and entrepreneur Otto Mears was pleased to invest in his service to the community. Historian Hall, really a journalist at heart, also did his best to explain how a San Juan mining camp in the midst of a Ute hunting ground could become a booming mecca to the gaming class. Hall writes:

> *In the summer of 1874, Saguache, then a town, but recently founded, had lofty aspirations, and its inhabitants were ambitious to strikeout for all the trade within reach. Otto Mears, the great road builder of the Southwest, to whom that entire country is mainly indebted for the greater part of its best and most direct thoroughfares, a man of tireless energy and constantly engaged in schemes of public improvement, was among the first to settle there. But of this hereafter. At the period named, the principal men of Saguache with the view of penetrating and capturing the growing trade of the San Juan, then a source of great revenue and prestige to its rival Del Norte, formed a company to build a toll road from Saguache to the Animas Valley.*
>
> *Enos Hotchkiss, a veteran builder, took charge of the enterprise, which involved the construction of a wagon road one hundred and thirty miles in length before the end of the following autumn. He reached the lovely valley where Lake City now stands, toward the last of August. Following on up the river, he observed upon the hillside some float rock which attracted his attention, for he had had much experience in prospecting and mining on the Pacific slope. He examined it closely and afterward traced out the vein from which it had been eroded, a work of but little difficulty, as it was quite large and distinctly defined. He staked off a claim, writing upon the stakes the names of James Sparling, Ben Hall, B.A. Bartholf, Monett Hotchkiss and his own, as the claimants.* [16]

There are some who challenge historian Hall's account, stating instead that his crew actually spotted the gold, but Hotchkiss had the presence of mind to trace the "float" to its source and file the claim. Such squabbles miss the point. Had it not been for Otto Mears' rivalry with Del Norte, his toll road, and gold,

ENOS THROOP HOTCHKISS

Enos T. was born on March 29, 1832, in Bradford, Pennsylvania, the second son of Samuel Sebra Hotchkiss and Medora Ackley. With wife Elisabeth McIntyre they raised four sons and three daughters. A veteran of both gold rushes to California in 1849 and Colorado in 1859, he is credited with discovering gold in 1874 near present-day Lake City, Colorado, that ignited the San Juans "excitement." Along with members of his road crew, he patented the Hotchkiss—renamed the Golden Fleece Mine—that lived up to its reputation. In 1880-1881 he began ranching in Delta County (Hotchkiss, Colorado, was named for him) where at age sixty-seven he died on January 20, 1900.

Having profited greatly from the sale of the Golden Fleece, Enos with two younger brothers and partners, drove a herd of two hundred horses from Lake City to their new homestead. This led to raising sheep and cattle, platting and selling lots in present-day Hotchkiss, organizing the first bank and opening (of course) a general store.[17]

Prior to homesteading, in addition to constructing toll roads to remote mining regions and gold mining, Enos operated a grain mill and lumber mill at Saguache and Lake City, and in 1879 scouted (trespassed) Ute territory for what became his ranch while living on a claim near Powderhorn. Enos filed his ranch claim late summer of 1881, mere days before the government opened the area to homesteading and the flood of settlers that followed.[18]

nothing in 1874 justified establishing a settlement in the upper Lake Fork of the Gunnison River Valley. As usual, news of what was described as Hotchkiss' gold vein (named for the claim if not the discoverer), later proved to be rich in tellurium ore, quickly reached the outside world. Large numbers of gold-seekers and camp-followers rushed to the scene. With the blessings of an effusive *Silver World*, the Hotchkiss Lode was celebrated for the abundance and value of its ores and Lake City for the promise of more where that was found. Accurately described or not, it mattered little. The divine purpose of the *Silver World* was to promote claims, the divine purpose of the prospector, miner, and investor was to exploit them or go broke trying.[19]

To be fair, Mears was no John Cantrell of Westport, Missouri fame, and H.M. Wood was no Denver William Byers.[20] Mears had far more integrity than Cantrell and H.M. Wood had far less talent than Byers. But when it came to promoting Saguache and newly established Lake City, in both cases they were all in the same league and pivotal in promoting their local interests. In Mears'

Enos Hotchkiss (1832-1900). While superintendent overseeing construction of Otto Mears Saguache-San Juans toll road, gold float near what soon became Lake City moved him to file a claim. To his credit, he also completed the road. *(Courtesy of the* Lake City Silver World*)*

case, unquestionably a quick learner, he became both an experienced City Father of Saguache and a Lake City visionary. If he hesitated ponying-up the capital needed to organize the Lake City Town Company and underwrite the *Silver World*, there is no record of it. There is record of his election to (arguably his new hometown) the first Lake City Board of Trustees. In keeping with his 1874 Saguache experience— Mears had hired Pennsylvania newspaperman David Downer to publish the *Saguache Chronicle*—there also is record he repeated this practice in 1875 by underwriting H. M. Wood and the *Silver World*. Both Downer and Wood shamelessly fluffed up their nests. Downer emphasized supply depot and transportation matters. Wood emphasized silver and gold veins beckoning any adventurous soul willing to stake claims along Mears' toll road or under the watchful eye of the Ute landlord. [21]

BOOSTERISM

Boosterism was the practice of shamelessly promoting one's hometown and its mining potential. The term most often described local journalists, but could describe any promoter, honest or otherwise. John Cantrell was not a booster in the journalistic sense of the word, nor was he honest, but from his perch on the Missouri frontier he crowed with the best of them when fanning the flames of the Colorado gold rush. William Byers' *Rocky Mountain News* was not only a classic example of the art of promoting one's hometown, he was the "Dean." Otto Mears' hand in this practice was far more subtle but nonetheless common. Print ads for merchandise and services in his stores were masterful. In Mears' world, more pilgrims meant more tolls and more products out his doors. In general, boosters were beloved, albeit belittled, members of usually raucous but tight-knit frontier communities.

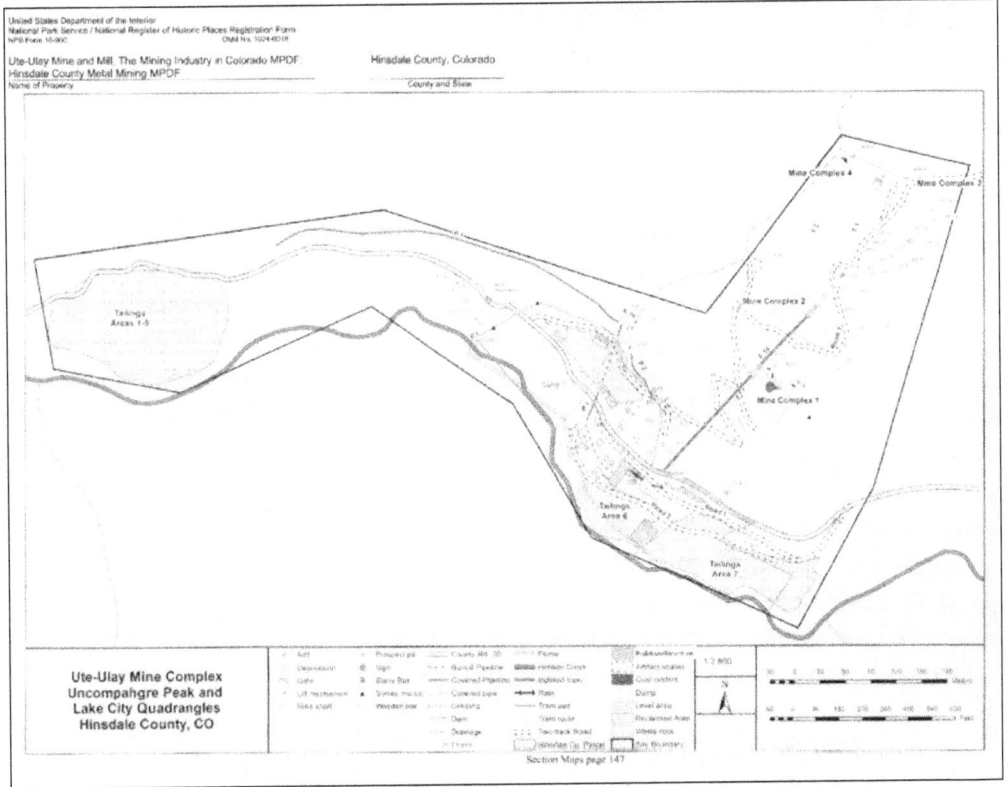

United States Department of the Interior
National Park Service / National Register of Historic Places Registration Form
NPS Form 10-900   OMB No. 1024-0018

Ute-Ulay Mine and Mill. The Mining Industry in Colorado MPDF.   Hinsdale County, Colorado
Hinsdale County Metal Mining MPDF
Name of Property   County and State

Ute-Ulay Mine Complex
Uncompahgre Peak and
Lake City Quadrangles
Hinsdale County, CO

Ute/Ulay Mine Complex. Tempting beginnings led to great promises and greater wealth. A series of owners developed what became the number one silver and lead producer in the Lake City mining district. *(U.S. Dept. of the Interior)*

As usual, the rapid influx of treasure seekers, just as in the case of the Front Range and California Gulch excitements,[22] quickly exhausted promising claim-sites along the Lake Fork of the Gunnison. Fortunately for disappointed late-comers, "late" measured in days or weeks, there was a handy option. Neighboring Henson Canyon also led west out of Lake City, deeper into the mineral belt and over Engineer Pass to the Upper Animas Valley (Bakersville, Howardsville, Arrastra Gulch, Silverton) and the incredibly mineral-rich future (ten years in the future) Red Mountain District. Surely Henson Canyon was equally blessed with treasure waiting to be unearthed. Were not early locations like the Ute/Ulay and less conspicuously the Big Casino tempting bait enough? [23]

Writing in 1879, mineral surveyor G. Thomas Ingham captured the tempo of the times and the national appeal of the region with a description of the Denver depot supplying men and materiel to booming San Juans camps and settlements. This very same description fairly depicted circumstances throughout the High Country, save for Lake City's one critical difference. It would be another decade before there was a Lake City railroad depot. By then the roar of the San Juan hullabaloo would be closer to a whimper. But not in 1879. Ingham described the

UNEASY LIES THE HEAD THAT WEARS A CROWN

—William Shakespeare, *King Henry IV*—

Lake City's reign as "Queen of the San Juans" was short-lived. By 1877, the population had swelled to 2,500, but in a few more years it dwindled to half that number. Despite scores of discoveries and still greater promise in Henson Canyon, the castle-keep was too remote and the quality of ores too inconsistent to be profitable. The Queen needed a king, if not a sugar-daddy, at least a rich mine or inexpensive rail service or higher silver prices. In 1880 frontier journalist Strahorn did his best to help:

> Lake City, 364 miles southwest of Denver, via Alamosa and Del Norte, or 285 miles from Denver via the Denver, South Park & Pacific Railway and Gunnison City, is the metropolis of northern San Juans. It contains some 1,100 inhabitants, two weekly papers, one of which, the Silver World, has a reputation throughout the country as one of the best mining journals in Colorado, and two extensive smelting establishments. Its altitude is 8,550 feet (sic). [24]

In the short seven years from the signing of the Brunot Agreement, in spite of an occasional Ute hostility, thanks to Mears' toll roads and no nearby competition, the San Juan queen managed to hang on. Just when total collapse seemed unavoidable, the *Silver World* trumpeted a new discovery, or better yet a fresh rumor that the Denver & Rio Grande Railroad was finally coming to town. That Lake City was Hinsdale County's seat of government also provided a worthy deterrent to ghost-town status.

Die-hard promoters, merchants, lawyers, doctors, clergymen, road builders, miners, and prospectors struggled but survived. On May 1, 1881, they welcomed telephone service, and in the following summer, lines threaded their way through the castle-keep to Silverton and Ouray, a few more fragile lifelines to the rest of the world. [25]

frenzied crowd swarming into Denver that year, and we are invited to image the impact the majority of them made upon arrival in the 1879 "Gunnison country" and its promising new boomtown.

> *Denver is six hundred and twenty-two miles from Omaha, and about two thousand miles, more or less, from New York. Its elevation is about five thousand and forty-eight feet. It is pleasantly situated on a gentle slope facing the South Platte River, surrounded by a sandy plain, in which there is plenty of alkali and cactus—to all appearance a desert—yet which with irrigation*

produces abundantly. It is a busy, bustling city, the streets being almost blocked at times with the rush of travel.

The city seemed to be full of strangers; the hotels were filled to overflowing; one hotel turned away over a hundred guests one night, being unable to keep them. The hotel arrivals had been nearly six hundred daily for a couple of weeks, and still they came. Many of them were "tender feet" and pilgrims from the East, bound for the mining camps of Leadville, Rico, the San Juans and Gunnison regions. Hotels and boarding houses were thriving, and the prosperity seemed to extend to merchants and tradesmen of all classes.

To all appearance there was a vast army of strangers here, crowding the hotels, thronging the streets, a restless, surging, eager mass of people, anxiously waiting for the snow to melt in the mountain passes, so they could reach the Gunnison country, which appeared to be the objective of two-thirds of all the people we met, and to which all the world seemed to be going en masse.

Here they were waiting for something to "turn up," or anxiously looking for employment, which many were seeking and few found, as there were a dozen applicants for every position save in the line of skilled mechanics alone; wages were low and board was high. Mechanics got two to two dollars and a half or three dollars per day, and paid seven dollars per week for board. Other laborers got from twenty to twenty-five dollars per month and board. We saw one poor fellow, with a sad countenance, inquiring "where the employment office was." Another sorry-looking young man came to our hotel, inquiring if any more cooks were wanted, and was answered "none." By the way, there are few women in this city comparatively, and the cooks are all men. The cooking and waiting at the hotels is all done by men; these men get from twenty-five to thirty dollars per month, while women as chambermaids are wanted and advertised for constantly, at the same wages per month. [26]

Some early San Juans and Lake City excitement was actually justified. Rightfully credited were promising discoveries south of Lake City beginning with the Hotchkiss mine, easier access into the Animas Valley afforded by Mears' toll roads, and Henson Canyon prospects. The *Silver World* faithfully printed report after report of rich finds or the likelihood of rich finds there. Having overcome most obstacles barring access, including fear of the Ute, more boosterism naturally fueled more prospecting. More boosterism also fueled more speculation, which in turn fueled even more prospecting and even more mines.

Of course some brave-hearts, men like J. K. Mullin and his companions, had never needed to be boosted. Gleaned from experience, their motivation to act early and daringly enabled them to beat the mob to the most promising claims. Four years after they pioneered the Engineer Pass/Henson Canyon route to present-day Lake City—incidentally a route that was essentially ignored four more years—the *Silver World* editor reminded his subscribers of that heroic event and their reward. It was H. M. Wood's way of explaining why the reasons it accomplished little in 1871 were obviously no longer the case in 1875.

> *Towards the close of the summer, 1871, J. K. Mullin and his partners started up the Animas River seeking a new field of discovery. Reaching its head and climbing a mountain, they saw as large a river below them, where the foot of prospector had never rested. They followed it to its mouth, and two weeks was required to reach the park where Lake City is now. Along the way they found many mines, notably the Ute & Ule. For three years it was unoccupied. In 1874 several mines were located notably the Big Casino. But in the spring of 1875 the real Henson Creek excitement began, reports & interest spread rapidly, every foot of space was taken by prospectors. On the 21st of July it became almost frenzy with the discovery of Little Chief. From then on everyone concentrated on Henson Creek—but little of the wealth could be utilized because of lack of roads. The trail was wild & rough, over hazardous streams, which caused the loss of at least twenty valuable animals, and thousands of dollars' worth of property. From the mines a little ore was packed to Lake City at great expense, and sent to Denver or Blackhawk with no profit.*[27]

Mullin and company were not about a Sunday afternoon outing. They were experienced prospectors, adventurers hungry for new fields of discovery. There can be little doubt that mineral veins and promising outcrops were noted as they followed Henson Creek down the canyon. The early location of Reynolds' last best chance is likely explained this way. Imagine, halfway through their journey, standing in the midst of a small alpine meadow looking north-eastward, an unmistakable yellow mineral vein in stark contrast to the drab native rock embracing it is clearly visible on the canyon wall. Tracing it upward, it tops a lateral ridge and continues down the backside into a lateral gulch. To the trained eyes of a prospector such a prominent vein, as certain as the finger of God, pointed the way to what became the Vermont/Ocean Wave Group. Like the scar left by a divine knife slicing through the mountain, this outcrop would warrant further investigation in safer times. Safer times would be several years in coming, but no matter. Equally promising outcrops closer to the future site of Lake City, safer and more readily accessible, also caught their attention.[28]

What manner of man accepted the challenges of the untamed San Juans? Members of the Mullin party epitomized this breed. They included Charles Godwin, Albert Meade, as well as Henry Henson, men we know something about. We can (and later do) speculate that early claims were filed by others not identified in this group. In addition to their pioneering trek earning them opportunities to locate promising mineral veins well ahead of more timid competitors, it also earned them the opportunity to name the creek they followed from its headwaters to its confluence with the Lake Fork of the Gunnison River. Oddly,

PATHFINDER MULLIN

Joel K. Mullin (also spelled Mullen) had not survived his Great Plains crossing a decade earlier to settle in with Front Range or California Gulch (Leadville) crowds. By 1871, Baker's Park was no different, and neither was Mullin's attitude. Post-Civil War reconstruction, America's industrial revolution, rapid increases in emigration, and extension of railroads throughout the West ensured a population boom and with it a return to exploitation of mineral resources. The upper Animas River Valley was the next bonanza. To Mullin, Baker's Park and the Animas Valley offered fresh prospects and treasure, but soon his wanderlust again set in. Even the surrounding mountains visible from the valley floor did not satisfy his adventurous spirit. Discovering what awaited him on their far side was a temptation too strong to resist.

There was no camp chatter about prospector opportunities in yet-to-be-named Henson Canyon situated a short but hazardous distance from difficult Stony Pass and the upper Lake Fork watershed. Of course the San Luis Valley was farther to the east, but appreciating what lay between Saguache and present-day Lake City was years away. In 1871 this no-man's land was uncharted, unexplored, unexploited for sure. With Henry Henson and a small contingent of equally adventuresome souls, Mullin determined to end the mystery.

J.K. was tight-lipped about his frightful reconnaissance. It took half a decade, a Lake City base-camp, and a zealous *Silver World* editor to unveil the many promising signs of rich mineral deposits, "mines" in the words of our newspaper friend. The Ute did not attack Mullin—that also was especially noteworthy. Less comforting was the thought that the trespasser's good fortune was simply due to going unnoticed. In any event, risk-taking paid dividends. The party spotted promising mineral veins and officially claimed them once the 1873 Brunot Agreement (not ratified by the U.S. Congress until 1874) made that possible. Several years later the editor of the *Saguache Chronicle*, slighting Mullin in favor of Henson (and confusing the actual location), added color to the harsh reality of their adventure:

> *Some years ago, Squire Henson and some of his companions were struggling through the mud, lifting out their burros by ears or tail and cursing things blue, until one fellow exhausted his vocabulary of epithets and wound up saying it was a "slumgullion of a place." They got out and the name stuck—and so have thousands of animals and wagons since.*[29]

Humorous as the editor's account was, "slumgullion" mud plagued the upper Lake Fork canyon, not Henson Canyon. The actual origin of the term is another matter altogether.

the creek was not named "Mullin" in honor of the expedition leader. It was named after Charles Godwin, perhaps the result of casting lots. How Godwin Creek became Henson Creek is less of a mystery. The story of their friendship and partnerships is equally intriguing.[30]

The simple answer to "creek-naming" is "patronage." While Mullin and Meade pursued silver and gold, successfully we might add, and Godwin returned to his home state of Virginia, Henry Henson pursued a political career in state government. Along with Lafayette Head, friend and future Lieutenant-Governor, he was a delegate representing the Twenty-Third District (Rio Grande and Hinsdale)

HENRY HENSON

Henry was born in Wayne County, Kentucky, November 12, 1824. He relocated as a small child to the Indiana frontier. He received a "common school" education and served as Treasurer of Martin County for four years before joining the Colorado gold rush in April 1860. Both disgusted with the overcrowded conditions on the Front Range and in possession of an abundance of courage, in December 1860 he accompanied Charles Baker into the upper Animas River watershed. Disappointed there, he settled in Fairplay where he made his way as a merchant, postmaster, and school superintendent. In 1864 he represented Park County in the Territorial Legislature and also served as Justice of the Peace. In 1865 he was a delegate to the Denver State Convention tasked with preparing Colorado for statehood (a task that did not bear fruit until 1876).

In 1871 he was back in the Animas watershed in time to join J. K. Mullin's epic trek over Engineer Pass to the future site of Lake City and on to the upper San Luis Valley. In Saguache he partnered in a general store, quite likely with Otto Mears. He returned to newly-established Lake City to file a claim on the Ute/Ulay—no doubt spied out in 1871—with J.K. Mullin, Charles Godwin, and Albert Meade. In October 1876, he was elected to the Senate of the first Colorado General Assembly. That same year the partners sold the Ute/Ulay for $125,000 and pursued other ventures together, notably the 4UR Ranch and Hot Springs Resort near Wagon Wheel Gap, Colorado — "taken up in October 1872."

Throughout his pioneer life Henson remained active in San Juan mining ventures as well as politics. Godwin Creek was renamed Henson Creek in his honor. The construction of a Ute/Ulay surface plant, cabins, and what rose to "town status" also was named in his honor.

According to the September 21, 1882, *Leadville Daily Herald*, "Senator Henry Henson, a former member of the Colorado State legislature; and a well-known citizen of Southern Colorado and New Mexico, is dead. He died at Los Angeles, California, last Thursday (September 14th)."[31]

at Colorado's December 1875 Constitutional Convention. In October 1876 he was elected to the Senate of the first Colorado General Assembly. Exactly when Godwin Creek ceased to appear in print is a quest left to others. What is known is Henry represented the region in the new state of Colorado and Charles relocated to his home state of Virginia with a new wife. Naming the gaggle of cabins in the heart of the Ute/Ulay properties "Henson" is clearer—his friends and partners insisted on that.[32]

And what became of Henson's partners? Charles Evelyn Godwin sometimes spelled Goodwin, almost always with an "E" instead of "Evelyn" no doubt for good reason, was born in Virginia on February 14, 1839. He joined the Union Navy in 1859, perhaps an early sign of his fondness for adventure. He served aboard the *USS John Adams*, participated in the daring Combahee Ferry Raid that abolitionist Harriet Tubman helped guide to liberate over 700 imprisoned slaves, and located to Colorado in time to join Mullin's pioneering trek. His friendship with Mullin, Meade, and Henson survived their harrowing two-week descent of Henson Canyon.[33] They partnered on the Ute/Ulay, and they partnered on the 4UR hot springs resort and ranch near Wagon Wheel Gap. If Charles took offense at losing naming rights to Godwin then Henson Creek, there is no known record of it. There is a record of his marriage to Ann Woodruff in Del Norte in December 1877. Apparently Ann was not enamored enough with Charles to share his penchant for Colorado frontier life. They sold their interest in the 4UR and moved to Birdsnest on Virginia's eastern shore, perhaps Charles' birthplace, perhaps a region that spawned happy memories, where they farmed the remainder of their lives. According to Sandra Wagner writing in *4UR Ranch and Resort*, Charley Goodwin made a return visit to the ranch in June 1881. On April 15, 1909, he died.

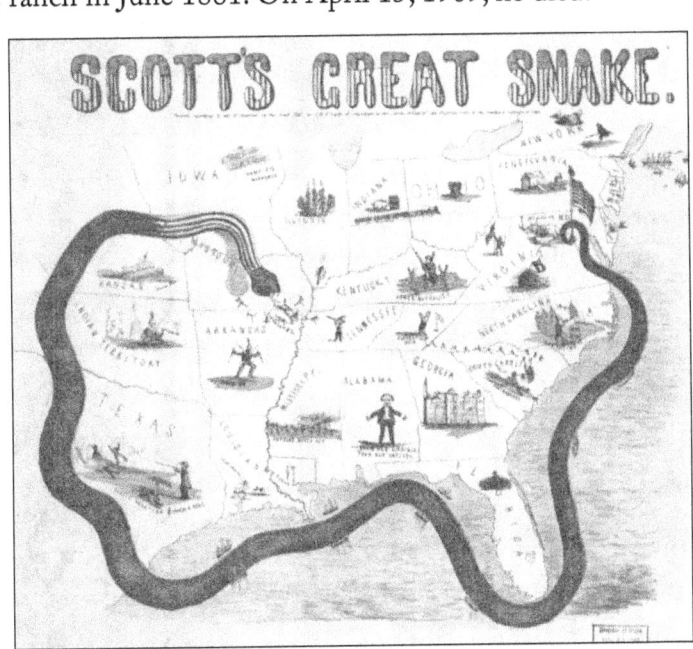

Scott's Great Snake. The Combahee Ferry Raid—June 2, 1863—was an offshoot of Union General Winfield Scott's strategy to isolate the Confederacy. It was spearheaded by the frigate *USS John Adams* assigned to Charleston Harbor blockade duties, Charles Godwin's duty-station throughout the Civil War. *(Wikipedia)*

HARRIET TUBMAN'S COMBAHEE FERRY RAID

While Charles E. Godwin served aboard the frigate *John Adams*, he participated in one of the most daring raids of the Civil War that no doubt stoked his appetite for later San Juans adventures. The raid on Combahee Ferry, Beaufort County, South Carolina, was organized with Union Colonel Montgomery by Harriet Tubman, former slave and Union operative. The *John Adams* led three steam-powered gunboats up the Harbor River to Port Royal, relying on local African-American mariners to guide them past mines and fortifications. The *John Adams* was built for speed and maneuverability, with a complement of 220 officers and enlisted men and an armament consisting of twenty-four 12-pounder and six 24-pounder guns. The squadron freed over 750 slaves and further eroded Confederate morale. According to Jeff W. Grigg's, *The Combahee River Raid: Harriet Tubman & Lowcountry Liberation*, Harriet Tubman was the first woman in U.S. history to plan and execute an armed expedition.

Born into slavery ca. March 1822, Harriet (born Araminta Ross) was an American abolitionist and social activist until her death March 10, 1913. She escaped slavery and subsequently was responsible for thirteen missions to free others. In 1858 she met John Brown and helped him plan and recruit supporters for his 1859 Harpers Ferry raid. During the Civil War she first supported the Union Army as a cook and nurse before volunteering as an armed scout and spy. In later years she was an activist in the women's suffrage movement; and, as so many others, a devout Christian.

Harriet married John Tubman ca. 1844. A free African-American, their "blended marriage," a term used to describe "free people of color marrying slaves," was common in that day. She changed her first name to Harriet about this same time. [34]

Albert Meade shared much the same story. Born January 22, 1846, in Pennsylvania, probably but not necessarily too young to join the "Pikes Peak or Bust" crowd or the young nation's Civil War, he found his way into the upper Animas Valley in time to bond with Mullin, Godwin, and Henson. He too partnered for a season on the Ute/Ulay and 4UR Resort and Ranch. Selling his share, he pursued various mining operations elsewhere in Colorado, obtaining a "cash entry patent" in 1881 for 160 acres at Loma near Grand Junction. Albert died in Rifle on May 22, 1914. [35]

Safer times accompanied better accessibility to Henson Canyon prospects and beckoning Ute/Ulay, Hidden Treasure, and Big Casino lodes, but development was slowed when in the spring of 1875 Otto Mears chose to route his toll road to the Animas Valley up the Lake Fork and over Cinnamon Pass rather than up Henson Canyon and over Engineer Pass. Not an easy route, it was a Mear's route and it was unwise to second-guess the seasoned toll road meister. Not even U.S. military expeditions including Wheeler and Hayden, full of Yankee bluster, who as late as 1873 considered Mullin's Henson Canyon route, decided to pursue it. Amazingly, one of Wheeler's tasks was to evaluate the feasibility of an Antelope Park (near the headwaters of the Rio Grande) to Lake City railroad grade. In so doing he must have seen potential in Henson Canyon few others imagined, albeit by a route that veered northward from Engineer Mountain. A right-of way up Henson Creek to American Flats and down to the Uncompahgre watershed also was deemed possible.[36]

Less visionary souls thought otherwise. Possible but impractical. Other routes scored more favorably including (to the disbelief of anyone who has been there) a death-defying route over Stony Pass, but they were not pursued either. Why was getting into this region so difficult? Remember the San Juans pedigree.

The topography of the southwestern quadrant of Colorado is the product of westward drifting and uplifting of the North American crustal plates, recurring volcanic eruptions, recurring collapses of calderas that were refilled with ash-flows and lava from other volcanoes near and far (i.e. La Garita, by far the largest in the San Juans), recurring glacial advances and retreats, and of course wind and water erosion. Not all of this geological churning occurred simultaneously. Some of it did. For example, the "San Juan volcanic depression, rather than being a single large oval collapse structure, consists of two intersecting smaller subcircular calderas."[37] This active volcanic period occurred twenty to forty million years ago highlighted by the growth of two nearby superstar volcanoes, the Uncompahgre (located on the oval nearest to Lake City) and the San Juan (located nearest to Silverton). Twenty-eight million years ago, both of these volcanoes erupted and collapsed, forming the San Juan and Uncompahgre calderas, but these eruptions were not the end of volcanic activity. The magma chamber deep in the earth's crust that was the source of the lava and ash refilled, pushing the center of the two calderas upward and forming a northeast oriented, elongated dome. The bulging of the dome stretched the layers of volcanic rock at the top, causing them to crack and form northeast oriented fractures. The crest of the dome subsided, and the resultant feature is known by geologists and mining people as the Eureka graben. Some of these fractures were focal points for the emplacement of veins rich with valuable metals. Eventually, the western part of the dome became the Silverton volcano, which erupted and collapsed 27.6 million years ago. Finally, the Lake City volcano grew within the Uncompahgre caldera, eventually erupting 22.5 million years ago before collapsing to form the Lake City caldera which obscures the east end of the Eureka graben. In due course all of these volcanoes filled with ash-flows and lava-flows from uncounted nearby and distant recurring eruptions.

When all was said and done, the Eureka graben situated between these collapsed calderas, suitably eroded by glaciers, wind, and water—roughly divided by Henson Canyon and its creek—presented to those with experienced eyes to see a bounteous mineralized zone. The zone is a mosaic of fissures often interrupted by the recurrent ash- and lava-flows, swelling, subsidence and calving of the calderas. Some fissures are aligned more or less with Henson Canyon. Some are perpendicular or nearly so. Some run deep. Some do not. Some are rich in metals. Some are not. Simply stated, the region resembles lasagna, the product of multiple cycles of volcanism resulting in multiple mineralization events not all of which were similar in nature or worth. Worse than lasagna, the region resembles lasagna that has slid off its plate and splattered on the floor. Is it a wonder that there were challenges unearthing its treasures? For those who prefer a more scientific description, consider this:

> *In the Lake City area, where an exceptionally complete stratigraphic succession allows determination of detailed age relations, at least three distinct stages of mid-Tertiary mineralization can be related to different local environments of deposition. Cores of four early intermediate-composition pre-collapse volcanoes around the periphery of the Uncompahgre caldera are altered and mineralized, with minor ore production from one. In addition, the caldera fill in the Uncompahgre caldera is cut by monzonitic intrusives and is locally hydrothermally altered. Many associated fractures were filled by quartz-sulfide veins that have supplied most of the production from this area. The altered rocks and veins are locally truncated by the Lake City caldera wall and clearly are older than this caldera. Finally, some ring-fracture intrusives and lavas around the Lake City caldera are intensely altered, and many of the distensional fractures within the resurgent core are altered and some contain metalliferous veins.* [38]

Put another way, fissures like those that characterize the Henson Creek watershed including El Paso Creek (a major tributary and site of the Vermont and Ocean Wave lodes), permitted steam and groundwater with enormous heat and pressure to bring valuable minerals from deep within the earth closer to the surface. As these fluids lost pressure and heat, they shattered the fissure walls, altered the chemical composition of the adjacent bedrock, and filled the fissures themselves with deposits of their mineral content. Recurring glaciers contributed to collapsing of the caldera walls. So did new magma domes, eruptions, ash- and lava-flows. Over perhaps two million years numerous ice caps a mile or more thick covered the northern half of the continent and filled mountain valleys even farther south. On each of their northerly retreats the melting ice and rain that followed generated hundreds of inches of annual precipitation century after century, millennium after millennium, until yet another global chill reversed their course. Above Henson Creek, above 9,000 feet, U-shaped valleys testify to the glacier's mountain-sculpting work. The saddle between Uncompahgre Peak to the east and Matterhorn Peak to the west gives way to a bowl-shaped glacial valley from which melting snowpack and springs feed the headwaters of El Paso Creek. The El Paso Creek watershed discharges into Henson Creek. The El Paso Creek watershed is home to A.E. Reynolds' Vermont/Ocean Wave lodes.

Now heavily eroded, the collapsed and most recent Lake City caldera situated in the collapsed caldera of the more ancient Uncompahgre volcano is barely discernable from the ground. It is difficult to appreciate thirty-five million or more years ago lava domes perhaps a hundred miles across swelled to the surface. It is difficult to appreciate the effects of lava and ash being intermittently cast out of these volcanoes perhaps for millions of years.

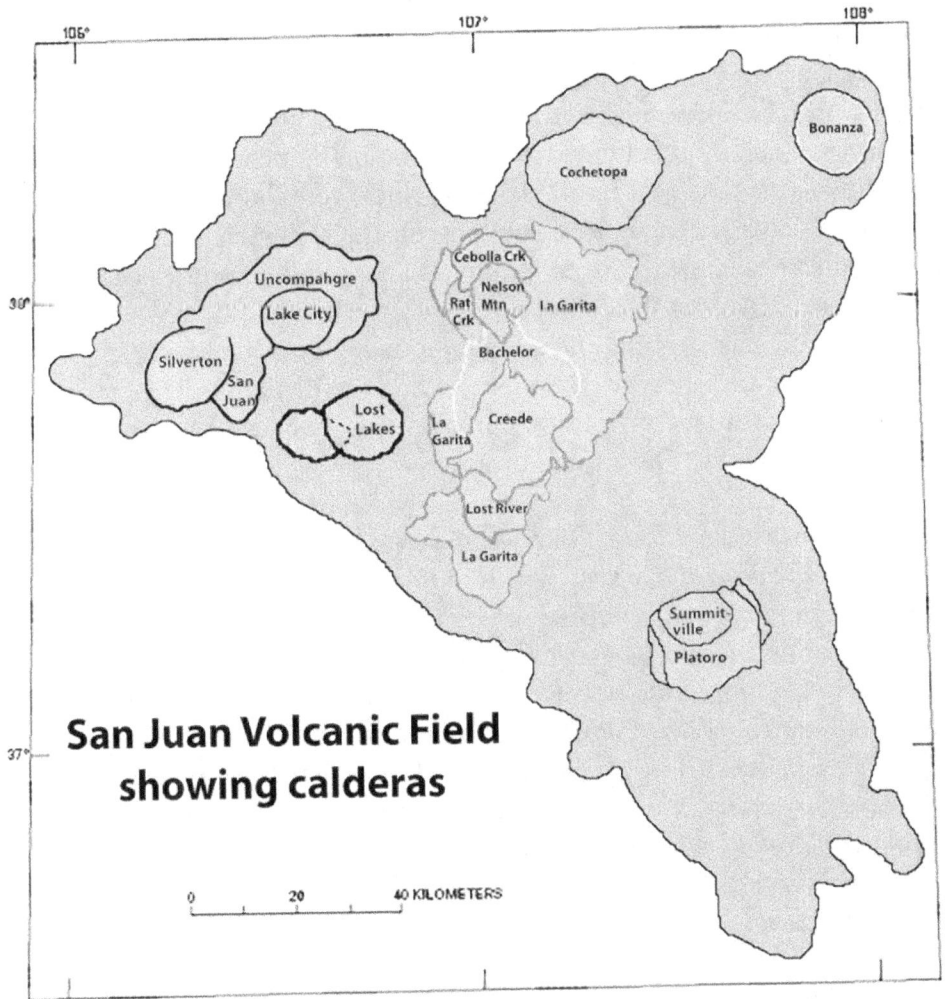

San Juan Volcanic Field showing calderas

Volcanic Fields. As suggested by this map of calderas, the Lake City region of the Colorado Mineral Belt is fertile ground for gold and silver ores, testified to by the heavy concentration of collapsed calderas and associated Henson Canyon mines. *(Courtesy of Mines Museum of Earth Science-Golden, Colorado, Ed Raines, Curator.)*

Thousands of feet of lava later, the earth quieted and cooled and was covered with glaciers. The glaciers carved canyons thousands of feet deep exposing and giving access to the mineral wealth left by the earlier volcanoes. Just 15,000 years ago, the site of present-day Lake City sat 1,500 to 2,000 ft. below just such ice, patiently waiting to emerge along with the peaks and valleys seen today. [39]

Of course the vast majority of the prospectors who first surged into Colorado and eventually Henson Canyon appreciated little of this, or how it would frustrate their quest for treasure. Nor would they have been concerned even if they did. They recognized placer gold when they saw it in their pans, and when they saw little of it in San Juans watersheds they learned to look for quartz veins or rotten, stained surface granite. And they slowly gained an appreciation for the rough neighborhood the forces of nature created and concealed for their very own good fortune. The miners and mine engineers that followed in their tracks knew more, but not those first on the scene. Their joy rested in the knowledge that the Henson Creek watershed with its El Paso Gulch were pristine, that their outcrops were incredibly sheltered from exploitation that could be witnessed just a ridge or two away, and that by all reckoning they were the first to tumble to its promise. Did they give thought to standing on the shoulders of generations of others who first challenged Fortress San Juans, that only a season earlier had outwitted the maze guarding the approach to its castle-keep? Did they give thought to geological enigmas awaiting them underground. Not at all.

One of the more helpful descriptions of San Juan Mineral Belt prospects is preserved in the writings of frontier journalist Robert Strahorn who graciously credited an anonymous (Fossett) contributor:

> There is probably more country standing on edge in this section than anywhere else beneath the sun. These mountains contain thousands of silver veins, many of huge size and some of great richness. In fact, well informed miners and geologists tell us that they present a greater number of true fissure mineral veins, easily traceable upon their towering fronts and summits, than any known region of similar extent on the globe. The silver belt is from 30 to 40 miles wide and nearly 100 miles long. It has taken years to build a few roads through this rugged and almost impassable country, and the heavy snows and long winters have also been a serious drawback to growth and development. It has been a quite recent thing to attempt to mine there in winter except in running a few tunnels, but the rapid approach of the Denver, South Park Pacific and Denver & Rio Grande Railways is changing the whole face of things. [40]

Ute "agreement" and "safer times" were not concerns of Otto Mears. Objectively speaking, his trust resided in his own shrewd judgment and raw courage. Realistically, his long friendship with the Ute including his ability to speak their language helped. He traded with the Ute and often negotiated on behalf of Ute chiefs with the U.S. Army. Chief Ouray, occasionally challenged but resilient leader of his people, was as close as a brother. In 1870, Otto was certain the increasing number of prospectors and settlers filtering into the San

THE LAST GATE

Obvious Henson Canyon invasion routes were east from Baker's Park, the audacious path struck by J.K. Mullin and partners, which required a hard climb up the westward face of the Engineer Mountain range and over what came to be named Engineer Pass before dropping into the narrow twenty-mile slash named Henson Canyon that led to present-day Lake City. (Later, rarely used trails from Animas Forks were widened to accommodate wagons leading to isolated Engineer Mountain mines—and Denver Pass, for example—but were even more difficult due to elevation and terrain.) Alternatively, a reverse route was possible, west from the future site of Lake City up the treacherous canyon and over Engineer Pass with barely an animal trail to lead one down the other side to the upper Animas valley. Even the Ute were leery of this choice, preferring instead to avoid the canyon altogether or venturing east or west along its ridges above tree line.

Mullin breached Fortress San Juans' last redoubt in the fall of 1871, violating but not lingering on Ute holy ground. Neither Henson Canyon terrain nor possible Ute hunting parties encouraged delay beyond the two weeks it took to follow Henson Creek from its Engineer Pass headwaters to its confluence with the Lake Fork of the Gunnison. Mullin and partners began their search for "a new field of discovery" by working their way up the Animas watershed. From the moment the party topped Engineer Pass and looked eastward at the narrow canyon descending below, they understood why it was a route to avoid. The pass was no more than a dip between mountain shoulders well above tree-line and still pocketed in mid-summer with the previous winter's snow. Mullin threaded his way down Henson Creek, sometimes on terraced animal trails above tree-line, sometimes struggling through downed timber and underbrush clogging the narrow canyon floor, sometimes retreating to bypass raging cataracts channeled by canyon walls too narrow and steep to get through.

Given the nearly impassable clutter of rockslides, avalanche debris, and tree-fall, it was natural for Mullin to wonder as he worked his way downstream if he was the first White-man to pass that way. Others, in fact hundreds of others over the past decade, are known to have crossed the continental divide separating the Animas Valley from what became the Lake City Park, but no one had reported traveling Mullin's way. To his astonishment, Henson Canyon revealed no signs of a prospector's claim despite colors he surely saw on the canyon walls. That was about to change, but not before the Ute agreed.

Luis and upper Animas River valleys would not have Ute problems either. His Saguache town site and his San Juan toll roads evidenced this belief despite an isolated hostility occasionally giving him pause.

By spring 1875, the confidence of scores of others also was high, including the vanguard of twenty-seven pathfinders poised to launch their great treasure hunt up Henson Creek once the weather broke.[41] Of course, they did not just appear there overnight. And of course some had been there with Joel Mullin in 1871. In a letter published in the *Silver World* in 1931, Eugene Barthoff recalled how such a mobilization began.

> In 1873 my two brothers, Byron and Will, went to Silverton in San Juans, by way of Del Norte, after locating some claims there. From Silverton they went in company with eight other men, following what I believe is called the east fork of the Animas River, to near the Mineral Point, then crossed over what they thot (sic) was the main summit of the Rocky Mountains, and struck the head of the Lake Fork of the Gunnison River. They discovered and located about 42 claims and formed a mining district, calling it Burrows Park, and elected Captain Burrows as recorder. At that time they thot (sic) they were on Pole Creek, tributary to the Rio Grande. They followed down the Lake Fork of the Gunnison to where Lake City now stands. As there were no trails, they had to make trails where needed. The Henson boys had been there and located the Ute and Ulay mines that year.

> By this time they knew they were still on the Western Slope. They travelled on down the river, watching for a pass to the east. They struck a trail leading up the creek and found a newly-made Indian grave. They named the stream Indian Creek. They crossed the divide into the Cebolla (Savoya), then up the divide to what they named Beaver Creek. They followed it up and across the summit and down Los Pinos to the Agency. They had run out of provisions and tobacco, and Captain Burrows and my brother, Byron, went on with saddle horses, the rest following with burros. When Burrows and Byron returned with provisions and tobacco, there was great rejoicing.

> They learned at the Agency they were still 45 miles from Cochetopa Pass, where they crossed the Continental Divide by Saguache, then home near Del Norte. They told my father that there would be a toll road built to the forks of the Animas River from Saguache by way of the Los Pinos Agency, so my father moved to Saguache that fall and with Otto Mears and Enos Hotchkiss got a charter for such toll road and early in the spring commenced work building it, finishing it late in September.

> That summer my father took up a ranch where the town of Lake City now is. We built a cabin just back of the Elephant Corral, which he built later. The cabin faced the cliffs, just west from the San Juans dance hall, which was built later. It was the first cabin built in Lake City. [42]

Eugene's account also did not fail to mention Enos's gold claim, or Pike Snowden, our drover. Barthoff wrote that the twenty-seven pilgrims included "… myself, father and brother; a few at the Hotchkiss Mine; Charlie Bunch (?) sic., and Will Hunter at the Falls. Pike Snowden and partner up Henson Creek a ways complete his thought on this matter." (Take note of Eugene's mention of the "Elephant Corral," an artifact of that era we will return to.) [43]

With the first tease of spring, the twenty-seven struggled upstream through willow groves and fields of avalanche debris, stumbling as they went over river rock churned up with every spring flood. To the extent there was a trail, it was tortuous at best, one that the Ute had abandoned as soon as practicable in favor of higher ground. Hundreds more soon followed, and then thousands, but these twenty-seven led the pack. They had paid their dues. Finally, Henson Canyon was open for business. Centuries of Ute stewardship had come to a shaky end. Chief Ouray and Otto Mears had done their part. The San Juans excitement had taken its place. Daily would come reports of one mineral strike after another until it seemed every stretch of canyon space had been staked. In fact a year later there would not be a quartz vein or streak of color in want of a claim. Wrestling control of the castle-keep was complete. Extracting its treasures would be a battle harder won.

Pilgrims like Pike Snowden were misfits in many strata of society, but not in the San Juans in the 1870s. With character traits common among men who left home young never to return, they were accepted and took their rightful place in the generation that fought this battle. In Snowden's case, his journey from Missouri farm boy to Texas drover to San Juans prospector forged relationships that produced a beloved Henson Canyon folk hero. His colorful story is a treasure tale all its own, like the Mullin Party a facet of the San Juans community too striking to pass by. His story is next.

Notes—Chapter Two: The Hunt Begins

1 *Lake City Silver World*, October 9, 1931. (Eugene Bartholf's letter introduces the first twenty-seven prospectors that wintered over in 1874-75 at the mouth of Henson Canyon when Lake City was little more than a glint in Otto Mears' eye. One of the most improbable pilgrims in the bunch—Pike Snowden—is the drover in Chapter Three. Part of his allure is he has no business being a prospector or mine owner. Uneducated, unemployed, untrained, a teenage vagabond much like our toll road king, he is now a thirty-year old prospector and miner on the cusp of great wealth. But for the greater balance of his life, he lived a humble, solitary life in Henson Canyon he knew well, a man of means by no means. Yet when he chose to engage his neighbors, he did so with country humor, a trait that local newspaper editors preserved for generations to come. In this regard, having befriended scholar and poet W.F.E. Gurley did not hurt.)

2 *Silver World*, April 14, 1921. (W.F.E. Gurley letter to Walter Mendenhall, editor. He is the cook in Chapter Four. "Bars" are island-like gravel deposits formed by creek currents, and "footlogs" are tree trunks that served as bridges.)

3 In the minds of those who stood in its shadows, the San Juans was not a fortress built by human hands but a fortress nonetheless (See Vol. I, *Fortress San Juans*). It was a natural hard

rock citadel almost too formidable even for the likes of the courageous early Spaniards accustomed to crossing oceans and conquering continents with a handful of men and a few horses. The dozen generations that followed them reached the same conclusion. The San Juans was a frightful barrier to their treasure hunts. Ridgeline upon ridgeline gave them pause. Try as they may, their seasons of fair weather were never long enough to probe much beyond the outer wall, the Sangre de Cristo and Sierra de la Plata ranges. Nor was there a great need to do so. Ute traders, responding to annual Spanish trade fairs known as "rescates," journeyed to Taos and Abiquiu and lesser New Mexico colonial outposts. Wearing neither gold nor silver jewelry (wisely concealed or truly of no interest is an ongoing debate), there was little Spanish motivation to follow these "impoverished" traders home.

More worrisome, Spaniards knew from trader's tales and limited incursions of their own that not far beyond the outer walls seemingly impoverished but certainly fierce Ute would bloody their approach. The practical effect was clear. The San Juans loomed large, an ominous hindrance for centuries to all but its Ute landlords ever watchful from its parapet-like walls. By the early 1870s the San Juans were familiar territory to encroaching Americans, many areas comfortably settled, others probed and left behind perhaps for another day, perhaps forever. Henson Canyon, effectively the fortress castle-keep, would be left behind until 1875 when suspected treasure justified a frontal assault.

4 "Two-Legged" was the demeaning name given to the early Spanish by the first Utes to encounter them. The Ute held them, all Whites for that matter, in total contempt. They did not merit the same respect as four-legged animals, much less indigenous peoples. (See: Pettit, Jan, *Utes, The Mountain People*, "Introduction by Eddie Box," pgs. ix, 1.) This term may have fallen into disuse by post-Civil War standards, but Ute hostility to Whites encroaching on their sacred homeland remained a serious deterrent.

5 Tucker, E. F., *Otto Mears and the San Juans*, pg. 11. (According to Tucker, Allen Nossaman in *Many More Mountains* writes that the Ute word "Saguache" means "Blue Earth". Otto Mears who claimed Saguache as his hometown believed it translated to "Blue Spring". Mears later explained that "Saguache" was misspelled, a clerical error. As a founding father, he intended to name the town "Swatch", which is what he called it. Chief Ouray also is a contender for special recognition. Generally simply called Ouray, he rose to prominence over all of the Ute factions and became their spokesman and principal negotiator. When his leadership was challenged, he acted swiftly and with lethal force if necessary. His willingness to accommodate American expansionism and promote peace was an indispensable feature of San Juans development. Also see *Ouray Chief of the Utes*.)

6 Tucker, pg. 3. (Also see: Helen M. Searcy, "Otto Mears," *Pioneers of the San Juans Country*, pgs. 5-46)

7 Ibid., pgs. 10-11. Mears later played a determining role in extending rail service (Rio Grande Southern) to Telluride and Durango, and construction of the Million Dollar Highway between Ouray and Durango.

8 Ibid., pgs. 4-9. (Also see Smith, P. David, *The Story of Lake City, Colorado, and It's Surrounding Areas*, pgs. 98-99; Becker, Cynthia S. and P. David Smith, *The Life & Times of Lafayette Head*, pgs. 184-185.)

9 Ibid., pgs. 27-28.

10 Ibid., pg. 28.

11 Ibid. pgs. 28-29.

12 The rapid development of the "new-fangled" internal combustion engine and introduction of trucks was certain to replace horses, mules and burros. They also were certain to replace wagons and often railroads.

13 On the American frontier, "city" was an important distinguishing feature of a settlement, carrying much more presumed stature than "town". The "City Fathers" of The Town of Lake

City covered their bases from the outset. The true measure of a settlement was the number of mouths that needed fed, either by their own localized industry and farms, or by supplies from elsewhere. Lake City grew rapidly in keeping with boomtown practices. Sadly, petals also fell quickly from the rose. By 1880 the town was still alive, but a shadow of its few glory years. At 1,100 inhabitants, it epitomized a struggling mining industry desperate for economical rail transportation for its low-grade ores. By the early 1900s the population of the entire county was half as much.

[14] Irving, John Duer and Bancroft, Howland, *Geology and Ore Deposits Near Lake City, Colorado*, USGS Bulletin 478, pgs. 12-18.

[15] This scope of professional knowledge was potentially available to prospectors and mine opera- tors addressed in *Reynolds' Last Best Chance*. No doubt another century of study and experience would challenge this science. More to the point, there is scant evidence that scientific knowl- edge of any caliber played a meaningful part in decisions regarding the Vermont/Ocean Wave Group. In its place reigned personal experience, hearsay, and hope.

[16] Hall, Frank, *History of the State of Colorado*, Vol. II, pg. 205.

[17] Wills, Thomas, "A Short History of Hotchkiss, Colorado," https://www.gregstratman.com.

[18] "Hotchkiss Homestead," pg. 10, National Park Service, National Register of Historic Places Registration Form.

[19] Hall, pg. 206. (According to Hall, Lake City was named in recognition of the mountain lakes nearby. P. David Smith writes in *The Story of Lake City* that more likely the town is named in recognition of nearby Lake San Cristobal, the second largest natural lake in Colorado. As for who actually located the "Hotchkiss gold", reportedly two of Enos's workmen drove a wagon full of rich gold ore to Canon City and sold it for $40,000, close to a million in today's dol- lars. That said, there is no question Hotchkiss with partners filed the claim. See Smith, pgs. 110-111.)

[20] John Cantrell played a significant role in 1858 in validating that gold along the Colorado Front Range was plentiful enough to risk crossing the Great Plains. A trader based in Westport, pres- ently a jurisdiction of Kansas City, Missouri, his questionable scruples did not seem to diminish the effectiveness of his boosterism along the Missouri River frontier. William Byers, editor of the *Rocky Mountain News*, was a champion booster of Colorado mining prospects and the ter- ritory and state at large. (See: *Fortress San Juans*, Chap. 4.)

[21] Tucker, pg. 16.

[22] California Gulch, near present-day Leadville, Colorado, was the site of a major 1860 gold discovery that drew prospectors and speculators away from overcrowded prospects along Colorado's Front Range.

[23] These promising properties were illegally located prior to ratification of the Brunot Agreement.

[24] Strahorn, Robert Edmund, *Gunnison and San Juans*, pg. 78.

[25] O'Rourke, Paul M., *Frontier in Transition: A History of Southwestern Colorado*, pg. 65. (Also: https:www.nps.gov/parkhistory/online_books/blm/co/10/chap6.htm, pg.7.)

[26] Ingham, G. Thomas, *Digging Gold Among the Rockies*, pgs. 252-256.

[27] *Silver World*, November 11, 1876.

[28] Smith, P. David, *The Story of Lake City, Colorado*, pg. 178. (The Ute signed the Brunot Agreement in 1873. The U.S. Congress ratified it in 1874. The Ute ceded the San Juans High Country to prospectors and miners, but not without caveats and not without continuing violence. In September 1879, serious hostilities erupted. The Northern Utes killed Nathan Meeker and all eight male employees at the Ute agency. Three women were taken hostage. The catalyst was Meeker's plan to plow up the Ute horseracing track to plant vegetables. On September 29, 1879, the Milk Creek "massacre" occurred when a U.S. cavalry rescue party was attacked by the Utes. Thirteen soldiers were killed, forty-three wounded. Thirty-seven Utes died.)

[29] *Saguache Chronicle*, June 16, 1877. (The first use of the term "slumgullion" may have been by

1849 California miners to describe the muddy slurry left behind in their gold sluices. It may have been a term used by whalers to describe what remained on their decks after processing blubber. It was a term used to describe stew served miners, ingredients left to one's imagination. In the Lake City region "slumgullion" is the name of the earthflows that blocked the Lake Fork of the Gunnison River north of Lake City to create Lake San Cristobal. Geologists believe this occurred about 1270 A.D. When the flows were first named is uncertain.)

[30] According to the 1879-1910 *Colorado Mine Directory*, J.K. Mullin was co-owner with H. Musgrave and John S. Hough of the Hidden Treasure Lode. Musgrave and Hough are not named members of the Mullin party, but were likely participants and likely located the Hidden Treasure during Mullin's 1871 exploration of Henson Canyon.

[31] Wagner, Sandra, *4UR Ranch*, pg. 98; *Lake City Mining Register*, June 17, 1881; *Leadville Daily Herald*, "Death of State Senator Henry Henson," September 21, 1882. (Also see Corbett, Thomas B., *The Legislative Manual of the State of Colorado*, pg. 332.)

[32] *Las Animas Leader*, December 3, 1875. (Lafayette Head was elected Lieutenant Governor of the State of Colorado and served from August 1, 1876, to January 14,1879.)

[33] Godwin was accustomed to harrowing experiences, beginning with his ship's Civil War raid deep into Confederate territory to liberate seven hundred slaves. Surely his trek with the Mullin party into hostile Ute territory was also harrowing.

[34] "Harriet Tubman," Wikipedia; and Steve Gould blog, "Harriet Tubman and the Raid at Combahee Ferry," South Hampton History Museum.

[35] Wagner, pg. 98.

[36] Smith, pg. 119.

[37] Lipman, Peter W., Thomas A. Steven, Robert G. Luedke, and Wilbur S. Burbank, "Revised Volcanic History of the San Juan, Uncompahgre, Silverton, and Lake City Calderas in the Western San Juan Mountains, Colorado," pg. 627. (Local geologist Harvey Duchene also warrants credit but no responsibility for the accuracy of the descriptions in this section of the manuscript.)

[38] Ibid., pg. 641.

[39] Curry, Thomas Sherrod III, "San Juans Scenery the Result of Successive Eruptions, Erosion," *Silver Thread Scenic & Historic Byway*, Summer, 2007, pg. 16; and Ellis, Richard N., "The Spanish," *The Western San Juans Mountains*, pgs. 215-222.]

[40] Strahorn, pg. 69. (The unidentified "one writer" Strahorn quotes is Frank Fossett writing in *Colorado, Its Gold and Silver Mines, Tourist's Guide to the Rocky Mountains*, pg. 509.

[41] Among the twenty-seven were H. Campbell and his partner Pike Snowden.

[42] *Silver World*, October 9, 1931.

[43] Ibid.

CHAPTER 3

The Drover

Pat was one of those who neither believed in heaven or hell. Finally, after many a rough voyage on the sea of life, he came to that ultimate end the poet describes as the inevitable. At the wake two old friends met at the coffin. One of them gazed long and sorrowfully at the still countenance of the deceased brother. The other, after a short scruting [sic.], began to laugh.

"And what are ye laughin' at," demanded the first.

"Well," answered the mirthful one, "ye know that Pat niver belaved in hivin?"

"Yes".

"And ye know that he niver belaved in hell?"

"Yes."

"And here is the poor divil, all dressed up and no place to go!"

Like Pat, Pike Snowden also endured many a rough voyage. He was an uneducated trail-hardened drover, before he was a Henson Canyon prospector, miner, recluse, and folk hero. Pike could neither read nor write. Most of what is known about him comes from the writings and recollections of others, most notably William F.E. Gurley, a new found Henson Canyon friend. Gurley was nothing like Pike. W.F.E. as he preferred to be called, provides the sharpest insight into the drover's character. W.F.E. became a world-renowned paleontologist while still a teenager and a brilliant Cornell University graduate before he was a San Juan camp cook, mucker, University of Chicago professor emeritus, and a founding member of the Geological Society of America. Yet his days in the San Juans remained his most cherished memories and his writings provide another first-hand perspective on early Henson Canyon developments. As improbable as any divine appointment, the contrasts between the drover and the cook illustrate the range of opportunities available to nineteenth-century adventurers determined enough to pursue them. Pike and W.F.E. exemplified another dimension of what became known as the "American Experience." On a personal level they exemplified how even a drover and a cook had parts to play in a king's last best chance to make a mine. First, the drover.

The occupation of drover, like so many other frontier callings, befell the very young as well as the very old. The services of the drover were introduced to the Western frontier with the life-or-death need to provision the Forty-Niners and the tens of thousands of emigrants that followed them to the Pacific coast. Settlers along the Oregon, Mormon, and California trails of the 1840s — homesteaders before there was a Homestead Act — typically were "off the farm" and capable of provisioning themselves. With the discovery of California gold at the end of the decade, providing for oneself took a different direction. Finding gold took obsessive precedence over cultivating fields or tending livestock and gave birth to a new class of entrepreneur. Long-held values of pioneer self-sufficiency gave way to mercantilism with markets stocked with all manner of produce and meat in exchange for legal tender, gold for the most part. Those who failed to find their fortune in the placer or hard rock mine often defaulted to shopkeepers who mined the miner in their country stores. Drovers helped supply the stores.

Walter Crow, Alexander Fancher, and cattlemen by the name of Thompson, Brown, and Waddle were among the first to appreciate just how lucrative trading beef for California gold could be. The Texas cattle industry and to a considerable

Drovers. Beginning in the 1840s, "drovers," an international term for "cowboys," drove Texas longhorns north to frontier markets, eventually intercontinental railroad depots, and west to Colorado mining camps. Cattle drives continued well into the 1880s and 1890s. (*Wikipedia*)

extent the food supply of the interior West was revolutionized when in 1850 they drove their first herd from Texas over the California Trail and South Pass to the newly discovered gold fields. Not to ignore an idea full of promise, others drove their herds westward along southern routes from Texas and Arkansas. In *With Golden Visions Bright Before Them*, Will Bagley puts flesh on these bones:

> *About eight hundred California-bound cows crossed the Missouri at Saint Joseph in mid-May, while William Bedford Temple found 'not less than 3,000 cattle on the ground' at the Big Blue in early June.*
>
> *Cyrus Loveland had served in California during the war with Mexico and made $18,000 during the seven months he spent in the California gold-fields in 1848. Eager to return west, he hired on with Walter Crow as a drover—the term "cowboy" did not come into fashion until after the Civil War.*
>
> *Throughout the gold rush, the cattle crowding the California Trail proved immensely profitable and became a major business, with large herds driven from Missouri, Illinois, Arkansas, and the Indian Territory (Oklahoma). California Trail cattle herds were smaller than the preferred size of about 2,500 head that became popular after the Civil War during the golden age of Texas-Kansas cattle drives, but in 1852, 90,000 head of loose cattle passed Fort Kearny on their way to the gold fields.*[7]

Proof of principal was demonstrated. Assuming the drover and his herd survived all manner of mischief or worse, a good living could be made driving livestock to an exploding Pacific coast population too smitten by gold fever to raise cattle or much else for themselves. Once etched into the prairie, this track was visible for a century to come. Herd after herd plodded along the northern Missouri-Platte River to the utter decimation of what little grass grew there to sustain the rapidly dwindling buffalo herds. With the discovery of gold along the Colorado Rockies Front Range, Texas cattlemen tumbled to the same money-making scheme. They pioneered cattle drives up the Arkansas, and eventually up the Pecos and Rio Grande to its upper reaches.

But profiting from a cattle drive was more difficult than it seemed. Rodman W. Paul summarizes the decades-long struggle in *The Far West and the Great Plains in Transition*. In 1858 Oliver Loving made history when he drove a herd of Texas Longhorns north through Illinois to the Chicago stockyards. When the Civil War erupted three years later, Oliver was in Denver selling cattle that he drove there through New Mexico to supply the ballooning Rocky Mountain mining region. Rodman Paul explains.

> *Then came the intervention of the war, with Texas cut off from external markets by the Union forces and with few men at home to tend the cattle. Left by themselves on the ample ranges, the Longhorns multiplied so freely that the*

returning veterans after the war found their ranges crowded with stock far in excess of the demands of familiar markets. Yet in the meantime the continued industrial and commercial development in the Middle West was constantly enlarging the urban market for food. A cow that would sell for three or four dollars in Texas was worth ten times that amount in the north. What is more, with railroad transportation now well-established west of the Mississippi and increasingly available west of the Missouri, there was no need to repeat Loving's exploit of trailing cattle all the way through Illinois; at any one of several railheads stock could be loaded for Chicago or St. Louis.[3]

Of course there were complications—the cattle were wild and loose on open range. But they also were free for the taking, or more accurately stated, free for the catching. Rounded up and driven north to Kansas railheads and Rocky Mountain boomtowns served important interests of a healing and growing Nation. Texans were gainfully employed and a westerly wave of northern emigrants had beef for dinner. Among the most appreciative were Rocky Mountain miners and settlers. A new industry was birthed.

Less appreciative were farmers in Arkansas, Missouri, and eastern Kansas who took offense to marauding Texan herds destroying everything in their path. The Texan's drives in the 1850s had shown that the trail herds could decimate everything in their paths, and that the South Texas cattle could infect local dairy and beef cattle with the "Texas fever." Not understood in its day, South Texas cattle were virtually immune to it because of long exposure. It was transmitted by ticks which naturally migrated to local cattle that had never before been exposed resulting in sickness and often quick death. As early as 1855 Missouri passed a law against the admission of Texas cattle. A stiffer statute followed in 1861. Kansas copied Missouri in 1859 and 1861. As one can

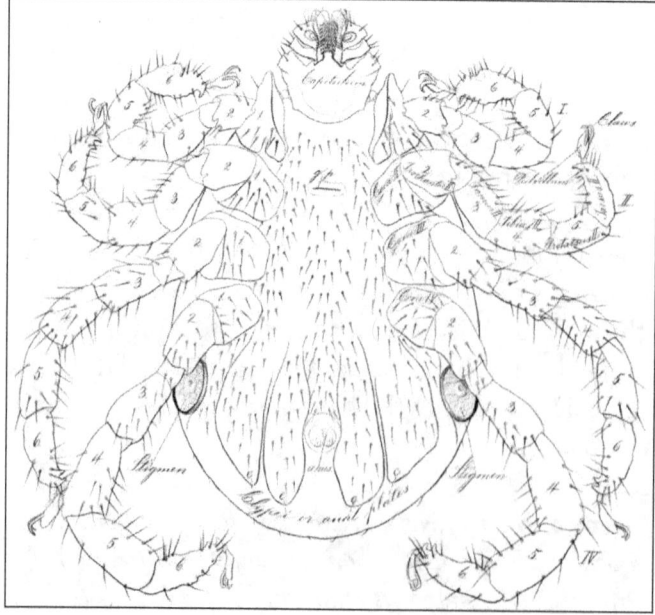

Texas Fever. The bane of all, at least Texas cattle were immune to their mortal effects. This rendering of the culprit that nearly ended Texas cattle drives to northern markets includes an evil grimace. *(National Agricultural Library, 1900)*

imagine, absent authorized law enforcement, armed gangs of farmer-vigilantes enforced the prohibitions by turning back trail herds at gunpoint.[4]

Matters worsened. The Kansas-Missouri-Arkansas borders became increasingly lawless as the secession of southern states and the outbreak of open warfare became more likely. Farmer-vigilantes morphed easily into cattle thieves that fomented violence and intimidation. A consequence of both trends was a new and relatively, (emphasis on "relatively,") safer route first westward across Texas, then north to Colorado mines and the rapidly approaching transcontinental railheads.

> *No one ever accused Charles Goodnight of lacking courage or vision, but in 1865 and 1866, as he debated how to market the stock that he found when he returned from wartime service, he decided that rather than strike directly north to Kansas, he would risk the hazards of fierce Indians and extreme aridity in order to sweep southwest through Texas to the Pecos River, then up that watershed and through the length of New Mexico to Colorado. In Colorado, he reasoned, there must be money because of the mines, and there would be ample free pasture in case he had to hold his cattle for a rise in prices.[5]*

Of like minds, Charles Goodnight and Oliver Loving joined forces and the Goodnight-Loving Trail was cut into Western history. In 1866 with a trail-hardened crew of Texas drovers that could have easily included young Snowden— he resided in Montgomery County, Texas in 1860, in Bents Fort, Colorado in 1870—Goodnight and Loving drove 2,000 head of cattle to Fort Sumner, New Mexico. Some of the herd was sold to a contractor charged with feeding starving Navajo and Mescalero Apache imprisoned there. Goodnight returned seven hundred miles to Texas to gather another herd while Loving continued on to Colorado to sell the remainder of their stock to John W. Iliff, soon to be known as the "cattle king of the plains."[6]

Not all Texas cattlemen shared Goodnight's and Loving's vision. Most, in fact, still preferred a more direct route north, if not to St. Louis or Chicago then at least to a railhead and freight service leading there. Texas drovers and northern buyers established a railhead west of Kansas farmland where Texas fever was not a concern. First Abilene and ultimately Dodge City, Kansas, and Ogallala, Nebraska earned bragging rights, but only for a time. Cattle trails and railheads were pushed ever-westward by the pressure of encroaching farmers. Rodman Paul reports:

> *The significance of the Long Drive was enormous. A well-informed Federal official estimated that from 1866 through 1884, less than twenty years, more than 5.2 million cattle were driven north from Texas. That meant that in a normal year a cattle army of 150,000 to 400,000 went plodding*

north, divided into herds of about 2,500, each shepherded by a dozen hands and advancing ten or fifteen miles a day, on a journey that might last two to three months—or might take longer, if the drive started at the Rio Grande and finished in Montana.[7]

Not only would the cattle industry be transformed, the entire nation's food economy and the western Great Plains would never be the same. Farms and ranches replaced roaming buffalo herds and Native American range lands. The transcontinental railroad system displaced freighters and stagecoaches. The land beyond the Mississippi and Missouri, bursting with life, displaced trackless prairie. And of course gold and silver discoveries, and a steady influx of wide-eyed emigrants, primed the pump.

This is the world of adventure and opportunity Pike (born Zenas) Snowden entered alone no older than sixteen at most. Handling livestock was a trade in demand and so were farm boys, illiterate or not, willing and usually eager to make their way in a boundless land. Pike's journey began near Westport, Missouri. Missouri is not often thought of as a State with a frontier legacy, or the ragged edge of civilization and the beginning of an inhospitable and threatening wasteland as late as the Lincoln presidency, but it was.

By 1803, American westward expansion had crowded the banks of the Mississippi River. St. Louis was a French village in French territory on the far bank, but the Louisiana Purchase put an end to that. The barrier to western expansion was breached and the Indiana and Illinois frontier would not contain another generation of settlers and treasure-seekers. By 1820, Ray County, Missouri, located along the Kansas-Missouri border, was tamed and would soon experience similar growth pains. Ten years later it boasted 2,657 residents. By 1840, 6,553 mostly homesteaders lived there. The 1850 census recorded 10,373 souls including six-year-old Zenas Snowden. A decade later, 1860 Ray County and its aptly named *Westport*, the new frontier, reported 14,092 men, women and children. Notably, sixteen-year-old Zenas was not counted among them. [8]

Pike Snowden was born on his family's Ray County farm in 1844. In the late 1840s nearby Westport was a scrappy frontier river port boasting all manner of supplies and distractions for traders, emigrants, and renegades willing to challenge the "Great American Desert," otherwise known as the Great Plains. Its legacy included provisioning Santa Fe and Oregon trail adventurers. The Rocky Mountains and the wilderness beyond was fair game if one fancied himself a mountain man. For those traveling from the far side of the Great Plains back to "the States," meaning civilization to the extent it existed in Missouri and all points east, Westport promised relief from all that troubled the harried soul. Within a short decade or two it would become home to a thriving industry promoting and provisioning settlements throughout the West. A few decades more and it would be a western suburb of a thriving Kansas City.

When Abraham Lincoln was assassinated Zenas was in Colorado Territory. Perhaps he had signed on with the Butterfield Stage Line and worked his way south to Texas and on to Colorado, or he may have worked his way to Texas by way of Colorado. He may even have been a "Fifty-Niner." Like other brave-hearts numbering in the tens of thousands, he easily could have been swept up in the excitement of the Pikes Peak gold rush, even adopted his nickname because of it. Let's just assume that is the case. In this scenario he walked to nearby Westport, or signed on with a riverboat headed upriver to Independence or St. Joseph. Westport was shrouded in adventure and opportunity, so-named for good reason. Ancestral trails of traders and marauders began there, etched deeper and broader by military wagons and Santa Fe traders, Mormon colonists, and Oregon-bound settlers that soon followed. Independence and St. Joseph were closer still to the prize.

In 1849, early reports of California placer gold reached Westport and the trading posts boomed. In similar fashion, a decade later John Cantrell's news of Rocky Mountain gold breathed new life into Westport along with its fledgling more westerly Missouri River sisters strung out along routes to the Colorado Front Range. Word of the Pikes Peak gold surely reached the Snowden farm. Sitting around the dinner table or in front of the kitchen fireplace, the Snowden children listened to talk of national politics and western opportunities. Open, peaceful lands and bountiful mountain treasures beckoned from the West. Imagine young Zenas's teenage dreams.

Whether motivated to escape a crowded home, or grueling frontier farm, or the increasing number of violent acts of northern and southern sympathizers edging ever closer to civil war, or simply enticed by dreams of a better life fending for himself, Zenas never said. In fact, there is no record from any known source of Zenas sharing the reasons why he chose any of the paths he took in his life. All we can be sure of is that the air was full of talk about Pikes Peak gold,[9] and

Tall Tales to Texas. Pike Snowden told a number of tall tales about his days as a stagecoach driver. Some of them may have been true. *(Wikipedia)*

that he turned his back on parents and siblings and never looked back. And we can be sure that he was comfortable around livestock, that the nearby Butterfield stage to Texas and beyond could always make use of another hand, and that in 1860 young Snowden lived with a Montgomery County, Texas ranch family at the southern arm of the expanding Butterfield line and the eastern arm of cattle trails leading west. [10]

Much of what is known about Pike's early years comes from census records and conjecture. Some conjecture is rooted in his tall tales, and of course friend Gurley's writings. Where Pike stood on slavery and the approaching Civil War, burning social issues of his day, also is unknown, but we can offer an educated guess. Pike's father, David Snowden, was a slave owner in Kentucky before the family moved to the Missouri frontier, but he seems to have repented before young Zenas left home. Missouri tax records list no slaves on the Snowden farm. More certain, in 1861 David Snowden returned to Kentucky, joined the Union Army, and served in the 3rd Regiment of the Kentucky Calvary. He survived the war and returned to Ray County. Little is written about Nancy Snowden,

---

TALL TALES

[Some taller than others.]

Tall tales can be the product of an active imagination and a keen sense of humor. Some can be true, or somewhat so.

Few of Pike Snowden's life-experiences are documented, but he was fond of sharing stories about his adventures with visitors to his cabin on Henson Creek who paused long enough to listen. Always entertaining, they also were usually well-beyond belief. His days as a young drover, perhaps even a Butterfield stage-coach hand, could have been real and thus the basis for the following tale. Told to Carolyn and Clarence Wright and shared in their first-hand accounts collected in *Tiny Hinsdale of the Silvery San Juan*, does it and several variations of it shed light on his life before settling in Henson Canyon? You decide. [11]

"Pike," I said one day, "tell me about some of your experiences of the early days." Pike scratched his head and thought for a minute before answering. Then he said, "Well I don't know what to tell you about onless (sic) I tell you about the stage I drove in the early days here."

"That will be fine," I said. "Where did you drive this stage?"

"Between here and Californie. I forget just how many horses I had, but I had so many, and the roads was so windin' that after I hitched up in the mornin', I never saw my leaders agin until night."

Zenas's mother. She was gifted musically, or at least nurtured musical interests in her daughters. According to tax records, the family bought a piano in 1866, an addition to family assets quite rare for hard scrabble frontier farmers.

Prodigal son (this one never humbly returned home) Zenas was at least six years into himself by the time his sisters got their piano and most likely knew nothing or cared anything about home. While we can only imagine what he had thought of the concerns of a genteel mother and a dutiful father discussing the makings of the war about to engulf them all, or the increasing violence among slave-holders and abolitionists, we do not have to belabor the action he took. Zenas left home. In fact, Zenas left the region. By the time Abraham Lincoln was elected President and the American Civil War was a foregone conclusion, Zenas was in Texas on a course that led west.

If Pike Snowden went west in 1859, he learned quickly as did most who hastily made that journey that the hardships of getting to what became Denver and Idaho Springs and Blackhawk and Boulder, even more so Charles Baker in Leadville and his

Pike Snowden. Uneducated and unremorseful, the trail and the mining frontier hardened Zenas into a self-reliant recluse. Somehow through it all he managed to retain a child-like heart and cultivate a pundits' sense of humor. (Lake City Silver World)

expedition into the San Juans, was no less challenging once there. Most discovered within weeks that placer gold worth panning was nearly impossible to find. Unlike California where placer gold nuggets were plentiful, most Colorado gold was bound up in lodes. Almost all of the hearty who survived the journey, as many as 100,000 and probably a great deal more, struggled back to the States before winter weather barred their retreat.

If Zenas did make it to the Colorado gold fields with the first frantic 1858-59 wave of Argonauts, he returned to the States, to Montgomery County, Texas, in time for the 1860 U.S. Census. If Pike was a Pikes Peak wanna-be prospector in 1859, according to the U.S. Census Bureau he was a Texas drover in 1860 and 1870. If not during the Pike's Peak excitement, where did Pike pickup his nickname and learn enough about prospecting to locate the rich Ocean Wave vein in Henson Canyon fifteen years later?

There *are* other explanations, of course. Pike may have labored in Westport quarries or mucked out nearby lead-zinc mines. As an entire generation of young Americans would soon conclude, Western mining was preferable to midwestern farming. Obviously teachable—a likeable sort—he could have learned enough about prospecting from partners in need of a strong hand. He could neither read nor write, but he was no dolt. We will soon see he had a keen sense of humor and a sharp if not civilized tongue. In time he proved to be a savvy underground "engineer." By some accounts he also was a shrewd investor and accomplished gambler. He did not need reading, writing, and arithmetic to master the ways of his world.

Directly or indirectly, the Butterfield Overland Stagecoach Line suited Pike Snowden well. Beginning in Saint Louis, Butterfield coaches followed the Missouri River valley jarring along rough trails toward future Kansas City before veering south through the Ozarks into Texas and points west. In due course the route widened, deepened, and became known as the Texas Road. (Later still it was part of iconic Route 66.) Coaches stuffed with all manner of adventurer and commerce passed through Missouri and corners of Arkansas and Oklahoma, through present-day Springfield, Joplin, Fort Smith and Atoka. Teams and teamsters labored between way-station after way-station 800 miles across Texas to the Rio Grande, northwest to Sana Fe and west to El Paso, through Tucson and Yuma to Los Angeles, and on north as far as San Francisco.

MONTGOMERY COUNTY, TEXAS

Why Montgomery County? Did young Snowden sign on with the Butterfield overland mail service as a stable-hand or teamster? Butterfield stages ran regularly across the breadth of Missouri between St. Louis and south Texas by way of Ray County. The "how" and the "why" are lost to history, the "when" is clear. The 1860 U.S. Census records Zenas Snowden residing in Montgomery County, Texas, a drover.

Why Texas? If Pike abandoned Missouri to escape the violence preceding the onset of outright war, or to avoid service in the Union or Confederate armies, Texas was not a wise choice. Missouri and Texas were much alike in that communities in both states were conflicted over slavery and state's rights. Missouri was a contested border state populated by both Union and Confederate sympathizers. Missourians provided soldiers, generals, and supplies to both sides. The flags of both Union and Confederate forces bore a Missouri star. Missouri maintained dual governments and endured vicious neighbor versus neighbor raids throughout the broader conflict. Texas was much the same. If avoiding the battlefield was the goal, Colorado was a better choice.

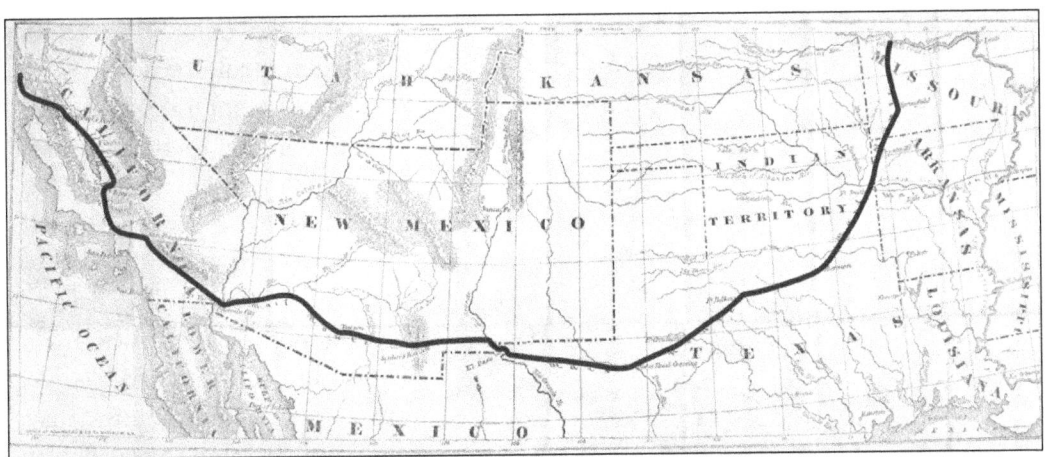

Butterfield Overland Stage Line. Short-lived but impressive, the first coach departed San Francisco on September 15, 1858. A westbound coach departed St. Louis a day later. *(Wikipedia)*

If the treasures of the Gulf coast appealed to one's fancy, Fort Smith accommodated with scheduled service south to Galveston. If Colorado was the desired destination, trails followed the Arkansas River west to Bents Fort and Taos/Santa Fe, or the Rio Grande north to its headwaters in the San Juans Range. Is it possible that a decade of adventures on these trails—with Butterfield or Loving or Goodnight—account for some of the most outrageous Pike Snowden tales?

On February 1, 1861, the reality of war reached Montgomery County. On that day Texas seceded from Lincoln's Union and a month later joined the Confederate States of America. Surprising to some, beloved Governor Sam Houston refused to swear allegiance to the Confederacy. Some 90,000 Texans served in the Confederate Army, but perhaps as many as 2,000 joined the Union ranks despite conscription laws that forced men of military age into the Confederacy. Often loyalties and volunteers to both causes came from the same families and communities. Brother against brother and father against son were not exaggerations. One segment of the population most opposed to secession was that of German descent. Those who did not change their views were in great jeopardy. Many had fled the state, or had attempted to do so. Often they had been pursued and executed. Pike Snowden could easily have been one of the fortunate ones who escaped west. [12]

The Haub family was of German descent, part of a growing "colony" of German immigrants in East and Central Texas, and most likely opposed to secession and slavery. Quite likely Pike Snowden, as was his Missouri family, was similarly disposed. If Pike's decision to seek his fortune in Texas had anything to do with Confederate sympathies, the prospect of serving in the army chilled his interest. More likely, his interests were limited to hitching a ride to wherever the ride was headed.

Sam Houston's Revolt. Revolt to the secessionist Confederacy, that is. Hero of the Mexican War, twice President of the Republic of Texas, Governor of the Lone Star State, Sam Houston and thousands of other Texans were not secessionists. Sam was deposed and lived the last two years of his life in virtual house arrest. *(Wikipedia)*

Making one's way in a Confederate culture, Missourian or Texan, absent military service was not going to be pleasant. Quite likely his German hosts advised that he continue moving west. They probably knew little of western allegiances—Coloradoans leaned toward the Union but not universally so—but western communities may be remote enough to stay out of harm's way.

Again, exactly how and when Snowden moved west is not known. Stages and freighters traveled the breadth of Texas throughout the war, and with the end of hostilities and the fragmented beginnings of reconstruction, Texans returning home greatly needed strong young lads like Pike. Pike was a drover, drovers were in short supply, emigration to Colorado increased, and quite naturally demand for beef was high. In 1870, Pike Snowden registered as a drover in Bents Fort, Colorado. His Texas days were finished.

Coincident with Texans returning home to neglected ranches were two developments in neighboring states that transformed these challenges into new opportunities. Along with increasing migration to Colorado came the accelerated construction of the intercontinental railroad system. Colorado recognition as a Territory, on the cusp of the Civil War, was the first step in achieving sufficient population to justify becoming a state in 1876. It also was a necessary precondition for growth of a statewide mining industry. Despite the dampening effects of the Civil War, the birthing of this industry quickly turned to Denver, upstart communities in southern Colorado, and existing communities in northern New Mexico for provisions. As a blessing to many Texans, in every Colorado mining camp and town existed a seemingly insatiable appetite for beef—mining after all was hard work.

Augmenting this demand was a growing Western military presence tasked with a growing obligation to "protect" Native American populations deprived of their traditional hunting grounds and food sources, namely buffalo. Doing their best to bankrupt freighting outfits and also trying to catch up with the Colorado market, two intercontinental railroads pushed steadily across Kansas and eastern Colorado from the east, and through California, Nevada and Utah from the west. Driving a golden spike (quickly retrieved and currently on display in the Stanford University museum) at Promontory, Utah, on May 10, 1869, symbolized the completion of reliable coast to coast commerce and the indisputable inauguration of a continental nation. While rail transport to Denver was possible by 1867, twenty-six year old Pike Snowden along with partner Henry Campbell were still employed as drovers near Bents Old Fort, Colorado Territory.[13]

It is not known how or how early Pike and his partner teamed up or found their way into the San Juans, but it is reasonable to assume they worked their way west from Old Bents Fort driving cattle to the mining camps or contracted gold fever when they learned gold had been located on the upper Lake Fork of the Gunnison River. It is known that Snowden and Campbell were camped at the mouth of Henson Canyon in the spring of 1876, half a decade after the Old Bent's Fort census taker ratted them out. Their whereabouts and occupations between 1870 and 1876 is anyone's guess, but there is no question their drover days were coming to an end thanks to the expanding railroads. They were about to become full-time prospectors and mine speculators counted among the first twenty-seven brave-hearts to assault Fortress San Juans' castle-keep. Of the two, Pike's journey would result in folk-hero status, at the very least an example of a small but not uncommon class of restless young men that settled the West. Partner Campbell was an example of a larger and more common class, an unknowable class that loses itself to history.[14]

Pike's transformation from drover to silver miner began at the mouth of Henson Canyon in a most unusual manner. It began with a divine appointment that revealed qualities in two men's character that surfaced and resurfaced for decades to come. What made this appointment memorable was the fact that the two men—Pike Snowden and W.F.E. Gurley—could not have been more starkly different, nor have taken more divergent paths. Snowden the drover and prospector "wanna-be," Gurley the eastern intellectual on a summer lark, nevertheless stayed bonded. Neither Snowden nor Gurley made much of their first encounter at the time, but over the next few months a friendship developed that defied logic and lasted a lifetime. Snowden discovered a valuable silver mine and was content to became a recluse. Gurley cooked and mucked for nearby prospectors and returned to an academic life back East. Separated by half a continent, neither lost sight of those early Henson Canyon days. For the balance of their lives neither were tempted to attribute their meeting to faithless handmaidens others called "Coincidence," "Good Fortune," and "Luck." In starkly different ways, both were enriched by the character of the other and held that experience close to their hearts. Their divine appointment was improbable, but thanks be to a cook who liked to write, we know it was unlike other frivolous drover's tales.

The Henson Canyon rush, a rush that quickly generated the "San Juans Excitement," had humble beginnings. Standing beside an evening campfire, men of the vanguard no doubt like men around countless prospector campfires before and since, entertained each other with adventure tales. When it came to Pike's turn, one could imagine him spinning one of his tall tales. Imagine standing with them, recently arrived William Gurley intently listened. His youthful curiosity and outward good-nature surely attracted Pike's attention. Maybe Pike was reminded of his own state of mind at that age, or earlier still in the family kitchen listening to tales of Pike's Peak gold, and the Forty-Niners a decade before then.

For Gurley's part, like so many easterners of his time, he was caught up in the spirit of Western adventure sweeping the nation. In response to news of the rush to the San Juans, he set aside his academic pursuits and found his way to Henson Canyon. In Henson Canyon he was no longer an easterner, he was welcomed as a fellow brave-heart, albeit in his case a lowly laborer brave-heart. Like most other mining camps, certainly post-Civil War Western mining camps, one's past or heritage was of no account. Rebel and Yankee, eastern gentry and frontiersman, all worked and lived side by side. Anyone willing to tolerate the hardships of frontier life was a friend until proven otherwise.

Gurley had joined a group of partners that had located the Big Casino Lode the previous season and were returning to work it. Enthusiastic and strong, his job was mucking and cooking. (Mucking was back-breaking removal of debris blasted down in the mine. Cooking was less strenuous but subject to hard-to-stomach criticism.) In a quiet moment, Snowden called Gurley aside and asked if he would be interested in joining his gang. Gurley declined, perhaps explaining

Snowden Cabin. Beyond humble, it suited Pike for the better part of three decades. It overlooked a meadow on his Owl Gulch claim, a site of many July 4th celebrations of nearby miners, and the county wagon-road leading into Lake City. (Author's Collection)

his commitment to the Big Casino men. What should have been the end of a tempting encounter instead marked the beginning of a life-long relationship. Learning more about Gurley's character does not leave us wondering why. The next day the drover and the cook went their separate ways, but they did not lose contact with one another. The Big Casino and the about-to-be located Ocean Wave were within sight of one another, a short distance across Henson Canyon.

The effects of Snowden's and Gurley's divine appointment lingered with both men, but Gurley was best equipped to express them. His writings in later years were laced with Pike-inspired insights and references to his uncouth demeanor and uneducated sense of humor. Like so many others throughout Pike's life, Gurley saw in Pike's clear sparkling eyes humility and simple charm even in the midst of his curious mix of simple lifestyle and braggadocio storytelling.

While Snowden rooted himself in Henson Canyon, Gurley wandered the Rocky Mountains for a season before returning east to the life of an intellectual. Even so, his Henson Canyon experiences were never far from his thoughts. Encounters with Pike were reflected in sometimes joyful, sometimes remorseful remembrances and poems. The cook and mucker that became an internationally acclaimed scholar never lost sight of what it was like being a cook and a mucker, or what it was like being a drover, hard scrabble miner, and recluse. The impact of this season on his life is revealed in a most interesting way in a March 28, 1921, letter written forty-five years after those cherished days in Henson Canyon. Reminiscent of Robert Frost's *The Road Not Taken*, Gurley recalled the threatening condition of the canyon and the details of his missed opportunity to share in Pike's Ocean Wave fortune:

> *Early in the spring of '76 I worked, as a miner, on one of the shifts at the Big Casino mine. In going to this job—with the mine superintendent—I plodded along the old Henson Creek trail which was primitive and very tedious owing to the considerable depth of snow, as well as the slides. At that time, due to the zig-zagging of the creek through the walls of the cañon, there were sixteen (gravel) bars and as many footlogs on the trail in the first mile and a half above Lake City. Just before we came to the last foot log crossing over to the Big Casino, we fell in with a bunch of boys who had just put up a dirty old wall tent and were preparing to get down to business as prospectors. These fellows soon arranged matters so that, while two were engaging the superintendent, the other was trying every possible way to induce me to go in with them as a partner, the condition being that they furnish the grub and supplies while I did the cooking. Somehow I was not impressed favorably with such a proposition and I even refused to try the thing "just for a day," for it was Saturday and I would not begin work "til the bone yard shift" late Sunday night. Had I "tried it for a day" then would I (sic) have been in on the stake which early the following morning was set up on the Ocean Wave and*

its extension, the Wave of the Ocean — one of the finest and most promising propositions at that time in sight.[15]

Gurley's fortune would have to be made by instinct, strength of character, and intellect in the normal course of tamer circumstances, in the normal course of lifelong pursuits. As for the Ocean Wave, it straddled a rich lead/zinc/silver vein that made Pike Snowden a man of means in a single day. During early 1876 the mountains and gulches on both sides of Henson Canyon filled with prospectors and soon all the veins that were cropping on the surface and easily found were staked and superficially examined. Well documented, "Zene" Snowden, George Boggs, and William R. Bernard began tracing mineral "float" that they found in the mouth of Red Rover Gulch opening into Henson Canyon opposite the Big Casino. The gulch is a steep and rocky watershed seasonally scoured by snowmelt and wet weather runoff. In early spring runoff typically ran strong enough to bring new treasure from above along with debris that covered high-grade ore from the year before. Working their way up the gulch, Pike and his partners located an ore outcrop, the likely source of the "float." On April 17th they staked their claim and named it the "Ocean Wave Lode." Why that name in the San Juans Range teases speculation that Pike's nautical tales may have had an element of truth. A month later they staked the adjacent Wave of the Ocean, thought to be a continuation of the same vein, and on August 22,1876 filed Mineral Application Nos. 31 and 32 at the U.S. Land Office in Del Norte. [16]

Lake City Mill. 1887 Lake City still lacks railroad service, but the Ocean Wave mill at the upper right of the photo testifies to investor confidence that concentrating ores can make up for this handicap. *(Courtesy of P. David Smith)*

OCEAN WAVE LEASES

The Ocean Wave vein underpins scores of mining claims including the Vermont Lode. The vein is a clearly defined fissure carrying ore bodies six inches to four feet wide. The ore is comprised of galena and gray copper. There also is some gold, speculators believing that the deeper the ore the higher the concentrations. Zinc concentrations are low which simplifies smelting. Leasing the right to develop veins was a common source of underwriting a project, either with direct cash contributions or through "sweat equity," work paid for with shares of future profits rather than a daily wage. Of course there were downsides for all parties concerned. According to the *Lake City Phonograph*:

> As with almost all Hinsdale County mines the total value of the Ocean Wave output is entirely a matter of estimate, but it is conservative to say that it was at least $250,000 and was probably considerably more. It has always been considered by those most familiar with it that the Ocean Wave was one of the best mining propositions in the San Juan and, like the Ute, Ulay and Hidden Treasure, would doubtless be working today (1910) if fair leasing terms could be obtained.[17]

"Fair leasing terms" was a common criticism of mine owners with the savvy of an A.E. Reynolds. Reynolds' extensive mining experience taught him the hard way that leases ruin the long-term value of a property if reckless short-term activities are tolerated. His approach to this common industry practice was lease agreements that contained stringent guidelines and mandatory payment milestones. Equitable or not, throughout the first decade of the 1900s leases were of no interest to Reynolds. If he could not continue to finance a project with investor money, he suspended work. A decade later he was more inclined to consider leases.

In fact, unappreciated at the time, the vein they claimed ran for miles in both directions along the west rim of Henson Canyon and in short order hosted scores of additional claims, the Vermont Group, one of several chief among them. In not so "short order," Albert Eugene Reynolds would appreciate the reach of the vein. The April 9, 1910, *Lake City Phonograph* revisited the historic occasion: "A splendid body of ore was soon established" in the Ocean Wave and "shipments of high-grade minerals were made to various places."

As is often the case, it was not long thereafter that investors far and wide sought out the former drover and his partners. A company was organized by Kansas City capitalists and John and Thomas Mastin along with Howard M. Holden

Snowden Meadow. A homestead of sorts with outbuildings no longer standing, Pike Snowden needed little more of what this world offered. *(Courtesy of Lake City Silver World)*

became the principal shareholders. Flush with optimism as well as cash, they erected the Ocean Wave smelter on the north side of Lake City for the reduction of Ocean Wave and regional ores. Snowden ("Zene" to the *Phonograph*) maintained his share and stayed on with the new partners to work the mine. The smelter operated intermittently for two or three years but never mastered the complex metallurgy of the Ocean Wave's lead-based ores. Similar metallurgy characterized most area mines and further diminished the usefulness of the Ocean Wave smelter. Ownership disputes soon led to suspension of mill activities and of Ocean Wave mining operations under company management, but work continued off and on under multiple leasing arrangements for decades to come. This turmoil scarcely affected Pike. Despite his peasant beginnings, he shrewdly navigated ownership and employee challenges and emerged healthy, wealthy, and wise. Nor would such turmoil trouble Reynolds. To the contrary, it piqued his interest and later presented him with a buying opportunity he could not resist.

Snowden Meadow was the epicenter of Pike's world even during his years of involvement with Ocean Wave matters. The 1880 Census listed "Zene" Snowden as a Hinsdale County silver miner and Lake City boarder. "Lake City boarder" is a curious entry, but there is no known record of the details. Pike surely enjoyed someone else's cooking, but surely dreaded having to pay for it. While wintering in Lake City had its good points, less congested surroundings closer to Henson Canyon mines were more to his liking. By most estimates Snowden built his cabin between 1880 and 1890 on a south-facing bench overlooking the wagon-road through Henson Canyon that connected Lake City with Engineer Pass and points west. He appeared in the 1900 and 1910 Census much as before, "miner of silver and lead in Hinsdale County (not Lake City)." Nor was there further mention in census records or town newspapers that someone else did his cooking or that he sheltered anywhere other than Snowden Meadow.

Whatever else he was or became, Pike Snowden made his way through life by his wits and his labor. In 1880, Zene, no longer "Zenas" and increasingly "Pike," enjoyed an abundance of mining opportunities. Scores of silver mines were working along Henson Creek, notably the Pride of America, Big Casino, Vermont, Ocean Wave, Ute/Ulay, Hidden Treasure, and dozens of others less accessible and thus less productive. This was the peak decade for Hinsdale County mining and Pike Snowden was both an occasional day-laborer and a savvy mine owner. He also gained a reputation as a skillful mining "engineer" (not to be confused with university-educated engineers of today). Investors and speculators sought his advice and valued his partnership in their ventures. From the front stoop of his log and rough-sawn cabin he dispensed his style of wisdom in the best tradition of a schooled stuffed-shirt. For some his manner of speech, a dialect all its own, could require a translator. His fondness for tall tales required patience. But wrapped inside it all was advice apparently worth considering, at least men-of-means thought so.

Men of Means. Pictured in Lake City's first automobile, a 1903 Peerless, are owner and son Thomas L. Beam and L.T. Beam in the front seat, with Pike Snowden seated between Jack Henderson and Nels Lee in the rear. With the possible exception of Pike, all were wealthy mine owners. (*Courtesy of* Lake City Silver World)

PIKE SNOWDEN — MINING MAGNATE

The source of Pike's income was a frequent topic of discussion among the Henson Canyon crowd. Of course there was the instant wealth derived from his share of the Ocean Wave. And there were rumors about winnings playing poker in Creede. There also was the secret gold mine above his meadow, and the inheritance from the Old Country, both of which were unfounded but persistent. Most likely, the small amount of income he required came from buying and selling claims, and working mines and odd jobs as a day-laborer. In the process of describing these activities, the *Hinsdale Phonograph* and *Lake City Times* also revealed more of Pike's personality and interests. Their characterizations also revealed how they and the community viewed the recluse.

> *Phonograph, October 18, 1890. Zenas Snowden (we all know him as the irrepressible Pike) who has been working J.L. Kinsey's wellknown Owl Gulch property, the '81', brought down a ton of the ore to the sampler the first of the week, the result, he says, of seven days' work on the mine.*

> *Times, May 21, 1891. Then comes the Yellow Jacket and Meat Augur owned by that old pioneer prospector Zenas Snowden, the 'positively only' and 'irrepressible' Pike has been dreaming for years of a fast team, a brown stone front and a spotted dog. And these prospects will 'fetch em' he thinks.*

> *Times, June 14, 1894. Pike Snowden is filling potholes between Capital City and Henson.*

> *Times, August 30, 1894. Pike Snowden claims to have struck it rich in a new prospect he is working up Henson. He says the ore contains ruby silver and gold, and he thinks he is very rich.*

> *Times, November 12, 1896. The only and original Pike Snowden of the upper Henson creek, spent several days in Lake City last week listening to the election news as it came in over the wires.*

> *Times, March 4, 1897. Pike Snowden is driving away on his tunnel across the creek from the Sacramento.*

> *Times, April 8, 1897. Sacramento Group, Yellow Jacket: Pike Snowden, who is authority on all mining questions in this locality, and besides being vice-president of the above named mining company (Snowden M&M), has several good properties of his own.*

> *Times, May 6, 1897. Pike Snowden is shipping two cars of Ocean Wave ore, a fine body of ore in the stope and in the breast of their tunnel.*

> Times, *April 28, 1898. Pike Snowden came down Monday to read the war bulletins. When asked if he intended going to war, he said the young men could go first and if they were not strong enough the old men could then be counted on.*
>
> Times, *May 19, 1898. Pike Snowden working the Special Payment on Henson Creek; shipped six sacks worth $108.79.*
>
> Times, *June 15, 1899. Pike Snowden sold the Meat Augur to the Red Rover Mining Co.*
>
> Times, *December 13, 1906. Pike Snowden last week completed the assessment work on the Copper King in Owl Gulch [Snowden Meadow].*

Notes—Chapter Three: The Drover

1. *Creede Candle*, February 14, 1920, "No Heaven—No Hell."
2. Bagley, Will, *With Golden Visions Bright Before Them*, Vol. II, pgs. 263-265. (Always alert to new opportunities, Uncle Dick Wootton relates in exquisite detail his experience driving 9,000 head of sheep to the California gold fields in 1852. *Uncle Dick Wootton*, pgs.161-174.)
3. Paul, Rodman W., *The Far West and the Great Plains in Transition 1859-1900*, pg.192.
4. Ibid. (Of course there were many lesser trails to northern and western markets, and a few other popularized ones such as the Chisholm Trail.)
5. Ibid., pg.193.
6. Ibid.
7. Ibid., pg.195.
8. "Zenas" is a shortened version of "Zenodoros." Translated from the Greek it means "gift of Zeus." The Judeo-Christian meaning is "lawyer." (One can assume from this and what we know of his father's actions regarding slavery that Zenas grew up in a Christian home. Son Zenas exhibited Christian values but words and deeds suggest he was far from devout.)
9. Gold-seekers joined parties leaving for the Colorado gold-fields daily, just as they had done years earlier enroute to Oregon, Utah, and California. Ray County and Westport had a rich pioneering legacy overflowing with exciting stories and tall tales.
10. In 1860 several bone-jarring but well-traveled routes south of the Santa Fe Trail led to Texas, the Gulf, and points west. The Butterfield Overland Mail Company operated from 1857 to 1861 when like just about everything else it was disrupted by the War Between the States. Until then, the Butterfield carried mail and passengers across the southwest to California, connecting St. Louis with Texas and San Francisco. The line through Missouri was an easy journey from the Snowden family farm.
11. Wright, Carolyn and Clarence, *Tiny Hinsdale of the Silvery San Juans*, pgs. 146-148.
12. "Texas in the American Civil War," *Wikipedia Online*.
13. Snowden and Henry Campbell are recorded in the 1870 U.S. Census taken at the Old Bents Fort post office. They also are documented as two of the twenty-seven camped at the mouth of Henson Creek in 1876 awaiting a break in the weather. Snowden's whereabouts and activities between 1870 and 1876 are anyone's guess, but time enough to accrue experiences we are amused with in his tall tales.
14. *Lake City Silver World*, April 14, 1921. (Sometimes spelled "Zenith," Pike was among the first twenty-seven prospectors to ascend Henson Canyon in 1875. He may have been one of the unnamed pilgrims who descended the canyon with J.L. Mullin in 1871. He may have adopted

his nickname as early as 1860 as the result of the "Pikes Peak or Bust" frenzy or his time near Old Bents Fort and Pikes Peak. Regardless, he was known as "Pike" in 1876 when he and three partners located the Ocean Wave group of claims. Among the richest of all the Henson Canyon mines, he sold his share and settled in to a primitive cabin in what came to be known as "Snowden Meadow." Sometimes employed by new owners of the Ocean Wave, sometimes prospecting and working other claims, maybe for a change of pace making his way to nearby and raucous Creede for a lively night of poker, Pike definitely spent much of the next several decades entertaining curious visitors with tall tales. There is no record he ever entertained or even met A.E. Reynolds despite his successful Ocean Wave laying the groundwork for A.E.'s treasure hunt two decades later, but they would have had a great deal to talk about if they had.)

[15] Ibid.

[16] If Snowden accompanied J.K. Mullin on his pioneering 1871 prospecting trek down the entire length of Henson Canyon, no one must have noticed or no one remembered signs of the Ocean Wave vein. By the same token, none of the twenty-seven pathfinders first to ascend the canyon early in 1875, Pike Snowden among them, must have seen Ocean Wave "float." This discovery awaited another year, one filled with great activity by hundreds of Argonauts. The likely explanation is that the float they observed was freshly deposited, a natural occurrence of freeze/thaw cycles and erosion. These cycles also explain why deposits from previous years could have been obscured by freshly deposited sediments in 1871 and 1875.

[17] *Lake City Phonograph*, April 9, 1910. Snowden's partners are incorrectly identified in this article. They are George Boggs and William R. Bernard. See Mineral Application Nos. 31 and 32 filed at the U.S. Land Office in Del Norte, CO on August 22, 1876, *Silver World*, September 16, 1876.

CHAPTER 4

Tall Tales

No Man is an island, entire of itself.... therefore
never send to know for whom the bell tolls:
it tolls for thee.

— John Donne —

If we were counting, for fifteen years Pike Snowden was a drover. For three decades Pike prospected, filed mining claims, bought and sold mining claims, and worked with partners or for others when needful. He was a recluse, but he was not a hermit. He welcomed visitors to Snowden Meadow, he flagged down and climbed aboard passing wagons headed to Lake City when he felt the urge. Full of opinions, he was a regular at the *Silver World* and *Lake City Times* offices. Unable to read, he kept up on the national news by gleaning what he overheard sitting outside the telegraph office. Appearing destitute and dangerous at first glance, to everyone who knew him—the rich, the poor, especially the children— his brand of humor and good-nature made many friends. All with eyes to see could see his clear blue eyes opened onto a lovable soul. All with ears to hear heard joy enshrined in his tall tales. Drover, miner, pundit, the heart of the man remained pure.

While rare, Pike did travel to other mining camps. The *Lake City Times* reported that he spent time in Aspen and Telluride. If there was any truth in some of his tall tales, maybe he drove ore freighters and tended locomotive boilers on the transcontinental railroad system as far away as Arizona and Nevada. Somehow he was conversant about borax freighters there. Perhaps reckoning the need to augment his income, the *Times* reported that he was preparing to enter the tourism business—serious or sarcastic is hard to say. Maybe Pike was not the only one who could tell tall tales. The *Times* editor wrote:

> *Pike Snowden has an enterprise a hatching that ought to be quite profitable when carried out as contemplated. He will this summer build a commodious cabin in his park at the mouth of Nellie gulch. Then the wagon road which runs as far as the lime kilns at the Old Spar lode will be extended to the base of*

Uncompahgre Peak. This will be done for the accommodation of tourists who wish to visit the highest point in Colorado. The tourist will be brought up from Lake City to the Snowden Park one evening, and the next morning get an early start for the peak, which can be reached by horseback or burro early in the forenoon. Then they can before returning visit Buzzard's Lake, in the breaks of the Blue, and get some petrified wood which lies above timberline. Pack and riding animals and a guide will be supplied by Mr. Snowden. Work on the Park Tavern and on the extension of the road will be begun right away. [1]

Pike did add what passed for a "room" onto what may have been intended to be his "tavern," but no more is written about this venture. It sounded like a great deal of hard work. He was accustomed to hard work, but managing the logistics of it all may have been the tavern's downfall. More in keeping with his recluse frame of mind, more than being a successful prospector and respected investor sought out for advice and partnerships by far more accomplished men, Pike was most remembered for being the kindly Snowden Meadow jester. Alex Carey writes in his unpublished *Memories, Scenes and Humorous High Lights of Lake City*, he was remembered by some for more than that.

> *Pike Snowden was one of his (Alex's) very most interesting (friends). Though he never had any schoolin' and was not able to read or write he did have a very active imagination – and used it. He lived up Henson Creek about seven [closer to five] miles in a beautiful little park beneath the mountains, all alone. The story, among the kids at least, was that Pike had a secret gold mine and whenever he needed anything [it provided him] with the gold he needed from a vein of solid gold!* [2]

Adults didn't buy the gold mine story, according to Carey, instead some of them believed Pike received a small income from the old country. The kids didn't buy the old country story. Secret gold mines were far more exciting, and besides their friend Pike always had a supply of candy on hand when they came by to see him which somehow seemed to bolster his credibility. More believable but no more reliable was the rumor Pike won a large sum of money in a poker game in Creede. This explanation was supported by the iron bars on his cabin windows, supposedly put there for fear of a sore loser hunting him down, shooting him, and retrieving their money. Scavenging bears would have been a better reason.

Snowden Meadow was strategically located for an enthroned folk-hero like Pike, a pauper's example of Apostle Paul on Mars Hill.[3] While the apostle of Henson Canyon was no Paul, he did lord over his fallen world, and Snowden Meadow did sit on a hill overlooking the heavily trafficked wagon road to Lake City. An hour by horse or wagon down to Lake City when the Spirit moved him, a mile in the opposite direction to the Ocean Wave and Vermont to work claims or check on lessors, Pike was at peace in the center of his domain. And strangers and town folks alike felt welcome there. Carolyn and Clarence Wright certainly did. Thankfully they spent enough time with friend Snowden to see his heart and write about it in *Tiny Hinsdale of the Silvery San Juan*. Thankfully, faithful to these occasions, they captured his trail-slang and avoided many opportunities to tame his tall tales. Instead their writings do much to preserve the nature of the age and a unique San Juans' soul.

Pike was a short rather heavy-set little man with twinkling blue eyes. He could neither read nor write, but he was nobody's fool. He found him a mine, built a cabin on one of the most beautiful spots one could wish to see, and settled down to working his assessments. His cabin was above the road that led to Capitol City, up Henson Creek. In the early days when there was a daily stage to Capitol City, Pike would be down on the road to speak to the stage driver, perhaps to send an order to town or to get what he had ordered the day before.

He always had a story to tell, no matter what subject came up. One time the conversation was about hunting and Pike came up with, "Speakin' of deer, reminds me of one time I was chasing a deer out on the plains with a bunch of dogs. That deer could shore run, but finally my dogs caught up with him and was just about to grab him, when he up and clum a tree." I said, "hold on there, Pike, you know deer can't climb trees." "But," said Pike, "this one had to."

One day Pike said he had his fortune made. He wondered why he had not thought of it before. Asked what he was talking about, he answered that he had made an invention. "What invention?" he was asked. "A contraption for battleships," he answered. "Instead of putting steel on battleships, I'm going to put rubber, yes sir, rubber thirteen foot thick. Bullets can't go through rubber that thick, and iffin they hit an iceberg, instead of being smashed, they'll bounce right away from it."

Another time Pike told about being on a train that was held up by bandits. He said he got away and was running down the hillside away from the train and while he was running, a jackrabbit jumped up out of a bush and ran along beside him. After stepping on the rabbit several times Pike said he yelled: "Git outen the way, and let somebody run what kin."

The Hough Fire Company gave a Masquerade Ball each year on February 2nd. Invitations were sent out to all eligible to attend. One year an invitation was sent to Pike. On the invitation were pictures of hook and ladder and bucket brigade. When the mailman had delivered the invitation to Pike, he delivered a thunderstorm. Pike could not read, but when he saw the pictures on the invitation he went wild. "Tarnation," he exclaimed. "Tarnation," was all he could say. Finally, when he could talk, he said, "I got the bucket, all right, but domned if I got the ladder and them other things, 'n bedad, if I'll pay for 'em." He thought the invitation was a grocery bill.

When the telephone line was put up to Capitol (City) Pike was asked if he did not want a telephone put in. "What do I want with a telephone?" he asked. "When I want to hear anything, all I got to do is hook a forked stick on the wire and put the other end in my mouth and I kin hear everything that's said."

It was as much fun to watch Pike's face when he was spinning a yarn as it was to listen to him. When he started to talk he would look straight at one for a second, blink his eyes, spit out his tobacco juice, and then start to talk. The gestures accompanying his yarns were worth seeing, and often he would pick up a stick and try to illustrate his story in the sand.

Pike's stories were often made more interesting by his dog. Spot had been with him so long folks said they looked alike. When Pike was telling a story Spot would watch his every move, and he always knew when the story included him. "Why should I get lonesome? Ain't I got Spot?" he answered when someone asked him if he did not get tired of living alone. When asked why he never married, he answered, "Git married and have some woman kick Spot around? I should say not. Besides Spot kin do anythin' a woman kin. Ef I get drunk, and don't come home, Spot comes after me and puts me to bed. And ef I don't feel like gittin up in the morning he puts the coffee on and calls me when it's done. A woman would probably want ME to build the fire."

Hough Volunteer Fire Company, 1905. John S. Hough, second cousin of President Ulysses S. Grant, often grubstaked miners as well as financed the Lake City fire department. *(Althea Knowlton,* Images of America, Lake City*)*

I had heard one of his tales about Mexicans, and asked him one day to tell it to me. "Mexicans?" Pike asked. "Oh, yes, Mexicans. Well, sir, I was firin' on the D&RG Railroad in early days and a bunch of Mexicans stopped the train. Afore I knowed what had happened, they was climbin' all over the engine. They killed the engineer, and started for me. I didn't have anything to fight with, so I just grabbed the shovel and started hittin' 'em. Fast as they came over the cab, I hit 'em over the head and the firebox bein' open, I just throwed 'em in the fire as I killed 'em. I cleaned up about fifty Mexicans, and then I moved over to the engineer's seat and started the train. An' by dad, I got her in on time too."

Another real wild tale told by Pike was about his little burro that he used to pack his ore. He claimed that one day he had the burro packed with three hundred pounds of dynamite and that as he was going along a rock fell off the cliff and struck the dynamite. "Well sir," he said, "Do you know that whole three hunert pounds of dynamite exploded at once. The cinch on the burro busted and the saddle went right up in the air with the dynamite. Thet pore little burro was so scairt, he started runnin' and ran all the way home 'fore he stopped."

Suffice to say that everyone liked the old man and grieved when he died. Henson Creek did not seem the same without looking for the dear old man and the thought of another wild tale.[4]

Alex Carey also memorialized the innocence of his friend with colorful characterizations, in his case recollections of a kindness common even during the harshest San Juans times and a bear tale apparently shamelessly shared with all.

Mrs. Brown who lived about a mile or so above Pike's place, and who had a few goats, had made up a batch of cheese. As she was going to town the next day she stopped in at Pike's to leave him a large piece. Pike wasn't at home, so Mrs. Brown left it in a bucket beside his door. Pike didn't notice it when he came home but discovered it the next morning. That day when the mail carrier arrived Pike said to him, "You know I never did believe that story about the moon being made out of cheese but I believe it now!"

"What makes you believe it now?" the mail man asked.

"Well you saw that big full moon last night didn't you?" Pike asked. The mail carrier agreed that he had.

"Well when it went over my house a big piece of it fell off and landed right square in a water bucket on my porch!" Pike said, "I found it there this morning!"

Another time Pike was telling about being out prospecting. He didn't have a gun along and as he came around a corner there was a big grizzly bear standing there on his hind legs growling at him. Pike threw his prospecting pick away, turned around and started running as fast as he could go, with the bear right behind him and gaining all the time as Pike told it to someone. "I looked around and saw that I didn't have a chance to get away, he was just ready to get me!"

"What did you do?" the listener asked.

"Well," Pike said, "I turned around real quick, stuck my fist down his throat, grabbed him by the tail, jerked him inside out and he was going the other way!" [5]

To the credit of the *Lake City Times* editor, he saved enough column space in his June 29, 1893, weekly to report a true Pike bear story:

> *Peter Walsh was riding a horse up Henson creek last Friday evening and when about one hundred yards above the Hannibal Mill his horse became frightened and started off on a keen run. After stopping the animal, Pete looked around to see the cause and saw a black bear standing at the edge of the creek drinking. He went to Pike Snowden's and Pike came out with a rifle and soon after shot the bear through the back bone in front of the hips. The animal was quite large though poor, and in the fall would have weighed about 300 pounds.*

Some recollections of Pike Snowden are more insightful than others. One in particular told through the eyes of five year old Helen Ewart revealed the tender

---

NOT ALL BEAR TALES ARE PIKE'S

Mrs. Al Johnson and Mrs. Chas. Ray met with quite a serious carriage accident Wednesday afternoon while returning from the Vermont Mine on Henson Creek. Just after passing the Hannibal Mill, the horse became frightened at a bear, it is supposed, and started to run. The ladies managed him for fully three-quarters of a mile, when coming to an abrupt turn in the road, which was impossible to make at the rate they were traveling, the animal rolled down the embankment, turning the vehicle completely over and throwing the ladies beneath it. It was some time before help arrived and the ladies were taken to the nearest shelter. Dr. Hoffman was at once summoned and on his arrival found that Mrs. Johnson had three ribs broken and was not otherwise seriously hurt. Mrs. Ray escaped with a scalp wound and a few bruises. The ladies were brought down Thursday afternoon and are now resting quite comfortably at their residences. (*Lake City Phonograph*, October 28, 1893.)

aspect of Pike's character, maybe a remnant of young Zenas on the family farm. In 1916 Helen's father, Rowland, was watchman at Reynolds' Vermont/Ocean Wave Group. During the summer of 1916 Helen's family joined her father and stayed with him at the Vermont boarding house just down the burro trail from the Ocean Wave.

Writing some seventy years later, Helen lovingly recalled her Henson Canyon summer. "Oh, those halcyon days!" [6]

Ben Hunt owned a Model T Ford, one of the few cars in town. I will never forget the day he came to our house to take us to the mine. We were wildly excited at the prospect of our first car ride and had been waiting at the front gate for what seemed hours. Each of us had a flour sack crammed with clothes, toys, and whatever. We were a motley group. My brother Bill had saddled old Nellie and ridden ahead driving Rose, the cow. Shep went along nipping at the cow's heels if she strayed toward the lush green grass growing by the roadside. It was the beginning of a perfect summer.

After we got settled in the boarding house, my three older sisters and I took empty lard buckets and went searching for raspberries and gooseberries. Our mother warned us about bears. And, sure enough, we thought we'd met one face to face when we rounded a corner and met Pike Snowden for the first time. He became our best friend that long summer ago.

We checked in with him at his cabin every time we went berry picking. Sometimes we carried something special for him in one of our buckets. Perhaps a loaf of warm baked bread, some hot rolls, or maybe a slice of apple or goose-berry pie.

I don't remember ever going inside his house, but we sat on a bench ad-miring his ore samples and listening to him spin yarns. If he was especially

Helen's Halcyon Home. The cabin in the center of the image is the cook house, the structure to the right is the boarding house. The Vermont waste dump is visible at the top-center; the Ocean Wave Mine is too far to the right to be seen. *(Author's Collection)*

busy we followed, like little sheep, while he puttered around his domain, hanging on every word he said. One story we still remember was how he had been out prospecting on the other side of the mountain and had come upon a cave of crystals. He promised to bring us some of these gleaming treasures on his very next trip. Of course, it wouldn't be right away, because it was a long, hard climb, but it never entered our heads that his next jaunt might be ten years away or whether there really was such a cave. Our faith in him was total! We waited with bated breath for the day he would cross over the mountain and bring back the shining crystals, but he never did.

He aroused our interest in prospecting and gave each of us what we thought were specimens of real gold. He didn't say they were gold, but he didn't say they weren't. We went home happily carrying our iron pyrite. We lined them up in a row along the kitchen windowsill, where they sparkled all summer in the sun.

One day Pike had a most delightful surprise for me. When we were not around, and after supper, he sat by his kerosene lamp sawing, whittling, and nailing a sturdy wagon. He had carved wheels with his pocketknife and had fashioned a wooden tongue for pulling and guiding. Best of all, I could ride in it. My sisters and I spent happy hours taking turns clattering down the hill from the boarding house to the road.

One day, when the leaves were beginning to turn and school was about to start, our father called Whinnery's store and told Olive Zeigler, a clerk there, to tell Ben Hunt to come for us the following Saturday. On the appointed day, we were down at the road, packed and ready to move on. When Ben came chugging up, we gathered our bags of clothes, and with ore samples in hand, bundled into the car. It became obvious that there was no room for the wagon. I wanted to drag it behind on a long jump rope we owned, but both my dad and Ben vetoed this. There was a great clamoring on my part. My father, a very gentle man, said not to worry. He would hide it under some bushes nearby and send it home on the next passing ore wagon.

Pike was down at the road waving to us as we bounced by. I never saw Pike or the wagon again. Like the ghost of a dear friend dead is time long past.

Pike's station in life was not defined just by post-mortem remembrances. He was a living legend, at least in Henson Canyon and the Town of Lake City. His mining exploits and Western adventures long behind him, he conserved his energy for officiating on affairs of the nation and all matters local that aroused his ire. Most often from his perch in Snowden Meadow, but regularly while patronizing town hotels, restaurants, and public gatherings; he counseled anyone who paused long enough to hear him out.

Exactly when Pike acquired local fame is difficult to say. His accomplishments at the Ocean Wave and other properties were dutifully reported by Lake City editors from the earliest days of mining in Henson Canyon. By 1896 he was recognized as a character likely to bemuse the sourest personality. Local editors were always pleased to report, albeit at times sarcastically, on his comings and goings. In addition to keeping up with Pike's mining interests and whereabouts, his thoughtless pronouncements always made good press. When he was derelict in this regard, his newspaper friends were not shy about putting words in his mouth. It is doubtful Pike knew anything about Mark Twain, but it is evident the editor of the *Times* saw similarities between Twain's style and Pike's wit. Reporting on the inauguration of the ambitious Montrose Tunnel that diverted Black Canyon of the Gunnison River water to the Uncompahgre valley irrigation system, the editor tried his hand.

> *Pike has observed the moon & stars are converging and on Sept. 20th the earth will be destroyed—sadly this will interfere considerably with the Gunnison Tunnel opening, Thanksgiving and Christmas.* [7]

Nor was Pike immune from snarky personal ridicule, perhaps retaliation for some barbed insult of a local mucky-muck[8] which could easily have included the editor. Little would it matter to a recluse who could not read, never would it elicit an iota of regret from the editor.

> *Pike Snowden is a veteran of the Civil War with 2 bullets in his person, one lodged just below his right shoulder blade, the other below his left shoulder blade—he put strong liniment on, dissolved the bullets, now no evidence except his "honorable record."* [9]

There is no record honorable or otherwise that Pike was a veteran of any war. To the contrary, he seems to have sought refuge in the West to avoid it. Likewise, there are few records of mean-spirited Lake City editors. In fact most of the time they were just the opposite. They usually were overly complimentary, not sarcastic, inclined to exaggerate the positive, boosters of mines and businesses, and more than willing to sacrifice valuable column inches to showcase local folklore. On the occasion of Wm. Gurley's 1921 tribute to friend Pike, the *Silver World* editor was more than accommodating.

> *The tribute in this issue to Zenas (Pike) Snowden by Mr. Gurley suggests the idea of collecting some of Pike's stories and publishing them in the Silver World. If those who can give the gist of some of the good yarns they have heard Pike relate will bring them in they will be published in a special series of articles, with due credit given to the one who may submit the thread of any yarn that will be typical of Pike's great ability.* [10]

In response to the editor's plea, Pike's friends and admirers submitted accounts of their Pike Snowden experiences. To the discerning they revealed extraordinary facets of both an ordinary man and the emerging Western culture his admirers epitomized. In fact, the tales they related and the manner of their telling added deeper significance to Pike Snowden tales already told. Pike lived in solitude in his meadow cabin, but his influence was anything but solitary or fleeting. His chroniclers lived in the world but not so much so that they could brush off an odd friend. True to his word, the *Silver World* editor published their recollections and credited them by name.

(O.J. Davis) At one time Pike had a dog, which with his two burros, Jack and Jill, were his only companions for many years. Whenever the conversation would revert to wild meat and the frequent difficulty of pioneers to get it Pike would point to a precipice of rocks back of his camp and say, "See that cliff there? Well, when I had Jack," or Pete or Jim or whatever name would occur to him at the time, "always had all the mountain sheep I wanted. When mountain sheep was gone I'd say, 'ol' pard, we're out of meat, and away that dog would go and I wouldn't see anything more of him until I'd hear a kind of bark which I always knew and would go out and sure enough there would be Jack holding a bunch of sheep on the cliff. And when I would shoot one Jack would let the rest go. Sometimes it would take him two or three days, but he'd always get the sheep." [11]

(O.J. Davis) "When a small boy I [Pike] ran away to sea. Once while in a sailing vessel we ran into a big school of sharks and they were so thick the ship couldn't move for four days and nights." One time Pike would say it was in the English Channel, then again by the Cape of Good Hope, then in the China Sea. His imagination took in pretty much the whole world. [12]

(Knowlton Wiley) Pike was an ardent supporter of Blaine and in the presidential contest between the latter and Cleveland was very much exercised over the telegraphic reports, which in Lake City were brought from the telegraph office at the depot to the Armory and read to the big crowd of people gathered to hear the election news. [Democrat Grover Cleveland of New York defeated Republican James Blaine of Maine in the 1884 Presidential election.] Not being satisfied with what he heard Pike started for the depot to find out for himself how they were getting the news. Reaching the depot Pike noticed through the windows the operator writing off the reports and handing the sheets as fast as they were filled to the messenger boy, and watching the performance a few minutes hurried back to the Armory and exclaimed loudly, "Don't you believe a word of it! They ain't a thing coming over the wires and that feller at the depot is just making up them reports and writing 'em down on paper jest as fast as he can. Was over there and saw him doing it myself and never a paper come over them wires." [13]

(Frank Wheeler) *"One time when I (Pike) was driving a big Concord coach and six span of horses in Nevada, with the coach full of passengers, we come to a big wash jest as a big flood was draining out, but I was behind time because of the soft wet roads and couldn't wait for things to dry so I started across the wash, but just as we got about in the middle the whole blame outfit, horses, coach, driver and passengers, sunk down plumb out of sight in the quicksand. But come to think about it, I wasn't driving that day."* [14]

(Knowlton Wiley) One day, about the time the late war was getting hottest, Pike came to town and stopped at the Occidental hotel. It happened that a number of traveling men came in the same evening and put up at the same place. After supper Pike casually picked up a late daily which had a picture of one of our newest dreadnaughts, about to be launched. Pike happened to pick the paper up upside down and immediately detected a stirring bit of news. Going up town Pike found the traveling men in a group in front of the stores and going up to them said, "Say, but that was a horrible disaster in the navy wasn't it? One of our biggest battleships torpedoed and busted all up and turned turtle."

"No!" cried the men, "we didn't hear about it. Where'd you see it?"

"Why, in the paper at the hotel. It's a terrible disaster," said Pike.

The whole group and Pike went down to the hotel and picked up the paper indicated by Pike, with the picture of the ship showing big on the first page.

"Hold on," said Pike, turning the paper upside down, "Don't you see what a horrible thing it was?"

Then those drummers filed out and up town with sheepish smiles on their faces, for they fancied Pike had been perpetrating a josh on them. [15]

(O. J. Davis) When the telephone line was built past Pike's cabin up Henson creek I (O.J. Davis) was passing one day and found Pike at the foot of a dead tree, which had been topped and trimmed for use as a pole for the line, with his ear close to the tree and apparently listening intently. I asked him

Pike's "Josh." Noticing a front page newspaper photograph of the Navy's newest dreadnought, Pike failed to notice the paper was upside down. He declared a naval disaster. Those who knew him considered it another tall tale. *(Wikipedia)*

what he was doing and he replied, "I'm lisenin' to them fellows talk. I can hear 'em, but can't quite make out jist what they're sayin." [16]

(Ernest Mendenhall) Once when a bunch of freighters were telling of the longest teams they ever drove or heard of some had gotten quite a ways beyond the limits of truth and Pike, who had listened attentively, said, "One time when I was driving one of the big borax freight outfits in Nevada most of the drivers got down with smallpox and I was the only driver who stayed on the job. So we joined all the teams and I started out, but the team was so long I had to harness on horseback and had to start before sunup and work until late at night to get in full time each day." [17]

On May 19, 1921, the *Silver World* wrapped up its tribute to Pike with two final conversations with friends.[18]

(J. F. Steinbeck) Pike had no use for the Boers of South Africa in their war with England. He said they worried him a lot when he was prospecting for diamonds in that country because he insisted on washing his clothes in the Vaal River, trumping up the claim that it polluted the stream too much to be fit for cattle and horses to drink.

(Professor H. G. Heath) Pike always claimed to be a great packer, and often related that one time when punching a big burro train loaded with ore in Nevada he came to a large wash in which a big flood was running. He couldn't wait for the flood to subside, yet the water was too deep to wade and the burros to heavy loaded to swim across, but he finally overcame the predicament by loading each burro down with a lot of sandstone, so heavy that it could stand up against the current, then tied the tail of each to the rear burro's saddle and then drove the train across on the bed of the wash under the water.

From these accounts we see many facets of Pike Snowden that would not be apparent from outward appearances. Some of them coincide with what is known of his life as a stagecoach hand, drover, miner, and recluse. By their very nature they tell us something about his humor if not his devotion to truth. That they were recollections of his friends tell us something about them and the times in which they lived, as well. Pike paid his final earthly dues working and selling Henson Canyon mines, but he earned his legacy in local folklore presiding with wit and a quick tongue over his Henson Canyon meadow and adopted Lake City. He could have been ignored, or shunned as old loners often were. Instead he was respected for being among the earliest and youngest pioneers in the canyon. Instead he was loved for his heart and selfless kindnesses. The combination of the two was a treasure of its own making.

NO MAN IS AN ISLAND

Writing four centuries earlier, no one has better described the impact of the loss of another than Pike's fellow countryman John Donne. As we have read, Pike's Lake City friends did the best they could.

> No Man is an island,
> Entire of itself,
> Every man is a piece of the continent,
> A part of the main.
> If a clod be washed away by the sea,
> Europe is the less.
> As well as if a promontory were,
> As well as if a manor of thy friend's
> Or of thine own were:
> Any man's death diminishes me,
> Because I am involved in mankind,
> And therefore never send to know for whom the bell tolls:
> It tolls for thee.

No one discerned Pike Snowden's true nature—the same nature that blessed young Helen Ewart with a handmade wagon—earlier or more profoundly than William Gurley. Their lifelong friendship that survived the briefness of their Henson Canyon times together defied reason. More intriguing still, what did Pike find worthy in the young cook? In later years Gurley returned to Hinsdale County for short visits with his many friends. Despite long absences, his bond with Pike was never broken.

Zenas died alone in Woodcraft Hospital, Pueblo, Colorado, on June 19, 1917. Friend Gurley reported in a 1921 letter to the *Lake City Silver World* that Pike left Henson Canyon for an operation. Woodcraft was a state-owned facility for indigents. Cause of death: cancer. His death and burial in nearby Mountain View Cemetery apparently went unnoticed at the time—after all he was a recluse—by even his distant friend. At least there is no known record of his passing. The best we can do for an obituary is the poem included in W.F.E.'s 1921 letter honoring a rough man with a tender heart who had obviously made a profound impression on the eastern academic and anyone else who knew him. He should make a profound impression on us.

Good Old Pike

There's a name unknown to fame,
A name I like,
For 'tis old Zene Snowden's name—
We called him 'Pike'.
In Owl gulch, up Henson Creek,
He had his shack;
He had nary kin nor chick,
Except his jack
He had come when men were few
And things were wild,
To that region, then so new,
So undefiled.
He had traveled many trails,
And often told
Funny, strange and thrilling tales
Of days of old.
With the yarns he used to spin
Pike would beguile;
He could make a jackass grin,
A preacher smile.
And, many times they were so ripe
That other folk
Wondered if he hit the pipe
Just as a joke.

One time old Pike struck it rich
And cleaned up well;
Then was sidetracked on the switch
That leads to hell.
Yet he never lost the hope
That some fine day
Old Dame Fortune with her dope
Would come his way.

Good old Pike turned up his toes
An quit the plan;
And now his campfire is with those
For whom we pray.
Good old scouts like Pike are few
And far between;
Good old timers, brave and true,
Are seldom seen.[19]

Notes—Chapter Four: Tall Tales

1 *Lake City Times*, May 6, 1897.
2 Carey, Alex, *Memories, Scenes and Humorous High Lights of Lake City*, unpublished handwritten notes. (Courtesy of Grant Houston, *Silver World*, May 7, 2014.)
3 It was from this location, appealing to Greek spiritual and academic curiosity, that the Apostle Paul focused attention on the Athenian altar to the "Unknown God" and delivered his famous invitation: "Now what you worship as something unknown I am going to proclaim to you. The God who made the world and everything in it is the Lord of heaven and earth and does not live in temples built by hands." Acts17:24.
4 Wright, Carolyn and Clarence, *Tiny Hinsdale of the Silvery San Juans* pgs. 146-148.
5 Carey, Alex, *Memories, Scenes and Humorous High Lights of Lake City.*
6 *Lake City Silver World*, August 10. 2007.
7 *Lake City Times*, August 1909.
8 "Mucky-muck" is borrowed from Chinook jargon. It is slang for a person of great importance or one who sees themselves as important.
9 *Lake City Times*, August 1909.
10 *Lake City Silver World*, April 14, 1921.
11 Ibid., April 21, 1921.
12 Ibid., May 5, 1921.
13 Ibid.
14 Ibid.
15 Ibid., May 12, 1921.
16 Ibid.
17 Ibid.
18 Ibid., May 19, 1921.
19 Ibid., April 14, 1921.

CHAPTER 5

The Cook

The Road Not Taken

Two roads diverged in a yellow wood,
And sorry I could not travel both
And be one traveler, long I stood
And looked down one as far as I could
To where it bent in the undergrowth.

Then took the other, as just as fair,
And having perhaps the better claim,
Because it was grassy and wanted wear;
Though as for that the passing there
Had worn them really about the same.

And both that morning equally lay
In leaves no step had trodden black.
Oh, I kept the first for another day!
Yet knowing how way leads on to way,
I doubted if I should ever come back.

I shall be telling this with a sigh
Somewhere ages and ages hence:
Two roads diverged in a wood, and I —
I took the one less traveled by,
And that has made all the difference.

— Robert Frost —

William Frank Eugene Gurley, from childhood known as W.F.E., by all outward appearances was as different from Pike Snowden as two individuals could be. Yet different appearances and life's journeys aside, the heart of each bore much in common. Pike Snowden discerned this as the two talked around that 1876 Henson Canyon campfire. Probably W.F.E. did not. At the time neither man probably recognized they were fulfilling a divine appointment. That revelation would come much later at least to W.F.E., and thankfully he would be moved enough to write about it to the benefit of the rest of us.

Gurley was quicker when it came to choosing which fork in life's road to take. A season in the San Juans was season enough for him to conclude his God-given gifts were not camp cooking and hard rock mining. Like so many others from his station in life, the West and the San Juans was a powerful magnet. Unlike so many others, it was not the harsh realities that drove him back home. For W.F.E., he was on an adventure to satisfy his curiosity. His labors in Henson Canyon would be short-lived, his memories would be life-long. Experiencing boomtown Lake City and the San Juans excitement first-hand would not lead to a life of mining. It would lead to a life of memories and a life-long friend.

W.F.E. Gurley. Incredibly adventurous from childhood, young W.F.E. set aside his academic pursuits and joined the San Juans' goldrush. He returned to the States, not with gold but with a deep appreciation for those who sought it.[1] *(Cornell Library, Division of Rare and Manuscript Collections)*

The Lake City town site was registered in the U.S. Land Office at Del Norte in October 1875. In the meantime, by spring the town could boast thirteen primitive log cabins. The first wedding was May 14, 1875. The first saw mill was erected that same month. Reverend Alex M. Darley organized the Presbyterian society June 18, 1875. The first issue of the *Silver World* was June 19th. The first child born in town was on July 8th. On July 11th the first Barlow & Sanderson coach somehow survived a rough trip from Saguache on the beginnings of an Otto Mears' toll road. The first mail was brought in on horseback from Saguache on July 20th. Mears' Saguache and San Juans wagon road reached Lake City in August, enabling Barlow & Sanderson coaches to begin making regular tri-weekly trips. Mears' second Lake City wagon road, the Lake City and Antelope Park Toll Road to Del Norte, was completed November 2nd. In November 1875 the town could boast sixty-seven finished buildings and maybe 400 residents. In 1876, Crooke's concentration works was completed in July and Van Gieson's lixiviation works was operational in December. [2]

By the end of 1876, the *Lake City Silver World* estimated the town's population was 800 to 1,000. A year later the population was "fully 2,000." Among the 500 buildings completed, there were:

> ... *ten assayers, three bakeries, two banks, three barber shops, two billiard halls, five blacksmith shops, three boot and shoe stores, two brick yards, two breweries, two cigar factories, one clothing house, five corrals and feed stables, two drug stores, one furniture house, fourteen stores dealing in general merchandise, four hardware stores, four hotels, two jewelry establishments, four Chinese laundries, fifteen lawyers, four meat markets, three news-dealers, three painters, one planning mill, six restaurants (two open all night),seven saloons, four saw-mills, one shingle mill, and nine surveyors. (Curiously, doctors and undertakers were absent, lawyers were well-represented at the trough.)* [3]

> *Buildings went up like magic, and arose on every hand. So great was the demand for lumber that the mills could not supply the demand, and the planning (sic) mill, although running night and day a large portion of the time, could not turn out dressed lumber as fast as it was required, while dry or seasoned lumber could scarcely be had at all."* [4]

How W.F.E. learned about the San Juans excitement and Lake City is a mystery easily solved. Unlike prior gold rushes to Colorado, post-Civil War communications and access were greatly improved. Every newspaper in the country could be expected to sing the siren's song. By the 1875 onset of winter, word of gold and silver strikes up the Lake Fork of the Gunnison River had circled the globe. The *Silver World* editor continued:

> *The increase in population during the year was not only rapid but substantial, and the class of newcomers far superior to those who usually rush into a frontier town, and especially a mining camp. [If this was boosterism, it was more subtle than usual.]*
>
> *The immigration began with the opening of the year, the coaches first coming in loaded, compelling the line to put on daily service as early as April 10th. The real rush came later, when teams began to pour in loaded with human freight. During April, May and June the roads leading into the town were perfectly lined with newcomers, pedestrians with packs on their backs or on burros and jacks, men on horseback and in wagons, a constant stream of humanity pouring into San Juans through this, the metropolis.*

Of course the largest share of these newcomers were disappointed. They came with no adequate idea of the country, totally ignorant of the character of the mines, or of mining. In fact, comparatively few were practical men, and the largest proportion were either adventurers or men who were masters of no trade, perhaps ready to do anything, but unable to or not knowing how or in what channel to direct their energies. The exodus of this class of men was about as rapid and great as was their incoming. Meanwhile business men, mechanics, men of capital or worth, came in great numbers and stayed and today Lake City can boast of the best class of citizens to be found in any town east or west.[5]

Young Gurley could be counted among those men who found their way to Lake City and Henson Canyon on horseback. When he returned to the States and his academic pursuits he re-entered a world in which the practical geology he had witnessed did not always match what could be ferreted out in an American classroom. Not until later in the century would geology along with its sister disciplines in science and engineering gain prominence as important adjuncts to prospecting and mining, basic building blocks nourishing America's industrial revolution. As W.F.E. witnessed first-hand in the San Juans, practitioners of science and engineering were few and far between. Instead, weathered prospectors

GEOLOGY AS A SCIENCE

One *History of Science* contributor, Martin Guntau, writes in "The Emergence of Geology as a Scientific Discipline" that geology as a classical science came into being around the second half of the eighteenth century, took root in European countries with notable mineral reserves that also were swept up in the industrial revolution—especially Germany and the U.K.—and slowly found its way to North America. When the mining industry developed to a certain point that practical experience about ores, veins, and the search for deposits handed down for centuries was no longer sufficient, scientific methods applied to geology became necessary. Essential elements of this transformation are specific institutions (e.g. Freiberg in Germany, eventually Cornell, University of Chicago, Colorado School of Mines), museums, journals, and scientific societies.

Guntau concludes that the rise of geology as a scientific discipline was not the product of a single event. There was no single defining theory, no life's work of a scholar, no publication of an uncontested scholarly book. The rise of geology as a science required a series of conditions, preconditions really, that had to develop over time. W.F.E. Gurley had a multi-decades role in this process. [6]

from all walks of life and strata of society ferreted out metal-bearing ores, and self-taught miners—happily ignorant of academic curriculums intended to advance their search and enhance their safety—followed in their tracks. While amazingly successful despite their lack of schooling, W.F.E. no doubt observed that "trial and error" was a poor substitute for predictability and design.

Europeans were far ahead, a century or two ahead, of North Americans in establishing mining institutes and professional societies, but the immigrants and discontents that answered the call of the West were not waiting for American institutions to catch up. To the contrary, for decades they contributed more skills and knowledge to industry than science and engineering could affirm, albeit inefficiently and often with avoidable loss of life and limb. Prime examples were the Cornish immigrants. Not to be ignored, although they often were in the mines, immigrant and investor graduates of Freiberg and London's Royal School of Mines eventually made their voices heard.

W.F.E. had a foot in both camps. He returned east to earn his place among the ranks of intellectuals and contributed much to the advancement of the earth sciences, but earning many honors in the process did not dampen his appreciation for the lessons taught him in Henson Canyon by the drover and the uneducated men like him.

Interesting how youthful adventures can displace far greater adult exploits when one reminisces. Mucking silver-bearing ores out of Henson Canyon's Big Casino Mine and cooking for the crew would have been the ultimate field camp experience for any student of the earth in that day and age. For W.F.E., it raised his already intense interest in geology to the stratosphere. More importantly, it sharpened his appreciation for how hardship and hard work that shapes the character of the common man produces a precious asset every man should cherish. Amazing what can be discovered half-buried in a silver mine if time can be found to pause, look, and listen.

The most prized treasure W.F.E. claimed for his season in Henson Canyon was being befriended by a hardscrabble drover who became a wealthy mine owner

Walker Museum - 1892.
Beneficiary of Wm. Gurley's world class fossils collection of 15,000 species and several hundred-thousand specimens, the University of Chicago also became his academic home until his death on June 27, 1943. *(University of Chicago Library)*

before his very own eyes. Rather than lament his missed opportunity—accepting Pike Snowden's offer to become his camp cook and by default one of his silver-rich Ocean Wave partners—W.F.E. considered his loss a blessing. At the height of his academic career Professor Gurley wrote:

> *I have for many years been glad I missed it, for, young as I was, the amount which would have been my share at the time of sale would likely have turned my head and placed me firmly upon those skids which shoot a fellow into the hopeless bunch of "has beens" who started young on the down grade.* [7]

How often the Professor's thoughts turned to that season in Henson Canyon is anyone's guess, but most likely it was often. Probably such thoughts also spread a knowing grin across his face. Ordinary San Juans miners like Pike Snowden could possess the most extraordinary character, proverbial "diamonds in the rough." Gurley's descriptions tell us a great deal about Pike Snowden, but also about himself. His descriptions also tell us a great deal about his generation and the West. We get a taste of this in his account of his first encounter with Pike:

> *Sunday morning, when I arose, I found the Big Casino bunch all on edge, as it were, over the display of a fine chunk of solid gray copper which was exhibited by the owners of the newly discovered (Ocean Wave) property, Steve Baxter, Bob Bastian and Pike Snowden, one of whom had picked up this piece of rock in the debris brought down by a snowslide and they had gone up the track of the slide and found the lode exposed and staked it under the names mentioned above (e.g. Ocean Wave and the Wave of the Ocean extension).*
>
> *Thus it was that I missed being "in" on that strike and thus it was that I got acquainted with three mighty good men, one of whom was old Pike Snowden, who had tried so hard to induce me to "fine (sic.) the gang." Pike was a veritable diamond in the rough. Unable to read or write, his deficiency in "book larnin" was more than made up by him in all those diversified attributes so essential to the old time mountaineer and pioneer, who was so frequently called upon to instantaneously solve problems and successfully cope with conditions of a character requiring an inconceivable stock of cool and clear headed judgment and quick and decided action under the most perilous circumstances.*
>
> *As is commonly the case, these necessary attributes go hand in hand with big hearts, warm hands, genial dispositions and what might be called "all round good fellowship" and in this Pike was well in line with those in the front rank.*
>
> *Like all others of his class Pike was a great story teller and he possessed the peculiar faculty—quite common with others of his type—of easily replenishing his stock when he was about to run out of those tales which have made many pipes famous. As a relater and a creator of interesting and thrilling yarns Pike*

*was easily the palm holder among past masters of the art, and I dare say that
all who knew him can readily call to mind one, perhaps many, stories told by
him which will bring a broad smile at the thought.*

   *In those memories of the past, within the sanctuary of my heart, are
many, many persons, whose acquaintance has had much to do with a career
which inspires the continuous thought that my life has been so full of blessings
and pleasant experiences. Genial, generous, unassuming, and good, old Pike
Snowden occupies a high place with the others—our old time friend, good old
Pike—yes, good old Pike!* [8]

There are others W.F.E. did not forget, and who received in the mail at least
until 1915 a fine cigar every July 4th by way of the *Silver World* editor and friend
Pike. Quoted in Thompson's *The Social and Cultural History of Lake City*, Gurley
explains why:

   *They were real men of sterling quality, belonging to that class which fu-
ture generations will delight to honor as pathfinders, trailblazers, and empire
builders. Oft indeed do I feel grateful that it was my good fortune to associate
with such men during the formative years of my career.* [9]

"Sterling quality," that was the ticket that transported pilgrims farthest in
the San Juans. Sometimes the pilgrim held tight to it through thick and thin to
the end of the line, sometimes a good Samaritan had to come along to pay the
fare. W.F.E. recognized "sterling quality" when he encountered it, and the most
unlikely wayfarer imaginable—a drover—recognized "sterling quality" in W.F.E.
In fact, nineteenth century America delivered to the West an abundance of men
and women of sterling quality, some of them long nurtured by their eastern families, some of them fresh from distant lands, some of them forged in the heat of
battle in the Civil War. If a pilgrim arrived without it, the rugged nature of the
San Juans would more often than not birth it.

   William Gurley had no angst when it came to character. He grew up in
a Christian home with an abolitionist stepfather when abolitionism could be a
capital offense. Riskier still, his step-father was an abolitionist in deed as well as
disposition. If any weight can be assigned to parental influence shaping the mores
and values of their children—the proverbial acorn not falling far from the tree—
how many of Daniel's characteristics found a home in stepson William's heart?
With the benefit of hindsight, William clearly exhibited profound love of his
fellow man, a belief in a God-given right to peace and equality, and the inherent
dignity and respect everyone regardless of station in life deserved. It also is not
difficult to see the origins of these values in his father.

   Daniel was born March 3, 1808, in Rupert, Vermont. At age eight, his parents
"removed" to Oswego County, New York, young Daniel making the trip barefoot.

At seventeen, he traveled alone west through Wisconsin, Michigan, and beyond the future site of Chicago. In his early life back in New York, he was a Presbyterian, in later years a "Spiritualist," whatever that meant in that day. More certain, to those who knew him, he "was always an abolitionist." And he was prone to action, demonstrated in 1851 by his role in the infamous "Jerry Rescue" in Syracuse, New York.

Jerry's Rescue. William Henry, who later called himself Jerry, was a runaway slave. Recaptured, Syracuse citizens freed him and saw that he safely arrived in Canada. W.F.E. Gurley's father David was one of the rescuers. (*Wikipedia, Onondaga Historical Association. Artist: Sharon BuMann*)

ABOLITIONISTS

The abolitionist movement was dedicated to ending the Atlantic slave trade and liberating enslaved peoples. In the wake of the American Revolution, northern states, beginning with Pennsylvania in 1780, passed legislation during the next two decades that abolished slavery, sometimes by gradual emancipation. Massachusetts ratified a constitution that declared all men equal. During the following decades the abolitionist movement grew in northern states and Congress regulated the expansion of slavery in new states admitted to the union. By 1804 slavery was abolished in all northern states. Abolitionists were in the forefront of political action groups often involved in violence that culminated in the election of President Abraham Lincoln and the outbreak of the Civil War. Many abolitionists actively participated in aiding runaway slaves make their way north by way of an "underground railway." The underground railway amounted to a series of safe-houses along a prescribed route north. Having anything to do with this activity was a dangerous proposition, particularly in the border states where hot pursuit of runaways by slave-owners was commonplace. Daniel Gurley maintained just such a safe-house in Oswego, New York.

William "Jerry" Henry was arrested in Syracuse, New York, as a fugitive slave, an unpopular move on the part of Syracuse authorities. Outraged citizens saw to it that this abuse of authority was not going to stand. Jerry was freed—the beneficiary of a jail-break, actually—and escorted north on the underground railroad to Oswego before crossing Lake Ontario to freedom in Canada. Apparently escaping retribution for his rebellious actions in this matter, Daniel did not leave Oswego for Danville until 1862. In the words of relative Albert Gurley, "his life was an open book. He was honorable, temperate, and industrious; had no difficulties with his fellow man; he never sued any one; was a good neighbor and citizen, respected by all." [10]

For much of the rest of the Gurley family story, we rely on Rollin T. Chamberlin's memorial to W.F.E. (William Frank Eugene) Reed, later Gurley by adoption, was born in Oswego, New York, on June 5, 1854, the son of Ben Franklin and Leonora Hall Reed. Ben, a printer, died when William was one year old. Three years later Daniel Gurley, a blacksmith, married Leonora and gave W.F.E. the Gurley name.

In 1863 the Gurley family moved to Quincy, Michigan, and the following year to Danville, Illinois, where ten-year old W.F.E. grew up to become a "leading citizen." Sadly, he also grew up to become partially blind. At age seven he contracted measles that left him completely blind for several months. Recovering to a degree, his vision thereafter was never more than fifty percent of normal. "Worse still, in 1897 his weakened vision was destined to fail again from proofreading by strong electric light and to vanish altogether in 1918."

Clearly endowed with great curiosity and intellect, W.F.E. also learned to make the most of his handicap. Despite his partial blindness, he took up collecting postage stamps, embossed trademarks, coins, stone Indian relics, and curios. By 1868, at age fourteen, his curiosity led him to geology. He read everything he could find on the subject. Better still, his family's relocation to Danville put him within walking distance of one of the richest fossil beds east of the Missouri River. In the black shale capping a coal seam exposed along the bluffs of Danville's Vermilion River, W.F.E. found beautiful fossils. Among his many giftings yet to be appreciated, the nearly blind young teen had an uncanny eye for spotting the form of half-buried fossils that others passed by.

The availability of Vermilion fossils seemed unlimited, and so attractive that before long W.F.E. was trading them to other collectors for fossils from different localities and distant horizons. Finding that most collectors of that period were not as interested in fossils found in their own neighborhoods as in showy minerals, relics, and attractive marine shells he found, W.F.E. corresponded with international brokerages, Greenleaf in Boston and Nickerson in New Bedford, and acquired mixed varieties of shells in barrel lots at reasonable prices.

W.F.E. did not limit his trading to New England collectors. Also a careful accountant, his records showed that in 1871 he made thirty-five exchanges as far afield as Weymouth, England and the Imperial-Royal Geological Museum in Vienna. The collection he sent to Vienna was so highly regarded that soon the "high-school lad is elected a corresponding member of the Imperial-Royal Geological Society of Austria." [11] Only four other Americans, all notables, were 1871 members of this prestigious Austrian museum, suggesting that no one imagined that he was not yet out of high school. Nor did W.F.E. feel compelled to clarify this matter. Instead, he did what any young entrepreneur would do, he expanded his network among the paleontologist community throughout Europe. For his efforts, in 1873 he was welcomed into this elite group of scholars and scientists who were in the final stages of organizing the Swiss Paleontological Society. Of course Gurley was offered membership.

Not inclined to rest on his laurels, in due course W.F.E. helped establish the Vermilion County Historical Society (1877) and the State Historical Society of Illinois (1879). Had his entrepreneurial stepfather not moved the family to one of the richest fossil beds in America, W.F.E. would not have found collectible fossils that led to his network of international paleontologists. Without this network of paleontologists, he would not have been invited to become a member of the Imperial-Royal Geological Society of Austria and the Swiss Paleontological Society.

All this said, none of these preconditions and subsequent accomplishments explain W.F.E. Gurley the mucker and cook. More intriguing still was his life-long friendship with Pike Snowden, our illiterate drover. Perhaps the best that can be said, the Gurley clan was adventurous by nature, and there was no more exhilarating adventure than a gold rush. Taking leave from academia to experience one first-hand was what this class of young Americans was apt to do.

Graduating from Danville High School in 1873, William returned to his birth state. In 1874 he enrolled in Cornell University's two-year non-degree "Optional Course" that was suited to his interests in geology and paleontology. Neither of these disciplines would be considered worthy of a degree program for another decade or more. W.F.E.'s "certificate," received in 1877 after his year-long San Juans "field camp," read "Engineering." Fellow students, later recognized as titans in the geosciences, and even their accomplished Professor, Charles F. Hartt, regularly "drifted into his room" where his European certificates must have caught their eye. These impressive wall hangings, especially his membership in the Swiss Paleontological Society, surely stimulated discussion of the benefit of similar institutions in America, the focus being "should we not have similar societies in this country?" [12] A decade later, in 1888, the *Geological Society of America* with W.F.E. Gurley inconspicuously among its founders, sprang to life in Ithaca, New York.

Student Gurley's 1876 Cornell sabbatical was no routine San Juans geology field camp. His adventure began with a tiring train ride to Pueblo, Colorado. What W.F.E. expected to find when he stepped off the train in Pueblo is anybody's guess, but based on his boundless curiosity it is likely he was simply delighted to be there. In 1876 Pueblo station was the end of the Denver & Rio Grande line, but the beginning of a great frontier experience. W.F.E. outfitted himself with a burro and trekked west over La Veta Pass to booming Lake City. Rollin Chamberlin writes:

> ... where he worked as a weighmaster, road builder, carpenter, and print- er, while prospecting extensively in the San Juans Mountains. He examined the upper Uncompahgre valley near Ouray and the San Miguel stream depos- its over the divide, locating placers which unfortunately had to be abandoned because of an Indian uprising. So he returned east with little gold but many more specimens for his collection.[13]

Overlooked in Chamberlin's account were W.F.E.'s life-changing Henson Canyon encounters [life-threatening in some cases], and his divine appointments kept and missed that endured in his reminiscences and poetry for the balance of his long academic career. Rollin acknowledges Lake City, but Henson Canyon and the Big Casino may have been bothersome details best left for the likes of the *Silver World* editor and W.F.E. himself. And how could he possibly have done justice to the drover? Exactly how long W.F.E. spent as camp cook and mucker is not clear, probably a summer season before 1876 winter snows returned, but we can be certain he fulfilled his obligations to his Big Casino mentors. Not one to dawdle, we also can be certain he made good use of his time in other San Juans camps, but was back in Professor Hartt's care in time to graduate with the Class of 1877.

As is usually the case, most gold-rushers wore out quickly and were just as driven to rush home. Most mining camps that boomed soon declined. Such was the fate of Lake City and its Henson Canyon, but not Wm. Gurley. Return to the States he did, technically a "go-backer," but he did not go back empty-handed nor was his friendship with Pike Snowden left behind. W.F.E. epitomized a class of young American's able to live a Western dream and still awaken to their previous life-style with wistful memories of what they had experienced and why it still mattered. His calling was in academia, but part of him remained on the frontier. To the contrary, Pike, the itinerant prospector and miner, was never the "go-backer" type. Nor was he shy. His unpolished wit and admirable character traits earned Gurley's respect long before it earned him Henson Canyon folk hero status.

By 1878, Pike was working the Ocean Wave, the Vermont was under new ownership, and W.F.E. was writing scholarly paleontology papers at his desk in Danville, Illinois. Perhaps it would have been different had he joined Pike's partners as camp cook and savored the taste of financial success at the Ocean Wave. Perhaps it would have been different had he not been preoccupied with preparing for the day when he would again be blind. After Cornell graduation, W.F.E. returned to Danville where he studied the law while working as a civil engineer locating railroad rights-of-way through the coal fields of eastern Illinois and western Indiana. He served as Danville's city engineer in 1885-87 and 1891-93, but his passion remained geology. Rollin Chamberlin picked up the narrative here, but politely leaves out that W.F.E. was driven by the reality that a prudent blind geologist must provide for his future income by some other means. Chamberlin writes:

> ... *as his ambition was to place himself in a position financially where he could settle down and devote himself entirely to geology, with characteristic energy he also carried on a real-estate and building-association business and entered the insurance field, all the while actively assembling the great Gurley collection of Paleozoic fossils.* [14]

Gurley's first professional publication on paleontology appeared in the 1878 *Proceedings of the American Philosophical Society*, followed by scores of additional scholarly works throughout the next decade. In the 1889 *Indiana Department of Geology and Natural History Report No.16* appeared the first of a long series of writings in collaboration with Samuel A. Miller, a Cincinnati lawyer by profession. This accomplishment resulted in "Miller and Gurley" becoming familiar names among students of Paleozoic paleontology. In July 1893, Illinois Governor Altgeld appointed Gurley curator of the State Museum of Natural History and State Geologist of Illinois, positions he held for the remaining four years of his active scientific career. During this time Miller and Gurley produced ten publications concerned with the description of new species and genera of Paleozoic fossils of Illinois and adjoining states. Their work comprised a total of 663 pages and fifty-one plates including descriptions of some 435 new species and eight new genera. "Science" by any stretch of the imagination, neither author was heralded in their day as scientists much less geologists.

The year 1887 marked the end of Gurley's public service and the beginning of the end of his sight. In the spring of 1887, an English specialist advised him that total blindness was imminent (in fact this did not occur until 1918) and that he should arrange his affairs in a way that would not require sight. At age forty-three, with a personal world-class collection of fossils, a nearly complete library of North American "geology," a comfortable home, and real estate investments sufficient for his needs, W.F.E. had done all he knew to do. And for all he knew, his professional life was about to end. The University of Chicago thought otherwise. Chamberlin continued:

> *Along about the turn of the century, President Harper and others raised the question of his coming to the University of Chicago. Receiving their proposals*

favorably, he became Associate Curator of Paleontological Collections, and through an arrangement—largely generosity on the part of Mr. Gurley—the University acquired his fossils. Appointed in 1900, Gurley continued as a member of the Department of Geology until his death on June 27, 1943—a longer span of years than has fallen to any other member.[15]

Part of what accounted for Gurley's contributions to the science he loved was a most uncommon mental faculty. In addition to his ability to see partially-buried fossils others passed by, he also was gifted with an uncanny ability to mentally catalogue and recall what he picked up years earlier. Again we turn to Chamberlin to explain.

In 1876 Mr. Gurley found an incomplete fish tooth in the Permian (Pennsylvania) bone bed near Danville, which was sent for description to the late Professor Cope of Philadelphia, by whom the specimen was described as a new species, and an illustration made in which the lost portion was restored in outline. More than ten years later the collector with his wife was again at the same locality, and Mrs. Gurley picked up a fragment of a tooth and handed it to her husband. It crossed his mind that this fragment was the remaining part of the tooth he had found so many years before, and on reaching home the two fragments were placed together and were found to join perfectly, together making a nearly complete specimen, which is less than an inch in length, and about one-fourth of an inch in width. During the period intervening between the finding of the two parts of this little tooth the locality had been visited many times, but the minute this little fragment was observed by Mr. Gurley it was recognized as the missing portion of the specimen already in his possession.[16]

Reflecting on the life of William Frank Eugene (Reed) Gurley, Rollin T. Chamberlin summed up the man: "Strong character, catholic interests, and very genuine friendship made Gurley a most lovable man." Rollin also tipped his hat to Gurley's helpmates in life. He was twice married, no children, first to Anna Graham Barnes of Maumee, Ohio, on June 17th, 1880. Anna wandered the fossil fields with him and died in 1918, quite possibly of the Spanish flu (or complications caused by it) that ravaged the world including the remote San Juans. In 1921 Gurley married Katharine Eberly Beard of Muscatine, Iowa. Widowed in 1943, she was praised for how much "her understanding, encouragement, and constant help... meant to him in his years of dependency."

An unmistakable part of Gurley was his eager desire to advance geology as a science, as well as culture and humanity. Where this desire originated is open to speculation. Did it arise out of some effect of his childhood blindness or his near-orphan status? Was it a consequence of his abolitionist, fundamental Christian homelife? Did his San Juans adventure account for it? Without doubt his divine appointment with Pike Snowden was a learning experience that profoundly affected him to the end of his life. Work among students and professors at Cornell was another learning experience. And what accounted for his generosity toward Cornell and the Chicago Art Institute, and service at Walker Museum? Chamberlin reports he was a:

> ...*helpful alumnus of Cornell; was prominent at Danville in all campaigns to raise funds for civic enterprises, industrial foundations, or charitable purposes; served as President of the Illinois Society, Sons of the Revolution, for 22 years, editing its organ,* The Minute Man, *with the assistance of Mrs. Gurley; and in 1921 he presented his collection of over 5,000 original drawings by old masters to the Chicago Art Institute. Fond of his fellow man, he was a Knight Templar, Knight of Pythias, a 33rd degree Mason, and a member of other fraternal organizations.*[17]

W.F.E.'s kindnesses extended to his San Juans friends, witness his annual box of premium cigars sent to the *Lake City Silver World* editor to be distributed to his Henson Canyon "colleagues." For his colleagues back East, he entertained with Henson Canyon tales. Chamberlin writes:

> *A seemingly endless supply of interesting experiences and anecdotes, which he related with a peculiar sparkle of wit, or shrewd understanding, never failed to entertain. Till his last year or two, he made it a point to attend the University homecoming dinners and those given by the Trustees for the faculty; always, well in advance, some faculty friend was making arrangements with him to be his companion for the evening. Even on his eighty-ninth birthday he reminisced with his charm of old.*[18]

As for his interest in humanity, his writings inspired by his San Juans experiences provided deep insight into his thinking and his character. Particularly revealing in this regard was his practice of writing his own Christmas cards. Christmas 1931 is a good example. Beneath the image of an engraving by Jacque Bossi of Raphael's Vatican fresco of the birth of Jesus, W.F.E. wrote *Soul Inspiring Story*.[19]

> Infant Saviour with His Mother,
> Three adoring Wise Men near;
> Sacred picture, like no other,
> Tells that story men revere.
> Story bringing peace and gladness
> To the weary souls of those
> Who may turn to God in sadness,
> Trusting Him 'midst direst woes.

Oh, that soul inspiring story
Which was born in realms above;
So transcending in its glory,
In its wondrous faith and love.
It began when those Three Sages
Came to Bethlehem of old;
It will live throughout the ages,
And forever will be told.

Based upon W.F.E.'s choice of poetic topics, his fondest reminiscences were of his San Juans school of hard knocks, his blessed opportunity to be a camp cook and mucker, and his prospector friends, especially ex-drover Pike. From time to time the *Silver World* reported on W.F.E.'s visits to Lake City, in August 1915 for example, and for several weeks in August 1919, to look after "mining interests," exactly what they were remains a mystery still.[20] Friend Pike squired him about the canyon in 1915. Friend Pike was long deceased by 1919. In fact, so were the rest of "the boys" that warmed themselves around that 1876 Henson Canyon campfire. At the end of his days, totally blind W.F.E. penned a final poetic epithet honoring his old friends. He sometimes recited it over the radio during broadcasts featuring his reflections on that road not taken. No better stated than in his own words, in memorializing a friend he memorialized himself. He also memorializes us.

Another friend has cast aside
His earthly dust
Another soul will now abide
With Him we trust.
Another spirit is enshrined
In realms above
Another memory is entwined
With all we love. [21]

In some circles W.F.E. was known as the "blind poet of Chicago." Among a handful of Henson Canyon miners he was remembered as Pike's friend. To us he is remembered as a chronicler of nobler times. To the Wright's who faithfully remembered so many of Hinsdale's pathfinders we leave the last word concerning a man who befriended and remembered all he met.

Among some of the notable men with whom Mr. Gurley was associated in the early days here were H.A. Tabor, Abe Roberts, Alva Adams, Enos Hotchkiss, and James and John Comstock, who discovered the Comstock Lode. He was also a friend of Captain Henson, for whom Henson Creek was named.

Tim Clawson, his oldest friend and partner, and who aided much in the history of this area, named his first daughter Gurley. . . . Mr. Gurley visited Lake City in 1940, at which time he and Mrs. Gurley visited with friends and with sons and daughters of friends who had passed on. His visit to our home will be long remembered. [22]

Notes—Chapter Five: The Cook

[1] Chamberlin, Rollin T., "Memorial to William Frank Eugene Gurley," *Geological Society of America, Annual Report for 1943*, pgs. 135-140.

[2] *Lake City Silver World*, January 5, 1878. [These mills relied on different technologies but had similar objectives: reducing transportation costs of low-grade ores by reducing the percentage of waste rock to increase the concentration of the metal-bearing ore.]

[3] Ibid.

[4] Ibid.

[5] Ibid.

[6] Guntau, Martin, "The Emergence of Geology as a Scientific Discipline," *History of Science*, XVI, 1978, pgs. 280-290.

[7] *Silver World*, April 14, 1921.

[8] Ibid.

[9] Thompson, Thomas Gray, *The Social and Cultural History of Lake City, Colorado*, pg. 88. [Also see: Smith, P. David, *The Story of Lake City, Colorado*, pg. 152.]

[10] Gurley, Albert E., *The History and Genealogy of the Gurley Family*, Willimantic, Connecticut, 1897, pgs. 102-103.

[11] Chamberlin, pgs. 135-140.

[12] Ibid.

[13] Ibid.

[14] Ibid.

[15] Ibid.

[16] Ibid.

[17] Ibid.

[18] Ibid.

[19] "William Gurley," *Archival Biographical File*, University of Chicago Library.

[20] *Silver World*, August 21, 1919.

[21] Chamberlin, pg. 139.

[22] Wright, Carolyn and Clarence, *Tiny Hinsdale of the Silvery San Juans*, pgs. 184-185.

CHAPTER 6

Silver Will Do

Once more on Hangtown's hills we delve,
On Murderer's Bar we mine,
At Niger's Tent and Boston Jim's,
You Bet, Red Dog, Port Wine.

On Poker Flat and Poor Man's Shack,
Once more our luck we try,
Where nuggets once were found as thick,
As planets in the sky. [1]

"It [takes] a gold mine to operate a silver mine." [2]

The story of San Juans' silver is not restricted to San Juans' mines. As important, it is a story of market forces and Federal Government politics.

The discovery and development of the Vermont and Ocean Wave mines, and the construction of a risky tunnel—Reynolds Tunnel—to exploit their silver reserves, exemplified a generation of Western mining history and a full spectrum of "young-American" culture. The drover turned prospector and hard-scrabble seekers like him stood at one end of this spectrum. The cook turned scientist and entrepreneurs like A.E. Reynolds anchored the other. Strewn between the two extremes were all manner of hero and horses'-ass.

The Vermont/Ocean Wave lodes and the men that fought Uncompahgre Mountain is a story of failures and successes seen through the eyes of those with the most to gain and the most to lose. In both cases we owe them, and those they epitomize, recognition and respect if for no other reason than for their grit. The editor of the *Lake City Phonograph*, no doubt having observed many a man who considered himself far wiser than his peers, thought so, too. He wrote somewhat awkwardly:

How men have tenaciously followed stringers and "leaders" until no flour, no coffee was left and the last slice of bacon was in the frying pan, giving up only because of crowning necessity, to be followed by others who reaped the benefits of their fruitless work and often only a little further on broke into bodies of ore that proved bonanzas in profit to the finders, is romantically demonstrated in the careers of the Ocean Wave and the Vermont. A number of fortunes have been lost and a number have been made in their operation, and there is no doubt in the writer's mind that with judicious handling there will yet be many millions of dollars' worth of gold, silver, lead, and copper developed and produced from both properties by deeper working.[3]

Every journey culminating in Henson Canyon and its gulches harboring prospects like the Vermont and Ocean Wave was heroic. Alpine seeps and springs fed the headwaters of the mighty rivers of the San Juan Mountains. They surfaced near passes shouldered by rugged ridgelines dividing watersheds. Ancestral trails never strayed far from the water and always converged on the passes. Engineer Pass was no exception. Tributaries to the upper Animas River flow from Engineer's western flank. A tributary of the Gunnison River, Henson Creek, gets its start off its eastern flank, cutting its way through Henson Canyon. Fifteen miles downstream, El Paso Creek and its gulch strike northward four miles to its source. On the walls of El Paso Gulch are hints of mineral veins that lured the first prospectors to the Vermont lode. Not far to the east, within

---

GRAY COPPER

"Gray copper" ore indicated high-grade silver content. The viability of any silver mining operation was a function of the grade of ore (measured in ounces of silver per ton of ore); the cost of mining, transporting, and processing the ore; and the market value of the recovered silver. During the late 1800s through the first half of the twentieth century the market value of silver fluctuated between $0.50 per ounce and $1.50 per ounce. When the value of silver was high, mining and marketing lower-grade ores could still be profitable. When silver values were low, lower-grade ores were profitable only if cost-cutting techniques could be employed. The quality of ores that were known to exist in the Vermont and the Ocean Wave lodes were moderate to good, and there was reason to believe that higher quality ores were present albeit yet to be discovered. A.E. Reynolds' risky haulage tunnel was a cost-cutting technique that promised better margins and an opportunity to exploit even lower-grade ores regardless of fluctuating silver values. Given other opportunities at hand, the Vermont/Ocean Wave project was his best chance to make a profitable mine.[4]

sight, sets the drover's Ocean Wave and south across narrow Henson Canyon, the cook's Big Casino.

Henson Creek is an immense drainage latticed with scores of mineralized gulches. One measure of its vast reach is the area of its watershed, 105 square miles give or take a few square yards. No better description than the one found in the 1888 *Hinsdale Phonograph* explains the last rush to the San Juans and the background for A.E. Reynolds' turn at unearthing Vermont/Ocean Wave silver. The editor wrote:

> *To the newcomer and mining investor Henson creek is one of the most attractive districts in the county."*
>
> *From Lake City to Capitol City is 9½ miles; to Roses Cabin 14½ miles. From Roses Cabin to the head of Hurricane basin is 3 miles; to the head of American flats 3½ miles; to the head of the main stream 4 miles. Numerous gulches between Roses Cabin and Capitol City drain considerable areas. At Capitol city the North Fork comes in, from three different sources six to eight miles away, and from the latter place to Lake City no less than eight gulches empty, each with drainage of from four to six miles in length. An estimate of the average length and breadth of the country drained by the main stream and its tributaries gives a territory 14 miles long by 7½ miles wide, level measure, or 105 square miles.*
>
> *Henson Creek, flowing west to east, diagonally crosses three great mineral belts of the county, and by its ages of erosion exposes their veins to easy prospecting and convenient development. [This assessment was boosterism at best, fraudulent at its worst.] The first of these belts, trending northeast to southwest across the headwaters of the northwest tributaries, possesses the same characteristics, and seems to be a continuation of the famous belt that has made Red Mountain [site of a number of incredibly rich mines between nearby Ouray and Silverton] such a noted producer. The ore of this formation occurs generally in chimneys or chutes, often of immense extent, and frequently broken and displaced by faults and slips, sometimes the ore jumping to one side a hundred feet from the vertical line of its original discovery. These chimneys contain more or less quantities of immensely rich ore, principally sulphurets and galena, in many instances a pocket yielding from a quarter to half a million dollars. [Chimneys or chutes thus described would be elusive or nonexistent in Henson Canyon mines.] Machinery and intelligent and systematic development are the requirements necessary to success in the mines of this belt. To companies and individuals commanding abundant capital it is an encouraging field for investment, but, for the poor prospector, who expects his mine to be his living, other districts of the county offer more promising inducements. And yet some surface strikes have been made in the copper stained porphyry of Copper hill and Engineer flats that have yielded to their fortunate owner's*

comfortable fortunes.

> *On the northeast of this and occupying the center and chief part of the country drained by Henson creek is the great lead belt of San Juans, extending from the northern limits of Hinsdale County through San Juans County to the southern slope of the La Plata Mountains. In this belt are found more forms and qualities of mineral than can perhaps be found in any other section of the United States, ranging from the highest grades of gold and native silver ores to the purist quality of galena, zinc, copper and iron pyrites. Its bodies of mineral are often astonishing in extent and purity, but are as yet unavailable as profitable producers.*
>
> *The third belt, of which Lake City may be considered the center of that part lying on the tributaries of Henson creek, is too well known to need general mention…. On the north side of Henson creek between Lake City and Capitol City are Modoc, Nellie, Pole and El Paso gulches, and on these are located the majority of the producing mines of lower Henson. The sources of all these creeks are heavily capped by a barren porphyry and if ore is to be found it will only be by expensive process. Numerous leads occur along the lower portion of all these gulches, however, and every year develops valuable properties in some of the claims.[5]*

El Paso Gulch channels El Paso Creek rising from Uncompahgre, Wetterhorn and Matterhorn mountain springs and builds to a thunderous roar at Henson Creek nearly five thousand vertical feet and four miles below. The two collide seven miles above Lake City and a few hundred yards below the Big Casino mine perched along the southern flank of Henson Canyon. Looking down from the Big Casino, little is seen of El Paso Gulch situated across the narrow canyon. Its course is serpentine and quickly lost sight of in its own narrow, high-walled canyon. Even so, its mineral outcrops did not go unnoticed. By 1874, despite the lingering threat of Ute attack, claims were staked, many of them by members of J.K. Mullin's 1871 trek. By mid-1875 the Ute had ceded the San Juans and the work of making them into mines was underway.

Of greater interest at the time, recall that Enos Hotchkiss and his toll road construction crew discovered gold in the nearby Lake Fork of the Gunnison watershed. The discovery, at the time deep in the sometimes hostile Ute homeland but far more accessible than nearby Henson Canyon, transformed the remote confluence of the upper Lake Fork of the Gunnison and Henson Creek watersheds into a metropolis by frontier standards. Two mines, the Golden Fleece and the Golden Wonder, proved to be well-endowed with rich gold ore, and the "Town" of Lake City, soon crowned "*Queen of the San Juans*," quickly became a legitimate "boomtown." But "Queen" was an exaggeration and exaggerated "gold claims" were lies. Other than the Golden Fleece and Golden Wonder, there was little to no success with Lake Fork claims. The vast majority of gold-seekers that rushed in behind the Hotchkiss crew learned this truth the hard way. Gold-bearing ore veins were elusive at the time and rare in Hinsdale County—in the end just the two—and Lake City never amounted to more than a town. As quickly as it bloomed, it plateaued and began to wither. For want of high-grade ores or a railroad to economically transport low-grade ores, the mining camp that would be Queen was dethroned. Gold was a "humbug." That said, there was silver, a lot of it.

While prospects in the Lake Fork watershed were disappointing, Henson Canyon prospects were not, at least in terms of silver-bearing veins. In short order, silver locations motivated community activists of the day to raise funds and construct a toll road that transformed nearly impassable Henson Canyon into a prospector paradise served by freight wagons and coaches. Hundreds of claims fueled a fresh rush, then sustained the community with promises of rich ore. However, like gold, an abundance of easily mined, rich silver ore also was usually a lie. Low-grade ore would have to do. Sadly, national economic policies and richer discoveries elsewhere in North America also conspired against Lake City prosperity. Not even the 1889 arrival of the Denver & Rio Grande Railroad (D&RGRR) guaranteed relief. In fact, it arrived a decade too late to save the queen. Meant to boost local spirits, *Resources and Mineral Wealth of Hinsdale County, Colorado— Past, Present and Future* was published in 1895. Intended to showcase mineral opportunities, embedded within its pages was a sobering confession that 1890s economic prospects of Lake City and Henson Canyon were declining. [6]

Part of the problem was competing gold and silver discoveries and rushes to new boomtowns. The great stampedes that started with Sutter's Mill in 1849 and Pikes Peak in 1859 shifted to easier to get to boomtowns. White Pine, Nevada in the late 1860s; and the Black Hills of South Dakota, Tombstone, Arizona, and Leadville, Colorado in the late 1870s were where fortunes could be made. During the early 1880s, Coeur d'Alene was hot. In the 1890s, Cripple Creek and Creede, Colorado would not disappoint. At the turn of the century the rush to Alaska and the Yukon was on. Skagway, Klondike, Forty-Mile, Tanana, and Nome were familiar names that fired the soul of any adventurer worth his kit. Henson Canyon, slow in rising, flashed in 1875 and was overshadowed in the 1890s by fresh finds elsewhere. Nor were falling silver prices on the global market helpful.

Students of human nature are well-acquainted with the state of mind of treasure hunters rushing from pillar to post. Rodman Paul quotes an 1898 gold seeker cheerfully declaring, a gold rush "being infectious attacks all grades and conditions of men...our hearts, our hopes, ourselves, are on board [our ship] for better or worse." Citing the June 27,1874, *Mining and Scientific Press*, Paul continues:

> *"Hundreds of lives were sacrificed... and many millions more of money spent than has been realized in these wild hunts after wealth." Ultimately "the*

remnant of this great army" came struggling back, "poor in pocket, with shat-
tered constitutions and wrecked hopes," to see what prospects there might be
in the older regions from which they had departed on their various odysseys.[7]

Such was the case with Henson Canyon and Lake City. Disappointing claims
located in the 1870s and early 1880s, and there were hundreds, were set aside for
more alluring ventures farther afield. Speculators once falling over themselves
to get in on the proverbial "ground floor" were lured elsewhere. Even producing
mines like the Vermont and Ocean Wave were not attractive enough to stem the
flight of the curious or the adventurous or the speculator flush with someone
else's cash. But in the case of the Vermont and the Ocean Wave, at least, the
Mining and Scientific Press author was prophetic. The drover along with others
like him would return to their San Juan digs, and A.E. Reynolds would invest his
profits from his Virginius' Revenue Tunnel overlooking nearby Ouray in developing what he expected would be a similar success in the Vermont and Ocean
Wave lodes.[8]

In the grander scheme of things, Henson Canyon played its best hand in
1875. Its turn at being a flash-in-the-pan gold rush darling was aided and abet-
ted by a number of other less obvious but fundamental San Juans developments.
Cattle herded from Texas became more commonplace than Great Plains buffalo.
Ancestral trails were widened and hardened by settlers, military fort builders, and
growing fleets of heavy freight-wagons capable of transporting mining equipment into the mountains in exchange for low-grade ore destined for refractories
in Leadville and along the Front Range. Completion of the transcontinental railroad spawned feeder lines and narrow-gauge branches capable of reaching the
remotest mining camps. And the press of immigrants, relentless "westering" that
in the case of Henson Canyon coincided with apparent relief from Ute threats,
provided manpower. All were preconditions for viable San Juans silver mining.
All required sacrifice and courage.

To sustain the influx of pioneers and settlers the heavy wagons and daring
teamsters probably deserve more appreciation than they received. Pack animals
and light farm wagons had served their purpose well, but their days were numbered. George Franklin's first-hand account of San Juans pioneer Major M. V. B.
Wasson's role in this matter illustrates the challenge.

> *On a return trip from California in 1872, Major Wasson found a load*
> *of mining machinery in Santa Fe, routed over the Santa Fe Trail, waiting*
> *for a freight outfit large enough to transport it to Arastra Gulch, San Juans*
> *County, (then a part of Conejos County), Colorado [just over Engineer Pass*
> *from Henson Canyon.]*
> *There were ten wagons in Wasson's train, each drawn by four yokes of*
> *fine big oxen; besides this array of equipment there were one hundred head of*

grade California mares, that he had bought on speculation hoping to sell them to some one of the cattle companies that began to appear on the plains with the disappearance of the buffalo.

The miners were willing to pay an exorbitant price even for frontier times, to anyone who could handle the freight. The time was late August. Wasson figured that he could make the trip from Santa Fe up the Rio Grande, then by doubling the teams on each wagon pull them over Cinnamon pass to the headwaters of the Animas, thence down the valley to Arastra Gulch. The road he took at the time he made the daring trip was but little more than the wagon tracks made by other pioneers in 1871, except in such places as where the slope of a hill had required a cut.

He left the main-travelled road at Antelope Springs and went over Alden Hill, past Lake Santa Maria (now called Mirror Lake) on up Clear Creek to a point about two miles above the falls, then followed Spring Creek to the top of the divide, crossed the headwaters of Cebolla Creek and hit the South Fork of Powderhorn Creek which was followed to the low pass at the source of Slumgullion Creek. From here down to Lake San Cristobal the wagons had to be snubbed to trees.[9]

Heavy Freight Wagons and their fearless teamsters were indispensable to San Juans mining. Boilers and mills could not be delivered otherwise. Like burros, mules, oxen, and horses, heavy freight wagons coexisted with railroads for decades. More threatening later were trucks which also could navigate treacherous mountain "roads" to reach remote sites. (Frank Leslie's Illustrated Newspaper, April 12, 1879)

Santa Fe to Lake San Cristobal was the easy leg of his journey. From the upper Lake Fork watershed Wasson cut a new track through a thick spruce forest and ascended narrow gulches and the upper Lake Fork Canyon to 11,000 ft. Cinnamon Pass. Descending the western slope of Engineer Mountain to the upper Animas River Valley, he followed the river down to Arastra Gulch and delivered a quartz mill at the Little Giant Mine to Major Hamilton who eagerly awaited its arrival. Wasson retraced his path to Wagon Wheel Gap and a new ranch where he had left his hundred mares. The winter of 1872 was long and hard, at times experiencing four feet of snow and minus forty degree temperatures. The mares, sheltered and nourished with good hay, nevertheless began dying. In order to increase their ration Wasson was forced to butcher his oxen.

What looked like a financial disaster in the making turned into an unimagined financial windfall. Prospectors camping at the future site of Lake City learned there was a supply of meat just fifty miles away ["*just*" fifty miles through heavy mountain snow]. Willing to pay dearly, the prospectors pack-trained back to camp with Wasson's butchered oxen, sparing him great loss. By winter's end, Wasson decided to make Wagon Wheel Gap his home. Having demonstrated heavy freighting was feasible, not to mention profitable, he also concluded that cattle and horse breeding were more to his liking than freighting. Similar epiphanies struck rookie prospectors and miners who quickly took up shopkeeping. Wasson named his ranch the "*W Oxyoke*" which became "the most famous horse ranch in all of Colorado." As for the silver mines the Major worked so faithfully to supply, despite making his home in the midst of one of the San Juans' richest mining districts, he was content to leave the pursuit of silver to others. No doubt well aware of the accounts of treasure pouring forth from all quarters, the Vermont and Ocean Wave included, by the time he learned of Reynolds' last best chance the old gentleman was long past caring.[10]

Of course the Major was not the only mountain freighter. Likewise, while he may have been the first to navigate the roadless San Juans, in the absence of railroads many others had to master the roadless Great Plains in order to get to the roadless San Juans. Little by little, beginning with tentative probes in the 1840s, freighters managed to keep up with supplying the West with the essentials. The West was in the first stages of an irreversible transformation. Horace Greeley attested to this in his own unique style while writing about his first-hand view of Colorado's gold rush. Rodman Paul sets the stage:

> *If the Indians, like the mountain men, had no great future in the West, with whom did the future lie? A partial answer rose dramatically before Greeley's eyes as he approached Leavenworth, on the Missouri River. "As we neared the California trail, the white coverings of the many emigrant and transport wagons dotted the landscape, giving the trail the appearance of a river running through great meadows, with many ships sailing on its bosom."* [11]

If this impression of transformation was not potent enough, Greeley received a booster shot farther south when he (with aspiring journalist A.D. Richardson in tow) approached the Santa Fe Trail. Again, Rodman Paul brilliantly captures the moment:

> *This time it was the big contract wagons of the professional freighters that dominated the scene, and near Leavenworth itself he visited the huge depot of Russell, Majors and Waddell, where that famous firm had in reserve literally acres of extra wagons, pyramids of extra axletrees, large herds of oxen, and regiments of drivers.*[12]

Professional freighters were the umbilical cord that delivered sustenance to Santa Fe, Tucson, Salt Lake City, Army outposts, reservations, and the rudimentary supply posts along the California and Oregon trails, the Colorado Front Range, and Denver in particular. They were the silent heroes of westering. More easily grasped and more to the heart of popular fascination were the mines and the pilgrims that searched for them. Not even Greeley was immune. Perhaps stemming from deep within his Christian conscience, he also was compelled to sound an alarm:

> *[A] few will be amply and suddenly enriched by finding "leads" and selling "claims;" some by washing those "claims;" some by supplying the mountains with the four apparent necessaries of mining life — whiskey, coffee, flour, and bacon; others by robbing the miners of their hard earnings through the instrumentality of cards, roulette, and the "little joker;" but ten will come out here for gold for everyone who carries back so much as he left home with, and thousands who hasten hither... will lay down to their long rest beneath the shadows of the mountains.*[13]

Greeley's instincts concerning the fleeting wiles of Rocky Mountain silver and gold, and the likelihood of dying, did little to stem the tide. Yes, disappointment and death were ever-present, but there was treasure to be had, and in sufficient quantities to energize the national economy. More on target, his instincts concerning the transformation of the Great Plains and the mountains beyond were prophetic. Without foreknowledge of names, in his mind's eye Greeley envisioned a thousand Major Wasson's taking up where the prairie freighters (and soon-coming railroads) would leave off. And in the final analysis, as coquettish as she is, silver would be the best play.

Of course gold was the dream, and the slightest trace was all that was required to spark a boom. But in Colorado geology, plentiful placer gold was not in the cards, and lode gold was rarely located and hard to mine. In 1867, Ovando Hollister did his best to shine light on the matter. He wrote *The Mines of*

Colorado, which was filled with authentic yet simple explanations of the fledgling geosciences and where valuable minerals could be found. Self-taught, nevertheless Hollister was a gifted observer and writer able to make persuasive arguments that may not have been valid but were plausible just the same. At the time, his "science" was as good as anyone else's. Mine engineering and mineralogy were not yet the provinces of prestigious universities and institutes akin to those found in Europe. Instead, journals and journalists, reprinting the work of others or sharing their own field experiences, schooled anyone who had an interest. Hollister was in step with his times. His focus was gold; but, for the most part, his advice held true for silver, and was consistent with European thinking. In any case, in the San Juans and Henson Canyon in particular, silver would have to do.

In typical Ovando Hollister style, he summarized late nineteenth-century mine geology usually in common language maybe even the drover could have understood if only the drover could have read. Dismissing placer mining as an "ephemeral business" [a term probably no one understood], Hollister declared "quartz or vein mining... among the most permanent pursuits of man." Further explaining the nature of quartz veins, it is easy in hindsight to see why Vermont and Ocean Wave circumstances tantalized but failed to fulfill owners, lessors, and Reynolds for half a century. What Hollister clearly described, Henson Canyon miners and investors experienced firsthand. Prospects looked promising if only they persevered. Ovando put words to what they saw, or more often what they hoped to see. Again, gold was rare. Silver would have to do. For the novice, he began with fundamentals. Forgive the lengthy quote, it is too packed with detail to sensibly unpack.

> *By a vein, as a geological or mining term, in general, is understood (to be) an aggregation of mineral matter of indefinite length and breadth and comparatively slight thickness, differing in character from, and posterior in formation to, the rocks which enclose it.*
>
> *Segregated veins are what their name implies. They are supposed to have been formed by the segregation of particles of similar nature from the gneissoid and schistose rocks in which they occur, while the mass was cooling down from a molten state. In other words, they are crystals on a large scale, and instead of occupying any preexisting fissure in the country rock, make way and room for themselves by force of chemical affinity. [Then he got to the heart of the matter.]*
>
> *The auriferous quartz veins of most gold regions belong to this class of deposits. They consist of belts of quartzose matter, with sulphuret of iron, which near the surface is decomposed into a hydrated oxide, and contain gold disseminated through these substances, and sometimes in the adjoining rock in fine particles, or, occasionally, large lumps. These belts run with the strata and dip with them, and in other respects exhibit the phenomena of segregated rather than of fissure veins.*

OVANDO (VANDO) HOLLISTER

Ovando "Vando" James Hollister, son of Loren Hollister and Sarah Center, was born October 7, 1834, in Colrain, Franklin County, Massachusetts. Married or not is difficult to say, but for whatever reason early in his childhood Loren and Sarah placed Ovando in the care of a Shaker community in eastern New York. He was largely unschooled, worked as a farm hand, moved to a Kansas homestead in the 1850s, and was swept up in the Colorado gold rush in 1859. Vando landed in Black Hawk June 7, 1860, where he took up residence with two other adventure seekers. The mines of Black Hawk taught many practical lessons. In 1861 he enlisted in the First Colorado Cavalry [with the rank of Colonel in one account, private in another], led his command in battle against Confederate forces in southern Colorado and New Mexico, and

Ovando J. Hollister (1834-1892). Civil War veteran, miner, editor and author, self-educated Hollister was as close to being a geologist and mining engineer as any formally educated "scientist." *(Images.findagrave.com)*

was discharged due to injuries received in the service of his state and his country. In November 1861, in partnership with General Frank Hall, soon to earn fame as a prolific Colorado historian, he established the *Daily Mining Journal*. He was the chief editor and proprietor from November 1863 through December 1865. His talents clearly included journalism and book writing.

In 1868 Hollister reached a broader audience as editor of the iconic *Rocky Mountain News*. He wrote a number of other books, filled a number of other offices and positions, and was held in high regard or low esteem depending on one's point of view regarding his use of "choice language" and his conservative political persuasions. All of this by way of saying that lack of formal education was no obstacle to Ovando mastering and sharing knowledge concerning the environment around him. Not known as a prospector or miner, or as a geologist or mining "engineer," he could pass for one. His insights were valued by most who knew of them, A.E. Reynolds for one.[14]

A true vein is a fissure in the solid crust of the earth, of indefinite length and depth, which has been filled more less perfectly with mineral substances; or, in other words, an aggregation of mineral matter, accompanied by metallifer-ous ores, within a crevice or fissure which had its origin in some deep-seated cause, and may be presumed to extend for an indefinite distance downwards. True veins sometimes attain a length of several miles. They vary much in thickness, and nobody has ever yet seen the under edge of one. They are the principal repositories of the ores of the useful metals, and their exploitation is a matter of lasting importance, involving the employment of both skill and capital. They are rarely found singly, but rather in groups, often in a compli-cated network crowded into a narrow space.

Usually but a small proportion of the matter in the fissure is valuable ore. The earthy or non-metallic portion is called 'gangue' or 'veinstone', and is most commonly composed of quartz, next of carbonate of lime in the form of calcare-ous spar, lastly of fluorspar and heavy spar. Different districts have vein-stones as well as ores peculiar to themselves, and the locality of an ore may often be de-termined by examining a fragment of its gangue. Sometimes pieces of the wall or country rock are recognized in the vein-matter. These are called "horses." The fissure itself is frequently of a complex character, forming parallel branches, and sending out ramifications from the main line of fracture, until it seemingly becomes lost. The branches that leave the main lode are called "droppers;" and when they concentrate and lead into it again, they are called "feeders." [If all this is not helpful, he continues explaining why fissures are so perplexing:]

The walls of veins are often smoothed and striated, as if there had been motion of the lode against them accompanied by pressure; these polished sur-faces are called "slickensides." The barren rock removed in excavating a vein is called "deads," "attle," "rubble." Fissures may be of different geological ages, and where this is the case, the phenomena attending them become doubly com-plicated. A system may be heaved out of place, or given a new direction by a newer one, and a younger system may heave both out of place, change their direction, and mix things up generally.

With regard to the filling of true veins there are various theories, the most popular one among miners being that they were filled by injection from below. This theory finds no countenance among scientific men, however, who find it impossible to reconcile it with the actual conditions presented by the veins and vein matter.[15]

So declared Ovando. Not satisfied, he had more to say of a practical nature. Sublimation, aqueous deposition, and lateral secretion were explanations contemporary science offered. Sublimation was characterized by the vein filling with metallic materials from the "ignited interior of the earth." Aqueous deposi-tion presupposed a chemical solution filled veins from above. Hollister dismissed this theory as "nonsense," as though he was a recognized expert. No matter, the lad was confident and he was articulate. Lateral secretion assumed a complicated series of phenomena that occurred concurrently over a long period of time. If these scientific explanations could be summarized in any meaningful way, it was to say that where there was quartz there was likely to be valuable minerals, gold in particular, but he would not rule out silver.

In fact, both usually were found together. If there was a greater concentration of gold, it was a gold vein accompanied by silver. If there was a greater concentration of silver, it was a silver vein accompanied by gold. As anyone involved in mining often experienced, market prices and governmental policies could easily upset this handy convention. When this happened, it could be more profitable to recover gold from "silver veins," or vice-versa. At times it even was preferable or mandated—during the two World Wars, for example—to extract associated metals like lead, copper, and zinc at the expense of the silver or gold.

One more perplexing Hollisterism: the highest assays could not be assumed to diminish with depth. Nor could it be assumed that the assay would increase with depth. In other words, a miner would have to follow the vein to find out, a fact of life that was not all that helpful, really.

Hollister addressed this "science" in a bantering, mocking style: veins could appear to pinch out, but in fact might soon reappear on the same bearing or maybe not, the same elevation or maybe not, or the same distance into the mountain or maybe not. Having trouble following this? Not Hollister. Again he helps us with a dose of layman's insight, the same common sense understanding our Henson Canyon miners acquired underground the hard way despite having little clue about scientific explanations and no clue who Ovando Hollister was or what he described. Hollister wrote:

> It must be plain to the reader by this time that very little is known as to how or when the lower sedimentary rocks were metamorphosed, the vein fissures made, filled with quartz or other vein-stone; or how or when the quartz or the whole rock strata in which it occurs, as the case may be, was impregnated, as the savans (savants) have it, with gold. We at least are most positively ignorant of the whole matter and confess to very little desire of being impregnated with knowledge of it. In the blaze of universal ignorance on the subject the Colorado rocks are likely to fare as well as any other rocks, and meanwhile it is of more interest to us how and when we shall get the gold out than how and when it was put in.[16]

"It is of more interest to us how and when we shall get the gold out than how it was put in." This is the operative thought, and it was the only thought that really mattered to "the boys" wielding hammers and drills. Had any of them read it, surely it would have brought forth a knowing chuckle.

Man's Work. Hand-drilling was not augmented with steam or pneumatic drills at the Vermont until 1899. The Ocean Wave never saw the use of power equipment. (*G. Thomas Ingham*)

But what about silver? Silver is found almost exclusively in the form of an ore. An ore is a metal combined with a "mineralizer." In the case of the Vermont and the Ocean Wave, the mineralizer is sulphur. Elsewhere it could be carbon. Also remember that in the case of the Vermont and the Ocean Wave, and virtually every other claim in Henson Canyon, ores are low-grade. Also remember gray copper, the common term for ores with high silver values and some gold, the greatest values usually occurring at greater depths, but (again) not always, was cause for great excitement.

Typical Vermont and Ocean Wave superintendent reports sent down weekly to *Silver World* editors, reports just like those from every Henson Canyon mine superintendent, never failed to titillate editors and citizens alike. Usually the reports praised the opening of a new vein showing gray copper. Gold was preferred, of course, but Henson Canyon was not blessed with much gold and sober folks had tumbled to that reality early-on. Silver in various forms was as good as it got, better than nothing and reason enough to move more dirt. The promise of gold had brought them, the promise of silver kept them. Gray copper promised ore yielding the highest assay. Other lower grade ores were shipped as well, but rarely at a profit. But who could know? The smelter run might yield more silver than expected. More often, the yield would be less than expected, and the smelter would be accused of understating values and profiting from the difference.

Coloration of rocks is often a good indication of mineral content. Yellowish-brown mine waste, commonly called tailings, is caused by iron hydroxide (limonite) resulting from the oxidation of iron pyrite (fool's gold). Other common minerals include Smithsonite (the green carbonate of zinc), Siderite (the brownish carbonate of iron), Rhodochrosite (the pinkish carbonate of manganese), Malachite and Azurite (the green/blue carbonates of copper), Pyrite and Chalcopyrite (sulfides of iron), Galena (a shiny lead sulfide similar in appearance to silver but brittle), Molybdenite (a molybdenum disulfide), and Scheelite and Huebnerite (ores of tungsten and manganese). A year or two of formal "engineering school" (geosciences are not yet "sciences") could have been helpful, but the typical Henson Canyon miner and many "engineers" learned their chops underground, especially when they could not read. [17]

As daunting as mining Henson Canyon complex-ores was, the chemistry of extracting silver or gold from their sulphur and base metal matrices at a smelter was more so. Despite the best efforts of Nathaniel Hill, Colorado's renowned Black Hawk metallurgist, the loss of anywhere between 30% to 70% of silver was common, a reality that struck mine operators more as pilfering and greed on the part of the smelting crowd than the metallurgy of the ores. But the nature of the ore was a legitimate, critical factor. Rodman Paul quoting the March 8, 1873, *Colorado Mining Review* explains the challenge:

GALENA DISTRICT

Precious metals like gold and silver are usually associated with other minerals. The most prominent Vermont and Ocean Wave mineral was galena, a lead sulfide which contains silver and looks like it. In keeping with Ovando Hollister's view, it usually was entrained in a quartz vein. A "lode" is ore found in hard rock formations. When a lode is eroded, gold and to a lesser extent silver is "freed" and can wash into streambeds and is known as "placers." The July 15, 1879, *Silver World* reported silver "float" in Henson Creek at the Burro Cabin mill site, downstream from the Vermont, but silver float is rare and the report was not exciting. It hardly mattered and in any event was not pursued. Instead, a quartz ledge was located a short distance up El Paso Creek which flowed into Henson Creek at the mill site. Regardless of whether or not this was a source of "float," the ledge was the prize.

In the 1882 *Annual Report of the Director of the Mint*, mineralization in the Galena Mining District was described as appropriate to the name given for that area: veins of principally argentiferous lead ores (sulfide and sulfate of lead), generally accompanied by auriferous copper and iron pyrites, gray copper, zinc blende, and quartz. Some of the most common minerals and ores in the upper Lake Fork watershed are quartz (an oxide of silicon), feldspar (a silicate of either potassium and aluminum or calcium and aluminum), micas (limonite and hematite which are iron oxides), clay comprised of aluminum silicate formed from weathered feldspar, and metal sulfides, notably iron, silver, lead, zinc, and copper. Talc also was common, not as exciting as gray copper, but sometimes an indicator it was nearby. All of these minerals are enticing treasure hunt clues — all of them were present in the Vermont and Ocean Wave lodes.

*In Colorado we are having the privilege of solving some of the most dif-
ficult problems of metallurgy.*

*We doubt if any other district on the continent can afford a more com-
plete and varied study for the metallurgist. Its gold is found nearly always
associated with iron and copper, the latter in quantities varying from three to
twenty per cent. Its silver is in a majority of cases carried in zinc or lead ores,
and often with an admixture of antimony and arsenic. Were only one or two
of these present the difficulties would not be so great. As it is however a very
small number of mines yield rock that can be properly handled in any other
way than by a long and complicated process.*[18]

As suggested above, the role of silver coinage in the global silver market
was another stumbling block repeatedly tripped over by Henson Canyon miners
and investors. Unfortunately, this stumbling block was not limited to Henson
Canyon, or the San Juans for that matter. It was bigger than that. The stumbling
block was in Washington, D.C. It was the Federal Government, the international
marketplace, and it was part and parcel of events that dated back to the Nation's
Civil War.

Oddly enough, the peaks and troughs of the price of silver and thus the value
of ores did not coincide with the peaks and troughs of mine activity in Henson
Canyon. Investment and production marched to their own drummers, which
could lead one to conclude that the hunt for treasure was little affected by its
expected market value. Treasure, after all, was simply treasure—gold and silver
have intrinsic and even eternal worth. Market value was someone else's concern
by this way of thinking, but probably not a concern for speculators who usually
dabbled with other people's money. As for locating the treasure, surely it was just
a few feet farther along, and high-grade at that. To the really clueless among this
class, the thrill of the hunt justified the game. To the miner, it was all about daily
wages.

More so than gold, the global market price of silver fluctuated wildly. Until
well into the twentieth century, the U.S. Treasury maintained a silver-gold price
ratio of 16:1, meaning it took the value of sixteen ounces of silver to equal the
value of one ounce of gold. When the U.S. value of gold was set in 1834 at $20.69
an ounce, the value of an ounce of silver became $1.29. U.S. government policy
was based upon the belief that maintaining this ratio was necessary to support
the value of U.S. silver coins. On the international market, however, this policy
often undervalued the silver content of U.S. silver currency. When this happened,
U.S. silver coins were melted down and sold as bullion because the value of the
silver content was greater than the face value of the coin.

In 1853 Congress, ever alert to short-term opportunities to create long-term
problems, responded to this debasement of U.S. silver coins by ending them with
the exception of silver dollars. How this exception was supposed to help is a

mystery, but apparently solving the mystery concerned no one that mattered. As unintended consequences go, the net effect was the country found itself on a de facto "gold standard" instead of on the well-functioning bi-metal standard. There was sufficient gold in circulation to meet the everyday needs of the economy, but capital formation for large projects was difficult. Economic development stagnated.

The Civil War not only ended 750,000 lives and the South's agrarian economy, the war ended both retarded national growth and widespread use of gold and silver coinage. Its demands resulted in government-printed paper money, "greenbacks" by another name. With no intrinsic value, public faith in their government was sorely strained but did not snap. During periods when the war was not going well for the Union, "greenback" holders were motivated to exchange their paper for silver dollars or gold coins of equal value. Devout Northern patriots did not consider doing so. Devout Confederates printed their own paper currency. Traders along the Texas-Mexico border sought Mexican silver to bolster Confederate commerce. Inflation on both sides of the North-South battlefront soared.

At war's end the currency gloves came off. Investors, bankers, and businessmen wanted paper currency totally replaced with gold coinage. They feared inflated paper currency would be used to repay loans and pay for goods sold on credit. Westerners and Southerners, often debtors, were just fine with a system

1862 Greenback. Gold and silver production could not keep up with the needs of a growing economy and the cost of civil war. Fiat [paper] currency was the solution, but also another nail in the Western mining coffin. (Wikipedia)

that enabled them to repay creditors with inflated paper currency. Silver interests were indifferent at this point—they soon saw the light—since gold was the issue and use of silver dollars was insignificant.

In 1873 Congress again dabbled in international economics. Government silver purchases and the minting of silver dollars that provided a price floor for silver was eliminated. Soon referred to as the "Crime of '73," silver mining prospects plummeted. Overnight the country was on a gold standard. Most countries not already on a gold standard followed suit. Sellers of silver far outnumbered buyers and prices fell. Western mining and agricultural interests were most directly impacted and did not go quietly into the night. Five years of bitter regional politics ensued.

Undaunted by prior missteps, Congress intervened again. The Bland-Allison Act of 1878 directed the Secretary of the Treasury to purchase two million to four million dollars of silver at "market price" monthly. The market price silver miners and investors were comfortable with was $1.29 per ounce. Secretaries of the Treasury from both major parties preferred lower prices as well as limiting quantities purchased to the lowest level—two million dollars a month. Silver interests won the battle on government purchases but failed on the issue of government backing currency with silver sufficient to achieve their price expectations.

Crime of '73. The Coinage Act of 1873 effectively placed the country on a gold standard to the detriment of silver. Ironically, silver production increased, further reducing its price per ounce. *(Library of Congress)*

In 1890, silver interests won a decisive battle in Congress. Political horse-trading yielded the Sherman Silver Purchase Act. It required the Treasury Department to purchase four-and-a-half million ounces of silver per month, which amounted to the projected total annual production of the entire country. Unlike the unsuccessful Bland-Allison Act, the purchase requirement specified in the Sherman Act was *ounces*, not *dollars*. Still, having failed to include a guaranteed price or price ratio, plenty of wiggle-room remained to undercut silver interests. At first, market forces pushed prices up to $1.07 an ounce by the end of 1890, but prices stalled and then steadily retreated to $0.78 an ounce by 1893. At the end of 1893, the country again was in a deep recession and the Sherman Silver Purchase Act was repealed. The silver euphoria in Colorado mining camps was also repealed.

As for Pike Snowden's Ocean Wave, he and his partners were not gaming the international silver market. They may not have known there was such a creature, much less how it affected them. They did understand the value of a dollar, and what an ounce of silver could buy. Every hardscrabble miner, as caught up in the adventure of a lifetime as they may be, quickly learned that much. In Snowden's case, the wages of a drover beat the wages of a family farmer, and the life of a prospector and miner beat the life of a drover.

Even so, it is doubtful he paid much attention to profit margins. Silver had to be valuable and he knew how to find it. That was all he needed to know. Had prices mattered to him, silver values were marginal when he and his partners located the Ocean Wave. Talk of $1.00 an ounce was common but rarely earned—$0.50 an ounce was more common after refractory costs were deducted. None of this really mattered to the prospector, nor to the miner unless at the end of another grueling shift the superintendent announced the investors could no

---

DEPRESSION-ERA INVESTORS

Neither growth of American industry into first place among the nations or a World War to end all wars improved the silver market. Prices cycled well-below the 1890 high of $1.07/oz., and bottomed out in the 1932-33 winter of the Great Depression at $0.25/oz.

Still, nearly beyond belief, established mines often idle for years attracted new investors. Silver was a coquette and some depression-era people still had plenty of money. Savvy regarding fickle markets, speculators—some honest, some not— were persuasive and the unemployed with hopes and dreams came to believe their venture would uncover the mother lode and reward them handsomely. If they heeded Vando Hollister's advice on where to search, or had uncanny instincts and were persistent, they did well. If they exhausted patience and faith, or funds, their mine went dark to await another speculator. Unlike silver, speculators proved easy to find. After all, even speculators with someone else's money knew to buy when prices were low. When it came to San Juan mines, even in a deep depression there was money to invest and money to be made. And, of course, gold was a treasure never out of mind for long.

longer pay. Until that moment arrived, mucking another shot and sorting out gray copper was all that was on their minds.

The Ocean Wave crew was the same save for one important difference. They were quick to find a high-grade vein, silver bearing ore with large pockets of gray copper.[19] The higher the grade, the less of a concern was the price of silver. They were also quick to find investors with pockets deep enough to fund development—at times supporting several dozen miners—and a smelter in Lake City to process the ore. "Zenas, the Missouri farm boy drover" became "Pike, the successful San Juan prospector/miner turned businessman" soon able to kick back and become a colorful Henson Canyon bard. One gray copper vein, and someone else's money, was all it took.

The partners accomplished a tremendous amount of development work at the mine. Much of 1877 was devoted to driving four tunnels at slightly different elevations to block out sections of ore, but production was slower than anticipated and marketable ore was not sufficient to cover costs. A year later, prospects remained positive, Pike Snowden was working the mine, but deep pockets still had bottoms and Ocean Wave investors had short arms.

Both the mine and the Lake City smelter shut down. That said, converting ownership to cash and employee-status had proven to be a shrewd move for Pike. Wages were far more reliable than future dividends. Still flush with ore, the Ocean Wave was far from done. The Company's next move was to lease the mine. The lessors shipped enough ore to achieve profitability, but in reckless extraction of the ore left its workings in a dangerous condition. As bad as that was, in 1879 prospects worsened. Additional capital to open new sections of the vein was not forthcoming and the old workings no longer offered easily mined ores. Having passed through the oxidation zone, the remaining "rebellious pay rock" also resisted smelting. Unfortunately, the Ocean Wave company designed its Lake City smelter to process only oxidized material. The design was incompatible with the composition of the ore presented to it. With the mill a failure and much of the best pay-dirt gone from the mine, the owners did what owners do. They bickered among themselves and the lessors shut down the mine in 1880 and sued each other.[20]

Over the next two decades a number of partnerships and lessors, including Pike Snowden, worked the Ocean Wave with mixed results. The best showing was in Level #4, what came to be known as the "Dago Tunnel," so named after the Italian immigrants that leased and worked it for a number of years. When A.E. Reynolds offered to buy the property years later, the owners were more than ready to sell.

Reynold's decision was no river-boat gamble. He was a student of Henson Canyon mines, and he quite likely was a follower of Ovando Hollister and certainly the *Silver World* editor who faithfully reported on the Italians. In typical fashion, Reynolds believed that with proper management and a strategic approach

REYNOLDS' DUE DILIGENCE

Always at risk of being victimized by "boosterism," Reynolds kept abreast of Ocean Wave and Vermont matters and bided his time. Early on, distant publications reported in detail on Henson Canyon mines. On May 3, 1877, the *Colorado Weekly Chieftain* wrote:

> The Ocean Wave was located in April, and the Wave of the Ocean in May [1876] following, by 'Pike' Snowden, Steve Baxter, H. Boggs and D. Bowyer. At the present writing there are four levels open, two of which are now being worked, in which the vein is uncovered; in all about 750 feet of levels and drifts. The work is mostly done by contract. Thirty-six men are employed on the mine, and nine upon other work. Mr. B. L. Riggins is superintendent, and L. H. Spilker, foreman. The paystreak is from nine inches to two and a half feet; fine galena carrying gray copper in great profusion.

William's pseudo-scientific *Tourist Guide to the San Juans* concurred: "The Ocean Wave, eight miles from Lake City up Henson Creek, is a five foot vein of fine galena, showing a great deal of gray copper. It is probably the best developed mine in the district." [21]

Far from being a booster or pseudo anything, H. C. Burchard, Director of the United States Mint, reported that "the Ocean Wave…vein is about 3 ½ feet wide, with 10 to 12 inches of splendid mineral, principally gray copper and galena. Up to the year 1880 the total product of this mine, treated at the Ocean Wave works, was 110,000 ounces. Since that time mine and works have been idle." [22]

Elaborating on Burchard's report, the *Colorado Mining Directory* described the Ocean Wave fissure vein as:

> 3½ ft. wide with a pay streak of 1-30 inches, averaging 7 inches wide comprised of gray and yellow copper with galena in quartz. Yield was 110 ounces silver/ton. Developments included 4 tunnel levels connected with shafts and winzes totaling 1500 ft.; stoping and drifting; output as of 1883 totaling 1,000 tons yielding 110,000 ounces of silver. [23]

"Yielding 110,000 ounces of silver as of 1883" is the same production reported in 1880, but probably was not as alarming as it seemed. "Idle" due to legal and leadership problems, and "development work" designed to locate ore bodies suitable for stoping, were more comforting explanations. The Galena Mining District as a whole continued to account for respectable silver production for another few years. By 1885-86 mining was considered "dull in this district." Charles Henderson's U.S. Geological Survey Professional Paper No. 138 paints a more complete and hopeful picture, albeit unavailable to A.E. Reynolds, who was quite comfortable operating on instinct. [24]

to development there was immense wealth to be recovered in the Ocean Wave. He also certainly was aware of Pike Snowden's accomplishments, and may even have respected them. For Pike's part, in atypical fashion he was content to sit on the front step of his primitive cabin a short distance down the canyon and lord over his old haunt and the district at large. Restless by nature, his contentment would not last long.

The Ocean Wave lode continued to meet every criterion for a bonanza mine without ever becoming one. The quality of ores that were known to exist in the Ocean Wave were moderate to good, but there was reason to believe that abundant gray copper was just another day or two's blasting ahead. For a shrewd mine investor who prided himself on understanding mining, A.E. Reynolds was fully aware of Ocean Wave history. Its production and its promise spanning more than a quarter century was reasonably well documented if not suspicious. Superintendents exaggerated "ore in sight" during weekly conversations with local editors—a necessary tactic designed to soothe the impulses of the impatient and often distant investor—and they understated revenues in reports to tax authorities.

By the mid-1880s, mining in the Galena District may have been dull but it was not dead. A number of older mines still produced paying quantities of silver. In 1887, considerable ore was shipped from the Ute/Ulay, Vermont, and Yellow Medicine. In 1888, the Ute/Ulay and the Vermont reported respectable shipments. In 1889, the Ocean Wave was back in full production with Pike Snowden, apparently bored or pressed for cash, back at work. Prospects in Henson Canyon were looking up. Profitability of the Ocean Wave again seemed certain, until it was not. Overshadowing it all were the less-than-helpful Federal mucky-mucks in Washington, D.C. And if politics, geology, and fickle silver prices were not enough to contend with, there also was the ever-present threat of accidents and avalanches, either one grounds for disruption, delay, or death.

On August 3, 1889, death knocked on the Ocean Wave door. Barney Mallon, had he survived, would have been the first to tell us that being a miner featured in a Lake City newspaper was not going to end well. For Barney's coworkers, productivity would sink, as would profitability. For the rest of us, maybe there is new found opportunity to appreciate the consequences of a more lethal facet of our San Juan miners, their times, and their daily lives. The *Hinsdale Phonograph* editor shared the rest of Barney's story:

> *The particulars of the accident at the Ocean Wave mine last Saturday morning in which Barney Mallon lost his life, indicate that it was one of those cases in which the long immunity of old miners from injury incline them to be a little careless in the use of the necessary but dangerous nitroglycerine explosives. The details of the accident are as follows: The whole force of the mine, consisting of about 25 men, were at the mouth of the tunnel preparatory*

to commencing work, Pike Snowden and one or two others having already started up into the workings. A new box of [blasting] caps was needed, and while the rest of the men were standing near engaged in various little duties, Barney with a pipe in his mouth picked up a box from the package of [blasting] caps and started to open it. Just as he lifted the lid it is supposed a spark fell from his pipe into one of the [blasting] caps causing an instant explosion, horribly mangling Mr. Mallon and stunning and shocking every man within twenty feet.

J. L. Kinsey was considerably bruised by concussion with the rocks and foreman McCauley severely cut in the face by pieces of flying caps. As soon as the men recovered Mr. Mallon was quickly carried to the house and everything possible done for him. But his injuries were too terrible and 45 minutes from the time of the explosion he breathed his last. The body was brought to town and taken in charge by friends of the family, and Sunday the remains were interred in their final resting place in the city cemetery north of town.

Barney Mallon was one of that large class of adopted American citizens of Irish birth, coming to this country when a young man and settling in Lake City almost at its foundation. He was well known all over San Juans and was heavily interested in mines in various parts of the county. He was 43 years of age and leaves a wife and four young children to mourn his untimely end, and to them the community will extend a universal sympathy in their loss and sorrow. [25]

Some mine accidents not only took the lives of miners but also ended the life of the mine. Not this time. Barney was dead and the Ocean Wave was crippled, but not for long. In fits and starts, work resumed. A decade later, in the spring of 1897, according to the *Lake City Times*, the Ocean Wave continued "turning out some good ore with Sam Jack as manager." By the same token, the death of Barney Mallon did not dissuade Pike Snowden from continuing to mine, just not in the Ocean Wave. The same *Times* article reported Pike "is driving away on his tunnel [the Yellow Jacket] across the creek from the Sacramento." [26]

Pike could not help himself. The Yellow Jacket and the Sacramento were within walking distance of his cabin. If he harbored any remorse or superstitions concerning his near-miss at the Ocean Wave or friend Mallon's death he never said so. He also never returned to work at the Ocean Wave. His heart was in mining, and would continue so as long as his body cooperated, but not there. Ocean Wave production also would continue as long as there was a lessor willing to work or investors willing to underwrite it. Likewise, with a silver legacy like the Ocean Wave, there also would continue to be buyers. None of these developments escaped the watchful eye of A.E. Reynolds. Nor did developments at the neighboring Vermont go unnoticed, nor the coming and going of the British, nor the running of one of the most heart-breaking avalanches in Henson Canyon history, nor the overall state of the San Juans mining industry and silver lobby shenanigans in the Nation's capital. Much about the Vermont and Ocean Wave interested Reynolds, but the risks and rewards did not yet justify an attractive price.

Notes—Chapter Six: Silver Will Do

[1] Everhart, William C., ed., *The Mining Frontier*, Forward, anon. [Author's note: Again, fidelity to the language of the era is preserved, not endorsed.]

[2] Smith, Duane A., *The Trail of Gold and Silver*, pg. 113.

[3] *Lake City Phonograph*, April 9, 1910, "Story of Our Mines."

[4] Copper pyrite or sulphuret of copper was one of the most common and best gold-bearing ores. Miners called it "yellow iron." "Gray copper" was usually high-grade ore, greatly encouraging to miners when uncovered.

[5] *Hinsdale Phonograph*, December 7, 1888. ("Rose" was not the first name of a woman, it was Croydon's last name.

[6] Eventually gold production at the Golden Fleece and Golden Wonder mines, and gold discoveries elsewhere along the upper Lake Fork of the Gunnison, prompted further interest in the region.

[7] Paul, Rodman W., *The Far West and the Great Plains in Transition, 1859-1900*, pgs. 254-255.

[8] Morse, Milo Z. and Faye Bielser, *A Brief History of Mining in Hinsdale County*.

[9] Franklin, George Cory, "Major M.V.B. Wasson", *DAR Pioneers of the San Juans Country*, Vol, II, pgs. 36-37.

[10] Ibid. pgs. 37-38.

[11] Paul, *The Far West and the Great Plains in Transition, 1859-1900*, pg. 12.

[12] Ibid.

[13] Ibid., pg. 13.

[14] Hollister, Ovando, Freepages.rootsweb.com/~bldr/folklore/Hollister.html, pgs.1-3.

[15] Hollister, Ovando, *The Mines of Colorado*, pgs.46-52.

[16] Ibid., pgs. 56-57.

[17] Steele, Joe M., *Guide to Lake City Geology*, pgs. 15-19.

[18] Paul, *Mining Frontiers of the Far West, 1848-1880*, pg. 123. (Vermont and Ocean Wave ore cannot be properly handled in any other way than by a long and complicated process. The significance of this sad reality was that the market value of silver, already by definition a small fraction of gold, and the burdensome cost of transporting low-grade silver ore, were all the more influential in determining whether a mine could be profitable. Our Henson Canyon heroes can do little to deal with their low-grade complex ores, steep losses at the mill, global silver market prices, and the misguided actions of their national politicians. Reducing transportation costs was a possible exception and an ever-present goal. Burros were a blessing, wagons were a Godsend, better than wagons were railroads. Again, rail service was beyond their ability to influence. Was there any other way to reduce costs? Maybe, but it would be costly finding out.)

[19] The Ocean Wave Lode, Mineral Application No. 31, was recorded August 22, 1876, on behalf of George Boggs, Zene Snowden and William R. Bernard. The Wave of the Ocean Lode, Mineral Application No. 32; was recorded August 22, 1876, on behalf of the same three partners.

[20] Twitty, Eric, *Inventory of Select Historic Sites, Hinsdale County, Colorado*, pgs. 74-79. [Also: 1882 *Report of the Director of the Mint*, pg. 474; Scamehorn, *Albert Eugene Reynolds, Colorado's Mining King*, pg. 178.]

[21] *Williams Tourist Guide to the San Juans*, pg. 7. [Cited in Smith, P. David, *The Story of Lake City, Colorado*, pg. 326.]

[22] *1880 Report of the Director of the Mint*, pg. 157.

[23] *Colorado Mining Directories*, pgs. 378-379.

[24] Henderson, Charles W., *Mining in Colorado: A History of Discovery*, pg. 51. (According to this professional paper, "there is much low-grade ore in this district, and associated with the low-grade ore is an enormous quantity of zinc blende, which should be amenable to proper treatment". However, determining the "proper treatment" was elusive and expensive. As a result, both affordable transportation and some processing of ores were critical to profitable mining ventures. A passable wagon road was not available to Henson Creek mines until late 1876. The railroad did not reach Lake City until late summer of 1889. Numerous mining companies built concentrating mills as soon as possible after determining sufficient ore existed to justify the expense, remnants of which are still observable on the Burro Cabin and Nellie claims (not to mention a small power plant on Nellie Creek and another one near the confluence of Henson and North Henson Creeks). But smelters were another matter. They had to be tailored to the type of ore they intended to reduce, and they were far more expensive to construct and operate than concentrating mills. The Crooke Smelter was built in 1878 and operated until 1883. The Ocean Wave Smelter operated from 1879 to 1880. Both were located in Lake City and were justified by rich discoveries and production dating back to 1876 at the Hotchkiss (renamed the Golden Fleece), Ute/Ulay, and the Ocean Wave. But neither were capable of extracting sufficient silver and other valuable metals to sustain operations.)

[25] *Hinsdale Phonograph*, "The Ocean Wave Accident," 10 Aug 89.

[26] *Lake City Times*, March 4, 1897.

CHAPTER 7

The Great Judge

"Greater love hath no man than this,
that a man lay down his life for his friend." [1]

The Vermont Lode interested A.E. Reynolds for a number of reasons. First, it straddled the same proven mineralized vein that enriched the highly productive Ute/Ulay, Hidden Treasure, and Ocean Wave lodes. Second, like the Ocean Wave, Vermont development history correlated well with his understanding of geoscientific and mining criteria governing the likely presence of silver-rich ores. Reynolds may have been a farmer by birth, but he was no country bumpkin. A merchant by training, he was a mining magnate by experience. Part of that experience was grounded in history and science. He followed Henson Canyon developments carefully, and he was a believer in Ovando Hollister's understanding of geology, validated by his own underground observations and by mine superintendents he respected. Third, the physical proximity of the Vermont and the Ocean Wave lodes, and the short distance between the Vermont lode and the county wagon road five-hundred feet below it, was ideal for construction of a cost-saving haulage tunnel leading from the deep lower workings of each mine to heavy-duty freight-wagons plying the county road. Costly hoisting of ore buckets up five-hundred feet of shafts and winzes to the surface only to be packed on burros back down a steep five-hundred vertical-foot trail to the county road and transferred to wagons could be avoided, thereby by saving a great deal of time and money. Finally, while Reynolds bided his time he was content in the knowledge that an incredible amount of development work at incredible expense was being funded by someone else. When the time was right—"right" in Reynolds' world meant bargain basement prices—and "everything else being equal"(meaning the price of silver was at the bottom of its market cycle), he would act.

Although the Henson Canyon boom came late in the San Juans treasure hunt, and in the final analysis there was not a great deal to show for all the hullabaloo when it did arrive, it nevertheless attracted more than its fair share of eastern and foreign investment. This was more often the rule than the exception. Ore production and profits of only a few claims usually met expectations or paid their way for long. But with rare exception every prospect was held in high regard by their developers, and especially the miners that daily risked life and limb to prove the worth of the veins they ferreted out. The Vermont was one of the exceptions. Despite being handicapped by its remote and rugged location, and absent the benefit of powered tools, thousands of feet of underground workings over four decades continually promised fresh returns. And fresh returns did come, just enough to reel in fresh investors.

What exactly led the first prospector to consider the site of the future Vermont mine worthy of labor and capital was probably the same as what led Pike Snowden and partners to the Ocean Wave. The vein the Vermont straddled, a yellowish-white gash on the south face of the mountain, was visible miles away from the floor of Henson Canyon. It stretched to the ridge line, suggesting it was a deep wound also visible on the far side of the ridge. In fact it was visible on the far side, five-hundred feet up El Paso Gulch's sheer western wall. It clearly etched the surface where the first Vermont portals would be opened. The same vein ran on the east face a few hundred yards to the future site of Snowden's Ocean Wave. The hope always was that sinking pick and shovel into such a vein would yield

---

VERMONT UNDERGROUND WORKINGS

Vermont's underground workings as of 1896, all accomplished without the aid of any power equipment, were nearly beyond belief. On January 16, 1886, a decade after hand-drilling began, Moritz Stockder began surveying the Vermont lode and the adjacent Delphi mill site for William Weston, an Englishman representing a London consortium. A decade later A.E. Reynolds was impressed enough to acquire the mine and adjoining properties. Improvements described in the Field Notes accompanying the Stockder survey included the following record:

- A discovery cut and tunnel, 7 ft. x 5 ft., 400 ft. long, partly timbered
- A second tunnel West, 7 ft. x 5 ft., 250 ft. long, partly timbered
- A third tunnel West, 7 ft. x 5 ft., 300 ft. long, partly timbered
- An interest in a tunnel East, 7 ft. x 5 ft. 750 ft. long, partly timbered
- A second tunnel East, 7 ft. x 5 ft., 140 ft. long, partly timbered
- A third tunnel east, 7 ft. x 5 ft., 200 ft. long, partly timbered
- A shaft 4 ft. x 7 ft., 53 ft. deep, timbered

(J.J. Abbott amended the Moritz survey and dated it Oct. 24th, 1894. Corrections were minimal, but he added the cost of improvements.)

- Discovery tunnel, valued at $8,000.
- A tunnel 150 ft. in rock, valued at $8,000.
- A tunnel 240 ft. in rock, valued at $3,000.

gold. On the east and west flanks of El Paso Gulch pick and shovel would yield some gold, but mostly silver.

By 1876 most San Juan adventurers searching for gold were willing to settle for silver. Originally named the El Paso Lode, the Vermont's promising vein was easier to see than to uncover. Its telltale colors bright only in the morning sun drew attention to the lofty outcrops, but by afternoon there was no light in the deep gulch and thus no such beacon. Those with experience may have focused on the outcrop regardless of time of day, but there were more appealing prospects nearby to investigate. El Paso Gulch was rugged, a hard climb over talus and fallen timber bordering the cascading creek. "Maybe a canyon ledge best left for another day," would have been a reasonable conclusion at the time.

The Vermont ledge did not have to wait long for closer scrutiny. The Ocean Wave and Wave of the Ocean kept pointing to it. In short order the morning "beacon" across El Paso Gulch was ignored no longer. First located soon after the drover and partners claimed the Ocean lodes, naming rights and owner-ship became a tale with many twists. The Vermont first named the El Paso by a Mr. Phillips was sold by him for $1,000 to W.C. Lewman who renamed it the Vermont. Unable to make the Vermont a paying proposition, Lewman also failed to make the required one-hundred dollar per year (for five years) improvements, thereby forfeiting his claim. No wonder. The site was a hard climb even for a mountain burro, the promising vein surfaced on a sheer canyon wall, and all drill-ing and mucking had to be accomplished by hand. So matters stood until 1880.

In the fall of 1880 Samuel S. Smith rediscovered good indications of min-eral on the abandoned El Paso/Vermont ground and on March 13, 1882, the Vermont [and Alabama] were relocated by Smith and Thos. L. Beam. They soon found a fine body of ore with a smelter value of $70 per ton. Illustrating the fickle nature of mining as well as what lures miners underground, Beam explained the source of their joy:

> *There was a body of solid mineral 8 ft. 4 in. wide which was shot down and shipped to the smelter without sorting, yielding an average value of over $70 per ton. After the mine was sold and when Walter Beam was manager the latter found a streak of mineral (alongside where the big ore body had been and supposed to be the wall of the vein by the first miners) 1 inch wide and yielding returns of $1,400 per ton – more than the eight feet of $70 stuff was worth.* [2]

As joyful as Smith and Beam were with their hard-won ore, they were more joyful with their quick 1883 sale of the property to William Weston and Frank Silvia of Ouray. Silvia was a well-regarded mine superintendent with unques-tioned integrity not always found among those in his line of work. Weston, a native of England and son of a London banking executive, was a trained mining

William Weston (1841–1920).
Multitalented and brave, William first sought purpose in life on the Canadian frontier, then in San Juans mining. (*Wilbur Fisk Stone*, History of Colorado)

engineer with decades of professional accomplishments and broad experience. His journey from London to the American frontier, common to many in his day, testified to the habit of rewards marching arm in arm with courage and hard work. Weston and Silva personified yet two additional classes of "young America" that would define American exceptionalism.

Like so many of his British peers, young Weston at age fourteen shipped out to Toronto where he somehow secured a position—probably through family ties—in the city's newspaper business. Five years later he was City Editor of *The Globe*, a Toronto daily.[3] True to his adventuresome spirit, he soon abandoned the editor's desk and joined Canada's secret service. Three years later, apparently bored with defending the Commonwealth, he resigned and pursued his first love, outdoor living. After two years on the northern lakes of Canada, and a stint as a militia artillery officer, Weston immigrated to the United States in response to an 1870 Kansas-Pacific Railroad advertisement seeking a land-agent for the Western frontier. Recognizing his many gifts, railroad superintendents advanced him rapidly to the position of "General Traveling Agent," and in 1875 sent him to London as General European agent, in hindsight *his* divine appointment.

Shortly after arriving in London, William learned from one of his childhood friends who had just returned from a sporting trip to Del Norte, Colorado, of "the marvelous gold and silver ores in the San Juans region." Gold and silver sounded more to his liking than promoting western railroad tours in London. Weston resigned from his Kansas-Pacific Railroad position in October 1876 and enrolled in the Royal School of Mines. Six months in the lecture hall, three months in the metallurgical laboratory assaying gold, silver, and lead ores; and William was a bona fide mining engineer with an assayer's certificate. He also was off to the San Juans. Arriving in Del Norte in March 1877, he outfitted himself with burros and assay equipment and crossed the "main range" by way of Stony Pass, Silverton, Red Mountain and on into the Imogene Basin. (One has to wonder if Weston and Gurley ever crossed paths—they would have gotten along fine.)

In Imogene Basin, Weston formed a partnership with fellow countryman George Barber. They staked six claims and financed their work by William selling his mule, saddle, and bridle. Evidently he was confident the claims would pay before he was in need of transportation, and they did. During the following four years Weston and Barber lived in a crude cabin at 11,200 feet and drove tunnels by hand over a hundred feet deep in each of their six claims, a total of eight hundred and fifty feet through solid rock. To occupy themselves when not tunneling, they did their own blacksmithing. Weston also did his own assaying. He built a small "drum muffle furnace" in their cabin and tested their own ores as well as ores provided by neighbors. To satisfy his intellectual nature, Weston also was a constant contributor to the *Engineering & Mining Journal of New York*. Most likely wishing for a mule, nevertheless he snowshoed ("cross-country skied" in today's terminology) weekly in the winter into Ouray regardless of the weather "in order to stay in touch." Obviously as strong as a mule himself, he also was fearless.

In 1881, Weston's talents and pluck came to the attention of Governor Frederick W. Pitkin who appointed him State Commissioner of Mines. Sadly, the Legislature did not fund the office, a loss for Colorado but a blessing for Ouray. Weston sold his share in his claims for $50,000 to a New York company and invested the proceeds in "enterprises and prospects which (were) the basic elements in the development and prosperity of Ouray." He was one of three who put in an electric light plant, was the largest subscriber to the building of the Beaumont Hotel, and was instrumental in securing the investment of large sums of foreign capital in the Ouray mining districts. When Weston sold in London the highly productive Guston Mine, a steady flow of British capital began to flow into the area and the San Juans in general. Henson Canyon would garner more than its fair share, the Vermont included. [4]

Worked under a variety of owners and lessors, the Vermont became a large and profitable producer. The 1883 *Colorado Mining Directory* reported that the Vermont contained native silver, galena, iron, and copper. It produced 238 ounces of silver per ton and comprised five tunnels totaling 535 ft. In the same directory, reportedly the adjoining Alabama lode also produced 238 ounces of silver per ton on the same vein as the Vermont to the west and the Ocean Wave to the east. Alabama's development as of 1883 was one shaft 65 ft. deep. All three mines also produced small quantities of gold, a welcome addition to both balance and publicity sheets. [5]

Moritz Stockder, Vermont Mine superintendent in the mid-1880s, proved to be one of the most successful "mining engineers" in the San Juans. In July 1887, thirty-eight men worked the Vermont on five levels spanning a depth of nearly 500 feet, exploiting a rich strike made the previous fall with silver running at 1,565 to 1,580 ounces per ton. During one campaign the mine employed as many as fifty miners year round. Weston's English investors were pleased and invested hundreds of thousands of dollars more. They also authorized surface plant improvements including a mine office and large bunkhouse erected close to the mine portal—far easier to appreciate than underground surveying, tunneling, and track laying—but not that helpful when it came to producing a tidy return on investment. While a welcome convenience given the precarious cliffside location of the portal and predictably severe winter conditions, the choice was unwise. The costly surface improvements sat in an avalanche chute sure to run sooner or later. And run it did.

VERMONT PRODUCTION

According to published figures, the Vermont produced $142,000 worth of primarily lead and silver until operations ceased in the late 1890s. Based on Colorado mine reports, values were considerably less, $115,343.84 to be exact. While this does not seem impressive, at least until 1910 this placed the Vermont among the top twenty producers in the Lake City area. By comparison, only Hinsdale County's Golden Fleece at $1,400,000 (gold), the Ute/Ulay at $12,000,000 (silver/lead), and the Hidden Treasure at $700,000 (silver/lead) did better. By some accounts, the Ocean Wave, which along with the Vermont held out such great promise for future investors, only records $26,000 worth of silver and lead values at the smelter. In light of everything else known about the Ocean Wave, this figure is probably grossly under-reported. (The "Italians must go" crowd claimed none of the Dago Tunnel gray copper was reported.) This production total, along with that of the Vermont, does seem low given the extent of the underground workings and the grades of the ores extracted. Indeed, plausible explanations are that far more ore was shipped to smelters and/or smelters lost or stole far more silver than reported. Something did not add up, a conclusion A.E. Reynolds surely reached as well.[6]

Vermont Silver/Lead Production
(Source: Mine Reports)

1884	$4,965.00
1887	40,436.00
	(Avalanche)
1888	62,648.00
1891	(Flu Epidemic)
1892	6,993.00
1895	1,182.24
1896	1,119.60
Total	$115,343.84

As if remoteness, high altitude, burro-only transportation, hand-drilling, temperamental explosives, preponderance of low-grade ores, volatile silver prices, and insufficient capital were not adversity enough for the Vermont, working under annual threat of avalanches added to the burden. It only took one destructive avalanche to put a mine out of business. An avalanche with fatalities was even more likely to do so, more likely even than a fatality underground. Cave-ins or blasting were errors in judgment, avalanches were acts of God. You did not have to be a superstitious Cousin Jack to believe that.

The year 1887 began with day after day of heavy weather, deep snows, and high winds. Ominous snow ridges, predictable harbingers of frightful snowslides, began appearing on ridges around mines near Lake City. Disregarding the pleas and threats of their superintendents and foremen, some miners from the upper Lake Fork valley and Henson Canyon came down to town. They knew danger signs when they saw them. But for others, work was scarce and the risk of being fired offset any fears stirred by danger signs. A small troop of Vermont miners elected to remain at their assigned posts.

An Annual Affair. San Juans avalanches are all too common and often harbingers of death. This 1888 slide between Ouray and Silverton (the Riverside Slide) is typical. Fortunately this one harmed no one. Two years earlier in the same spot a mail carrier and sixteen mules were killed. *(Courtesy of the* Lake City Silver World.*)*

Already cash-strapped from days off for the Christmas holidays, they dreaded loss of a day's wage or worse yet loss of their job more than a slide.

While the majority of the winter crew retreated to Lake City for a weekend of carousing, four men stayed behind—George Lampshire, Patrick McEnany, John Strom, and Henry Repath. Repath and Strom, married with young families, stayed to make up time lost over the Christmas season. Lampshire and McEnany, also married, stayed for reasons unknown. All four were in their forties and well-acquainted with the hazards of winter mining. The prior winter a small snowslide ran, but the mine buildings withstood the impact. The 1886 slide was a harbinger for those with eyes to see. A hundred and ten years later almost to the day, the January 9, 1997, *Silver World* recounted the tragedy.

The great Vermont Snowslide of 1887, as it was to be called in later years, came thundering down the mountain, through the Vermont Mine buildings and down into frozen El Paso Creek late in the evening of January 13. Strom, McEnany and Repath were in the boarding house, comfortably visiting and reading, when there was a roar and then, almost instantly, everything went utterly black. The bunk house was crushed by the slide and then carried down into the gulch bottom. Repath and Lampshire were uninjured and almost immediately, in the swirling snow and blackness, waded back into the slide to rescue Strom and McEnany. It was to be a futile, fatal effort. 7

During the night of January 13-14, 1887, the threat had become reality. The *Silver World* editor explained in a literary style common to his trade yet equally suited to a memorial service. On January 15. 1887 he wrote:

With grief we are once more called on to chronicle another of those curses of the San Juans country—a snow slide! It occurred last Thursday evening at the Vermont, and caused the death of one of the best men who ever trod the earth—Pat. H. McEnany. The snow had been falling for two days, and most of the men quit work in the morning and came to town, as they had every reason to believe that a slide would take place, for the buildings were right in the track of one. Last winter the buildings managed to withstand the slides, but this year they have been swept completely away. Why anyone placed in the position of mining superintendent should not use better judgement in erecting buildings for the accommodation of their men seems strange indeed, and we think this is a matter which demands the consideration of the Legislature. We cast no blame on the present superintendent, as the buildings were put up before he took charge.

When the news reached town on Friday afternoon, quite a force of men volunteered their services, and Aaron Richart hitched up a four-horse sleigh, with the intention of taking them to the scene of the wreck, but they could get no further than the Ute and Ule, and were compelled to go afoot the balance [four miles] of the way. They could see that there was less snow on the mountain side than in the gulches, giving indications that the slides had been very numerous.

On their arrival at the Vermont they found that P. H. McEnany and John Strom had been caught in the slide, but through the noble exertions of George Lamshier and H. Repath (the latter rupturing himself very severely) for thirteen hours, John Strom was taken out alive, but Pat McEnany was dead, and on examination it was found that his neck and back were both broken and the only consolation his friends have is, that he did not know what killed him. 8

Patrick Henry McEnany was born of Irish parents in Port Henry, New York, April 2, 1846. In 1866 or 1867 he worked his way west along with so many other of his brethren building railroads, and like so many of his brethren he settled into the life of a San Juans miner. In 1882 at the age of thirty-six he married Maggie Connor. Five years into their young married life the *Silver World* editor wrote:

> *[W]e hope that in this great trial the snow, so pure in its whiteness, may teach to the distressed widow that a pure life, of which her husband was an example, is the best legacy to leave behind. May she have strength given to her to bear the burden, and accept with a humble trust the decree of the great Judge who doeth all things well.* [9]

A week later the editor was as much in the spirit as any pastor would likely be. Reporting on the final rites accorded Patrick, he wrote of "one of nature's noblemen,"

> *Though almost a giant physically he was as kind and gentle as a child. To know him was to be his friend, and if he had an enemy in this world it was not the fault of the heart. He was a friend to all, an honorable citizen, a true and affectionate husband, and his bereaved widow has the sympathy of the whole community.* [10]

Patrick was buried in the Lake City Independent Order of Odd Fellows (IOOF) cemetery after a brief service in his home lead by John Mendenhall. The Silver Star Lodge of the IOOF, of which Patrick was an honorable member, performed their solemn ritual at the grave. Mendenhall wrote, we can imagine with teary eyes, "there was a large turnout of the citizens to pay their last respects to the dead." [11]

P. H. McEnany was not the only victim of the 1887 Vermont avalanche. There were two more. Henry Repath, who worked so long and hard trying to save Patrick that he severely ruptured himself, died from his injury two days later. As with the eulogy for Patrick, the editor's compassion for the ordinary man was evident.

> *"The name of friendship is sacred: What you demand in that name I have not the power to deny you. – Longfellow." Such was the motive that prompted the late Henry Repath in the heroic exertions he made to save the lives of his fellow-workmen, nobly sacrificing his own in his superhuman efforts to rescue them from that terrible snow slide. It was the love for our common humanity which animated him, and it was done with the inward satisfaction—and it alone would have been reward enough—that he only did his duty. The good book says—"Greater love hath no man than this, that a man lay down his life for his friend."* [12]

INDEPENDENT ORDER OF ODD FELLOWS

The IOOF is an organization that aims to provide a framework that promotes personal and social development. The fellowship emphasizes a leaving of the old life and the start of a better one focused on helping those in need. The command of the IOOF is to "visit the sick, relieve the distressed, bury the dead and educate the orphan." Specifically, IOOF members today are dedicated to the following purposes:

• To improve and elevate the character of mankind by promoting the principles of friendship, love, truth, faith, hope, charity and universal justice.

• To help make the world a better place to live in, by aiding each other, the community, the less fortunate, the youth, the elderly, and the environment in every way possible.

• To promote good will and harmony amongst peoples and nations through the principle of universal fraternity, holding the belief that all men and women regardless of race, nationality, religion, social status, gender, rank and station are brothers and sisters.[13]

Of Purest Character. Henry Repath lived a faith common to his generation, that there was no greater love than laying down one's life for another. (Courtesy of the Silver World)

Henry was born in Colebroom, England, and immigrated to America in 1870. He lived in Pennsylvania a short while, likely working in the coal mines, moved west to Hancock, Michigan where he worked in the copper mines, and made his way to Lake City in 1879 to work the lead and silver mines. Like so many others who worked their way through life in the mines, "he was a man of the purest character, and of the strictest integrity," declared the *Silver World* editor, a man of deep convictions himself. "May the sorrowing ones who are left behind bow in submission to the great Ruler of the Universe, and say 'The Lord gave and the Lord hath taken away, blessed be the name of the Lord'." Strong words for some preachers much less a newspaper man.[14]

John Strom was the third victim. Born in Skaraborg County, Sweden, in 1844, he immigrated to Nebraska in the 1870s, married his Swedish wife in Omaha in 1882, and settled in Lake City shortly thereafter. Daughter Alice was born March 1884. The Vermont avalanche buried John fourteen hours, crushing him beneath broken timbers and frozen snow before being freed by his fellow miners. John passed away peacefully at home. Our editor writes:

> *Every care and attention was given him during the night he lay at the mine, and in the morning rallied so far as to be able to be placed on a hand sled and brought (seven miles) to Lake City. He was a man of iron nerve, and bore the tedious and dangerous journey nobly, and strong hopes were entertained of his ultimate recovery; but on Thursday evening his remarkable nerve began to fail, and he gradually grew weaker and weaker, until he had to obey the final call. Dr. Hoffman attended him faithfully until the last, but he was beyond medical skill.*
>
> *His many friends did everything in their power to alleviate his sufferings and at the same time console his disconsolate wife... whom with (their daughter) he leaves to mourn his untimely and sad death. He was about 42 years old, and was a loving husband, a kind father, a good citizen and a true friend. The sympathy of the entire community is extended to the bereaved widow and orphan.* [15]

Of all the classes of society sure to be found in mining camps, none were more valued than doctors, newspaper editors, and the clergy. Perhaps the assayer could be added to this list. Each had vital roles in serving their community and were respected for doing so. Less respected but quick on the heels of the earliest prospectors came the saloon keepers, faro dealers, and camp-followers. Peppered among them were the rare selfless servants, surprisingly found in every class.

By the late 1870s, Lake City amenities and worldly distractions were equal to the best San Juan boomtowns. Among the Henson Canyon miner class the adage that idle hands were playthings of the devil was demonstrated all too often. No one knew this better than Reverend George Darley. The *Silver World* editor and Dr. Hoffman in their own ways had their hands full trying to foster a more vibrant economy and healthy workforce. Reverend Darley joined the fray to foster a more God-centered community. As so often the case, Darley knew that the spirit-man deep within the pioneer was easily rekindled by memories of home and church even in the midst of daily temptations and toils, and especially in the midst of tragedy. Darley's accounts of his saloon ministry and presiding over dancehall funerals illustrates how powerful this dimension of Henson Canyon mining could be.

George Darley was a skilled laborer in his thirties when he stepped into his life's calling. His greatest attribute was his love for the souls of his community irrespective of their station in life. Leaving school at age fourteen to learn

Reverend Darley. Self-taught, George Darley was not self-directed. Early in life he heeded the call of his Lord and devoted himself to frontier folk in need. (Pioneering in the San Juan)

carpentry from his father, a Nebraska grasshopper plague motivated him to relocate to Galveston where he put his skills to work lining Danish grain ships. Gifted with a command of the Gospel, he also was quick to share the Good News with his fellow dock workers and with Galveston's jail community. Comfortable in the midst of men accustomed to the dark side of society, he was no stranger to the debauchery hard times and hard hearts could lead human behavior. His experiences in Galveston would serve him well in the San Juans.

In 1876, George joined his brother Alexander in Del Norte, Colorado, where Reverend Alexander served as pastor of that thriving community's first protestant church. When word reached the brothers that Lake City was booming, they recognized a mission field in the making. On June 18, 1876, the brothers organized the Lake City Presbyterian Church. Alexander returned to Del Norte and George the carpenter took charge of building what became the oldest protestant church on the Western Slope of Colorado. He also built the pews and pulpit, was ordained a Presbyterian minister, and founded the Presbyterian College of the Southwest. Of greater consequence are examples of his bold Lake Fork ministry, his love of his fellow pioneers, and the compassion he extended to those in need regardless of their character.

Reverend Darley was a common man, was recognized as a common man, and "the common man" respected him as one of their own. No more insightful characterization of the frontier mining society he cared so much for can be found than what he wrote about shining God's light into dark places.

No class of men knew better how to treat a minister they liked in a royal manner than the men who went into southwestern Colorado during the great San Juans "excitement" of '75, '76 and '77. Nor could a more intelligent, plucky, warm-hearted set of men be found; men who knew what was right. Among them were many who had been taught in Eastern homes, by pious parents, that "man's chief and highest end is to glorify God and fully enjoy him forever."

When entering camps where no religious services had been held I invari-
ably went to the right place (gambling hall) to find an audience; and in ev-
ery case was courteously and kindly received and generally told: "Just wait,
Brother Darley, until the games can be stopped, and we will give you a chance
at the boys." It was not always an easy matter to stop the games; winners were
usually willing, while the losers were not. But so [sic] soon as the games closed
then "roulette," "keno," "poker," and "faro" would give place for a time to the
Gospel.

A more convenient pulpit than a "faro-table" could not be found; nor a
more respectful and intelligent audience. In what occasional singing we did
have, men with trained voices, rich and sweet, would sing without books those
grand old hymns: "Jesus, Lover of My Soul" and "Rock of Ages, Cleft for Me."
With bowed heads they listened to the prayer; often with tears in their eyes to
the "old, old story," being told as they had heard it "back East," while sitting in
a pew beside father, mother, or fond wife and dear children. [16]

Nor did faithful Darley turn down an opportunity to preach a funeral, in
a church or in a dancehall mattered not. Everyone deserved a respectful fare-
well, anyone could be forgiven. More importantly, funerals provided tender
moments where hearts of the living could be touched by a glimpse into eter-
nity. While editor Mendenhall held his own when it came to eulogies, George
Darley's burden for his neighbors was never stronger than when he stood
beside a coffin, even when that coffin cradled the remains of a tragic figure like
Magg Hartman.

When asked if he would preach Magg Hartman's funeral, Reverend Darley
consented without hesitation. It was his calling. Over the years he was acquainted
with all classes of "the deceased." Magg Hartman lived and worked in "Hell's
Acre," politely described as the town neighborhood "largely given up to the
sporting class." In the Reverend's vernacular he opened more than a physical door
for those in the world she left behind. Magg was the reason they gathered there.
They were the reason George preached. You, too, are welcome to find an empty
chair and join the service.

As I entered the house a very tall, well-known character, who was sitting
on the floor, rose and said as he took my hand: "Well, Parson, this is the way
we all go."

I replied, "Yes, we all must die, but it depends on how we have lived, and
in whom we have believed, as to the place we go when we die."

I then stepped to the side of the coffin and looked at Magg Hartman's more
than ordinary face; for few faces were more remarkable looking and few lives
had been stranger than that of this many-sided woman. As the "girls" came
in from the "dance-halls" I took each one by the hand and spoke a kind word.

CAMP CLERGY

Nearly all mining camps of any standing or longevity boasted of at least one man of the cloth. The shepherd and the flock of every persuasion stood in sharp contrast to one another, seekers from all strata of society, united for a time only in an hour of need. Typically the camp shepherds, at least the most effective ones, bore little resemblance to city cathedral bishops or robed pastors manning country white-washed clapboard churches. More likely they carried a bowie knife and long-gun as well as Bible and cross. They were accustomed to surviving in the wilderness, pen-niless and hungry. They were as comfortable with the sporting class in the saloons as with fellow pilgrims in a house of worship.

The frontier pastor usually worked out his own salvation in a solitary struggle in a hostile land. Daniel Tuttle, on the good authority of historian Rodman Paul, was "one of the most loved and most universally remembered of all the mining-camp missionaries." Paul quotes Tuttle:

> *Next to the sense of loneliness, I was most oppressed with the sad conviction of the prayerlessness and godlessness of the people among whom I found myself. Of them, women, especially good women, were a very small minority. Men were kind personally, generous in giving money, respectful and courteous; but I was appalled to discover day by day how almost universally given up they were to vicious practices.* [17]

Samuel H. Willey, another pioneer clergyman no doubt also speaking for his fel-low-laborers remarked, "One of the lessons my California life has most thoroughly taught me is that transplanted people do not begin life on new ground on as high a plane as they occupied before removal".[18] Willey surely had a point. Fleshing out the condition of the spiritual nature of that era, Paul concludes:

> *Most people had come to the mining West to seek wealth and to enjoy excitement and change. How fortunate it was that a few had from the begin-ning a sense of public responsibility, and that as the frontier era passed, an increasing number came to value and even to love the strange, demanding, and sometimes beautiful country to which they found themselves devoting their lives.* [19]

Sadly, fewer still returned to their spiritual roots, casting off their recently acquired bad habits in favor of devotion to practices and cherished memories of home. George Darley testified to the same.

When all was ready for the funeral service I noticed a strained attempt on their faces to "take it," which plainly said: "You hold a full hand now, so just wade in."

George Darley, a carpenter by trade, a Galveston dockworker by necessity, a mountain-man missionary and practitioner of God's Word by divine appointment, understood completely the condemnation they expected. The eighth chapter of the Gospel of St. John was his text of choice for just such a time as this. Not to disappoint the girls, he "just waded in."

> Vs. 1:   *Jesus went unto the Mount of Olives.*
>
> Vs. 2:   *And early in the morning he came again into the temple, and all the people came unto him; and he sat down, and taught them.*
>
> Vs. 3:   *And the scribes and Pharisees brought unto him a woman taken in adultery; and when they had set her in the midst,*
>
> Vs. 4:   *They say unto him, "Master, this woman was taken in adultery, in the very act."*
>
> Vs. 5:   *"Now Moses in the law commanded us, that such should be stoned: but what sayest thou?"*

(Some sitting before him stiffened, some squirmed. It did not take a student of the Gospel to imagine where this could be going.)

> Vs. 6:   *This they said, tempting him, that they might have to accuse him. But Jesus stooped down, and with his finger wrote on the ground, as though he heard them not.*

Neither Do I Condemn Thee. Music to the sinner's ears, the balance of the thought was usually quickly forgotten. Nor was "go and sin no more" what Reverend Darley was accustomed to seeing. *(Guercino's Adultress, 1621, Wikimedia Commons)*

Vs. 7:   *So when they continued asking him, he lifted up himself, and said unto them, "He that is without sin among you, let him first cast a stone at her."*

Vs. 8:   *And again he stooped down, and wrote on the ground.*

(With the reading of verse eight, Darley reported, the atmosphere in the room changed. Some arms unfolded, some strained looks drained away. Who indeed was without sin?)

Vs. 9:   *And they which heard it, being convicted by their own conscience, went out one by one, beginning at the eldest, even unto the last, and Jesus was left alone, and the woman standing in the midst.*

Vs. 10:   *When Jesus had lifted up himself, and saw none but the woman, he said unto her, "Woman, where are those thine accusers? Hath no man condemned thee?"*

Vs. 11:   *She said, "No man, Lord." And Jesus said unto her, "Neither do I condemn thee: go, and sin no more."*

Watching the girls quietly rise from their seats and file away, George Darley knew in his heart he would see them again, one by one in a coffin, not one in a church. Years later he lamented, "and as words void of severity were spoken tears began filling their eyes. Soon every head was bowed and, had I not witnessed such scenes before, I might have believed everyone would leave the paths of sin and seek a better life." [20]

Among miners and town folks alike, the need of local rail service was as consequential a matter as the health of body and soul. It is doubtful anyone thought the Denver & Rio Grande would diminish the debauchery of saloons and dancehalls, but the efficient and economical transport of low-grade ores to distant smelters would surely diminish the availability of idle hands. Avalanches and accidents aside, neither the Vermont nor the Ocean Wave were consistent producers (not to mention high volume, high assay producers), but neither were most mining properties of that era. They all had ownership disputes, investor disputes, and labor disputes. Natural disasters, man-made disasters, health disasters, and economic disasters had their way with the best of them, and the Vermont and Ocean Wave lodes were no exceptions. Still, mining had a seductive charm. Still, the Vermont and Ocean Wave, consistently thought to harbor high-grade ores yet to be found, charmed the speculator class. [21]

Among the charmed, A.E. Reynolds watched and bided his time. He did not acquire a reputation as Colorado's mining king for no good reason. He was analytical and he was patient and he was wealthy, on paper at least. His formula for success was simple yet strategic. Let others invest their capital in development

---

THE SPORTING CLASS

One more unfortunate,
Weary of breath,
Rashly importunate,
Gone to her death.

Who was her father?
Who was her mother?
Had she a sister?
Had she a brother?

— Thomas Hood —

George Darley's account of Magg Hartman's funeral epitomized another class of society and frontier lifestyle common to San Juan boomtowns. Such funerals added yet another facet to the complex convergence of circumstances and opportunities that defined the San Juans frontier. Within a single century, five decades really, the United States had grown from an Atlantic Ocean nation to a continental nation, the vast interior between the Appalachian Mountains and the Pacific Ocean overflowing with adventurers and seekers from around the world. The "sporting class" and the "madams" with their covey of "soiled doves" caught up in their own addictions and depression in a society yet to provide a safety net or safe harbor were an integral part of this "westering." So were the doctors that treated their bodies and the shepherds that treated their souls.

---

work. Invest one's own funds when profits and prices were low. If low-grade ores are likely, look for innovative solutions to lower costs and wait for the arrival of rail service. If neither were forthcoming, look elsewhere for the next best chance to make a fortune. Thus, it was no surprise that Reynolds, undeterred by troubled times, acquired the rights to the Vermont and the Ocean Wave when they were idle, silver prices were low, and the long-promised Denver & Rio Grande railroad finally was sure to reach Lake City.

As for innovative solutions for profiting from low-grade ores, Reynolds had a proverbial "ace up his sleeve." A disciple of Ingham and Ovando, and encouraged by the success of his Virginius/Revenue Tunnel in the Sneffels Mining District near Ouray, he was confident he would succeed. He would eliminate hoisting and burro-trains by driving a risky but promising haulage tunnel from the county wagon road into the deepest workings of the Vermont and Ocean Wave lodes. Little did he know—how could he—that the Vermont/Ocean Wave would be his last best chance to make a mine. If that revelation ever came to Reynolds, he never said so. The *Lake City Phonograph*, always prepared to boost expectations, did not help in this regard.

> *That these two properties [Vermont and Ocean Wave lodes] have every indication of becoming big mines with work is undoubted. The vein is a huge one and but a small part of it has yet been exploited. Great masses of low grade ore still fill the stopes of the old workings. The total value of the output from the two mines was probably $500,000, the Vermont producing nearly all of it. It was once a great mine and we are satisfied again will reach such a station.[22]*

In fact, faith in a bright future for the Lake City mining district never entertained a cloudy day on the pages of the *Phonograph* or its sister-in-arms the *Silver World*. Not even avalanche deaths, the total destruction of the entire Vermont surface plant, and the prospect of more slides every year, overcame either the Vermont's resilient lure or Lake City scribes' shameless encouragement of continued investment. Part of the explanation rested with the determined nature of the fraternity of miners, part with the pioneer spirit of the community that nurtured them in their day. And part rested with Reynolds' vision. He did not focus on the small quantities of silver extracted from the Vermont and the Ocean Wave. He focused on the large quantities that he was convinced still remained. He did not focus on risks, he focused on opportunities and innovation. Buying into adversity was a habit of his. Doing so meant some below-market prices that increased his chances for earning above-average profits.

It is impossible to say with certainty whether news of Denver & Rio Grande management's decision to provide service to Lake City affected Reynolds' timing on securing rights to the Vermont and Ocean Wave. Likewise, even construction of the line, albeit in fits and starts, was no guarantee it would be completed and operated. What is certain is that reliable rail service was a precondition for investing in his haulage tunnel and he would cautiously, patiently wait until that was assured.

Denver & Rio Grande management delivered in 1889. Lake City merchants and miners, giddy over the prospects of the long-awaited rail service and increasing signs that a major A.E. Reynolds project was in the works, were not timid. They rejoiced at the prospects of improved sales, and mining interests rejoiced in the resumption of suspended operations in their historic mines. Still, prior broken promises and a decade of false starts made for a great deal of public skepticism that was not vanquished until the chants of the approaching track-layers could be heard. Years of disappointment was replaced with the sights and sounds of Italian gandy-dancers—how amusing their dance, how heartening their chant.

GANDY-DANCERS

Linin' Track
Oh boys, is you right?
Done got right!
All I hate 'bout linin' track,
These ol' bars 'bout to break my back.

"Gandy-dancer" was a railroad term used to describe tracklayers, also known as "section hands." The term likely gained widespread acceptance as a result of the dance-like movements of the laborers and their habit of coining colorful terms in the course of job-site bantering. The term may have come from the crews' "waddle" as they straddled a rail and shifted their weight from foot to foot as they carefully edged the rail into place. Using a 5-ft. long "lining bar" called a "gandy" to leverage the rail, the process required coordinating the actions of an entire crew numbering as many as two dozen men. Little by little, they positioned the length of the rail on cross-ties and gravel ballast.

Coordination was accomplished by rhythm, by simple work songs, and chants led by "callers," foreman by another name. Rhythm enabled a large number of men to move a long heavy rail a fraction of an inch at a time into precise alignment with the rail preceding it. Once aligned, they drove spikes into the cross-ties to secure it and the process was repeated. Gandy-dancers were nimble, mastered the work routine quickly, or were relegated to picks and shovels. There was no substitute for the teamwork required to move and precisely position rough-cut ties and 39-ft., 1,200 to 1,800-lb. iron rails.

The gandy was a straight pry bar with a sharp end. The thicker bottom end was square-shafted to better fit against the rail, and pointed to dig into the ballast underneath the rail. The top end was lighter and rounded for better gripping. Each man would face the rail and work the chisel end of his lining bar down at an angle into the gravel under it. Then all would take a step toward the rail and pull up and forward on their pry bars to lever the track. [23]

Gandy-Dancers. A sure sign rail service was imminent, rhythmic chants and "dance," mimicking the gait of a goose, characterized their method of aligning heavy iron rails. *(Wikipedia)*

The routine and vernacular were the same on every rail line regardless of the nationality of the crew. But the chants were limitless with a seasoned "caller" capable of leading workmen an entire day without a single repetition. The typical song was structured around a two-line, four-beat couplet, "to which members of the gang tapped their lining bars against the rails until the men were in perfect time and then the caller called for a hard pull on the third beat—on the huh—of a four-beat chant." Before *"Linin' Track"* found its way into folk culture, famously Leadbelly's rendition, it could be heard at the working end of any new line.

> *Oh boys, can't you line 'em, Jack-a-Jack-a.*
> *Oh boys, can't you line 'em, Jack-a-Jack-a.*
> *Oh boys, can't you line 'em, Jack-a-Jack-a,*
> *See Eloise go linin' track.*
> *Moses stood on the Red Sea shore,*
> *Smotin' that water with a two-by-four.*
> *If I could I surely would*
> *Stand on the rock where Moses stood.*
> *Mary an' the baby lyin' in the shade*
> *Thinkin' on the money I ain't made.* [24]

In fact, the working of any line west of the Mississippi River was a sight to behold. Long before anyone knew much about Colorado treasures or much cared, transcontinental rail service was a long sought after goal for commercial and geopolitical reasons even the dullest of politicians grasped. President Polk envisioned it. Military expeditions surveyed routes for it. Settlement along the Pacific coast and gold discoveries in California and Colorado demanded it. Not even the Civil War derailed efforts to build railroads westward. In 1862, in an astounding example of multi-tasking—in the midst of the 2nd Battle of Bull Run, the Battle of Antietam and the Battle of Fredericksburg with combined casualties totaling nearly 60,000 Americans—the Lincoln Administration mustered the resolve and resources to award two transcontinental railroad construction contracts. Beginning in Sacramento, the Central Pacific largely employing Chinese laborers, was to build east through the Sierra Nevada range. From Omaha the Union Pacific largely employing Irish laborers, was tasked to build west across the Great Plains and South Pass of the Rockies until they met their Chinese counterparts.

Work began in earnest in 1863 and ended on May 10, 1869, when the two lines joined at Promontory Summit, Utah. Progress was slow for the Central Pacific, often as little as 8-inches a day. By contrast, benefiting from more favorable terrain [but harassed by unfavorable Plains war-parties], the Union Pacific often logged ten miles a day. As the rails snaked forward, infrastructure including villages and farms sprouted along the way. To the alarm of miners and merchants alike, neither Denver nor the balance of Colorado was on the route.

Cheyenne, Wyoming made for a better hub and South Pass just to the west an easier grade through the Front Range. If Denver and Colorado mining camps were your home, being bypassed by the transcontinental railroad could not have been comforting.

Denver City Fathers were not comforted. They understood how little daylight there was between opportunity and disaster. Rail service promised life, no rail service ensured stagnation and possible death. The City Fathers chose life. If the Union Pacific would not reach out to Denver, Denver would reach out to the Union Pacific. The marriage did not take long to consummate. On June 22, 1870, the newly organized Denver Pacific's first train south from Cheyenne entered Denver city limits. Great news, but a frontier pulsating with ravenous entrepreneurs was not content with just one railroad. The Denver Pacific had competitors.

In August the Kansas Pacific in the capable hands of William Jackson Palmer arrived. At last the Queen City of the Prairie (again, for some reason, "Queen City" had to be attached to any metropolis with a grain of self-respect) was firmly linked with the States, both city and country now poised to grow into regional and global powers. Servicing the high country mining camps was another matter. Bolstering Denver's economic capability as a regional supply depot was a necessary but insufficient precondition for mountain development. Local rail service was also required. Sadly, railroad equip-

Ten Miles a Day. The construction of the Union Pacific leg of the Transcontinental Railroad had considerable advantages save for skirmishes with tribal peoples who failed to appreciate such improvements to their ancestral hunting grounds. *(A.D. Richardson,* Beyond the Mississippi)

ment suitable for the prairies and Western deserts was not suitable for servicing Rocky Mountain mines. William Jackson Palmer would be credited with the solution. If not his brain-child, at least he could pass as its mid-wife. Narrow-gauge railroad equipment was the ticket. With Denver's success in becoming a robust supply hub, all Palmer needed was capital and that should come by way of the Kansas Pacific Board of Directors. How could they refuse an opportunity to launch what in all probability could go where no standard-gauge competitor could go? How could they refuse to build what in all likelihood could become the largest narrow gauge rail system in the West?

Of course, to start with there were competitors for the "regional supply depot honor." Cheyenne first and foremost, but fledgling Colorado Springs and Pueblo would eventually showcase their wares as well. [Ironically, Palmer was responsible for their rise from the arid prairie.] But on balance Denver, flush with natural attributes and aggressive City Fathers, would remain the dominant beneficiary of rail service as long as routes could accommodate standard gauge track. Denver's well-being, however, was not a foregone conclusion.

Quoting from Jerome C. Smiley's "excellent history of Denver," Rodman Paul writes:

> *Prior to 1870 Denver was distinctly a little frontier "city" presenting the aspects apparently inseparable from every community depending wholly on stage-coach communications. The town was crude.... The pioneer manners, practices and customs still held sway.... In size the population was virtually the same in 1870 that it had been in 1860.*
>
> *The little "city" made varying impressions on visitors. In July 1863 a Congregationalist missionary wrote home to his Eastern sponsors that Denver stood in the midst of plains so hot, dusty, and bare that he was tempted to make his congregation sing Watts' hymn, "Lord, what a wretched land is this!"*
>
> *Yet, he went on, "some of the Denverites think they have found the best spot on earth. Poor, deluded mortals! The population of the place is now about four thousand. Much of the society is good, business is brisk, and many of the buildings really fine for so young a city."* [25]

Denver's "revolution in transportation," according to Rodman Paul, was the game changer. Ideally situated at the base of the mineral wealth of the mountains and the resources of the East and far West, the Denver frontier outpost did grow into a city. Depending on who was asked, Denver would always be an outpost. But to others, boosters of course, surely it was destined to be a queen. In 1867, according to Paul, a visiting Frenchman struggling with a snarky attitude was of the former persuasion. Attitude aside, he painted a clear picture just the same:

> *[Denver] is well built; the houses are attractive, constructed of brick, stone or wood. Denver has numerous buildings, a theatre, a mint, a race track.... M. Talleyrand was right when he said that in North America he had found only one dish and thirty-two religions. There are no cooks in this country, but everyone is a little religious... Everywhere are stores, banks, hotels, saloons. As in all the Union, one partakes freely, several times a day, of the sacramental glass of whisky, or some of the iced drinks which the 1867 Exposition brought to the Parisians.* [26]

Denver's population in 1870 was 4,759. In 1880 it was 35,629. Along with people came warehouses, stores, industrial plants, hotels, and homes. The city was a natural choice when it came to transshipments between long rail routes crossing the Great Plains and steep mountain ruts passing for roads leading to the mining camps. Tonnage off-loaded from standard-gauge railcars went into warehouses or onto burros, mules, or wagons destined for the mountains. Palmer envisioned a better way. He not only had railroad experience, he had courage.

Palmer was a civil war hero, a cavalry officer, a scout, a Congressional Medal of Honor recipient, and a daring entrepreneur. He also was savvy enough to know he could not compete against the likes of the mighty Union Pacific, Central Pacific, Denver Pacific, and Kansas Pacific railroads, especially in light of federal government largesse that further inflated their bank accounts. He also was savvy enough to sense his Board of Directors was satisfied with a railroad that ended in Denver. Not accustomed to defeat, Palmer dealt himself a new hand and

Medal of Honor. Arguably "king of Colorado's narrow-gauge railroad system, William Jackson Palmer demonstrated incredible skills along with courage in the corporate boardroom as well as on the battlefield. *(Wikipedia)*

played the "innovation card," the card so common in America's industrial revolution. Unlike his competitors, Palmer envisioned narrow-gauge lines to mountain mines financed by the emerging money-class and communities he would construct and promote along the way.

America's railroads began flourishing when America's railroad pioneers agreed upon a standard track gauge that enabled any and all enterprises to enjoy use of an ever-increasing network of tracks. A number of other factors were also in play, chief among them technology like George Westinghouse's airbrake that slowed and stopped a long line of heavy railcars individually and simultaneously as opposed to simply braking the locomotive and having the railcars bunch up and often derail. A half-century later the American railroad web spun by restless iron spiders was networked across the East and soon across the West.

Standard-gauge trains ran on rails four-feet, eight and one-half inches wide. Why this odd dimension? Bureaucracy and a horse's ass is the simple answer. No, not a bureaucratic "horse's ass," although that would be a good guess, but a Roman warhorse's ass. A Roman war-chariot was pulled by two horses with a combined rear

WILLIAM JACKSON PALMER
(September 18, 1836 – March 13, 1909)

Born on the Quaker family farm near Leipsic, Delaware, at age five William's family moved to Germantown, Pennsylvania where he attended the private *Friends School*, then public schools. In 1851, at age fifteen, he went to work in western Pennsylvania as a clerk for the Hempfield Railroad's engineering department. Two years later he worked directly for the chief engineer. William was interested in finding ways to convert railroad engines from burning wood to burning anthracite coal which was more plentiful and more energy efficient. Obviously a bright lad and entrepreneurial to boot, he was well-equipment to benefit when this transition gained steam.

Following a six-month "tutorial" in England, Palmer returned to Pennsylvania and a management position at the Westmoreland Coal Company, and a year later at the Pennsylvania Railroad. Future industrialist and accused "robber baron" Andrew Carnegie was a peer. William, also a candidate in later years for "robber baron" status, reported directly to Thomas A. Scott, soon to be President Lincoln's Assistant Secretary of War responsible for military logistics during the Civil War. As one might expect, Scott was partly instrumental in Palmer overcoming his Quaker pacifism in favor of his Quaker abolitionist leanings. Palmer volunteered for the Union Army, organized and took command of a Pennsylvania cavalry regiment, and survived numerous engagements including the Battle of Red Hill, Alabama in which he earned the Congressional Medal of Honor.

After the war, Palmer resumed his railroad career. In 1867 he joined the nation's mass migration west with the Kansas Pacific Railway, first as secretary and treasurer, then as managing director. The Kansas Pacific reached Denver in 1870. From Denver, Palmer envisioned extending the line south through New Mexico and El Paso to Mexico City. Seeing matters differently, the Kansas Pacific board vetoed the idea. Not dissuaded, Palmer organized his own company, the Denver & Rio Grande Railroad. Innovative in more ways than its choice of markets and routes to reach them, Palmer introduced narrow-gauge track (three-feet between the rails) that enabled rail service to reach remote mountain mining camps. He also was instrumental in establishing communities along the way, chief among them Colorado Springs, Pueblo, and Trinidad; and new industries including coal fields, iron and steel works, and hard rock mines and quarries. Westward looking, he founded Salida, Alamosa, and Durango, and connected Colorado and Utah communities with rail service reaching to Salt Lake City.

William did not abandon his humanitarian roots. He funded Colorado College, numerous municipal parks, the Colorado School for the Deaf and Blind, a tuberculosis sanatorium, and multiple libraries. He also founded the *Colorado Springs Gazette*. All told, his philanthropic kindnesses exceeded four million dollars, over $120 million in twenty-first century dollars. [27]

breadth that governed the width of the chariot and thus the wheels. Roman roads built during the Roman occupation of Great Britain were rutted by Roman chariot wheels. Rather than fight the ruts, better to avoid damage to wheels, carts, wagons, and carriages by everyone else adopting the same dimension. Centuries later the British maintained this gauge when they built pre-railroad tramways. Being known as creatures of habit, naturally they followed suit when railroads replaced tramways. Flash forward to the American experiment. British expatriates designed American railroads utilizing specifications long-established by Imperial Rome.

Palmer was not impressed with the limitations standard-gauge track imposed on routing service to mountain communities. Major problems with standard-gauge track were the right-of-way required extensive excavation and grading, the size and weight of the cars on the steep grades required large steam-powered locomotives, large steam-powered locomotives required enormous quantities of coal and water, and the track alignment required wide gentle curves and expansive yards to supply, maintain and turn around trains. As a result, feasible mountain routes were scarce and uninviting, and costs were prohibitive. All said, affordable mine-to-market railroads, with a smelter stop or two along the way, were preconditions for widespread mountain service. Palmer understood the problem, Palmer understood the solution. Downsizing from standard gauge to narrow gauge track was a precondition for supporting the growth of mountain communities, Lake City and Henson Canyon mines included.

Palmer's plan was to construct a north-south narrow-gauge railroad system along the Front Range from Denver to Mexico, with branches west into the mountains and east into the agricultural Great Plains. It would climb steep grades, navigate sharp curves and constricted canyons, utilize smaller engines, and cost less to build and operate than its standard-gauge brothers. Ironically, his plan also appealed to British investors willing to set aside principle for profit. In the fall of 1871, Palmer's Denver & Rio Grande (D&RG) railroad reached Palmer's new community of Colorado Springs, then drove southward until southerly construction halted in 1873 due to a deteriorating national economy. Westward construction was another matter.

Reaching out for the treasures in the high country camps fared better than reaching out to Great Plains and Mexican markets. Branch lines, Palmer's and a few others, continued to work their way westward. The Lake City Branch was one of them. As narrow-gauge mountain railroads went, the D&RG Lake City Branch was not the most difficult to construct, but it probably ranked among San Juan's top ten. As the D&RG branched out from Alamosa and approached Gunnison in late summer 1881, surveyors began laying out the 35.7 mile right-of-way between Sapinero (a short distance to the west of Gunnison) and Lake City. By fall, construction crews began mobilizing and grading commenced. Three hundred to five hundred laborers made steady progress but failed to complete the roadbed before winter set in. Work ceased until spring.

Spring came and went. Work did neither. D&RG priorities had changed, the project was suspended indefinitely, and Lake City on the cusp of another boom busted instead. Desperate for rail service, the City Father's encouraged other companies to take up where the D&RG left off. Exclusive rights to the Sapinero-Lake City right-of-way were due to expire in 1889 if the D&RG did not resume construction, meaning that a great subsidy could befall any other railroad willing to complete the line. D&RG management was not impressed. Nor was A.E. Reynolds. Neither made a move.

The Lake City Branch, only thirty-six miles long, originally was estimated to cost $207,000. The actual cost was $770,996.80. The Branch required uncommon valor and diligence. The available workforce was comprised mostly of Italian immigrants who were paid a sub-standard wage of $1.75 for a ten-hour day, six days a week. What spare time they enjoyed was filled with card playing, story-telling, and singing. Not to be confused with gandy-dancers who brought up the rear, these crews were the shock troops who blasted a narrow shelf in the tight canyon wall and graded the roadbed on which tracklayers and gandy-dancers would eventually work. Marril Lee Burke puts meat on their bones:

> Thirty-five to 125 men occupied several camps along the Lake Fork Canyon at any one time. Most of the men who lived in the camps were separated from their families for months on end. Living quarters were constructed of whatever branches, logs, earth, and rock was available at the site. Sometimes standing trees and large boulders would act as part of their structure, and some even had crude fireplaces. A few of the more unfortunate men had only a gravel platform and a canvas tent to keep out the cold winter winds.
>
> The laborers, who were working dawn to dusk, must have been famished by evening. They had to prepare their own meals. Large quantities of bread were baked in dome-shaped ovens. The ovens were circular structures, enclosed on the top except for a small opening to allow smoke to escape. When the fire inside had subsided and only the hot coals remained, the food was inserted through a small opening at the bottom of the oven. The locals often referred to these ovens as "dago ovens." [Ovens, tunnels, if an Italian had anything to do with anything it was likely to be called "Dago," no malice intended.] [28]

The year 1881 witnessed ovens baking bread, blasting and grading, but no tracks being laid. Frustration and skepticism on the part of our Lake City and Henson Canyon pilgrims was palpable. Where were the gandy-dancers?

Up and down this road I go,
Skippin' and dodging a .44.
Hey man won't you line 'um ... huh.
Hey won't you line 'um ... huh.
Hey won't you line 'um ... huh.
Hey won't you line 'um ... huh. [29]

In 1881 the sight of an approaching track bed excited Lake City folks, but no tracks were forthcoming. Instead, season after season, D&RG white-shirts and cuffed Denver and Washington politicians blustered about plans and predictions until most people and most editors quit paying attention. Reluctantly jaded citizens and investors would reserve their banter for the day they heard the Gandy-dancers chant, the only trustworthy banter signaling a locomotive with cars was not far behind.

Instead of a locomotive, much of the construction work suspended in 1881 was eroded from seasonal storms and slides, and was never restarted where the canyon walls were most challenging. Not until December 1888 did D&RG work crews return, two hundred men strong, and resume cutting a way through the Lake Fork Canyon narrows. Without mechanized equipment the laborers, again mostly Italians, shoveled rock into railcars, graded the rail bed with picks and shovels, and hand-drilled and blasted canyon walls.

Skilled rock drillers, using hand tools, laboriously drilled holes in rock and used small amounts of dynamite to enlarge the holes. Then over 100 bags of black gunpowder were packed into the holes. Huge explosions echoed through the canyon as the solid rock walls were blasted into rubble. [30]

The Lake Fork Canyon narrows were four miles of sheer granite walls with the Lake Fork of the Gunnison River cascading between them. The only way through required blasting a shelf for the track bed. The right-of-way through the lower canyon was widened and small bridges were built. Meanwhile carpenters worked on the Elk Creek and High Bridge, two major engineering projects midway to town. Track neared the town limits in June 1889. Not inclined to accept D&RG progress at face value, Lake City officials sweetened the kitty, a normal practice. In addition to pledging that local mines would ship more than enough ore to ensure a profitable branch line, a guarantee everyone knew they had no way of fulfilling, they gave what they could. The D&RG insisted towns grant the D&RG a right-of-way through town at no cost including ground needed for track, depot [also built at town expense], and maintenance facilities. This was a sweet deal, standard practice to be sure, but sweet just the same.

Still, even with reports of laborers in the canyon, skepticism lingered. D&RG management had unexpectedly reversed course before. Not until June 1889 did the citizens of Lake City nod approvingly. The gandy-dancer's telltale chants testified to nearby track being laid. All signs pointed to the D&RG's imminent arrival save for one unmistakable omission. Work on the Lake City rail-yard and depot remained undone. Thanks to Lake City largesse, legal issues were moot, but track was leading to the yet to be built station was missing. Also missing was track looping around the rail-yard in order to reverse the engine, and several sidings including one to the engine house. Carpenters still needed to build a water tower, scales, and coaling shed. The depot complex, a classic structure two-hundred feet long and fifty feet wide with a loading dock around the building would be a major undertaking in and of itself. The passenger area alone was a two-story, twenty-four foot by twenty-eight foot structure connected to an express baggage and freight section sixty-foot by twenty-foot.

Amazingly, on August 15, 1889, at 10:00 A.M., with all necessary construction complete, the first scheduled train eased alongside the Lake City depot loading dock. The carpenters had done their part. The graders and gandy-dancers had done their part. Their chants were music to the town folks' ears even if their behavior at days' end was not.

For some time our observant *Hinsdale Phonograph* editor had noted with alarm the increase of laborers in town, and soon lamented their carousing. He longed for the day they would be gone, after completing their track-lining of course. Were there not enough idle locals to keep the saloons and dance-halls full?

> *In the space of one short week Lake City has been transformed from a quiet, peaceful town into a perfect sheol [hell] of brawling graders, the streets disgusting with a carousing crowd, many of its members making one almost ashamed to be called a human being. We suppose it is a necessary evil, but it is a relief to believe that it will last only until the grading camps have moved away.* [31]

A week later, the line camps were dismantled and love returned at least to the heart of the *Lake City Sentinel* editor—struggling rival of the *Phonograph*, it should be noted—who welcomed the long awaited railroad with an uplifting poetic prophecy:

> *This coming of the railroad means revival of hope, revival of business in all its branches, revival of the development of the hidden treasures which have been sleeping in the recesses of our rugged mountains for so many years, waiting for the arm of the sturdy miner to bring them to the surface.... At the beginning of our business relations we meet as friends and not rivals.... Welcome thou agent of a higher civilization to our humble mountain city, and may each arrival and departure bring nothing but increased friendship between us.* [32]

So began a new era in the lives' of our San Juan pioneers. Gold-bearing ores were not in the cards, but silver would do. The long hoped for link to the outside world and in particular Front Range smelters lusting for low-grade ores was a reality, a God-send really. Henson Canyon mines had another shot at profitability. Indeed, so did the entire Lake Fork valley. The gandy-dancers had chanted, economic rail service had actually arrived, and the last major precondition for regional prosperity and the success of A.E. Reynolds' last best chance was fulfilled.

When Reynolds' attention returned to his Henson Canyon holdings, he considered all factors beyond his control were aligned in his favor. All that was required now was digging more dirt, which of course required more money (an abundance of which the Revenue Tunnel/Virginius investment produced).

GRAVITY

Rather than hoisting buckets of ore up from deep workings through lengthy shafts only to be returned to lower elevations in sacks carried by burros, A.E. Reynolds the innovator would turn gravity to his advantage by dropping the ore into ore cars pulled out to wagons waiting on the road. The only problem: the haulage tunnel at the bottom of the shaft had to be constructed. This concept was not lost on others, but every site presented unique challenges, and Reynolds was one of the few willing to risk funds on such an expensive and uncertain project. Site conditions at the Vermont and Ocean Wave favored success, but Reynolds' confidence was not based solely on site conditions. He had proven the haulage tunnel concept with his Revenue Tunnel at the Virginius mine. Doing so had earned him a sizeable portion of his personal wealth and his reputation. He intended to bolster both by digging similar dirt at the Vermont and Ocean Wave. [33]

Notes—Chapter Seven: The Great Judge

[1] John 15:13.

[2] *Lake City Phonograph*, April 9, 1910, "Story of Our Mines, Historical Synopsis of Their Discovery, Situation, Minerals & Production, The Hannibal, Big Casino, Lellie, Ocean Wave, Vermont."

[3] *The Steamboat Pilot*, April; 7, 1920, "Wm. Weston Succumbed in Denver." (Rather than sometimes reported as the *Toronto Leader*, Weston's obituary states he was City Editor of *The Globe*.)

[4] Stone, Wilbur Fisk, ed., *History of Colorado*, pgs. 296-298.

[5] *Colorado Mining Directories, 1883*, pg. 389. (Indicative of title issues that plagued San Juan mining, exactly who owned the Vermont and when title changed hands regardless of when possession changed hands is difficult to unravel. What is certain, A.E. Reynolds would not have invested in his Vermont and Ocean Wave project without title or other legal arrangements concerning ownership or development of the properties. In 1902 he acquired the Vermont

outright; he already had title to the Ocean Wave. The Vermont was named the El Paso originally, but another claim that never was patented lying along both sides of El Paso Creek between the Burro Cabin and current Vermont Lodes also bore that name. Phillips sold his claim to the El Paso to W.C. Lewman for $1,000. Prior to 1880 there was no ore produced. In 1882, Smith and Beam owned the El Paso/Vermont and soon found ore worth $70/ton smelter value. In 1883 the Vermont, and probably the Alabama, was purchased by William Weston and Frank Silvia and apparently "relocated" in that year as well. Weston was granted a patent on the Vermont as well as the Alabama and Alhambra on April 15, 1896. At some point he sold the Vermont along with the Alabama and Alhambra to English investors organized as the Vermont Mine Syndicate, and a warranty deed was recorded to this effect on August 30, 1897. However, a "Decree" recorded in April 1896 entitled "E.B. Hendrie vs. the Vermont Mine Syndicate" contradicted this. There was some indication that in April 1910, the mine was again owned by Hendrie and Bolthoff Machinery Company of Denver, and on March 13, 1924, Edwin B. Hendrie conveyed by way of a "Mining Deed" the Vermont, Alabama and Alhambra to Castlewood Investments Corporation. Contradicting this, Reynolds or his estate leased the Vermont and Ocean Wave well into the 1930s.)

[6] Steele, Joe, *Guide to Lake City Geology*, pg. 28.
[7] *Silver World*, January 9, 1997.
[8] *Silver World*, January 15, 1887.
[9] Ibid.
[10] *Silver World*, January 22, 1887.
[11] Ibid.
[12] *Silver World*, January 22, 1887
[13] Independent Order of Odd Fellows, The Sovereign Grand Lodge, https://odd-fellows.org.
[14] Ibid.
[15] Ibid.
[16] Darley, George M. *Pioneering in the San Juans*, pg. 19.
[17] Paul, Rodman W., *Mining Frontiers of the Far West 1848-1880*, pg. 192.
[18] Ibid. ("Removal" is a curious term for describing "relocation" or "moving" – its origins date to Biblical times and appropriately is part of the vocabulary of the frontier preacher.)
[19] Ibid.
[20] Darley, pgs. 27-30. [John 8:1-11 KJV]
[21] (Trouble, trouble, trouble. Inadequate underground development work was performed in 1885-1886. A murderous avalanche destroyed the Vermont surface plant in 1887. Yet another blow to Vermont viability was the 1891-92 influenza epidemic. Four or five people died each week, eventually totaling more than a hundred residents and miners before spring brought relief. There was another flu epidemic in 1918, less lethal in Hinsdale County than the 1891-92 bout, but debilitating just the same. And then there was the ever-present problem of silver prices.)
[22] *Lake City Phonograph*, April 9, 1910, "Story of Our Mines."
[23] Leadbelly folk song.
[24] *Wikipedia*, "Gandy Dancer," pg. 1-10, https://en.wikipedia.org/wiki/Gandy_dancer.
[25] Paul, pg. 125.
[26] Ibid., pgs. 125-126.
[27] *Wikipedia*, "William Jackson Palmer," pgs.1-8.
[28] Burke, Marril Lee, *Ghosts of the Lake Fork Region*, pg. 88.
[29] *Wikipedia*, "Gandy Dancer," pgs. 1-10, https://en.wikipedia.org/wiki/Gandy_dancer.
[30] Burke, pg. 87.
[31] *Hinsdale Phonograph*, June 22, 1889.
[32] *Lake City Sentinel*, June 29, 1889.
[33] Smith, P. David, *The Story of Lake City, Colorado*, pgs. 239-252.

CHAPTER 8

Dirt

Dirt is just matter out of place,
So scientists aver;
But when I see a miner's face
I wonder if they err.
For grit and grime and grease may be
In God's constructive plan,
A symbol of nobility,
The measure of a man.

There's nought so clean as honest dirt,
So of its worth I sing;
I value more an oily shirt
Than garment of a king.
There's nought so proud as honest sweat,
And though its stink we cuss,
We kid-glove chaps are in the debt
Of those who sweat for us.

It's dirt and sweat that makes us folks
Proud as we are today;
We owe our wealth to weary blokes
Befouled by soot and clay.
And where you see a belly fat
A dozen more are lean....
By God! I'd sooner doff my hat
To washer-wife than queen.

So here's a song to dirt and sweat,

A grace to grit and grime;

A hail to workers who beget

The wonders of our time.

And as they gaze, though gutter-girt,

To palaces enskied,

Let them believe, by sweat and dirt,

They, too, are glorified. [1]

Not all dirt is created equal. Dirt stands between the miner and paying ore, what his kind appropriately calls "paydirt." Dirt enriched with valuable ore is paydirt. Without ore dirt is just that, dirt. Worse yet, it is expensive.

Tunneling through dirt is the domain of burrowing mammals, man not necessarily chief among them. Tunneling through hard rock is another matter. Hard rock tunnels are man's sole domain. While they may not produce treasure, they are expected to clear away the dirt standing in the way of where treasure can be found. With faith in one's purpose and sufficient capital, the length of such a tunnel was of little concern. In its season, Nevada's Sutro Tunnel accessing Comstock paydirt was American West's finest example of this axiom. A.E. Reynolds' hugely successful Revenue Tunnel, accessing Virginius paydirt above Ouray, Colorado, was patterned after it. So too, Reynolds envisioned, would be what came to be known as the "Reynolds Tunnel" accessing Vermont and Ocean Wave paydirt in Henson Canyon above Lake City.

Adolph Sutro, Otto Mears, and Albert Eugene Reynolds had a great deal in common when it came to heritage and character. Sutro and Reynolds had a great deal in common when it came to tunnels. In 1860 Prussian Jewish mining entrepreneur Adolph Sutro began promoting the idea that silver production at the Comstock Mine in Nevada could be vastly improved by driving a horizontal tunnel from the surface to the lower workings of the mine. Born in present-day North Rhine-Westphalia, Germany, Adolph was the oldest of eleven children. The family emigrated to America in 1848, first settling in Baltimore. Adolph was caught up in the California gold rush and arrived in San Francisco in November of 1851. Wisely forsaking the gold fields, he became a shopkeeper and eventual owner of several tobacco shops. In 1860 he left San Francisco after silver was discovered in Nevada with plans to sell cigars. By 1865 he had recalibrated himself into a mining entrepreneur. In 1866 he incorporated the Sutro Tunnel Company and was granted an exclusive charter by the U.S. Congress to build what became his world renowned tunnel. Financed with other people's money, Adolph leased the tunnel to mines it accessed for an average of $10,000 a day and moved back to San Francisco where he was the city's 24th mayor from 1894 to 1896.[2]

Sutro's Tunnel.
Adolph Sutro pioneered the excavation of large U.S. access tunnels not intended to recover ore but to open the way to it. A.E. Reynolds took note. *(Library of Congress)*

In its time, 1878, the Sutro Tunnel was a technological wonder, a mining marvel at least. In the midst of the nation's full-throated assault on the world's industrial revolution, such accolades were noteworthy. Simple in purpose and execution, extraordinary in effort and expense, the Sutro Tunnel spawned a number of prominent imitators in Colorado and inspired A.E. Reynolds to replicate it in concept if not design. Adolph Sutro engineered and constructed his tunnel in order to undercut the incredibly rich Nevada Comstock vein and the cluster of

THE SUTRO TUNNEL

The Sutro Tunnel was the nineteenth century poster-child for large drainage, transportation, and ventilation tunnels in the United States. Nine years in the making, it was wide enough for mule or burro-pulled carts to pass one another. It also was straight, an accomplishment all tunnel constructors valued but few tunnels could boast. In Adolph's case, topography and southern orientation were friends that facilitated maintaining a constant bearing for the length of the tunnel in a unique way. Calibration with a mirror reflecting a beam of sunlight into the tunnel every noon ensured that it was aligned and its axis was true.

On September 1, 1878, tunnel workers hit their target, or nearly so. They broke into the Comstock catacombs just eighteen inches off-center. An indication of the sought after airflow between upper and lower workings, characteristic of all naturally ventilated mines, was a strong howling draft as pressure differences equalized. The project cost investors on the order of two million dollars, well worth the price for fresh air, easy rail access to the surface, and easy access to a fortune in silver ore. [3]

mines that worked it. At a depth of seventeen hundred feet below the Comstock's uppermost portal, it was nearly four miles long from its adit to the Comstock catacombs it drained and ventilated. Like Reynolds, Sutro and investors had hoped construction of the tunnel would fund itself by uncovering paying ore, but that was not its purpose and would not be the case.

Like the Sutro Tunnel, the Revenue Tunnel proved to be a risky, costly, but economical method of tapping and transporting ore, removing large volumes of water, and ventilating workings at great depths. Early in 1893 the Virginius tunnel vein was evidently in sight of its vein. The tunnel crew had cut into a thin lead at a distance of 7,335 feet from the entrance. Reynolds was not so sure, but he remained expectant. Biographer Scamehorn explains:

> *Although uncertain, Reynolds concluded this was not the long-sought pay streak but a spur or feeder of the Virginius vein. Two weeks later miners reached the elusive goal. The vein comprised a total of 24 inches of ore separated by approximately 12 inches of barren rock. It was located at a vertical distance of 3,040 feet from the surface.*[4]

With the vein as their fickle guide, the tunnel was about to mate with the Virginius mine. Excavating approximately 800 ft. overhead at a fifty-degree angle, what became a 7 ft. x 12 ft. winze (shaft) was cut to the fourteenth level of the Virginius. Once divided into three chutes to accommodate ore, waste, and an electric skip, the winze ventilated the tunnel and deep workings and allowed ore to be trammed from the lower levels of the mine. Once in operation, the Revenue Tunnel was credited with profits in excess of $330,000 a year until the end of the century [yes, the end of the century], a commendable achievement for the day. In raw capital the project netted Reynolds an estimated fifteen million dollars. In sound mining experience, the return in raw confidence was incalculable. Reynolds' reward bankrolled him along with his faithful investors on numerous other mining projects throughout Colorado. It bankrolled his Henson Canyon tunnel. It earned him recognition throughout western mining communities, unwanted but valuable, as well as in eastern finance centers, very much wanted and even more valuable.[5]

Hubble Reed, the Revenue Tunnel superintendent, and Reynolds, having kept the faith despite years of criticism and ridicule, were eventually recognized in the most meaningful of ways. Reed's reputation as a mining engineer could not be more complimentary. Reynolds' ability to raise capital and develop additional properties seemed unlimited. By 1900, he was arguably Colorado's mining king, princely at the very least, uncrowned but acclaimed, nevertheless. Sadly, not far into the unknowable future he would be a pauper at best.

In the meantime, Adolph's and A.E.'s pluck impressed other Colorado high rollers. As detailed in P. David Smith's *Mountains of Silver*,[6] the idea of constructing deep haulage, drainage, and ventilation tunnels gained popularity elsewhere in Ouray's Red Mountain mining region. In1896 the Treasury Tunnel was started to access the lower workings of older mines and hopefully open promising deep veins along the way. Yet more ambitious was the Meldrum Tunnel. Started in 1898, Andrew S. Meldrum envisioned a tunnel "large enough for a normal narrow-gauge freight train to go from the Red Mountain area almost directly west to tie in with the Rio Grande Southern Railroad near Telluride." As usual, in addition to "blasting ore chutes into several of the larger mines" along the way, the project anticipated the sale of ore encountered as work progressed. As usual, locating ore as work progressed was not in the cards. Two years into the Meldrum project, Scottish financing dried up and six miles of tunnel—started at both ends—was suspended with less than four miles to go.

Even grander in scale was the Joker Tunnel. Construction began July 1904, and by 1907 cut forty-eight hundred feet into Red Mountain. It was ten to eleven feet wide and seven to eight feet high. While none of these projects were blazing successes, neither were they failures. The Treasury Tunnel survived as an asset to adjacent mines into the 1970s. While financing for the Meldrum Tunnel dried up two years into the project, operations remained well under budget as long as new money had flowed. The Joker Tunnel contradicted its name by working profitably until 1914, then sporadically well into the Second World War.

Such was the optimistic mood in the San Juans, often reflecting local perspectives remoteness can engender, often contradicting national trends. Forty miles east on the Henson Canyon side of Ouray's Engineer Mountain awaited the Vermont/Ocean Wave lodes, also subject to optimistic moods, which gradually took on the mining king's name. Reynolds Tunnel was blessed with topography and orientation that was almost a mirror image of the Virginius' Revenue Tunnel. To the timid, Reynolds' vision for exploiting the lower workings of the Virginius had been foolishness. Many viewed prospects of reopening the old workings of the Vermont and Ocean Wave with similar distain.

To Reynolds who was anything but timid or foolish, the Reynolds Tunnel was simply a natural and simpler replication of the Revenue Tunnel and far less ambitious than it or the Treasury, Meldrum, or Joker Tunnels. After the decade-long success of the Virginius project, he was more confident than ever that he had learned valuable lessons well. He was also confident that the lifespan of even the best of mines was limited. He needed another Virginius to fund his industrial age life style and his unquenchable thirst for new mining ventures.

When it came to the Colorado Mineral Belt and San Juan mines, frontier adventurism characterized the 1890s and early 1900s seemingly irrespective of the underlying condition of the national economy or seemingly more attractive investment opportunities offered by the nation's industrial revolution. What could be more promising than industries built upon electricity, or internal combustion engines powering automobiles, or aviation. Employment beckoning from urban factories appeared far more rewarding than from rural mines.

Nevertheless, while there might be serious competition for capital, or a recession, a dismal silver market, a war or two, a flu pandemic that would kill fifty million souls worldwide and scores in Colorado mining towns, there remained plenty to get excited about in the San Juans. When a mining venture stumbled over production costs or high-grade ore played out or other people's money dried up, other mining ventures promising high returns still found a way to lure new investors. Some were fraudulent, as we will see. Many were honest, but the victims of honest misjudgments. Some paid dividends, enough to encourage more ventures. When narrow-gauge railroads welcomed to town with parades and brass bands fulfilled the last major precondition for San Juans prosperity, A.E. Reynolds launched his last best chance to replenish his coffers. Well-experienced in such matters, still the journey required the better part of a decade.

Reynolds' tunnel strategy for the Vermont and Ocean Wave was conceived amidst plenty but executed amidst scarcity. Why the mines were worked when they were, and why they sat idle in-between, was no mystery, at least not to Reynolds. Idled for months or years only to be revived again and again was their legacy. Ownership squabbles were common complications. Fatal accidents and avalanches did not help. Money, always the governing vestige of any enterprise, often ran out before hope and hype could yield a return.

But typical of his generation, Reynolds' hope was not groundless. It was the product of experience, first-hand knowledge of a property of interest, and boundless confidence born of hard work not easily shattered and an overcomer's attitude. And he was a risk-taker who did not like to lose, who did not confess a bad decision. Midas' golden touch was mythical, but A.E. Reynolds' silver touch was real. Somehow he seemed to "know" whether a mine should bear silver before he bought it. He knew how to extract silver profitably before it was profitable. He was a legitimate digger of dirt before he was a respected Denver mining magnate. Of course he was not always successful, witness his earlier Lake City ventures.

Early in Lake City's first boom era, mid-career for Reynolds, he brought his ingenuity, daring, and considerable financial resources to the Lake Fork Valley. At first he was welcomed into the ranks of the high mucky-mucks calling municipal tunes. His large mercantile establishment, freight line, and numerous mining ventures, tangible wealth by any measure, substituted for elected office, fraternity ties, or gentry pedigrees, but not all of his investments worked out well. Sadly, the warmth of his welcome ebbed and flowed in step with the balance in his bank account. It also ebbed when his vision outpaced the comfort zone of the citizenry.

There is no better insight into these matters than that provided in Scamehorn's biography. Reynolds' Lake City story began while the "Queen of the San Juans" still enjoyed boomtown status. In 1882 A.E. diverted his attention from his highly profitable Texas Panhandle ranch to San Juans merchandising and mining. Turning the ranch over to brother Charles, A.E. moved to Lake City, opened a general store, and introduced himself to the Henson Canyon mining community. According to Scamehorn,

> *Reynolds was attracted by Lake City's prosperity and the likelihood of greater wealth when mines then under development became regular producers of ore. The community, in his judgment, was an ideal place for a general merchandise store. The supervision of the retail business, including the wagon trains that hauled goods to and from Alamosa, Del Norte, and Gunnison, was entrusted to Charles F. McKenny, leaving Reynolds time to pursue other business opportunities.*[7]

Yes, an ideal place for a general merchandise store, and a great revenue generator, but apparently not what A.E. wanted to face when he woke up every morning. If the proverbial "gold-bug" had a "silver-cousin," one or both had bitten Reynolds. A large proportion of the balance of his entrepreneurial life would be devoted to profiting from mines. Of first importance was the Palmetto, a property high on Engineer Mountain along the headwaters of Henson Creek. Scamehorn writes:

> *The Palmetto offered, in Reynolds's view, the best hope for a successful mining venture. That mine had been developed in a limited way by John Hough, in partnership with George A. Smith and son, prior to 1880, when the Reynolds–Thatcher–Maugham pool secured an interest in the property. That year the owners organized the Palmetto Consolidated Mining and Milling Company to open the mine on a large scale and to erect and operate a mill to reduce the ore to silver bullion.*[8]

Both mine and mill failed. Despite hiring Hubbell W. Reed, a highly regarded mining engineer and superintendent; despite Malter, Lind and Company of San Francisco erecting an $80,000 "state-of-the-art" reduction mill, by 1882 both mine and mill went dark. In keeping with his nature, Reynolds placed no blame on either, certainly not Hubbell Reed who remained a trusted ally Reynolds would call on time and again. Not a whiner, nevertheless the Palmetto did not fill Reynolds' heart with joy, nor did it discourage him from pursuing similar opportunities. Circumstances beyond any man's control had spoken loud and clear— ore had been difficult to retrieve from the high-elevation mine and the mill was ill-suited for its metallurgical composition, surrendering over sixty percent of its values to Henson Creek instead of partnership coffers. He would have to be more careful going forward.

But the Palmetto was not Reynolds' last disappointment. His investment in the Frank Hough Mine met a similar fate. Partner John Hough discovered it in 1879, named it after his son, and ignored it until Reynolds Thatcher Maugham funding enabled Reynolds to develop it. Soon sold for $125,000, the sales contract was terminated after payment of $25,000. Hough took over management of the mine, and matters worsened. Scamehorn writes:

> *Thereafter, according to Reynolds, the property was managed by Hough, who, unknown to his partners, ran it for his own benefit. He sold the ore without accounting for the proceeds and without paying for supplies used in working the mine. Operations ended in 1884, with the mining company in debt almost $3,500, including goods purchased from McKenny on credit. [Worse still, local creditors sought payment from Reynolds rather than Hough.]* [9]

Reynolds managed to settle Frank Hough Mine accounts, but his troubles were not over. As long as Lake City boomed, his mercantile did well. By 1883 the boom was over, and so was payment by debtors of more than $15,000 owed the store. With no relief in sight, A.E. asked his landlord—sometimes partner John Hough—for a reduction in rent for the space his mercantile occupied in Hough's Lake City building. Hough agreed, then four months later reneged. That was the last straw for Reynolds. He and McKenny liquidated store goods and fixtures, twenty yoke of oxen, four freight wagons, and a smaller wagon. What remained was shipped to Ouray on the other side of Engineer Mountain, which would become the epicenter of Reynolds' mining interests for the next fifteen years.

All that remained on the Lake City side of the range was Reynolds' ownership and interests in local mining claims. Despite his assessment of Lake City and its business class—"dead and stagnant... barnacles of the community"—that "robbed him on contracts and beat him in every way," he held on to his belief that the nearby mountains held more treasure. Curiously, he also believed that emerging technology utilizing electricity was ideally suited to these very same mountains. When in his judgment the time was right, he would return to exploit both. [10]

Hands-On Manager. A.E. Reynolds did not always manage his mining properties from his office in Denver. Standing to the left, he is on his way to the Frank Hough mine near the top of Engineer Mountain in the dead of winter, 1907. (*Courtesy of* Lake City Silver World)

When it came to electricity, Reynolds was more than a believer, he was a doer. He not only introduced electricity-powered "mules" to his Revenue Tunnel, he built a hydroelectric power plant to supply it. (Satisfied with the results, he invested in electrifying Ouray.) Apparently by the mid-1890s Reynolds' love-hate relationship with the Lake City community had tipped toward "love" enough for him to revisit nearby opportunities. Preparing to drive his Vermont/Ocean Wave tunnel was one of them. More ambitious, electrifying the Lake Fork valley was another.

Electrifying the valley involved securing permits on behalf of the Argenta Mining Company to convert the waterpower of Lake San Cristobal and Argenta Falls into electric power. By 1900 he had acquired all necessary properties around the lake with the intention of raising the water level at least eleven feet to drive turbines capable of delivering power throughout the Lake Fork and Henson Creek watersheds. More ambitious still, the project would include an electric tramway from the Lake City terminus of the Denver & Rio Grande Railroad up Henson Creek twenty plus miles to the mines on Engineer Mountain, some of which he owned. By reducing the cost of transporting ore just half that distance from Capitol City to Lake City, ten dollars per ton by wagons to an estimated two dollars per ton by tram, Reynolds' scheme would be certain to encourage the reopening of several mines. Need we be reminded, the projects' electricity and tram—highly profitable at the Revenue Tunnel would also offset the cost of the Vermont/Ocean Wave haulage tunnel.

Not all that surprising but underestimated by Reynolds, the ramifications of his vision alarmed not only local capitalists, his Lake San Cristobal hydroelectric plant in particular horrified residents quite content with their near-pristine surroundings. Lake City infatuation with the likes of A.E. Reynolds again veered into troubled waters. Again his former perch among the mucky-mucks proved unsound. Again his vision and love for the town collapsed. What never collapsed was A.E.'s belief that Henson Canyon was the site of great mineral wealth, and that in due course he would profit from it. [11]

Of course San Juans' mines were not A.E.'s only interests. A much more robust life began to blossom in the backwaters of the Civil War when the American West exploded with diverse opportunities regardless of ones station in society. Possessed with an extraordinary abundance of confidence, in Scamehorn's judgment the West was "ideally suited to Albert Eugene Reynold's ambition, drive, and talents." [12]

"Loyalty" could be added to these traits. A. E. was loyal to friends and associates alike when they exhibited the same ethics and virtues he prized. At times this aspect of his character extended to competitors. Relationships dating back to his earliest days as an Army post sutler, rivals and partners included, resurfaced time and again as he developed his retail, ranching, and mining empire.

Of particular interest in this regard was Reynolds' friendship with John A. Thatcher and his brother Mahlon. John and A.E. were merchants at Fort Lyon east of Pueblo, Colorado. Both men and often Mahlon partnered repeatedly, first as investors, and, in Mahlon and John's case, later as Pueblo and Lake City bankers willing to underwrite Reynolds' speculative mine projects. As became apparent in this phase of Reynolds' business activities, his near-term successes or failures often depended on the urgent infusion of other people's money.

A. E. REYNOLDS

Albert Eugene Reynolds, often referred to as A.E., was born in Newfane, New York, on February 13, 1840. He grew up in Lockport where the family relocated when he was an infant. Parents Henry A. Reynolds and Caroline Van Horn Reynolds owned and operated a Lockport general store and a nearby farm, both pursuits no doubt providing young Albert with valuable grounding for his own adventurous life. As the eldest male among nine siblings, biographer Scamehorn reports that:

> Albert was the natural leader, the achiever, and he invariably succeeded at any task to which he devoted attention and effort. This characteristic not only set him apart from his siblings but also prompted them to look to him for their well-being. Albert was ambitious, self-confident, aggressive, tenacious, and competitive, qualities that his brothers and sisters lacked in varying degrees. He was uneasy when dependent upon people but willingly encouraged others to become dependent upon him. He readily accepted responsibility for the actions of his siblings and supported and looked after them in numerous ways throughout his adult years.[13]

For reasons one can only imagine, the call of the West surely among them, in 1866 A.E. took flight with eighty dollars to his name and landed in Junction, Kansas on the outskirts of Leavenworth, future site of Fort Riley and home to the U.S. Army's 1st Infantry Division. Employed a short while in a local general store, then a mercantile of his own in Richmond, Missouri, then in Fort Lyon, Colorado Territory, as an agent of a Leavenworth merchant responsible for a trading post where his western legacy began.

Fifteen years hence—several partnerships and business ventures including freighting and ranching later—A.E. rooted himself in Lake City, Colorado. Married in Columbus, Wisconsin on April 25, 1883, to Dora (Eudora) Earll, the Reynolds lived in Lake City until the birth of their only child, Anna Earll on January 26, 1884. That year, A.E., disgusted with Lake City shenanigans, and Dora, uncomfortable on the frontier, moved to Denver where they lived for the balance of their lives. For A.E., that balance ended March 21, 1921, while tending to business in Nashville, Tennessee.[14]

Rancher Reynolds with Banker Thatcher ca 1900, Channing, Texas. Dating back to their early days as young Army sutlers, friend Mahlon D. Thatcher and brother John established banks in Pueblo and Lake City that funded many A.E. Reynolds business and mining ventures. *(Courtesy of* Lake City Silver World.*)*

The Lee and Reynolds partnership was another example of Reynolds' ability to make life-long friends who often became long-term business associates. Initially rivals—W.M.D. Lee was a former U.S. Army quartermaster turned post sutler like Reynolds—the two men chose cooperation over competition and organized the Lee and Reynolds company to trade with the Cheyenne and Arapahoe. Scamehorn explains:

> *The firm of Lee and Reynolds remained active for more than a dozen years. The Indian trade was immensely profitable as long as the Arapahoe and Cheyenne had buffalo robes and hides to trade for merchandise. After the slaughter of the herd on the southern Plains, completed by 1878, Lee and Reynolds sold the Indian agency store and limited their merchandising effort to retail outlets at Fort Supply, at Fort Elliott in the Texas Panhandle, and at places designed to serve the military during temporary field operations or cattlemen driving herds of longhorns out of Texas to the railroad at Caldwell and other points in Kansas.[15]*

Reynolds and Lee did not limit themselves to stocking mercantiles. If there was money to be made in a particular venture, they engaged in it including saloons and billiard rooms. They sold cord wood and hay. They operated a freighting business between Dodge City, Indian Territory, and the Texas Panhandle; and, later with Colorado mines. And as if all that was not enough, they ran cattle, operated slaughter houses at Fort Supply and Fort Elliott, transported U.S. mails and served as postmasters. They even provided the army with cedar poles for a telegraph line strung between Fort Supply and Fort Elliott. Flush with cash, they bought the large ranch in the Texas Panhandle and invested in Utah and Colorado mineral lands and large blocks of railroad and other securities.

For reasons unknown, Reynolds and Lee parted company in 1882, both pursuing their own destinies and both accumulating even greater wealth. Reynolds
continued merchandising and freighting for several years, but savoring the
suspense mining hidden treasures must have entailed, he became increasingly
infatuated with Lake City opportunities. Inclined by nature to take big risks so
long as they promised big rewards, he began investing in upper Lake Fork valley
properties which then led him over Engineer Pass to Ouray, Mount Sneffles, and
the Red Mountain District. Famously, the purchase of the Virginius Mine and
construction of the Revenue Tunnel testified to his vision and good judgment.

Of equal significance, Scamehorn identifies several other A.E. attributes that
also explain his confidence in his approach to his Vermont/Ocean Wave project
fifteen years hence.

> *The Virginius Mine revealed Reynolds's (sic) unusual talent for organiz-
> ing and managing mining operations. Whenever he acquired a potentially
> valuable property, he placed the responsibility for day-to-day operations in
> the hands of a highly competent superintendent. Hubbell W. Reed, an engineer
> of wide experience, held that position at the Ouray property for twenty years.
> Angus Snedaker, Charles F. Palmer, and David G. Miller, managers and
> mining engineers of unquestioned competence, had charge of other properties.
> Reynolds required that his managers keep him informed of day-to-day opera-
> tions. No detail was too technical, or too obscure, not to merit his attention.* [16]

Throughout the development of the Vermont/Ocean Wave project, and the
construction of what became known as the "Reynolds Tunnel," these practices
were evident. We observed as much in A.E.'s brave winter ascent of Engineer
Mountain to oversee Frank Hough Mine progress. Reynolds relied on self-taught
engineers and superintendents, but trust had its limits.

These men who you will meet soon, in addition to their loyalty, field experience, and work ethic, possessed two other attributes Reynolds highly prized. First,
like so many of his entrepreneurial and industrial contemporaries, formal education and privilege were not required. Reynolds boasted of neither, saw merit in
others of like kind, and was teachable by anyone he considered honest and knowl-
edgeable. Second, Reynolds valued managers that were diligent record-keepers.
Reynolds himself was a near-obsessive record-keeper, as was Charles F. McKenny
who served him thirty-seven years beginning as a clerk for Lee and Reynolds in
Indian Territory. C.F. McKenny earned in due course the position of confidential
adviser, friend, and overseer of day-to-day operations. When Reynolds settled
in Denver in 1884, McKenny settled there, too. Humbly referred to as office
manager, in fact he functioned much like a silent partner or Chief Operations
Officer. On occasion he was a shareholder in a Reynolds mine. Often correspondence with Reynolds' trusted associates at distant ranches, stores, and mines was

initiated or followed up by McKenny. When Reynolds' appetite for new ventures exceeded McKenny's ability to keep up, J.P.M. Humphrey was brought on to assist. Humphrey also earned Reynolds' trust, succeeded McKenny in 1910, and proved equally adept at mastering an enormous volume of records and correspondence.

Savvy and loyal associates were not the only assets Reynolds relied upon for mining successes. His cost-cutting instincts and application of innovative techniques and technology were also always in play. Finding paying ores, even low-grade ores, was not the greatest challenge. The greatest challenge was managing the costs of surfacing, transporting, and separating paydirt from dirt. Reynolds' precious metal mines yielded mostly silver, the prices of which fluctuated greatly and began trending downward beginning in 1873. By 1883, when Reynolds was heavily invested in silver properties and the most promising, the Virginius chief among them, were finally beginning to produce good ore, a dip in silver prices threatened to crater the entire region.

This market environment and Reynolds' reactions to it perfectly describe his mode of operations throughout his entrepreneurial mining career. Largely the victor in this classic struggle to remain operational and profitable, he was not infallible. His Vermont/Ocean Wave project stretched him to the breaking point. But the history and ultimate success of the Sutro Tunnel bolstered his confidence, and the Virginius bolstered by its Revenue Tunnel served as a fitful harbinger of better days to come. For the Vermont and Ocean Wave Mines, he might have abandoned his vision and his last best chance to deliver another bonanza. Instead, in the face of downward pressure on silver prices and less than encouraging reports from the boys working San Juans mines, Reynolds gambled even more on technical innovations. [17]

Technical innovations included more than experimental equipment powered by electricity. It included untried milling protocols. It included economical transportation which to Reynolds meant narrow-gauge branch lines connecting mining districts to smelters and markets, and tunnels (some actually constructed) connecting the interior valleys to the Front Range. The success of his lobbying railroad interests is impossible to say, but branch lines were built to Ouray and Lake City and tunnels were blasted through the Front Range.

Mining rewarded A.E. Reynolds well, and success bred success. As both promoter and operator of mines, he was adept at producing silver and at raising abundant funds. In both cases he was adept at ensuring funds were prudently spent. His oft-repeated business model was acquiring promising mineral properties, organizing a mining company, selling all but enough stock to retain control, and using other peoples' money to fund operations and pay dividends. While not an uncommon model, in an age of robber barons his renowned integrity made his ventures refreshingly uncommon. He not only forecasted—not guaranteed— dividends, he usually paid them, or bought back shares. Even in the face of losses and missed milestones, his investors accepted such risks believing that he was truly mining minerals and not simply mining them. As a result, he was a success-ful entrepreneur which meant he was wealthy, usually meaning his investors also were wealthy. He also was wise. Scamehorn explains.

> *The gross profits from all of his mines reached a staggering $60 mil-lion during his lifetime. The Virginius Mine, developed in part through the Revenue Tunnel, produced ore worth approximately $15 million over a pe-riod of slightly less than twenty years. The Durant and Smuggler, celebrated mines at Aspen, yielded large returns. The Commodore and adjacent properties at Creede were similarly productive, paying substantial dividends to stock-holders over a period of about a decade. Highly profitable but less spectacular was the May Day Mine near Hesperus.*
>
> *The secret of his success, according to one editor, was his ability to see "into the ground," meaning that he was unusual in the thoroughness of his under-standing of mines and mining practices. According to this view, Reynolds, because of hard work, daring, and determination, became Colorado's greatest mine operator.*[18]

Greatest mine operator? Uncanny gift of sight? Uncommon instincts? Perhaps. Newspaper magpies of the day did their best to understand, but Reynolds was a private man and such claims were not his own. According to biographer Scamehorn, not even his wife and daughter were aware of the full extent of his business activities that would take years after his death to unravel. His civic kind-nesses were equally impressive and equally obscure. Not particularly known as a religious man, A.E. devoted forty years to serving as a trustee of the University of Denver and the Iliff School of Theology. He also was a trustee of the City Temple Institutional Society whose purpose was consolidating the management of a number of religious, educational, and benevolent organizations funded by the Episcopal Church. Chief among these were The Haven, an industrial school for girls; the Belle Lennox Nursery; the Young Women's Friendly Club; and the City Temple Institutional Church.[19]

In pace with his devotion to privacy, Reynolds' aversion to newspaper editors was due largely to his belief they were all "busybodies" publishing "misleading and mischievous trash." Underlying his ire was concern that exaggerated claims were sure to prove false and therefore undermine the confidence of investors in the integrity of mine owners and stock companies upon which he and so many other honest operators depended. In November 1902, Reynolds wrote a particu-larly colorful complaint to Frank Hall, among Denver's best historians and most honest mining editors:

> *"I wish to call your attention to a lying, false, misleading and mischief making article published in yesterday's Evening Post, in regard to a great strike*

of gold ore in the properties of the Revenue Tunnel Mines Company above Ouray." The vein of ore in question was supposedly worth more than $2,000 per ton. "I am sorry to have to annoy you with this matter," Reynolds continued, "but I do not like to see published such an absolutely rotten, lying article about properties in which I am interested." [20]

When it came to politics, Reynolds was a conservative, or perhaps better described as a hybrid libertarian if such a class existed. He was neither Republican nor Democrat. He supported those who supported silver coinage. He opposed anyone who supported a gold standard. He abhorred both unionized labor and organized management. "Unhampered freedom of action" was Reynolds' mantra. Left to his own devices, he was confident he could work his properties peacefully and profitably.

This too helps explain Reynolds' decades' long infatuation with the Ocean Wave and Vermont Lodes. Persistence and innovation without the help of unions made the Revenue Tunnel and the Virginius jaw-dropping successes. Surely they were harbingers for Reynolds' Henson Canyon gamble if their lessons-learned were applied.

As for Reynolds' personal life, his passions ran far deeper than business and philanthropy. He was devoted to his siblings as well as his bride and daughter. He supported his unmarried sisters, most of whom lived together in New York City, providing them with the means to travel West in the summer and South in the winter. (After his marriage in 1883 the sisters spent their summers in New England.) Brothers Andrew and Charles, and to a lesser degree George,

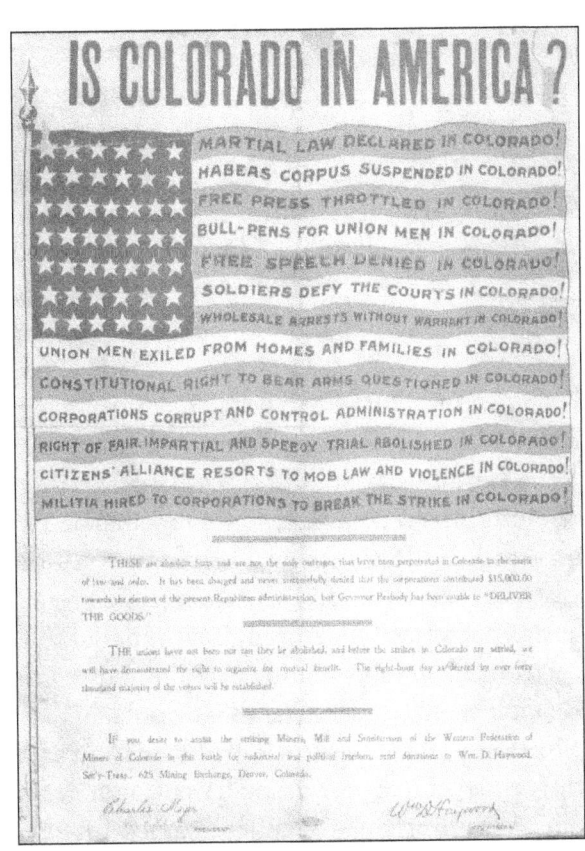

Is Colorado in America? A.E. Reynolds, staunchly opposed to unionized miners and management alike, could easily have wondered the same thing. The Western Federation of Miners is credited with this political poster. Reynolds successfully fended off every attempt to lure his miners into the brotherhood. *(Wikimedia Commons)*

worked for A.E. in one capacity or another most of their adult lives. In effect, Reynolds had two families deftly portrayed by historian Scamehorn in the following series of quotes.

His sisters and brothers were for many years his primary concern. His attachment to them was unwavering. He shared his success with them, and they were content to depend upon his judgment and support. Reynolds thrived on giving advice and was flattered when people, including siblings, accepted his recommendations. Eventually this created problems for the woman who became his wife, and the key member of his second family, in 1883.

A bachelor aged forty-one residing at Fort Supply, western Oklahoma, had few options when it came to romance, but A.E. was not one to stand by passively.

Eligible non-Indian females were almost nonexistent in Indian Territory, and Reynolds lacked the time and opportunity to search for a prospective bride during frequent business trips to Leavenworth, St. Louis, Chicago, and New York. Probably for that reason he enlisted the aid of his partner's wife, Orlina (Lina) Whitney Lee, who suggested that he correspond with a longtime friend from her hometown of Columbus, Wisconsin. Orlina, who married Lee in 1877, had grown up with the four Earll sisters, the daughters of Dr. Robert W. and Angeline Lawton Earll.

A.E. and Dora Earll began a correspondence courtship in the spring of 1881, followed by a brief June date in Milwaukee. Formal engagement quickly led to plans for an early wedding, January 1882 to be exact. Alas, Reynolds' business interests intervened. A.E. and Dora married a year later in Columbus, Wisconsin, on April 25, 1883. After a brief visit to Chicago, the newlyweds "removed" to Lake City to look after the mercantile store. For reasons easily imagined, Dora left remote, frontier, and high altitude Lake City which was often fatal to newborns in favor of hometown Columbus to deliver their only child, Anna Earll Reynolds, on January 26, 1884. Soon thereafter, mother and daughter reunited with A.E., not in Lake City but in Denver, where they spent the remainder of their thirty-three year union. Albert married at age forty-three; Dora was thirty-one. According to biographer Scamehorn, less due to their age difference than to their natures, their worldviews were indeed worlds apart.

A.E.'s optimism sharply contrasted with Dora's pessimism. Unlimited faith in his own judgment was seldom tempered by reasonable caution. In mines, corporate stocks, and silver futures he was willing to gamble to the limit of his resources. Of an opposite view, Dora wanted certainty, security, and safety. Gambling in any form, even if called business enterprise, was fraught with extreme danger. She could not enjoy her husband's successes because of her preoccupation with the possibility of failure. For this reason she was content to know little, if anything at all, about his entrepreneurial ventures and pursued interests of her own outside of the Reynolds household.[21]

Worldviews aside, Dora appreciated luxury when she saw it. In 1913 A.E. rented a mansion at 1555 Sherman Street from mine and smelter magnate Simon Guggenheim, and subsequently agreed to purchase it in their daughter's name for the sum of $25,000. Sadly, by 1913 his financial problems were beginning to overwhelm him . He could only pay $5,000. Guggenheim did not need the money, and apparently was a patient man. In the course of settling Reynolds' estate years later, son-in-law Bradish P. Morse completed the purchase.

But financial problems notwithstanding, A.E. Reynolds was a fighter. He had faced hard times often and had usually prevailed. Nor should the importance of his successful innovations at the Revenue Tunnel, his reliance on the devotion of the men who had served him well in the past, and the prevailing optimism characterizing the mining industry at large, be underestimated. The early years of the twentieth century were not kind to Reynolds and mining interests in general, but he could shrug all that off as temporary setbacks. More representative of a life lived well were the 1880s and mining ventures that made him a millionaire—when a million dollars was a lot of money—before age fifty. Accustomed and pleased to learn from others, not every good idea had to be his own. His Revenue Tunnel and innovative development of his Virginius Mine that made him and his partners rich men, patterned after precedents set by Adolph Sutro, testified to this feature of his character.

Beginning in 1882, Hubbell W. Reed in close consultation (of course) with Reynolds, managed the Virginius and Revenue Tunnel projects for twenty years. Reed, blessed not with formal education but by hard-won experience, was just the sort of "engineer" Reynolds respected. They were alike in many ways. Self-taught himself, Reynolds easily grasped the most technical and scientific concepts of his day in large part because he was hands-on and humble enough to listen to others who were hands-on, too. Reynolds could stand his ground with the best geologists and engineers the San Juans had to offer. Hubble Reed was just such an engineer, and men like Reed tended to respect owners like Reynolds who were hands-on, too.

Nor did Reynolds achieve his kingly millionaire status by worrisome thoughts that any investment opportunity he deemed worthy could be "a last best chance." Only hindsight led to that conclusion, hindsight of others, not him. Moreover, contrary to logic and common sense, a" last chance" could knock more than once. In Reynolds case, it knocked twice at the Vermont/Ocean Wave, once falsely with his Revenue Tunnel money that would run out, again for real with someone else's money. In fact, "last chance" was so much a cultural norm that it showed up everywhere whether real or anyone believed it or not.

Last Chance. Nothing like a sense of urgency to promote goods and services, or a last chance for a drink. Sometimes it could be prophetic. The owner pictured in front of this business was killed in a gunfight a few years later. (*Courtesy of the* Lake City Silver World.)

In the final analysis, A.E. Reynolds' understanding of geology and mine engineering accounted for much of his success. It was cobbled together not just from experience—his own and others like Adolph Sutro and a handful of superintendents like Hubbell Reed—but also from the works of G. Thomas Ingham and Ovando Hollister. This foundation, coupled with his careful attention to Henson Canyon details, helps explain Reynolds' infatuation with the Vermont and Ocean Wave lodes, and his conviction that great treasure awaited him there if he was persistent. His business acumen punctuated with a reputation for rarely losing even small fortunes, and underpinned with other people's money, also was a shaper and finisher of his faith in these properties. More a factor still, he was fixated on the Vermont and Ocean Wave lodes—obsessed, really—in part due to chips left on the table dating back to his earliest Lake City ventures and perceived mistreatment. Mine and mercantile failures aside, he had a score to settle with the haughty city and county mucky-mucks that scorned his innovations, refused to pay his invoices, and called in his loans. He would show them a thing or two and doing so with the Vermont and Ocean Wave, both with checkered pasts, would sweeten his revenge. He would pull the proverbial rabbit out of one of their own cock-eyed hats. He would settle old scores by playing his haulage tunnel card, his proverbial "ace-in-the-hole."

The Ocean Wave showed great promise and even produced respectable quantities of silver ore over its two-decade existence, but there were red-flags. In addition to recurring, lengthy idle periods (that could be explained by typical ownership disputes), poor engineering of the underground workings and its burro-dependent location were concerning. Reynolds was not adverse to risk, but neither did he make his millions speculating foolishly. Here especially his grasp of circumstances served him well.

Likewise, the Vermont had more than its fair share of glory days and idle seasons. Stoping in extensive tunnels on multiple levels produced most of the early returns, but was the mine depleted as a consequence? Did the owners/operators extract far more pay-dirt than they reported? The volume of mine waste dumped from the portals suggested this was the case. More importantly, were there greater or lesser reserves at greater depths? And, like the Ocean Wave, getting ore from the Vermont portal to the county wagon road a half-mile down the mountain required hoisting it to the surface, loading it into sacks, and trailing it on burros, lovable creatures for the most part but an expensive and inefficient choice for transporting heavy sacks of ore. Could a haulage tunnel like the Sutro and Revenue tunnels nullify this cost?

Reynolds opted for cautious investment. He purchased the Ocean Wave, leased the Vermont with an option to purchase, and commissioned a haulage tunnel that would retire the burros. Patterned after his Revenue Tunnel, the project also could have been pursued with the writings of G. Thomas Ingham in mind. Ingham's analysis of the characteristics of paydirt and where to find it was impressive, perhaps advanced for their time, albeit not necessarily correct by later standards and not all that clear. Ingham never set foot in the Vermont or Ocean Wave, but comparing his work to the progress reports of Reynolds' miners could have led one to think so. If A.E. compared his writings to his miner's reports, he would have been encouraged.

In fact, if Reynolds and Ingham had met, they would have become the best of friends. Far from a schooled geologist, Ingham was a self-taught U.S. Deputy Mineral Surveyor in the 1880s. Like Reynolds, he was gifted with a sharp mind and practical eye for mine conditions likely to produce valuable minerals. Without reference to any basis for their judgments, Reynolds and Ingham were on the same page when it came to what mining claim was worth further investment, which veins should be developed, and which veins would surely pinch out. Reynolds never shared his thoughts on the matter. Ingham thankfully did. In a curious way we can see Reynolds' vision for his Vermont/Ocean Wave project through Ingham's eyes. Ingham's view of mineralization supported Reynolds' belief that Vermont and Ocean Wave veins ran deep, and the deeper they ran, the richer their ores would be. Ingham wrote:

> *Of the origin of minerals, authors disagree, but a theory very commonly accepted is, that their origin in the form of veins of ore may be considered as the result of infiltration from the surface to which class many of the iron and copper ores belong, or that the deposits have been formed in the bottom of the sea, as those of the coal measures, or that the minerals have been injected from below, raised by the power of internal heat, to which class the gold and silver ores belong.*[22]

Whether the extent science mattered or was even considered among the mining class of Reynolds' day, the schools of thought available to them can be summarized with an unanswerable question: "Upon discovering a promising vein of silver-bearing ores, have the richest deposits eroded away from above, or do they lay at greater depths?" Thus, a major challenge for miners, mining "engineers," and men with money being asked to finance mine development was judging what to make of the vein to be worked. One common variety of mineral vein was a wedge that decreased with depth. Another variety was spheroidal with "masses or pockets." A third variety was a wedge that increased with depth. Poor judgment, either abandoning treasure ahead or plunging farther into the depths and debt, spelled the difference between a profitable mine and bankruptcy. Ingham explained:

> *These wedges, described as increasing with depth, are termed by miners, in gold and silver regions, as true fissure veins, and a genuine true fissure vein has never been found to become exhausted as depth is attained, though it is sometimes "pinched" or narrowed, with horses or otherwise to a very small streak of ore, yet farther down it usually widens out again to its usual thickness. (When a fissure is formed at the plane of least resistance, that is, at the point of contact between two rocks, large masses of country rock from the hanging wall falling into the fissure form what was called "horses". Horses keep the fissure open.)*
>
> *Hence it is where true fissure veins are discovered, the only question of successful mining is, in regard to the richness of the ore, such veins having never been known to give out entirely. From the foregoing it will appear that gold and silver are usually found in regions where the granite or primary rocks have been pushed up to the surface, from great depths below by volcanic action, and are the prevailing country rock of the section in which these metals are found, the secondary or tertiary strata not abounding, this having been displaced or swept away by the elements which exposed the granite and older formation.*[23]

Well, Henson Canyon is clearly blessed with millions of years of volcanic activity. The canyon also has been ground away by millions of years of glaciers and erosion. Given an opportunity to solve the mystery, he compounds it:

> *It will, therefore, appear that it is nearly useless to look for gold or silver ore, or rich auriferous gravel deposits, in sections where there are no primary rocks to be found; nor is it to be supposed that, because these rocks do abound, that gold can be discovered. Indeed, such rocks are abundant in some localities where no valuable metal has been discovered. It is safe to say that it will hardly pay the prospector to search for auriferous or argentiferous veins in other than the granite or metamorphic rocks and the older limestone and other formations which belong to the primary class. There may be exceptions to this rule, of course, but only a practical geologist could determine where the exception exists...*[24]

How clear is that? Can you hear the old gentleman chuckling?

Ingham also probably chuckled as he worked at balancing his assessment of the significance of quartz veins, most often the first signal a mountain flashed to the observant seeker that treasure was close at-hand. Quartz often was the surface thread on which a prospector staked his claim.

As before stated, quartz veins, as found in the rocks, vary greatly in the richness and quality of the ores they contain, and also in the ease or difficulty with which the metal can be extracted from the ore. The same is true in regard to the size and thickness and general formation of veins of ore. Sometimes a vein is discovered of but a few inches in thickness, and again another will be of many feet. Frequently their length is limited only by the length of the mountain on which they are found, and sometimes they are only a few rods in length. In regard to the depth which they may extend into the earth, there is the same variation. Sometimes the plane of the vein is but a few degrees from level, and frequently it is nearly vertical. Sometimes they are exhausted of ore, but a few feet in depth from the surface; but often they extend down seemingly to the center of the earth, and are never exhausted, their production being only limited by the expense of working mines at great depth, and the cost of machinery for draining the mine or pumping out the water. [25]

So what was a prudent man with money or a hungry man in need of work to do? In the case of the Vermont and Ocean Wave, prospects looked favorable, but not certain. All geological criteria for rich veins at depth were met, including the possibility that all the geological criteria for rich veins pinching out were also met. Of course there were historic production reports, but could the past predict the future? Were the Vermont and Ocean Wave "played out" or a prize? Were the wedges pointing up or down? Did the wedges extend to the center of the earth or were they scarcely present near the surface, scoured off over time, at that? Did the vein run from Lake City to Capital City? Did it run east to the Ocean Wave and no farther? And about those production reports, were they boasts or understated to deceive the tax man. Reynolds believed he knew how to find out, what to look for along the way, and how to profit or cut his losses from what he learned. A. E. was not afraid to put money down, including someone else's money entrusted to his honest care. Not exactly a gambler, he was a speculator.

Nor was he a scam artist. In an age when ruthless robber barons reigned, stock fraud fleeced the unsuspecting, and "wild-cat mines" and tunnel schemes were commonplace, Reynolds scammed no one. His stockholders saw their investments rise and fall at the whim of geology and silver prices, but not at the whim of A.E. They understood that his mines and tunnel projects were consistent with science and circumstances as understood at the time, but also undeniably reliant on risky, innovative technology and governed by informed but imperfect judgment. In contrast to extravagant claims of other promoters, some Reynolds' projects did underperform, but rarely did they disappoint. When they did, he paid his debts and boldly invited his shareholders to join him in other ventures. Many did.

At times Reynolds was a very wealthy man, so too those who partnered with him, but not always. Even when wealthy, his notion of wealth was operational mining properties, not cash-in-hand. As a result, wealthy or not, he lived hand-to-mouth. Revenues from profitable mines paid the monthly expenses of developing other mines. When his reservoir of cash and especially credit ran low, this business model did not work well. Driving the Reynolds Tunnel fell into this latter category. He routinely was forced to delay paying his miners until revenues from other properties came in. When cashflow was tight or nonexistent, he made do with partial payments allocated among many properties. Unable to square accounts on all of his projects at the same time, some disgruntled employees laid down their tools, some continued to work fully expecting to be paid "soon." When "soon" did not arrive soon enough, Reynolds turned to lessors willing to take a stake in lieu of wages. While no one accused A.E. of unscrupulous behavior throughout these difficult times, there was plenty of whining.

In Reynolds' day capital came in a few familiar packages all of which could be manipulated to the detriment of the naïve investor. Sometimes manipulation was in the hands of owners, sometimes in the hands of the workforce. Like two scorpions circling in a jar, owners and miners kept a watchful eye on each other. This was the world Reynolds circumnavigated for decades, the world in which he earned his crown. He rarely got stung, he never stung others. G. Thomas Ingham summarized the matter this way:

> "Gold and silver mining being a business which requires a large expenditure of money and heavy investments of capital, often for a considerable length of time before returns or profits can be expected, it very naturally happened that the operation of mines by means of stock companies and large corporations became the favorite method among capitalists, as the risk is very great for private enterprise. Undoubtably the organization of stock companies, when properly officered and honestly managed, is the proper method of operating mines. And there is no question, but that the bona fide, actual sale or purchase of mining stock, carried on with honest intent, is as legitimate a business as any other..." On the other hand, "there is a large class of operators in mines who care nothing whatever for the profits that may accrue to them from legitimate mining, or the production and profits from ore extracted from the mine or mines which they may control. Such is too slow a method of accumulation for them; they seek only the profits which may come from their manipulation

of the prices of the stocks they own, and the rise and fall of the market for the shares of the mines which they control." [26]

Common to the dishonest owner was the practice of nursing share values skyward by paying large dividends frequently, then secretly selling their shares. When the ability to pay dividends ceased, usually because new sources of investment dried up, and share values plummeted, they lost little whereas the unsuspecting investor lost everything. The ability to pay large dividends was usually a combination "Ponzi scheme"—a term yet to be coined but a practice all too common—and exploitation of ore in sight instead of forward-looking development in anticipation of ore bodies yet to be uncovered. [27] Often this practice yielded large profits immediately at the expense of an owner's ability to extract paydirt safely or efficiently over a longer period of time. When the owner or lessor had unethical or short-term objectives, the long-term value of the mine suffered. Having witnessed this practice often, Reynolds drove hard bargains on leases and enforced them. The consequence was often a broken lease and an idle mine, albeit a mine vacated in workable condition ready for the next lessor.

Ingham warnings regarding "wild-cat mines" and barren tunnels could have been especially relevant to the San Juans given the region's volcanic history. Its abundance of eruptions could have supported an equal abundance of fraudulent behavior, but they were rare. Nevertheless, wildcats and barren tunnels were jokers in the investors deck that Reynolds chose to address head-on. He did not promise what he knew did not exist or that he had no intention of pursuing. In the case of the Vermont and Ocean Wave, he did not even look to New York, Chicago or Kansas City for investors. When he ran short of his own funds, he raised capital by selling shares to friends, relatives, and the miners and superintendents that trusted him and he trusted to work the mine responsibly. Later, when health issues forced him to give up active management of his holdings, he leased properties, usually to locals who had first-hand knowledge of the project

Innocent-Looking Enough. Charles Ponzi, Italian immigrant and Boston businessman, personified the ease of swindling money from the naïve and/or greedy, mining industry practices that far and away pre-dated his 1920s rise to fame. *(Wikipedia)*

and faith in its prospects. Often these miner/entrepreneurs worked for a percentage of revenues rather than daily wages.

As for barren tunnel scams—there was a greater risk of these—Reynolds' decades-long reputation for fair dealing shielded him from such charges. His Revenue Tunnel testified to his integrity as much as to his ingenuity. Less so for his Henson Canyon tunnel, still it too was never deemed a fraud. Despite its troubles from time to time, time and again its treasure clues fueled investor dreams. Ingham described what actual tunnel fraud looked like.

Another species of "feline" is in the well-advertised shares of tunnels to pierce a "well-known mineral belt." A tunnel is started in some mining

WILDCAT MINES
G. Thomas Ingham

An advertisement appears in all the mining journals, and mercantile newspapers and others, giving a glowing account of the rich assays from the mine or mines in question, describing it as in close proximity to some well-known, valuable mine, or as upon some "great mineral belt," or as an extension of some valuable lode. A prospectus is issued and sent out, giving the graphic description of some professed mining engineer and expert, who has examined the property, and who, although his name is unknown to the public, and far from familiar, finds "millions in sight" in the lode. The capital stock is one million dollars, divided into one hundred thousand shares of ten dollars each (which is a very common way of capitalizing mines). "It is expected," the circular reads, "that the stock will speedily advance to par as soon as the mill is completed and begins to crush ore; but in order to build a mill and further develop the mine, twenty-five thousand shares will be disposed of at the low price of two dollars per share; and when these are disposed of the price will be advanced to three dollars per share, when twenty-five thousand shares more will be offered." The innocent investor pays his money and receives some finely-lithographed certificates of stock, duly signed by the officers of the company.

A few months pass away and nothing is heard from the mine. Finally the investor writes to the secretary of the company for information, and is told that "sufficient stock" not having been sold to erect a mill, work is not progressing at the mine. "But as soon as the mill is erected," dividends will soon be forthcoming. A few months more elapse, in which nothing is heard from the mine, when the investor writes to some reliable mining journal, and is told that the mine is a "Wild-Cat;" that there is such a hole in the ground in some mining region; but there is nothing in it, and that the officers are unknown and irresponsible persons; that his stock is worthless; the officers having pocketed the money. [28]

region, in which the mines are well known to the public; such as the Black Hills, Nevada, or the San Juans region, Colorado; and it is stocked and the shares offered for sale. The tunnel is advertised as sure to pierce a mineral vein "well known to exist as a continuation" of some valuable lode, at a distance in and accordingly a few thousand shares are disposed of, the money expended in driving the tunnel and in paying the salaries of officers. No mineral is found, and the stock becomes worthless. Moral: "There is no safety in investing in a tunnel or mine in which there exists no paying mineral when the investment is made." [29]

On a superficial level Reynolds' Virginius Mine and associated Revenue Tunnel, more so Reynolds' Vermont/Ocean Wave Tunnel, fit Ingham's profiles. Upon closer examination neither do. Unlike barren-tunnel schemes, the goal of both projects was clearly stated: drainage, haulage, and ventilation, not silver or gold. Moreover, the costs of ownership of both projects were predominantly on Reynolds' account, and management of the tunnels and mines was clearly in the hands of Reynolds and his hand-picked surrogates. In the case of the Virginius and Revenue Tunnel, evidence of good faith was validated with every dividend check and added up to millions of dollars paid out regularly for nearly two decades. In the case of the Vermont/Ocean Wave Tunnel, dividends were nonexistent, but clues to the mine's treasure were honestly reported. To this end, funds were devoured by miners' lengthening underground workings, not scam artists laughing all the way to their banks. There was no mistaking that the Vermont/Ocean Wave Tunnel had the characteristics of the treasure hunt that it was. There was no mistaking the thrill of moving more dirt for the thrill of unearthing treasure. There was no mistaking the thrill of the recurring vote of confidence from the successful recruitment of still more investors.

Notes—Chapter Eight: Dirt

[1] Service, Robert, *The Best of Robert Service*, pg. 206.

[2] "Sutro Tunnel", www.onlinenevada.org/articles/sutro-tunnel, pg.1; Wikipedia, "Sutro Tunnel." (Later examples included the Argo Tunnel at Idaho Springs, the Leadville and Yak Tunnels at Leadville, and the Roosevelt Tunnel in the Cripple Creek District, and of course Reynold's two tunnels above Ouray and Lake City.)

[3] Ibid.

[4] Scamehorn, Lee, *Albert Eugene Reynolds, Colorado's Mining King*, pgs. 115-116 (Lee Scamehorn's comprehensive biography of A.E. Reynolds is unmatched in its research and presentation of facts and circumstances surrounding one of Colorado's pioneering giants. Of particular excellence is his treatment of the complicated partnership and financial aspects of Reynolds mining properties that explain in great detail his legal problems and his great debt. The History Colorado library is the custodian of the "Reynolds Collection" and source of an impressive volume of original documents. The "Reynolds Collection" and Lee Scamehorn's scholarship are heavily relied upon in the pages that follow. How could it be otherwise? There are no comparable alternatives.)

[5] Ibid., pgs. 114-116.

[6] Smith, P. David, *Mountains of Silver*, pgs. 189-197.

[7] Scamehorn, pgs. 87-88.

[8] Ibid., pgs. 88-89.

[9] Ibid., pgs. 89-90.

[10] Ibid., pgs. 90-91.

[11] Ibid., pg. 180; *Denver Times*, August 3, 1900. (Hydroelectric works on the Lake Fork were never the issue. Over the years there were a number of them, the most ambitious at Crooke Falls. The issue was raising the level of Lake San Cristobal.)

[12] Scamehorn, pg. 7.

[13] Ibid., pg. 5.

[14] Ibid., pgs. 5-7.

[15] Ibid., pg. 9.

[16] Ibid., pgs. 9-11.

[17] (The downward spiral of silver prices that began in 1883 did not stabilize until World War I and then not for long. At the end of 1883 the average market value of silver was $1.10 per ounce. At the end of 1893, in the shadow of a national financial panic and the repeal of the Sherman Silver Purchase Act, the average market value was $0.69 an ounce. Throughout successive decades prices cycled between $0.70 and $0.50 an ounce.)

[18] Scamehorn, pgs. 19-20 (Also see: Cripple Creek (Colorado) Citizen, June 20, 1898.)

[19] Ibid., pg. 20.

[20] Ibid., pg. 22.

[21] Ibid., pgs. 24-27.

[22] Ingham, G. Thomas, *Digging Gold Among the Rockies*, pgs. 105-106.

[23] Ibid. ("Had it not been for the fact of these masses falling into the fissure, it would in all probability have closed up again. But in this manner there was left an open channel down to an indefinite depth, which gradually became filled, probably by means of thermal agencies, or possibly by volatilization, according to the different theories which scientific men accept." Pg. 115.)

[24] Ibid.

[25] Ibid., pgs. 108-109.

[26] Ibid., pg. 384.

[27] (Charles Ponzi was a depression-era fraudster so successful that his scheme, oft repeated before and after he took it to new heights, became synonymous with his name. A Ponzi scheme attracted new investment by promising extraordinary, literally overnight, returns. It thrived on greed that overrode reason. Greed was cultivated by actually paying extraordinary returns to the early investors. Seeing this, early investors elected to keep their money invested to generate even greater returns, and new investors were attracted. It was their funds that was used to pay dividends if ever asked to do so. The fraud was revealed when new investments were insufficient to cover requested withdrawals, an inevitable outcome at some point since there was no actual investment in products or services to generate profits, a fact that eventually dawned on investors.)

[28] Ingham, pgs. 391-392.

[29] Ibid., pg. 393. (Other stock-manipulation schemes also were prevalent, as was "salting" a tunnel or mine or hiring a dishonest engineer to produce a report that inflated or flatly misrepresented the ore potential of a property.)

CHAPTER 9

Pig-in-a-Poke

She was thinner than a bed-post

Taller than a rail;

As yellow as a pumpkin,

And slower than a snail.

She lived in Indiana,

Had just come out of school;

She was hell on a piano,

But she couldn't ride a mule.

— Anon —

Our observant Lake City *Silver World* editor was on to something when he published this verse, where he found it he does not say. For the less discerning among his subscribers, he explained his revelation this way:

If [this] beautiful verse correctly describes the 'points' of its heroine we notify her that she won't do for San Juans. She fails in an essential feature, as is evident in the last line.[1]

Given some thought, this humorous ditty did say a great deal about the frontier in a few words. A.E. Reynolds would have understood. He supported with large sums of money the culture and fine arts Denver offered. His wife and daughter were musicians. At the same time, the frontier required getting your hands dirty learning new skills. It required strength of character only borne out of hardship. He had an abundance of it. He was fully capable of visiting his mining properties by whatever means was necessary regardless of the season—snowshoes if required—or his age, to see that work progressed even under the harshest of circumstances. He also was fully capable of avoiding the pitfalls of "pigs in a poke." He was willing to invest in the "uncertain" but not the "unknown." Development of his Vermont/Ocean Wave lodes was a Henson Canyon treasure hunt that seemed to contradict this practice, making its tale all the more intriguing.

In simple terms, A.E. was a student of geology when it came to Henson Canyon, well-characterized by contemporary standards but coquettish just the same. He was a student of human behavior when it came to fickle newspaper editors and speculators. And he was a student of history when it came to investing in mining properties risky by definition. He knew a buyer's market when he saw one—he knew buyer's remorse when he misjudged it. London capitalists, also fully capable of riding mules, were no different.

Acquiring rights to the Vermont and Ocean Wave, two troubled and complex properties, was carefully calculated, carefully timed, and carefully executed by British capitalists long before A.E. Reynolds did the same. Interestingly, Reynolds and the British came to different conclusions in the 1880s about the worth of Henson Canyon mines, notably the Vermont and Ocean Wave. British capital flowed into the San Juans, into Henson Canyon. Reynolds' capital also flowed into the San Juans, but not Henson Canyon. Reynolds invested in the Ouray and Red Mountain district to the west, into the Virginius and its Revenue Tunnel, and into the Commodore Mine above Creede to the south. As matters eventually developed, the British lost their investment and moved on. Reynolds made his millions. A decade later when his interests returned to Henson Canyon, he saw a buyers' market and a chance to make millions more, ironically where the British had failed.[2]

The *Silver World* editor was never shy about extolling San Juans mining attributes and what mattered most in the region. Even his frontier humor reflected cultural values and judgments that permeated every aspect of daily life including the relative merits of mules and piano players. The viability of Henson Canyon mines depended on mules and burros for half a century. Reynolds appreciated pianists, but his mines succeeded or failed on the backs of mules and burros, and more so on the availability of nearby railroads.

The Vermont and Ocean Wave vein was clearly visible on the surface even to the untrained eye, but the vein was difficult to reach. Where it straddled rugged El Paso Gulch, it tested the prospector and the miner with forbidding terrain, deadly avalanches, and most importantly the lack of a decent trail much less a wagon road. Lurking in the background were uncertain silver values, hunger and disease, insufficient capital, and until 1880 the threat of Ute attack. Those who would work the Vermont and the Ocean Wave broke much ground and were broken in turn. Despite what they considered natural inconveniences, prospects were good. In the process of coping, their character was forged as hard as the drill steel they hammered into the mountain.

Success was fleeting, forced retreats assured; but still they rallied and returned to the fight. The more driven among them needed no convincing that the mother-lode would show herself with the next round of charges, and many a daily wage was paid to test this belief. Year after year more tunnels and shafts were drilled and blasted—all by hand—and mucked out around tempting mineral veins.

Sadly, between pockets of paying ore teasing still more just ahead, great expanses of worthless dirt would eventually end the quest. But only for a time.

The Vermont/Ocean Wave vein breached the El Paso Gulch's surface near the top of a precipitous three hundred foot bluff and a steep talus slope that fell away to El Paso Creek raging below. It was 10,100 feet above sea level, 700 feet above Henson Creek, 500 feet above the rough but passable county wagon road. From there an even rougher road built in 1884, routinely washed out by spring rains or winter avalanches, never much more than a burro trail, led from the base of the talus slope to the county road. Leading to Lake City and the eventual rail-head, this wagon road also washed out regularly. The 1880s were the Vermont's best decade despite it all. The Ocean Wave story was much the same. For remote mines wholly dependent on burros, mules, and hand tools, they produced and shipped enough silver ore to interest investors as far away as Kansas City, New York and London. Paydirt and funds surfaced, paydirt and funds pinched out, all under the watchful eye of A.E. Reynolds. Being the patient contrarian that he was, where others saw only dirt, he saw clues leading him to believe that where there were clues, there eventually would be treasure.

In the age when the sun never set on the British Empire, a rumored treasure in the San Juans did not escape the notice of British capitalists. Mining camp newspapers, birthing an emerging class of journalists, did more to attract these investors than any assay report could ever be expected to achieve. Every camp with any prospect of surviving more than a season needed two allies, rail service and at least one newspaper. Often rail service could wait, a newspaper editor afflicted with a healthy dose of "boosterism" could not. Local sheets and big city tabloids boasted of the most unlikely successes and downplayed the most damaging setbacks. They reported incredible accounts of rich veins, some of which were actually true.

Nor could Denver editors resist reporting the tales. Nor could the British resist following the leads. Buckling under the weight of their colonial wealth, commoners, royalty, and parliamentarians made their way to the San Juans, and to the Vermont and Ocean Wave.

(Denver Republican, June 10, 1882.) There arrived in Gunnison by special train from Denver, early yesterday morning, a number of gentlemen who are likely to be conspicuous and important factors in the development of the mineral resources of Western Colorado. The party consisted chiefly of Robert Tennant, member of the British Parliament, and Vice-President of the Mining and Smelting Company of London, England; Charles Argles, the solicitor of the company; Mr. Boyd, Resident Director of the Duke of Manchester's company, which has recently purchased 15,000,000 acres of land of the Canadian Pacific Railroad; a son of Mr. Tennant; Mr. Green, and Lieutenant-Governor Dorsheimer, of New York. The party reached Gunnison

at 6 o'clock in the morning, and after breakfasting at the Tabor House, took their special car to Kezar, at the end of the track, where they were met by three carriages from Doyle's stables at this place, and started at once for Lake City.

Owing to their early arrival and quick departure no opportunity was given to the people of Gunnison to welcome them, or to extend any of the courtesies which are so gladly and freely extended by the people of the West to all foreign visitors.

The Mining and Smelting Company of London, England, is an organization with a paid up capital of $1,500,000, with $200,000 reserved as a working capital, and with promises of more if needed. Its President is Professor Theodore Rogers, Member of Parliament, and its Vice President is Hon. Robert Tennant, Managing Director of the Great Northern Railroad of England and Scotland. Its Board of Directors embrace such men as Balfour, Member of Parliament, Gilman Ewing, the great Indian merchant; Dixon, the engineer who brought the Thames embankment obelisk from Egypt; Maynard, of the Argyle Manufacturing company, and Mr. Grenfell, a brother of the President of the Bank of England.

This company has recently purchased the group of about fifteen mines owned by the Crooks, of Lake City, and their trip to Lake City has undoubtedly been undertaken to arrange for the development of this property and for the construction of complete reduction works.

Not lost on Gunnison's City Fathers was the likelihood that such an impressive delegation of British capitalists would motivate the Denver & Rio Grande Railroad to complete their branch line to Lake City. If this was a troubling thought—somehow a loss of Gunnison business—the City Fathers had little to worry about. Not even the Queen of England could accomplish such a feat. Little did it matter. Just the prospect of large sources of capital, British or otherwise, was enough to spur the opening of Lake City regional mines. The Vermont was located (relocated actually) March 1883 on what turned out to be a five-foot wide quartz fissure containing galena, iron, copper pyrites and native silver with an initial mill run of 238 oz. of silver per ton. The *Lake City Mining Register* was all over it.

(Mining Register, July 31, 1883.) Two men are at work on the claim, and at present have several tons of high-grade ore on the dump. It is the intention of the owners to commence shipping ore this week. Assays recently made gave $1,500, $700, etc., to the ton, with 28 percent copper. About two weeks ago, the body of mineral was opened up in the first level west of the gulch. Assays over $1,000 per ton. Last Friday, still another body of high grade ore, carrying gray copper, was exposed in the second level east of the gulch. This last strike consists of from four to six inches of gray copper, assaying over $1,000 per ton.

Throughout 1883 and 1884 enticing reports from the Vermont flowed as stoutly as Henson Creek during spring run-offs. Paying ore abounded and underground workings increased accordingly. Yes, local gray-beards predicted low-grade ores at best, but pockets of high-grade ore were not uncommon and of course argued on behalf of the exception being the rule. Who but the venerable *Rocky Mountain News* could be more certain.

(Rocky Mountain News, *December 29, 1883.) S. Smith, who is working the Vermont, took down $200 worth of that handsome gray cooper ore in two weeks – not bad wages. The ore is from the drift, eighty-two feet in and from a body heretofore hidden by the gouge and supposed to be a wall....The Rogers brothers, who have contracted to run the drift, are on hand and will make the rock fly under their sturdy blows and steady blasts.*

(Rocky Mountain News, *May 30, 1884.) The Vermont continues to improve. In the drift where the stoping is being done a block of ore is exposed of eleven tons (estimated) of galena gray copper and black sulphurets of silver. Recent assays show a valuation of from 65 to 1300 ounces of silver; with an average of 500 ounces out of six careful tests.*

Not to be outflanked by the *Rocky Mountain News*, bully of all competing mining camp journalists, on July 1, 1884, the *Lake City Silver World* mounted a counteroffensive with a slew of seasonal Vermont and Ocean Wave puff-pieces. "Puffs" aside, what better source of insights than first-hand accounts from the frontlines.

(Silver World, *July 1, 1884.) The example set by Beam and Smith in the case of the Vermont is a good one to follow, and the results achieved by them certainly ought to encourage others. Without money, but with plenty of pluck and will and with confidence in their property, they worked all last winter, first doing dead work to open the property, then in running levels, and in consequence took out and shipped on or about June 15th a car load of ore which netted them nearly enough to pay all costs of developing and of mining, shipping and treating the ore....There is 2 ½ tons first class sacked ore on the road near the mine and about four tons on the dump....Besides this, there must be a large amount of second class ore on the dumps. Figures do not lie, and the foregoing presents a proud exhibit for the Vermont and its owners. Who will be the next poor man to emulate the example?*

(Silver World, *November 15, 1884.) Beam Brothers & Smith signed bond and lease of the Vermont mine, Monday, to J.J. Silva, an old-timer in San Juans and now working properties in Marshall basin. Mr. S. was in* *the city and informed us that he would systematically develop the property, working eight men at the start and running levels both ways....He has ample means of his own, beside he is backed by an English company which has placed to his credit $30,000 for developing this one property. Buildings will be at once erected at the mine. E.E. Broad has been given the contract for building a wagon road from the Henson creek road up El Paso creek to the property.*

The El Paso Creek wagon road, short, narrow, and steep, was better than a burro trail, but a poor excuse for a road. More likely than not, it served more burro trains than wagons. Still, investments like roads and surface buildings were not undertaken frivolously. The Vermont had given up treasure; seemingly more was clearly at hand. A month later the *Silver World* editor was not so sure.

(Silver World, December 13, 1884.) Mr. T.J. McKenna, of Tin Cup, Gunnison County; superintendent of John J. Mastin's mining properties at that place, arrived here a week ago and will spend the present winter on the Ocean Wave mine, the controlling interest in which is owned by Mr. Mastin. The property has long been idle, involved in legal and other complications arising from the failure of the Mastins in the banking business in Kansas City, in 1879. We understand that Mr. McKenna will merely fix up the mine, clear the levels and shafts of the accumulated debris, re-timber where necessary and then exploit the mine with a view to ultimate operations....The mine is certainly one of the richest and best in San Juans, and systematically developed and worked would prove a large and paying producer.

(Silver World, December 27, 1884.) Greatly to the surprise and disappointment of everybody, particularly the employees, the Vermont closed down this week. The reason given is that the heavy snow caught the lessees unprepared – timber for the mine and tramway not being on the ground and but little cut; the new road being rendered impassible for teams for hauling up supplies or hauling ore down; and the development already done on the west side having opened up such a body of ore ready for stoping that to continue was unnecessary, while the result of the investigation of the shaft on the east side failed to disclose any ore body which would warrant development there.... Looks to us as if the mine is in a good shape to sell and that this may account for the shutting down. [Well, all this sounded reasonable and not all that discouraging. No doubt more skeptical observers saw matters differently.]

Scooped but far too aloof to be shamed, the *Rocky Mountain News* was quick to pick up the storyline. No doubt A.E. Reynolds took note as well. Notice the probably well-founded presumption that "Eastern readers" also were paying attention.

(Rocky Mountain News, December 30, 1884.) The Vermont shut down Tuesday night for some reason known only to Manager Silvia, for the reason set forth is incompatible with business judgment....We do not mean to dictate to Mr. Silvia, but the excuse for discontinuing work does not harmonize with $60,000 worth of ore in sight – some calculate $80,000. If several black eyes had not already been administered to the county the past year we would probably pass this suspension by without a word; but we would like our Eastern readers who have been watching development on the Vermont to understand that the mine is not a failure, and that it could have been worked all winter and would have paid its bond before spring as easily as falling off a log. Mr. Silvia's stated reasons for suspending are that he did not get a good wagon-road completed in time, nor his ore chute finished, and there is now too much snow in the gulch to do that kind of work.

The year 1885 birthed more ominous developments for Lake City and Henson Canyon. In March news spread that A.E. Reynolds was closing his Lake City mercantile business. Nothing was said about his mine interests. The Ocean Wave was sold for debt, but no one bet that would be the last of it. J.J. Silvia came over from Telluride to arrange for resuming work on the Vermont, but was caught up in a blizzard. He scurried home until the snow was more manageable up El Paso Creek. According to the Silver World, he was encouraged when he returned. The mine showed better than ever, and the dumps, stopes, and chutes were full of ore ready for sacking.[3]

(Silver World, June 6, 1885.) The Vermont has jumped to the front as one of the great bonanzas of the country – one of the heaviest and richest producers in the State.... The purchase price of the mine is already in sight; every dump, bin and available storage place on, in and about the mine is full of ore and the work of sorting, dressing and shipping gives the mine a very gratifying appearance.... Mr. Herbert Strickland, sent out from London by the English gentlemen who are negotiating for the mine to examine and report upon the property, returned here Tuesday evening accompanied by Wm. Weston, of Ouray, one of the promoters of the sale, J.J. Silvia, the bonder and lessee, and D.C. Hartwell, agent of the Pueblo S.&R. Co. The latter came to examine the ore with a view to its purchase for the company he represents.... Mr. Strickland is one of the best read men in his profession – a graduate of the Royal School of Mines and of Freiberg, and has spent many years in the study of mineralogy, metallurgy, chemistry, etc., and is thoroughly up in his profession. (The Vermont might be a mine filled with more enigmas that treasures, but it would not be a pig-in-a-poke.)

The *Silver World* editor rang more than one bell with his June 6th proclamations. Referring to the Vermont as "one of the great bonanzas of the country" was boosterism at its best, yet there was verifiable evidence his claims could be true. Dropping Wm. Weston's name was a nice touch. He was almost legendary in the San Juans for his pluck, accomplishments, and integrity. J.J. Silva and D.C. Hartwell, an agent for a prominent reduction mill, lent further gravitas to the Vermont assessment team. And finally, mention of the world renowned Freiberg Royal School of Mines, delivered the knockout punch. Indeed, there was no need for a Paul Revere to alert locals that the British were serious about coming, and that the Vermont was a mine worth investing in. Our faithful editor was up to that task.

(Silver World, *June 27, 1885.) The reports from the Vermont continue to encourage, even increase, the enthusiasm first created. Extensive and rich ore bodies, piles of ore on the dumps and active operations, is the steady report.... The Honorable Arthur Loftus Tottenham, M.P., one of the syndicate negotiating for these properties, who had come from London upon a hasty trip to examine the mines, arrived here quite unexpectedly Saturday and remained a few days watching the development work, examining the property and awaiting the results of the sampling tests of a 27 ton lot, made Monday at the Argenta Falls sampling and concentrating works...*

Again, not to be scooped, the *Rocky Mountain News* ran with the June 27th *Silver World* lead. The *Silver World* counterpunched on August 15th. The *News* hit back October 15th with what looked to be a reprint from the *Silver World* and *Telluride News*.

Freiberg, ca 1850. Europe was far ahead of America when it came to earth sciences. Freiberg was established in 1765 to produce skilled miners and scientists. By the nineteenth-century it had earned worldwide acclaim even in the San Juans. (Wikipedia)

(Rocky Mountain News, July 1, 1885.) Lake City was honored this week by the presence of a live M.P., the Honorable Arthur Loftus Tottenham, a Tory, member of the House of Commons from County Leitrim, Ireland. He is a magnificent type of manhood, standing 6 feet 2 inches in his stockings and weighing 250 pounds. He was here to examine the Vermont mine, as one of the syndicate who are negotiating for it. L.P. Ward killed a mammoth mountain sheep Sunday afternoon, on the mountains above the Vermont mine. It had one of the finest heads we have seen — horns unusually large and finely shaped — which he presented to Hon. A.L. Tottenham, M.P., who had just come to inspect the Vermont. Mr. T. took it with him to Ouray to have his friend Weston mount it, with the view of taking it home to the old country.

(Silver World, August 15, 1885.) Few of our citizens realize the magnitude and importance of the recent deal on the Vermont. The syndicate which now owns it is possessed of immense capital and great experience in mining. It will, however, organize a stock company and enlist others in the operation of the property — in fact the organization is well on the way. Work will not, however, wait upon the completion of the organization, but the development of the mine will proceed under the direction of Mr. Strickland. Some idea of the magnitude of the operations planned may be gathered from the statement that $75,000 will be put up for development work, a shaft will be sunk 500 feet and levels will be run 500 feet at every 60, and connected — all this before any stoping is done. Sampling and concentration works will be erected at the mine in due time. Roads and buildings will soon be constructed and other work begun. The present force on the mine will, we understand, be continued pending the arrival of orders.

British Gravatas. Never mind the fact British elites were often portrayed as buffoons, nothing like an incredibly wealthy member of Parliament to lend credibility to a delegation of mine speculators touring prospects in the Lake City district. *(Wikipedia)*

The significance of these developments was not lost on A.E. Reynolds. Neither was the importance of paying attention to what came next. Some mines were obvious bonanzas that reliably delivered high volumes of rich ores from the git-go -- the more obvious, the higher the price. Some mines were more speculative, sleepers – the price might be correspondingly low, but the mine might never awaken. To Reynolds' way of thinking, neither proposition was attractive. If the Vermont had the makings of a bonanza, he was already too late to the party. If it was going to be a bust, better his British competitors learned that lesson instead of himself. If it was a sleeper that could be awakened, that was Reynolds' cup of tea. That was what he was expecting at the Vermont/Ocean Wave. That was what he was patient enough to wait to see.

What accounted for the Vermont's [and Ocean Wave's] checkered legacy and its longevity was no mystery to A.E. Reynolds, nor was he intimidated by what he knew. He knew a pig-in-a-poke when he saw one and he did not see one here. Better yet, where others saw depleted mines, he saw clues to treasure troves of high-grade ore yet to be unearthed. Better still, he appreciated the value of the vast infrastructure paid for my someone else's money—shafts hundreds of feet deep with hundreds of feet of drifts every sixty feet—that he could acquire free of charge. If doubts ever troubled his sleep, he could count on reports filed by diligent editors to bolster his confidence. Whenever there was a treasure hunt worth telling, our diligent editors did not disappoint.

> (Rocky Mountain News, *October 15, 1885.) Mr. Walter Beam, foreman of the Vermont, was in town last Tuesday looking for twenty-five more men. He will put them to work as soon as they can be secured. It is now a sure thing that the mine will be worked all winter with a force of from forty to fifty men. This begins to look like business, and we hope to see the Vermont mine working 200 men before long.*

Two hundred men working the Vermont seemed somewhat of a stretch, but with capital no longer a limitation, who could say? Apparently there was sufficient ore in sight to justify such a large workforce, and with experienced management it appeared the Vermont was positioned for long-term profitability. Mapping the underground workings two decades later revealed that indeed multiple levels and shafts had been constructed, but in 1885 for reasons not entirely clear operations were not assured. One likely complication, common among early mines, was title and survey errors that put ownership in question. Need we be reminded: other complications included accidents, avalanches, persistent shortages of burros (yes, burros), mules, and wagons, and of course the recurring low-grade ores that had to be sold into a recurring low-value silver market. This latter factor, an unpredictable global silver market with a nasty habit of trending downward and sticking there, probably accounted for most of the Vermont and Ocean Wave drama.

But a more troublesome factor soon surfaced. Internal management disagree-ments among men with boundless egos took their toll. Still, Reynolds watched and waited, but he was far from idle. He was preoccupied with growing his min-ing empire elsewhere in Colorado, notably in the nearby mountains to the west, notably at the Virginius and its Revenue Tunnel. As for his former home town, Henson Canyon, and El Paso Gulch, albeit with a suspicious eye, he mulled over local reporting, noted the loss of key personnel, and puzzled over the fact none of this seemed to diminish productivity. Could there be more to the Vermont not to mention the Ocean Wave than what met even his experienced eye?

(Rocky Mountain News, November 11, 1885.) William Weston, M.J. Silvia and Walter Beam have resigned from the management of the Vermont mine.

(Silver World, January 2, 1886.) The Ocean Wave, which is known to be an exceedingly rich mine, shipped out 60 tons of high grade ore. This mine can ship hundreds of tons. The Vermont is also a first-class mine (working a full shift of 30 men.) The ore shipment for the past year is only about 150 tons, but it can ship many times that amount. The ore shipped was all first-class. During the past three months the men working on the Vermont have been engaged in developing the mine. In fact, the last three months represent dead work almost exclusively.

Silver World interest in Vermont and Ocean Wave matters waned throughout late winter and spring of 1886. Reasons why are unclear. Perhaps it was due to the threat of avalanches. Perhaps work was suspended for any number of reasons. Perhaps work continued without any newsworthy milestones. Perhaps the editor was suffering from winter doldrums. Perhaps it took the new superintendent, Capt. Stockder, a few months to gain the confidence of the editor. Whatever the problem, the news blackout ended in late July 1886. On the 24th of that month the *Silver World* reported that the Vermont was working two shifts sinking a new shaft on the vein, and the boys were getting "some fine mineral" out of both the shaft and drift. Two months later there was more good news. The British were back on site.

(Silver World, October 2, 1886.) Mr. A.L. Tottenham and brother, lately arrived from England, and heavily engaged in mining enterprises in this country, spent Saturday, Sunday and Monday last in Lake City, being here for the purpose of examining the Vermont mine in which they are largely interested. They are greatly pleased with the new ore bodies, so much so that they have ordered an increase in the working force and numerous other im-provements about the mine. Capt. Stockder is to be congratulated on the strike

[what a coincidence] just at a time when our distinguished visitors could see it for themselves. [A week later there was even better news.]

(Silver World, October 9, 1886.) As announced in last week's issue, we now present a report of the recent rich strike on the Vermont, and which is still increasing now undoubtedly one of the richest strikes which have ever been made in Hinsdale County, and we are indeed pleased to see the owners rewarded for their energy and perseverance. Its chief value to the people of this county is the encouragement it will give to other mine owners to stay right with their claims, and pay no attention to croakers and grumblers....The last two tests which Cap. Stockder made on ore which was taken out last week, ran respectively 1565 and 1580 ounces of silver to the ton. For more than a year the company has worked the mine, running hundreds of feet in barren ground, not even striking a small pocket to relieve the monotony, or give them some encouragement....But about the middle of last August a change began in No. 3 tunnel, little streaks of ore appearing here and there through the quartz, increasing in number and size until the first of September, when a fine body of ore a foot wide was uncovered, and which has increased to eighteen inches, and is now maintaining that width. [When high-grade ore 'relieves the monotony' of low-grade ore at 1,560 and 1,580 oz. of silver to the ton, the mine is a candidate for 'bonanza' status.]

(Silver World, December 31, 1886.) In the beginning of September a fine and quite extensive lot of mineral was discovered about eighteen inches wide, but owing to the inaccessibility of the tunnel in winter, nothing is being done in it. In the spring, however, men will be put to work there to take out the large body of ore now in sight.

But work was not deferred, the hardships of winter and the Vermont's January 1887 avalanche notwithstanding. Oh, the deadly and destructive slide

what are other words for croaker?

grumbler, growler, mutterer, toad, sourpuss, frog, polliwog, doctor, medico, physician

Croakers and Grumblers. An irritable and complaining (and other unprintable synonyms) person. A commonly used term in nineteenth-century English-speaking lands. *(Thesaurus Plus)*

derailed progress long enough for funerals and eulogies, but within weeks men returned to the site. With respects duly paid, wages needed to be earned and investor expectations needed to be fulfilled. To the boys working underground, perhaps the greatest incentive was the thrill of finding abundant treasure among the muck following every shot. After all, the Vermont slide was not Henson canyon's first nor the worst, and no one believed it would be the last. Like so many other risks mining presented, San Juans avalanches were simply an occupational hazard only worth mentioning when fatalities occurred. The 1887 Vermont slide was no exception. The boys were eager to return to work, but were the investors eager to pay to rebuild?

(Silver World, February 5, 1887.) Cap. Stockder has a small force of men at work on the Vermont, and as soon as the elements will allow, a new bunkhouse will be erected in a safe position out of the way of snow slides, and the full complement of men put to work. A body of ore has been struck in the main shaft, and some rich mineral is being taken out....The Vermont has $5,000 worth of work done, and shows from ten to fifteen inches of high grade ore. The Ocean Wave has in the neighborhood of $10,000 worth of work done. It has always paid more than the cost of working when well-managed, and will continue to do so. It has about eighteen inches of high grade ore, and is worth $100 per ton.

(Silver World, May 7, 1887.) Quite an important and valuable strike has been made in the Vermont mine. Capt. Stockder, while prospecting the old workings in No. 3 level, found an old stope which had been abandoned by the former manager as worthless, and believing the indications justified, set men at work opening it up. The result is a fine body of ore has been developed, two men in the stope taking out as much ore as three can sort, and the ore body is steadily growing larger and improving in quality as well. Average 300 lb. lots of ore from the ore chute opened up last summer, which were sent to Denver in April, gave returns of $155 to $167 per ton. Manager Stockder will work 16 men in the stopes during the summer besides those employed in development ore sorting.

From a community perspective, the murderous slide had made local headlines through much of January, but by February it was just the latest tragedy in a world of tragedies. Respect had been paid to the dead and now it was proper to return to the business of making a mine. Life went on and work at the Vermont did, too. As for the Ocean Wave, matters were not as rosy. One could have thought an avalanche had struck there. Instead, burros were the problem, more accurately the lack of them. A new manager, Judge McKenna, was having trouble finding pack animals to get his ore down to the county wagon road. At the Vermont, the ore coming out of the stopes grew larger with every shot, but transporting it to waiting freight wagons suffered a similar fate. Given that Vermont shifts were exploiting a high-grade deposit, two feet wide in places, nearly solid gray copper by some accounts, with consistent assays of 1,000 to 1,500 ounces of silver per ton, imagine the frustration cultivated by of all things a shortage of burros.[4]

BONANZA OR BUST?

Is it any wonder that everyone but A.E. Reynolds witnessed a hung-jury when it came to categorizing the worth of the Vermont and Ocean Wave mines? Were they pigs-in-pokes, their true nature unseen, or profitable ores absent all together? Were they bonanzas in the rough or were they teases? Were they populated with clues ultimately leading to high-grade treasure, or were the clues simply remnants of depleted veins and chimneys? In hindsight we can see that the Vermont and Ocean Wave mines were among the most profitable mines Henson Canyon had to offer, and gave up clues suggesting massive reserves awaited further development, but neither produced to their fullest potential. Reynolds observed them at their best and at their worst. When he needed a bonanza mine the most, he put his money down on opening Vermont and Ocean Wave reserves. On balance, their best was yet to come.

But as usual, frustration was short-lived in the face of fresh clues, and the Vermont stopes did not disappoint when it came to rich and extensive deposits. If anyone doubted this they were welcome to view samples at the *Silver World* office, a repository of treasure second only to the offices of local assayers. Editor Mendenhall proudly declared, "We have some fine specimens showing the quality of the ore and the width of the streak." In fact, Vermont levels No. 2 and No. 3 were now connected by a winze (shaft) and plans were afoot to increase the workforce greatly. Our vigilant editor also reported that "eight new men were put to work last Monday," and that "Manager Stockder will give a contract for packing the ore from the mine to the road." The editor continued, another contract was required to freight the summer's production from the Henson Canyon road to the railhead in Sapinero (a long, rough way from Henson Canyon and a poor substitute for a railhead seven miles away in Lake City), with "magnificent bodies of rich gray copper" and fine streaks of ore literally full of wire and native silver remaining in No. 2 stope. [5]

In July 1887 the *Silver World* reported that ore chutes were being installed in Vermont stopes so ore could be loaded directly into cars without shoveling.

Left unsaid, presumably trammers wheeled the cars along the lowest or first level to its portal where the ore was sorted and sacked for a burro ride down to the wagon road. By all accounts, the ore in No. 1 and No. 2 stopes in the third level remained plentiful, "five sorters being not nearly able to sort the ore as fast as the miners take it down." No. 4 level, about forty ft. above No. 3 level, also opened a splendid vein of nearly solid gray copper. By the end of the month thirty-eight men were working the Vermont with more to be hired when "enough accommodations were available." Ore considered worth shipping to Sapinero totaled thirty-two tons. At the same time, Ocean Wave work was suspended due to lack of profitability. [6]

In August 1887 the first hints of changing seasons also foretold changes at the mine. Generally speaking, changing anything was seldom good news, but in the case of the Vermont its charmed fortunes were not exhausted. Dutifully the *Silver World* reported that Capt. Stockder had turned over Vermont site operations to Crit Hart for reasons unknown. Wise in all matters pertaining to mining, Crit's first change was hiring a woman cook. Seemingly a noneventful matter, in fact there was no better way to bolster morale than good food and lots of it. A woman in the camp also improved the caliber of conversation around the dinner table, not that there was much interest in talk in the first place. Crit was a big success and Stockder remained manager. The Vermont remained a big success, too, shipping twenty tons of ore, some of which was high-grade peacock, "pure gray copper." [7]

In September, the *Silver World* reported that the Vermont shipped another seven tons of ore, a good quality of bismuth with an assay of 42%, a high return of silver, and Stockder had been ordered by the owners to clear out the mine and prepare for winter work. Sounded promising. Manager Stockder "made haste" to prepare the Vermont. He also took advantage of the moment to commence sinking the long-awaited shaft that would descend along what was believed to be the principal high-value vein to great depth. He let a sizable contract for 300 cords of firewood and for mine timbers. New boarding and bunk houses near the mouth of El Paso gulch were pushed as fast as possible to completion. In the sincerest words our beloved *Silver World* editor could muster—remember his kind are boosters—he penned: "this is one mine which we can be reasonably sure will work a full complement of men this winter." As prophetic as those sentiments were taken to be, fulfillment was unlikely. On the other hand, the Vermont had earned a reputation for miraculous recoveries from repeated setbacks. It entered the winter of 1887-88 with haunting memories of the January slide but also with a tailwind of good monthly reporting by the faithful *Silver World*. Ignored and maybe forgotten by all but the likes of Pike Snowden and A.E. Reynolds, the Ocean Wave was left in its wake.[8]

(Silver World, October 1, 1887.) Probably the greatest strike in Hinsdale County and certainly the richest strike yet made in the Vermont was made last

Tuesday in No. 2 stope of the third level, west. A vein of ore between four and five feet wide was uncovered, nearly two feet of which is almost pure grey copper that will return per car load from $10,000 to $12,000. Manager Stockder estimates that four to five tons of this ore can be produced every day…. He says that in addition to the immense ore body now exposed in No. 2 stope, No. 1 and No. 3 stopes in the third level and No. 4 stope from the winze connecting 2nd and 3rd levels all show good bodies of mineral. He estimates that if the ore now exposed in the stopes continues with the certainty they indicate, the 3rd level will furnish, alone, stoping ground for two years' steady work.

Success bred success, every miner knew that, and in the case of the Vermont, flush with British money, there was no better time for success than just before an infrequent visit from abroad. While an efficient and even comfortable surface plant, and an extensive rabbit-warren of tunnels, shafts and winzes on multiple levels was impressive, it was the quality and quantity of ore that really mattered. Not even back-biting from neighboring mining districts gained traction under those circumstances.

(Silver World, October 29, 1887.) The Messrs. Tottenham were greatly pleased with the showing of the Vermont, the immense pile of grey copper ore, which has not yet been shipped, being much greater and of much better quality than they thought the Vermont capable of producing. They gave Manager Stockder full authority to erect ore bins and other necessary buildings, and to run levels and sink the shaft, which certainly shows that they have great faith in the mine and its management.

(Silver World, November 5, 1887.) Last week's output of ore was the largest in the history of the Vermont mine. Four sorters sorted and sacked 205 sacks of ore, and moreover, the grade is the best grade yet taken from the mine. An increase in force will be made as soon as the new ore bins are completed. This is the mine, which the report is being industriously circulated in Red Mountain, Ouray and other places, has shut down. Still, it does not hurt the mine and when the truth is known a credit to us will be gained.

(Silver World, November 26, 1887.) One great improvement and consequent saving in cost of operating the (Vermont) mine has been the connection of the different levels of the mine, rendering the use of pack animals unnecessary hereafter in getting the ore down within reach of wagons. The ore is now sent to the surface through the 1st level and from there it is loaded directly into the wagons. The stopes continue their production of ore, and Mr. Stockder reported the first of the week that they looked better than ever…. It is to be hoped that the next move will be to resume work on the shaft.

Completing "the shaft" was the next best opportunity to confirm the direction of the high-grade vein and to further reduce transportation costs. Costly to construct, once completed it would pay dividends quickly. In and of itself, it would improve ventilation throughout each level as well as provide a means of hoisting ore from lower levels to the No. 1 portal and waiting burros or wagons. Left undone was connecting the bottom of the shaft "on the level" to the surface, eliminating the need for burros or mules altogether. Of course connecting the bottom of the shaft directly to the surface at the county road level was dead-work—expensive dead-work with no expectation of pay-dirt—fifteen hundred feet of dead-work.

(Silver World, *January 21, 1888.) Splendid improvements are shown in the Vermont stopes during the past week. The stopes were looking lean and thin last week and Manager Stockder was becoming discouraged, but a week's work [twenty-five tons shipped] has changed all this and the mine is as well now as at any time in its history. In No. 3 stope of 3rd level a continuous body of gray copper and galena is exposed forty-six feet in length, and the other stopes are showing up good and improving grades of ore.*

(Silver World, *February 4, 1888.) Supt. Crit Hart seems to be the lucky star of the Vermont, for since his return the stopes in the 2nd and 3rd levels have shown a decided improvement. The production of sorted ore last week was the largest to the man in the history of the mine. If the stopes hold out as they now are for a time it will not be long until active work will be started on the shaft. The mine once developed from the shaft we confidently predict the opening of ore bodies to which the present chutes will be insignificant.*

(Silver World, *February 18 and 25, 1888.) The ore body in No. 1 stope of 3rd level of the Vermont is holding out well and the quality of the mineral coming out is fine. It is too bad for the company that they cannot conclude to commence work on the shaft. Good ore once found in the shaft will quadruple the value of the mine.... The first stope in 3rd level of the Vermont has shown an immense body of ore last week and this. The output of ore for the two weeks has been very large, steady and of an excellent quality.*

(Silver World, *March 10, 1888.) The Vermont has worked almost constantly since it was purchased by the Vermont Mining Company in 1883, and has borne an important part in keeping this camp afloat during our hard times. [Faltering production or outright abandonment of most Hinsdale County mines was reducing Lake City to 'camp' status, a telling admission from the district's chief booster.] Under Capt. Stockder's management the mine has been a regular shipper of ore since last June, and at present is producing in* *greater quantity than at any previous time in the history of the mine. The ore bodies of the Vermont are of a remarkably high grade, some of the gray copper being worth one dollar per pound, and considerable of the sacked ore running $1,000 per ton. Most of the production of the mine thus far has been from the 1st and 3rd levels to the west, and consequently, from its close proximity to the surface, the ore exists in pocket or chimney form. An extensive system of development from the shaft, which is contemplated by the management, will unquestionably open up mineral bodies more extensive and of greater continuity.*

A promising strike was made last week in the No. 2 stope of the 3rd level. A vein of gray copper ore five inches wide and nearly solid was opened up and has improved with every shot since. Foreman Joe Hobisel says if it holds out as it is at present two tons of first class ore can be produced each day. Several tests of the strike have been made and uniformly show the ore to be worth over $1,000 per ton. The result of Manager Stockder's visit to Denver will be the purchasing of necessary machinery for the erection of a light concentrating plant for the handling of the second class ore, about 600 tons of which is now lying on the dumps. But the news which best gratifies us and which we believe to be by far the most important for the mine is the statement that work will soon commence on the shaft. With work once resumed on this enterprise the finding of a good body of ore in any of its workings would surely convince the company of the value of gaining depth on this property.

On March 31, Stockder shared with the *Silver World* his annual report to the Director of the Mint. Production in 1887 was 172 tons, grossing $29,000 for a net profit of $24,080 or $140/ton average net proceeds. Given the intermittent reporting from the mine, these values seemed greatly under-reported. No surprise here. High values were for investors, not the government. Whose numbers were correct? A gambling man would bet the investor performed better due-diligence. [9]

Of course, better due-diligence meant investigating a mine "on the ground," not just through the eyes of newspaper editors known for their helpful exaggerations. But exaggerations usually were anchored in at least some truth. This was the case with *Silver World* reporting on the Vermont and Ocean Wave mines. Embedded in most articles were hard facts supported by accepted geological knowledge. When it came to forecasting future developments or the magnitude of ore bodies was the time to be wary, but those moments did not diminish the significance of the reported progress or production. In the final analysis, in an age when boosterism was not only rampant but recognized for what it was, movers and shakers in the mining industry and the financial community that funded it were fully capable of keeping *Silver World* reporting in perspective. Men like A. E. Reynolds also were fully capable of cutting their losses. In the case of the Vermont and Ocean Wave, Reynolds believed there had to be more there than met the eye.

"Men like A.E. Reynolds" included some of the most influential "scientists" of the day. Reference to paying veins "gaining depth" would not have surprised Thomas Ingham and Ovando Hollister. Did veins improve with depth or did they degrade the farther they were from the surface? Our newspaper editor was in the camp of the former. but in the end it did not matter. Abundant winter production and associated optimism did not last long despite the *Silver World's* best efforts to promote both. Rosy forecasts conveyed in one issue after another ultimately failed to impress distant owners. The Ocean Wave fared even worse. Owned by "eastern people who did not seem to care whether their mine worked or not," its potential was barely tested under lease to Judge T.J. McKenna. Perhaps more damaging than any internal development of either property, the *Silver World*— beacon of optimism shining into this darkness—for reasons never explained went dark in April. Not until mid-October did its successor, the *Hinsdale Phonograph*, report on El Paso Gulch mining activities. When it finally did, the resumption of coverage scored poorly on the "boosterism scale," a further sign that the days of either the Gulch mines or the newspaper or both probably were numbered.

(Hinsdale Phonograph, *October 19, 1888.) As we promised in preced-ing issues we herewith give a general review of the work done and the strikes made in Hinsdale County mines since April last. In considering the progress we have made it must be remembered that the county labors under the disad-vantage of an average freight rate of $22 per ton of ore from mine to smelter; that there are no sampling works in the county, and there are few prospect owners who can afford to wait until a car load of ore is out before they ship. And the experience we have had thus far teaches that it is not worthwhile to ship smaller lots to smelters.*

The progress of [the Vermont] has not been what was hoped for, as no development work has been done during the summer with the exception of sinking two winzes from the first level just under the upper stopes of the mine. While waiting the action of the company, Manager Stockder has employed three men in sorting and jigging the second-class ore, and from this work he has shipped several car loads of high grade concentrates during the season, the returns of one car, that we saw, giving a profit above shipping and smelting expenses of $1,207. It is not certainly known what is delaying the Vermont company in resuming work on the shaft but it is probably their desire to be sure that Lake City is to have a railroad soon. When work on the railway is commenced we believe active work will be renewed on the mine. (Again and again, not far from the thoughts of any astute observer of these matters is "the shaft" and "the railroad.")

Mentioning the darling Vermont and the "phantom railway" in anything but the most optimistic of terms surely struck sour notes around about town and up

Henson Canyon. Coincidence or not, scarcely a month later the *Phonograph* editor was gone and the needle on the "boosterism scale" ticked northward again. It did not hurt that Manager Stockder's planned trip to London to talk with investors at least sounded promising.

> *(Hinsdale Phonograph, November 9, 1888.) The Vermont has been closed down for the winter, or until Manager Stockder's return. The secretary of the company, writing Capt. Stockder respecting the future of the mine, said, "While it is necessary to close the mine down at present, I feel certain that arrangements will be made to resume work early in the spring, with ample capital necessary to conduct and complete a deep, thorough, and systematic plan of developing shafts and levels." In Capt. Stockder's visit to England we can expect the influence of his personal advocacy of the needed improvements for the mine to result in strengthening the syndicate in their conclusion to devote a considerable amount to the intelligent development of the mine, with the prospective certainty of placing it on the list of dividend payers.*

Gushing optimism notwithstanding, the damnable cost of transportation owing largely to the lack of rail service continued to have its way with Henson Canyon profitability. But what a difference a year could make. As early as March 1889 the town awaked to undeniable sounds signaling the railroad was finally coming to Lake City. Strangers, a lot of Italians with heavy accents, seemed to be everywhere one cared to look. Of course, the rowdy railroad crews and camp followers were a mixed blessing. On the one hand, the City fathers and merchants were cautiously optimistic their long economic drought was coming to an end. On the other hand, indeed it was, but not without eroding the peace of mind of the law-abiding citizenry.

In late summer of 1889 a reassuring sound was heard, the rhythmic work chant of the gandy-dancers. A Denver & Rio Grande (D&RG) locomotive could not be far behind. The prayers and dreams of a weary region were finally being answered. Even the *Phonograph* got the story straight. Even the eastern owners of the Ocean Wave, soon followed by their Vermont British counterparts, were incentivized to play. In the March 9th and again in the March 22, 1889, issues of the *Hinsdale Phonograph* the editor wrote, "a large number of people on the streets now. Strangers coming in every day, so fast the local editor cannot keep track of them. The new places of business which are opening up give a decidedly busy appearance to the streets compared with a few months ago." [10] Of greater significance, the Ocean Wave was back in the news in June, followed in September by the Vermont.

> *(Hinsdale Phonograph, June 8, 1889.) Ever since his arrival Mr. R.A.H. Drennon has been busy with preparations to commence work on the*

Ocean Wave, and Wednesday started the work of cleaning out the mine. Pat. J. McCauley, who is interested in the lease and who will have charge of the work, had the lower level cleaned out Wednesday and that night began breaking rock in the tunnel. The face of this drift shows a small streak of good ore, and it was improving with every shot. In other levels good ore has been found, and evidently a little work will open up some bonanza ore chutes. No system of development has yet been decided upon, Mr. Drennon rightly feeling that the mine should be subjected to a rigid prospecting before a plan of work is adopted. It is likely, however, that whatever else is or is not done a crosscut tunnel will soon be started to cut the vein 150 feet below the present workings.

And in the old workings enough ore has been exposed to permit of regular shipments. All the force available is now working and within another week the number of employees will be doubled. Messrs. Drennon and Wilson are greatly pleased with their investment, stating that the mine was much better than was represented to them, and there is no doubt that with their associates, Messrs. McCauley and Stone, the means will be forthcoming for big work, and with this there is no doubt the Ocean Wave will soon resume its old place in the front rank of San Juans mines as a productive and valuable property (despite having been on the delinquent tax list for 1888.)

Sometimes "boosters" somehow managed to stick to the truth. Rarely completely idle for long, the Ocean Wave was on course for another round of extensive development. Apparently of little interest to the editor, a change in Ocean Wave ownership and the resumption of serious work proceeded without fanfare until September when $200-$400/oz. ore was uncovered at the breast and in the stopes of Level 4. Improvements on the surface also signaled a brighter future. A bunkhouse and bins were constructed at the mine, and an ore chute was built

Unintended Consequences. After decades of political wrangling over silver- and gold-backed currency, in 1890 Congress passed the Sherman Silver Purchase Act. The intent was to support silver prices. The effect was just the opposite. *(Watson Heston in* Sound Money)

WHAT THE GOLD BUGS ARE DOING FOR UNCLE SAM.

down to the Henson Creek wagon road, thus eliminating most of the need for burros or mules, or so it was hoped. Of greater significance, the U.S. Congress passed the Sherman Silver Purchase Act, no friend of the Western miner.

UNINTENDED CONSEQUENCES HIT HENSON CANYON

Enacted on July 14, 1890, the Silver Purchase Act authorized an increase in the amount of silver the government was required to purchase to 4.5 million ounces per month. It fell short of the silver lobby goal of setting a minimum price per ounce. The silver industry needed higher prices to cover production costs. Farmers and others with high debts believed higher silver prices would lead to inflation which would help them retire their debts. The effects of the Act were counterproductive. The Act stimulated production to the extent supply outran demand, silver prices plummeted, and deflation rather than inflation ensued. Loss of confidence in silver created a run on the government's reserves of gold and the "Panic of 1893" ensued. To protect the government's gold, President Cleveland oversaw the repeal of the Act. The silver industry was worse off than beforehand and the political wrangling between silver and gold interests intensified once again.

The July passage of the Silver Purchase Act of 1890 did not go under-reported. After decades of political haggling in one form or another, this Congressional action had a greater impact on Henson Canyon mining than systematic development or rail service or English investors combined. Initially, the Act inflated silver prices 50%, from less than $1/oz. to as much as $1.50/oz., and prospects along Henson Creek brightened accordingly. Not only would the arrival of the D&RG reduce transportation costs, now the value of silver in low-grade ores could be mined profitably. Nowhere was this more encouraging than among the Vermont and Ocean Wave miners and owners. (The unintended consequence, of course, which would soon become apparent, was overproduction and deflated prices.)

Still, A.E. Reynolds bided his time. He would wait for a buyer's market, in his judgment the certain outcome of high silver prices that would encourage high production that would lead soon enough to a highly oversupplied global market resulting in low prices. Sure enough, oversupply resulted in low silver prices, record low silver prices, and inevitably low prices for silver mines. That was when Reynolds preferred to buy. In the meantime, Vermont miners did their part to contribute rich ore to the market and fresh clues pointing to even richer ore hopefully to the delight of investors. Of course, the fawning press was on top of it, even daring to use the term "bonanza."

(Hinsdale Phonograph, September 27, 1890.) Supt. Ray has materially increased the mining force on the Vermont, and is rapidly placing it in the condition of a mine. The stopes in No. 3 level are proving better than was expected, and there is no doubt that much good ore will yet be taken from them before they are exhausted. No. 3 will be driven west for some distance into the Scotia ground (the latter now under control of the Vermont Company) and it is the intention to extensively develop this part of the vein. If No. 3 shows up good ore, No's 2 & 1 will also be extended into the ore chute.

(Hinsdale Phonograph, October 25, 1890.) It is reported that the Vermont is showing up the latest bonanza strike, No. 1 level having broken into a fine ore body. We do not know the extent of the strike, but rumor is that it is large and shows a fine grade of gray copper ore.

(Hinsdale Phonograph, November 15 & 29, 1890.) Supt. Chas. Ray is pushing development on the Vermont and has a smile on his face when in town that reflects a promising outlook for the mine. A force is at work driving No. 1 tunnel and several men are steadily employed in the stopes.

Manager Schwartz was in from Denver during the weekend and paid a visit to the Vermont. He is well pleased with the appearance of the mine and with Mr. Ray's superintendency, and it is quite probable he will soon direct a large increase in the force on the tunnels, and will also probably begin work on the shaft. Sorters are kept busily at work but it is not likely shipping will begin until spring, when there will be enough to make it an object to freighters to give the best rates for hauling.

Later reports show that we were mistaken in regard to shipments, as Supt. Ray is now looking for packers to get three cars of ore down to the road for shipping. [Wow, a rare retraction.]

Reference to "packer" as opposed to "loaders" or "freighters" suggested burros were back on the payroll. A return to burros or possibly mules instead of the use of wagons on the El Paso Creek "road" suggested the "road" was no longer wagon-friendly and a change in operations was required. The practice of loading ore directly into wagons at the portal of Level No.1 must have run into problems, perhaps with navigating wagons in the steep, narrow gulch, perhaps because burros and mules competed better than expected with light wagons capable of transiting the road but still requiring the transfer of their cargo to sturdier freight-wagons plying the Henson Creek wagon road, perhaps because seasonal erosion made the road impassable even for light wagons.

On balance, 1890 looked to be a decent year for Lake City and Henson Canyon mines overall. D&RG locomotives pulling freight and passenger cars arrived and departed daily. Silver prices were improving. Fifty-six mines employed

229 miners. Patented claims, 275 of them, beckoned to investors near and far. But the shrewd observer was unimpressed. The Ocean Wave for all its fuss and financing only shipped 108 tons of ore worth $5,640. The Vermont, also well-endowed, shipped none. Maybe the boosters were not so truthful after all. Maybe hand-drilling and mucking was taking its toll. Maybe the region, edging into another recession blindly or not, was shedding its most ambitious workers. Most did not see trouble coming. A.E. Reynolds did—still he bided his time. [11]

Like prior years, 1891 was ushered in with predictions of the best of times. On February 7th and 21st the *Hinsdale Phonograph* reported that the Vermont would begin to ship ore, three or four carloads once snow and avalanche danger subsided. Indeed, numerous slides did run, but nothing like January 1887. On February 12th and 21st the *Lake City Times* reported:

> *the boys to lay off a few days, but this (avalanche) danger is now past unless another heavy snow fall should set in; and they have gone back to work. One of the slides took away the powder house, but did no other damage.*

Reports from other mines were sketchy, but this was not surprising for that time of year. What was surprising was the sudden demise of the *Phonograph*. Apparently boosterism had limits.

Like the *Silver World* before it, without warning to its readers the *Phonograph* published its last issue on February 28, 1891. And like the *Phonograph*, quick to rise from the ashes of the iconic *Silver World*, the *Lake City Times* quickly picked up the pieces and ran with news of the mines. The *Phonograph* and the *Times* had competed for years, but the depths of disdain between the two of them may have come as a surprise to the community. On March 19th the *Times* editor wrote what he really thought about the *Phonograph*, an epitaph that surely spread grins on many a face:

A Century of Winters takes its toll. The Vermont powder-house awaits a new roof, stone work, and stock of explosives. *(Author's Collection)*

The word "phonograph" means, "to speak without thinking," but this is probably no news to those unfortunate people who were obliged to put up with the feeble squeak of a publication of that name until a real newspaper was established here. The name is generally admitted to be very appropriate, very. [No love lost here. Ironically, also no time lost before the Times *suffered a similar fate at the hands of a resurrected* Silver World.*]*

Slow out of their own chute or short on mining news generally, the *Times* did not report on Henson Canyon developments until mid-April 1891:

The Vermont is keeping two ore sorters busy, shipping high grade galena while development continues. This is a mine that has always paid its owners a handsome profit. The Vermont is adding men to develop and produce.[12]

On May 7th the *Times* followed up with a short note that Vermont work was "progressing vigorously" with the workforce "materially increased…twenty tons of fine ore is ready to ship by the end of the week." Slow perhaps but no less a shameless practitioner of boosterism just the same, the *Times* tried to hold up its end of the civic bargain. When presented with a slow news week, the editor was not above digging deep into the past to wax poetic about personalities he found entertaining. As one might expect, our drover Pike Snowden was a recurring attention-getter and worthy addition to any mining article.

The *Times* did not have to puff Pike into a larger than life caricature, Pike was fully capable of accomplishing that on his own. But the *Times* could and did give him a stage. Recalling that Pike was one of the earliest pilgrims—a bona fide honor—and one of the original owners and miners of the Ocean Wave—the truth—the editor underpinned Pike's growing reputation as a colorful recluse by documenting his continuing Henson Canyon mining interests. Like the Vermont and the Ocean Wave treasure tale, a recluse's story always reeked of adventure and reward. Imagine sitting at breakfast in Lake City's Occidental Hotel, or sitting on the D&RG platform awaiting departure of the morning train to Sapinero and the world beyond. Imagine opening the May 21st *Times* to learn that Henson Canyon treasure hunts were alive and well.

(Lake City Times, May 21, 1891.) Then comes the Yellow Jacket and Meat Augur owned by that old pioneer prospector Zenas Snowden, the "positively only" and "irrepressible" Pike. Pike has been dreaming for years of a fast team, a brown stone front and a spotted dog. And these prospects will "fetch em" he thinks. Just across the creek is the well-known Ocean Wave Mine owned by Mastin Bros. of Kansas City, Mo. This property was one of the wonders of the camp when discovered (by Pike), the ore milled 600 oz. per ton at the grass roots, and has produced more mineral than any other mine in the district; the

Ute and Ulay excepted. The Vermont owned by an English syndicate is being systematically developed and shipping quantities of very rich ore.

There you have it, further evidence the Vermont and Ocean Wave were worthy investments, further example of why investors continued to hunt treasure there. Also note that it was prudent—self-serving really—for the new editor to work in a tribute to Henson Canyon's lovable pundit.

Whether due to Pike Snowden's involvement in the Ocean Wave or the deadly avalanche at the Vermont or the interests of "English cousins" involvement in both, these hometown mine favorites were perennially acclaimed despite their jaded production legacies. Everyone enjoyed suspense; everyone enjoyed come-from-behind drama. In June 1891, the *Times* again did its best to counter an increasingly dark mood in a community sensing decline. Usually the Vermont could be counted on for good news, if not true and current, then "just around the corner" good news. Without ever saying so, the Vermont and to a lesser extent the Ocean Wave served as economic barometers, at least one could draw that conclusion based upon the amount of printer's ink devoted to them. Other mines could have their day in the sun, but none of the others including the far larger and more profitable Ute/Ulay, seemed to garner the same fascination. Yes, there were reports of gold at other Henson Canyon and Lake Fork prospects and mines, but little if anything seemed to come of them. Could the promises and pitfalls of the Vermont and Ocean Wave (and maybe their folklore mystique) more so

D&RG Lake City Depot. Completed in autumn of 1889, the impressive station, rail yard, and link to the outside world was the pride and hope of the community for the next forty years. *(Courtesy of Hinsdale County Museum)*

than their tantalizing but intermittent production account for this? More so than other mines in the district, even the Ute/Ulay, the community seemed comfortable with the notion that "as the Vermont and the Ocean Wave went, so went the region."

(Lake City Times, June 11, 1891.) C.H. Ray superintendent of the Vermont was in town Sunday and reports that work on that valuable property is progressing nicely, and the output increasing both in quality and quantity. The Vermont is now working 20 men; no machinery is needed as it is being worked altogether through tunnels. This mine has been producing three carloads of good ore per month, since the first of January, and the output will be increased to five carloads this month. The shipping ore is of a good quality, being rich gray copper and galena. The pay streak averages about a foot wide besides which there is a large body of good concentrating ore which will yield a profit as soon as a concentrator is placed on the property.

The *Times* reported favorably on Vermont activities nearly weekly. Superintendent Ray, beneficiary of the latest management change, was adept not only at exploiting mineral veins but also friendships at the newspaper office where he paid regular visits. In September he advised our faithful—some would say gullible—editor that the Vermont was working thirty men, shipping five cars of ore per month, and [characteristically] "working of the mine would probably continue all winter." In December he advised that the mine was working four levels with twenty-two men. From the frost-rimmed window of the *Times* office the future looked bright to both the superintendent and the editor, and they shared their optimism at every turn. If the remote Vermont was working this hard in the dead of winter, imagine what spring would bring. If the Vermont could work this hard, what was standing in the way of other mines?

In January 1892 Vermont work did start strong. With minor changes in the number of men working, the mine hit mid-year with thirty laborers and regular shipments. But with August came more than the typical thunderstorms. News usually reserved for winter came early.

(Lake City Times, August 4, 1892.) The Vermont has shut down and all the men laid off that were employed thereon. The low price of silver probably had as much to do with it as anything else. The report that the mine has played out is without foundation, for parties who have been working in the mine say there are several tons of ore knocked down in the mine, besides a car at least on the dump, so that it is very evident that our English cousins could not stand the pressure brought to bear on the price of silver by the governors of the Bank of England. It was English money and dishonest Congressmen that demonetized silver in 1873, and now the British syndicate have to suffer on

account of it.... This is the first mine in this vicinity that has stopped work on this account, but if the price of silver continues to drop more will follow suit. With silver at 80 cents when it should be 100 cents it is difficult work for mine owners to make both ends meet.

The unintended consequences of the 1890 *Silver Purchase Act* were hitting Henson Canyon mines hard, but a call for volunteer pallbearers was premature. Barely two weeks elapsed and the *Times* reported the Vermont would be working again. The British were ready to cut their losses, but they were not ready to abandon ship. Leasing a mine, in whole or in part, was always an option, a method of spreading the costs and risks while still paying a dividend to investors and owners. In fact, often a lessor would sub-lease a portion of their contract to a number of others [multilevel marketing at its best]. The major risk to owners was reckless exploitation of the silver-bearing ores for short-term gain at the expense of long-term, systematic, thoughtful development. Short-term exploitation could do so much damage that long-term development was unaffordable. [Mid-grade ores would be cast aside in favor of high-grade ores rather than sorted for higher assays. Failure to properly timber drifts and stopes could result in unstable ground or collapses.] Ensuring this did not occur and that the lessors honestly reported and paid their production-related royalties were the responsibilities of mine managers

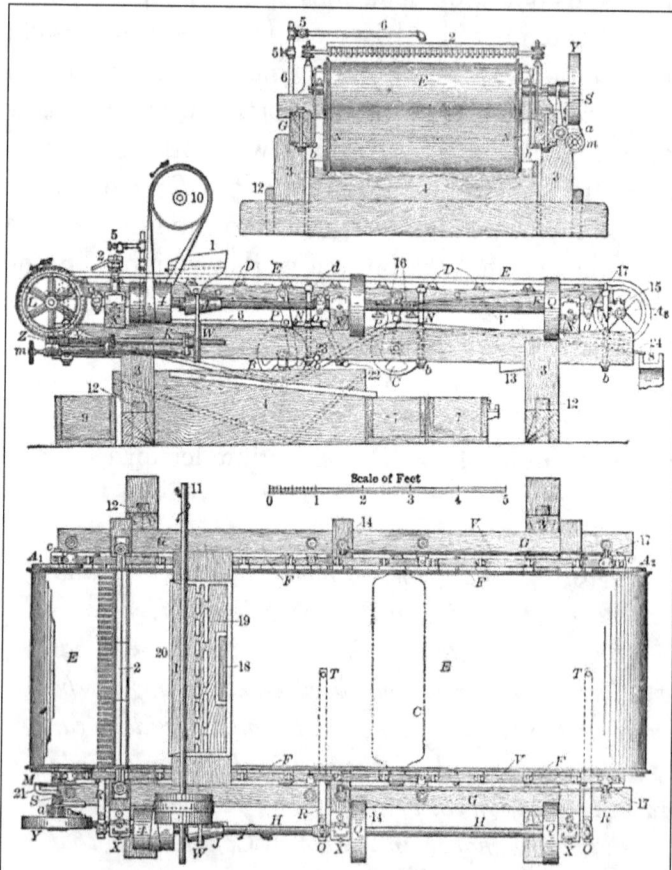

Mechanical Ore Separation. Reducing the volume of waste rock and increasing assay values could be achieved by sorting ores. This was done by hand for course materials or by crushing course materials and separating the finer materials with equipment like the Luhrig or Frue Vanner concentrator. *(Wikipedia)*

and superintendents. In light of the worsening global silver market, the British were now prepared to play this end-game. Better to run the risks associated with leasing than those associated with ownership.

In mid-August 1892, Thomas, Charles, and James Ray secured a lease on the Vermont and neighboring Scotia and Alabama mines and commenced work. They planned on employing only three or four men at first, but increasing the force as the output justified. Initial working capital would come from several tons on the dump that would be hauled down to Crooke's sampling works and run through their concentrators. Longer term, if possible one of these mills would be put up at the mine.[13]

By October Ed O'Brien joined the ranks of Vermont lessors which now included several sub-lessors. The October 13th and 20th *Times* reported that the Vermont was shipping considerable ore. To his credit, in the best of journalistic traditions our erstwhile editor took it upon himself to inspect the mine before harsh weather set in. His thorough report soon followed.

(Lake City Times, November 3, 1892.) Leaving the Ulay we reached the Vermont mine about noon. Here we found great activity and nearly all the levels producing good ore. The mine is being worked mostly under sub-leases, Chas. Ray having the lease on the mine. From the mouth of the third level in 100 feet, with stoping ground extending up to the fourth, John Marshall, Henry Wood and Al Croft have a sub-lease. They made a shipment of a car load of ore recently, returns of which were received last week, netting them $525. Chas. H. Ray is working the remainder of the third level on the Vermont ground, and made a shipment last week. At the end of the Vermont ground, in the third level, begins the Scotia (now considered part of the Vermont Group). Here for 125 feet on the Scotia, Philip Ralph, Frank Stobaugh and Ed Kenan have a lease, and have taken out some good looking ore. They are at present working in some stopes. At the end of the ground held by above lessors, Ed O'Brien, Goldie Ray and Isaac Wilhelm have a lease, comprising the remainder of the Scotia between levels three and four. They are working in a nice body of gray copper and galena and will ship a car load this week.

From the mouth of the second level, extending westward to within 200 feet of the Scotia line, and upward to a point 60 feet below the third level, is the ground under sub-lease by David Jamison and Ed Jury. They are getting out what is considered the best ore in the mine. Between the second and third levels on the Scotia, west from the Vermont line, Arthur Carter, Mr. Curtis and Chas. Stanton hold a sub-lease. On the east side of El Paso gulch, also a portion of the Vermont, Peter Faulk and Andy Johnson are working a sublease on the third level, and are taking out good ore. The Vermont is a mine that has always paid its way, and the lessors are nearly all making more than regular wages, while some of them are making a big thing.

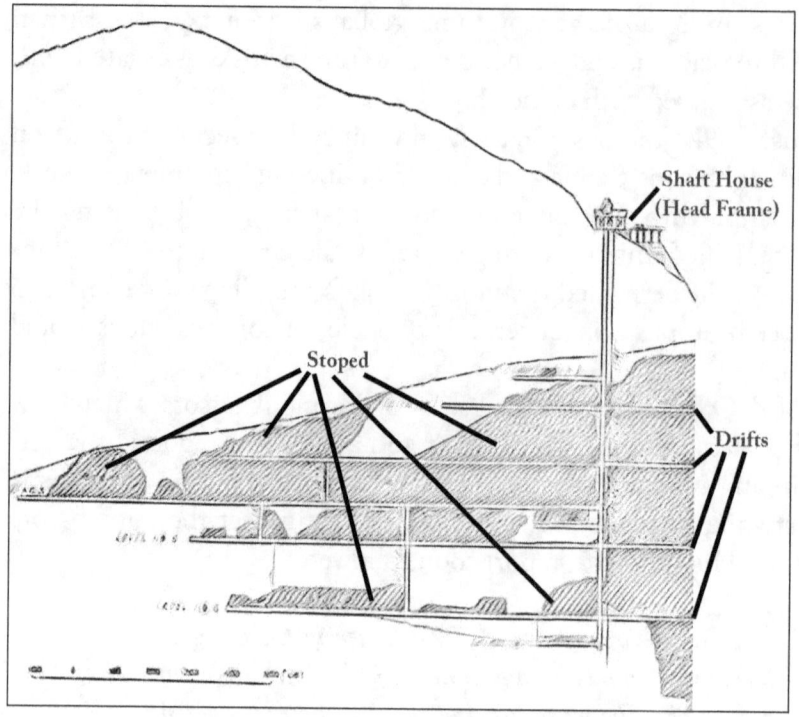

Treasure Troves. Unlike veins threading their way through the mountain, high-assay ores could be found in pockets, quite large pockets at times. When mined, these "stopes" created underground caverns rivaling the largest European cathedrals. (Irving & Bancroft)

James L. Ray is running the boarding house and nearly all the lessees are boarding with him. John H. Pappe, the gentleman in charge, fully satisfied two appetites that would make a chipmunk hunt its hole, or a garbage wagon driver push on the ribbons.

If all that Vermont activity did not make our editor's head spin, nothing could. It certainly described the nature of hard-rock mining in Henson Canyon. The year 1892 ended well for most Vermont miners and for the reputation of the mine itself. According to the December 22nd *Times*, "the Vermont has probably the largest force working in the tunnels and stopes of the mine." As important as this holiday good-tiding, prospects for a prosperous 1893 looked promising throughout the region save for two troubling developments. The first and closest to home was the influx of Italian immigrants and increasingly deep resentment for Italian miners. Cousin-Jacks were one thing, after all they were "cousins." Gandy-dancers and track-layers could be tolerated, they were transients and would go away soon enough. But Italian miners were a class of immigrants that stayed on. They were family-oriented, large and extended-family oriented, which further compounded the matter. Italian miners begat Italian miners accustomed to their cultural enclaves and largely independent from their host community. Their growing numbers in mining communities produced a call for their "removal," much like the movement two decades earlier regarding the Ute.

The second troubling development was a pesky nationwide depression. Part of that problem was the 1893 repeal of the *Silver Purchase Act* that would ensure silver prices remained depressed for decades to come. The contraction of the nation's economy would depress employment and investment opportunities nearly as long. For the Vermont, work and shipments continued through 1893, but at a far slower pace than before. The Ocean Wave resumed work at the end of that year, but for the most part, the San Juans did not escape hardship and a loss of population. Still, miners and their investors were creatures of habit. The slightest hint of opportunity could lure them back underground.

As signposts of the times, local blacksmith Richard Kilvert in1894 began working as a miner but soon returned to blacksmithing. By mid-year he was back to mining. Three saloons closed for the winter, a stark harbinger of hard times. Most Italians left the district for parts unknown, but they too would soon return. Two ice cream parlors opened in 1895, a harbinger of a return to good times. A larger number of Italians had returned than had left. And in the midst of it all, mines opened, closed, and opened again depending on word of the latest ore deposit or ability of an out-of-work miner to scratch together enough funds to "hire" himself and maybe one or two other die-hards to take up a bond and lease. The only constant, it seemed, was the low price of silver. Even notable personalities responded in unaccustomed ways. Pike Snowden filled potholes between Capital City and the Ute/Ulay, belying the belief harbored by some that he did in fact support himself with a secret gold mine. In stark contrast to Snowden and the others, A.E. Reynolds accompanied by wife and daughter came in from Denver to fish.

For the balance of the 1890s Lake City and Henson Canyon were in the doldrums. But as is often the case, neither completely idle nor strategically worked, the Vermont and the Ocean Wave enjoyed spurts of new life from local interests. And every episode fanned another ember of hope that the old mines were far from depleted, that their elusive treasure was worth renewing the hunt.

(Lake City Times, February 11, 1897.) Last fall Rev. Chas. Fueller and Press and Charley Hix obtained a bond and lease on the Vermont, at a very reasonable figure, and immediately commenced work to open up some new ground in the old tunnels. Last week they struck a large body of good ore which they have in both the upper and lower tunnels, with a hundred feet of stoping ground between.

Recurring reports of lessors striking new bodies of rich ore would have been music to Reynolds' ears. Such reports would have confirmed his belief that El Paso Gulch geology portended not simply silver-bearing ore veins, but large concentrated pockets of high-grade ore. The deeper the shafts and drifts, the more frequent they would be uncovered. Yet to be discovered were treasure troves in

Uncompahgre Mountain near Ouray. Still, A.E. bided his time. His focus and shrinking capital would remain concentrated on his numerous other properties for a while longer.

Nevertheless, good news brought forth many cupbearers. Perhaps flush with new money, perhaps for lack of it, neighbor Snowden set aside filling potholes and returned to mining. A little farther up the road the Vermont was being worked under the management of Charley Hix — some good ore was being sorted and sacked ready for shipment. Setting on the same vein, one also would expect good reports from the Ocean Wave, and there were some. Our *Times* editor did not fail us:

> (Lake City Times, *March 4 and 18, 1897.) The Ocean Wave is turning out some good ore with Sam Jack as manager. Work in the above property is being pushed with flattering results. Sam Jack, who has the property under a five year bond and lease, recently made another shipment of ore, the shipment being second class ore, and a few days ago Mr. Jack showed a check for $750, the net return for the car of ore.*

> (Lake City Times, *April 8, 1897.) A little over a mile further [from Pike Snowden's Yellow Jacket Mine] we come to a formation somewhat different from what we have passed through, and on the side of the stream high up on the mountain, we find our Italian friends, Sam Jack & C. (sic), working the Ocean Wave mine and producing large quantities of rich gray copper ore, and making regular shipments. A short distance further brings us to the Vermont mine, which as in former years shipped large quantities of galena and gray copper ores. After laying idle for a couple of years, it is now in the hands of Fueller & Hix, who are working a force of men and putting the property in excellent shape for producing. In the last few weeks large bodies of high grade silver ore, running well in gold, has been opened up, and as soon as the roads are in condition, will make regular shipments.*

As usual, skepticism was in order, skepticism regarding gold and high grade silver, and especially regarding Italian "friends." Historically, there usually was some quantity of gold associated with silver-bearing ores, but never enough to transform the Vermont into a gold mine. As for "Italian friends," by the late 1890s there was no mistaking community resentment at the mention of Sam Jack and his Ocean Wave crew. They made short work of the high-grade ore in the fourth level of the Ocean Wave that came to be known as the "Dago Tunnel." Their success was an accomplishment that earned them a great deal of wealth. It also earned a great deal of jealousy. It also heightened A.E. Reynolds' interest in the Ocean Wave and by extension the Vermont.

To say nineteenth-century America was rife with racial slurs is an understatement. Displacement of native populations, enslavement of one native population by other native populations, Black-American slavery, the Civil War and its aftermath aside, virtually every immigrant population encountered it the moment they stepped off their ship. In the West, particularly severe discrimination plagued the Chinese and the Italians. In Henson Canyon, it was the Italian miner. They worked in any mine that would have them. Most mine owners or lessors "would have them" because they were hard, skillful workers. The Vermont and Ocean Wave were no exceptions.

The Ute/Ulay employed as many as 150 Italians at a time. In the case of the Ocean Wave, circumstances differed in one important regard. The Italians there were savvy enough and financially secure enough to appreciate the advantages of leasing, putting their own hourly wages at risk in exchange for a share of the profits. And they were savvy enough to appreciate the potential of the ore deposits located in the fourth level. In due course the identity of the Ocean Wave was less about the quality and quantity of valuable ores in the mine at large, and more about high-grade ore viewed by the community as an unjustified Italian windfall. From Sam Jack's perspective, the "windfall" was an ocean-voyage back to the home-country in long-deserved style. From a student of history perspective, it provides sharp insight into the cultural norms of the age. From the perspective of the editor of the *Lake City Times*, fancying himself somewhat of a linguist, it was a subject ripe for ridicule.

(Lake City Times, *April 18, 1897.) If you have never heard of the big strike in the Ocean Wave mine it is no doubt because you do not understand the Italian language. The writer, on seeing quite a crowd of Italians, who were making as much loud talking as a flock of Guinea hens, and gesticulating as*

Little Rome. As development of the Ute/Ulay Mine gained momentum, so too did the construction of nearby cabins, a boarding house, mine surface plant, and not surprising what passed for a general store and probably a saloon. "Henson" a.k.a. "Little Rome" afforded miners (predominantly Italian) many of the benefits of Lake City four miles away. *(Courtesy of P. David Smith)*

ITALIANS

As early as December 1892 Lake City society unequivocally raised its hackles in its love-hate relationship with Italian immigrants.

> *(Lake City Times, December 1, 1892.) The writer was informed this week that the Dagos employed on the Ulay mine, were all being laid off. If this be true, the new management should be highly complimented for the good it has already done. There are exceptions of course, but the general class of these mahogany-faced creatures is filthy and undesirable to have around. While they may be good workers, they are of no benefit to a town in the way of patronizing its merchants, neither is there anything enterprising or public spirited about them. It would be a wise scheme for all the mines to adopt, not to employ a single Dago, and fill their places by respectable and industrious men, who are a credit to a community. A Dago is all right in his place — peddling cheap jewelry, or selling 'de banan', but when it comes to mixing them up with, and working them alongside able miners, far superior in every respect, here is where the line should be drawn.*

Lake City was a microcosm of the nineteenth-century Western frontier. How odd this seemed for a country populated by immigrants until competition for work and pressure on wages is considered. In the case of Lake City, regarding Italians and the adventurers that preceded them, it was difficult imagining two more dissimilar cultures. It was also difficult imagining nineteenth-century journalists giving minorities a pass. A January 1893 *Times* editorial is representative of this clash of cultures. If the good citizens of Lake City experienced the Christmas Spirit, the Spirit did not linger into January. Insulting characterizations of fellow immigrants were tolerated if not welcomed when the local economy was experiencing a hangover.

> *(Lake City Times, January 19, 1893.) Almost every community is infested with a certain class of people that are anything but desirable citizens. Lake City is probably no worse in this respect than any other town in the state, but there is one nationality of people who find employment in this county that we would be much better off without. These are the Italians, or more commonly known as Dagos. While they are nearly all industrious and law abiding citizens, their objectionable features arrive from the fact that they send nearly every dollar of their earnings out of the country to sources from where the money never finds its way back. About Lake City there are probably twenty Dagos employed and last month they sent out of this camp over four thousand dollars, most of which went back to Italy. This is one of the secrets to the scarcity of money. Had this amount of money been in the hands of men who have the interest of this great mining region at heart, instead of sending it away, it would have been expended in the development of mining claims, and the money would have remained here among us. As it is, it will be an accident if any of it ever gets back into the money channels of the Rocky Mountains again.*

*though war was about to commence, made inquiry of one of their number who
talked a little pidgin English, as to what was up. He says, "You no hear him
strike in Ocean Wave heap eighteen inch gray cop. One car load him sell $1300.
Nudder car down to depot, same kind ore. Car more every week, mabeso."*

*Notwithstanding the difficulty the Italians always have in making them-
selves understood, yet they have no trouble in forcing people to realize that they
have a good mine, when checks come in for returns on ore varying in size from
$750 to $1300 per car load, and shipments being made at the rate of a car per
week. Something like two hundred thousand dollars have been taken from the
mine in years past. The ore at that time running about $60 to the ton. But a
400 foot cross cut tunnel had to be run, which discouraged forming any lessors.
When Sam Jack took hold of the mine on a five year lease, he started the tunnel,
drove it to the vein and is being amply rewarded.*

Despite inhospitality bordering on open hostility, Italians were attracted to
mining camps wherever they sprang up. They came not by chance, but frequently
at the hands of agents who recruited them in Italy and provided them and often
their families with everything necessary including a job in a San Juans mine.
When work dried up in one camp, they were helped to find work elsewhere. The
Times took it upon itself to keep track of what was considered their unpatriotic
acts. Especially egregious was depriving Americans (which of course included
immigrants from many countries) and adding insult to injury by sending their
wages elsewhere, usually back to Italy.

*(Lake City Times, January 19, 1893) Forty or fifty Dagos left Lake
City last week for eastern points. Quite a colony of them are left, however, at
the Ulay mine.*

*(Lake City Times, September 28, 1893) A couple of Dagos came in on
last Sunday evening's train, expecting to get work in this case.*

*(Lake City Times, February 8, 1894) Fully one hundred Italians are
at work in the Ute and Ulay mines. This means all the way from $1000 to
$5000 sent from this camp to Italy every month...*

*(Lake City Times, August 5, 1894) Dagos are coming in from all sec-
tions of the country by the wholesale. They all expect to find employment at the
Ute and Ulay.*

Alarms had been sounded, ground zero being the Ute/Ulay, but when it
came to the Ocean Wave, resentment was muted if not negligible. Again, the
difference was the Ute/Ulay hired hourly laborers, the Ocean Wave was worked

by long-term lease holders led by likable Sam Jack. For the more tolerant in the community, Italian investment in a five-year lease went a long way toward defusing the complaint that Italians did not invest in the community. Producing good returns from their own labors suggested that they were hard-workers and maybe even wise and diligent stewards of someone else's property. But for the bigoted class, their successes fueled more resentment than admiration, and did nothing to offset the complaint that local merchants did not share in their good fortune. And there was the seasoned mine owner class—quite often absentee landlords—that often discovered late that the lease-holder had not extracted ore in a responsible manner, in a way that respected the mine owner's property rights or preserved the structural integrity of the mine.

To manager Jack's credit, he was a gifted businessman as well as miner. Early in 1897 he worked nine or ten men and held an option which he sold to Mr. Kearney for $100. The option term expired and Mr. Kearney forfeited the $100. Neither man knew how valuable the Ocean Wave could become, but in hindsight Sam Jack knew his day of reckoning had not yet come. As 1898 approached, instead of seeking another buyer or abandoning the venture, manager Jack wisely invested in developing levels No. 3 and No. 4, a decision A.E. Reynolds was well aware of despite not knowing a word of Italian.

While little was heard of the Ocean Wave outside Italian circles, those who visited the mine appreciated the skill of the men Sam Jack employed, and Sam's willingness [vision] to invest in dead work [infrastructure not expected to yield paydirt, but helpful in opening access to it]. While one shift of men in a stope took out one car-load of high-grade ore a month, the main force was engaged in sinking a shaft and making an upraise which when completed would connect levels No. 3 and No. 4. Connecting levels No. 3 and No. 4 provided good air to the entire mine and increased production. What was not appreciated at the time but complained about later were unstated shortcuts that had to have been taken to account for the profitability of the lease. Hard work and good luck alone could not be the reason. An inescapable article of faith in these matters—true, verifiable, or not—was that a lessor's immediate needs and wants would always trump preservation of an absentee owner's property rights and values. Reynolds also was acutely aware of this axiom. [14]

First-class ore, along with expected dead work, continued to be opened through 1897 and into 1898 at the Ocean Wave and Vermont, but was largely under-reported to the government or not reported at all. Official production records and the volume of waste rock [dirt] removed from drifts, shafts, and stopes still do not correlate well even when refinery losses are considered. Although suspicion of wrongdoing was most often associated with the Ocean Wave and the Italian lease in particular, Vermont leases were no less subject to similar practices irrespective of evading similar complaints.

(Lake City Times, *March 3, 1898.) The Vermont property, operated under bond and lease by Hicks & Fueller, is once more on a shipping basis. This property has shipped a fortune of ore in its history, but when the present company accepted the bond and lease there was 1,000 feet of dead work to be done. The task has recently been completed and a high pay streak has been cut in an upraise near the breast of the tunnel. The streak shows a thickness of 6 inches of solid ore. There is a streak of bismuth lying next to gray copper running 18,000 ounces in silver. They brought down 200 pounds of this Wednesday. They have already one car of ore out for shipment the first of next week, and they expect to make shipments throughout the present season, which will bring their property back up to the old standard as one of the best up Henson.*

When the *Times* was not boosting or belittling mining initiatives, it turned to reporting on who came and went. In addition to Italians, accounts of English syndicates always increased newspaper sales. A visit by A.E. Reynolds did likewise. When Reynolds, accompanied by his Pueblo banker friend M.D. Thatcher, visited Lake City for two days in October 1898, the editor suspected more than brown trout was on their minds. On the 1st of February 1899, A.E. signed a two-year lease with E.B. Hendrie of Denver for the Vermont Group. The deal included purchase of the Ocean Wave, and Reynolds' commitment to drive a tunnel to access the lower workings of the Vermont mine as partial compensation for the lease. The lease also granted Reynolds an option to purchase the property. Interestingly, prior leases on the upper workings of the Vermont would be honored by both parties. Surprisingly, leases on the Ocean Wave, notably Sam Jack's lease, also would be honored and work continued without landlord oversight. In retrospect, this was a calculated risk that turned out badly.

Thus began the Vermont/Ocean Wave treasure hunt. In the finest boosterism tradition, the vigilant *Lake City Times* took upon itself the duty of faithful scribe. Sometimes known as the Reynolds Tunnel, the Vermont Group, or the Vermont/Ocean Wave, the project would be puffed as incredibly valuable. With the lodes squarely in the hands of A.E. Reynolds, the future of the project and thus the town could not be brighter. On the 16th of February with the ink scarcely dry on the Hendrie-Reynolds contract, the *Times* published the first of many years' worth of Reynolds Tunnel reports. Not all of them were puff-pieces. None of them belittled the mine as a pig-in-a-poke. All of them fueled the Vermont/Ocean Wave mystique and the growing realization that this project was Reynolds' last best chance to make a mine.

Notes—Chapter Nine: Pig-in-a-poke

[1] *Silver World*, May 24, 1879. ("Pig-in-a-poke" is common slang conveying the thought that something is offered or appears in a way that obscures its real nature or worth. It aptly describes some people and some San Juans mines, but not Reynolds Vermont/Ocean Wave.)

[2] (Reynolds grew up on a New York farm and lived much of his life in the rural West, but he was never known for buying a "pig-in-a-poke." He knew his way around money-men often found in New York, London, Chicago, Kansas City and Denver. Leveraging his own assets with the abundance of others was a life-long practice.)

[3] *Silver World*, March 14 and 28, 1885.

[4] *Silver World*, May 14, 21, and 25, 1887.

[5] *Silver World*, June 18 and June 25, 1887.

[6] *Silver World*, July 9, 16, 23, and 30, 1887.

[7] *Silver World*, August 13, 20, and 27, 1887.

[8] *Silver World*, September 17 and 24, 1887.

[9] *Silver World*, March 31, 1888.

[10] *Hinsdale Phonograph*, March 9 and 22, 1889.

[11] *Hinsdale Phonograph*, January 10. 1891.

[12] *Lake City Times*, April 9 and 23, 1891.

[13] *Lake City Times*, August 18, 1892.

[14] *Lake City Times*, August 5, 1897.

CHAPTER 10

Ace-in-the-Hole

"I've been hittin' some hard-rock minin',

I thought you knowed,

I've been leanin' on a pressure drill, way down the road,

Hammer flyin', air hole suckin', six foot of mud

And I shore been a muckin'

And I've been hittin' some hard travelin', Lord.[1]

February 16, 1899, marked the beginning of a new era in ferreting out high-grade silver in the Vermont and the Ocean Wave lodes, thereafter commonly known as the Vermont Group or Reynolds Tunnel. Croakers and grumblers notwithstanding, that wintry day also marked the beginning of A.E. Reynolds' personal commitment to bringing the Vermont Group treasure hunt to a glorious conclusion. Of course no one imagined viewing the project quite that way at the time. Instead, if anyone imagined anything other than a wonderful job opportunity was at hand, they may have concluded that Reynolds simply deemed the time right to implement his long cultivated vision for a Henson Canyon rerun of his Virginius/Revenue Tunnel glory days.

In fact, based on his reading of geology and site conditions, Reynolds commitment to the Vermont and Ocean Wave lodes was grounded in the belief that these mines were far from "played out." They may have been mismanaged, they may have been handicapped by natural disasters, carelessness, greed, and unhelpful international silver markets exacerbated by political dolts; but the Vermont Group was not only worthy of further investment, it would be gross negligence to do otherwise. It just so happened that everything needed to launch the venture did not come into alignment until 1899. In 1899, under the watchful eye of J.J. Abbott, his trusted Virginius/Revenue Tunnel supervisor brought over from Ouray, Reynolds played his "ace-in-the-hole." [2]

What exactly motivated Reynolds to finally pursue his Reynolds Tunnel vision? He never said. The answer could be as simple as E.B. Hendrie was eager to sell at a price A.E. could not resist. It could be A.E. needed more than ever before a replacement for other properties that were playing out. It could be new technologies—more powerful explosives and powered drills—were available to greatly improve efficiency and thus the ability to make a profit. Doing so required a large investment in a surface plant to produce the steam and compressed air that drove the drills, but Reynolds was no stranger to large investments. It could have been that he convinced himself the nationwide depression triggered by the "panic of 1893" was actually ended. Any of these factors could have been the trigger for action, clearly all of them were present.

Also present, considered but not brought to bear, was "electricity." Electricity was one of Reynolds greatest Revenue Tunnel gambles and successful innovations. Could replacing the high cost of a coal-fired boiler with hydroelectricity, like at the Virginius and Revenue Tunnel, have spelled the difference between profit and loss at the Vermont Group and its Reynolds Tunnel? We will never know. Other challenges relegated the cost of coal compared to hydroelectricity to a position low on his priority list, so low he never got to it.

Dawn of a New Age. The end of the 19th Century witnessed a flood of inventions and innovations, electricity among the most profound. A.E. Reynolds was one of the first mining entrepreneurs to invest in it when doing so was economical. Electrifying the Virginius/Revenue Tunnel was economical; electrifying the Vermont/Reynolds Tunnel was not. This 1895 photograph of the Ames Hydroelectric Plant near Telluride, Colorado, captures the moment. *(Wikipedia Commons)*

As others would demonstrate in years to come, building a hydroelectric plant in Henson Canyon or elsewhere in the district was feasible, but not on Reynolds' critical path. Within weeks of finalizing his deal with E.B. Hendrie the Reynolds Tunnel would be underway. But "underway" and "headway" were two quite different matters. It would take months to procure and install surface plant equipment, leaving the tunnel crew no choice but to drill the old-fashion way. Within months the tunnel crew would discover the rock they pounded drills into was the hardest they had ever faced, so hard that work songs could be (and were) written about it. In the meantime, our local editor reported more encouraging news.

> *(Lake City Times, March 9, 1899.) Two men have been at work this week on the Vermont property excavating for the blacksmith shop, powerhouse, etc. The contract for cutting and supplying the timbers for the Vermont tunnel and houses has been awarded to C.A. Wiers. The largest contract ever let in this county was awarded to George Staples and Dan McLeod today by J.J. Abbott, A.E. Reynolds' representative in this county. The contract is for the driving of a tunnel from Henson creek level to cut the Ocean Wave and Vermont veins, the estimated distance being 1,200 feet. Messrs. Staples and McLeod are miners of great ability and many years of experience and, although the contract is a large one, they will prove equal to the occasion. (The height and width of the tunnel, 8 ft. by 5 ft., are considered large by current standards. The length could be challenging for any small-town contractor.)*

Consistent with his nature, A.E.'s specifications for his tunnel and everything associated with it were detailed. Every condition accompanied by penalties for non-compliance spoke to Reynolds' experience dealing with contractors that apparently had not always been satisfactory. The portal of the tunnel needed to be exactly one hundred feet above Henson Creek at the confluence of El Paso Creek. Tunnel work needed to commence no later than May 1, 1899, "and be prosecuted diligently with not less than thirty shifts per month to completion within said stipulated period of two years." Local miners Staples and McLeod had no experience—neither did anyone else—with contracts as carefully crafted as A.E. Reynolds' contract, nor with an owner as diligent concerning enforcing its every stipulation. They focused on the promised compensation instead of warily assessing the terms and conditions regarding what was required of them. This would not be their first miscalculation.[3]

Reynolds was no less legalistic when it came to contracting for lumber. Unlike Staples and McLeod, C.A. Wiers did not need an attorney or a priest to counsel him that A.E. Reynolds was no one to trifle with. Also entered into on March 9, 1899, Wiers committed to furnishing and delivering mining timbers to the mouth of his tunnel cut exactly to the following dimensions:

- *Round timbers 17 ft. and 2 inches long, ten inches at the small end.*
- *Round timbers 14 ft. 10 inches at the small end.*
- *Lagging 12 or 18 ft. long, not less than 3 inches at the small end, or split lagging of the same lengths, made by splitting straight grained logs not less than six inches at the small end once in tow.*
- *Timbers 9 inches in diameter at the small end, any lengths from 12 ft. to 20 ft., also timbers 6 inches diameter, 11 feet and 17 feet long.*
- *Ties three feet long, 5 inches thick and hewed on two sides (opposite) to a face of not less than four inches.*

REYNOLDS' TUNNEL CONTRACT

A.E. Reynolds had learned many painful lessons during his decades-long ownership and operation of scores of hard-rock mines. By 1899 he had learned the value of tightly constructed contracts for any goods and services required. He understood the value of performance metrics and he understood owner liabilities and measures required to mitigate them regarding an increasing body of labor laws. He also may have been too arrogant to appreciate the risks of few if anyone wanting to do business with him.

    This Contract and Agreement made and entered into this ninth day of March A.D. 1899 by and between A.E. Reynolds of the County of Arapahoe and State of Colorado, Party of the First Part, and George Staples and Daniel McLeod of the County of Hinsdale and State of Colorado, Parties of the Second Part, WITNESSETH:

    1. That the said parties of the second part, for and in consideration of the covenants and agreements hereinafter set forth to be kept and performed by said first party, hereby contract and agree to run a tunnel from a point near the mouth of El Paso Gulch to intersect the Vermont vein. Said tunnel shall start at a point to be fixed by said first party, and shall run on line as given by first party and on an exact grade of four (4) inches to each one hundred (100) feet. Failure to keep grade or line will work forfeiture of the contract at the discretion of said first party. The width of the tunnel shall be five (5) feet in the clear, top and bottom, and the height eight (8) feet in the clear. The tunnel until under cover of solid rock shall be timbered eight and one half (8 & 1-2) feet in the clear from mudsill to cap with timbers of round red spruce not less than ten (10) inches in diameter at the small end and framed to true joints, with mudsills and collar braces. Tie shall be laid two and one half (2 & 1-2) feet apart from centre to centre. The rails shall be laid on the exact grade as above fixed, well spiked to the ties, and be kept carefully in line, with nuts and fish plates always tight and secure. Lagging shall be laid tight and close on the outer sides and top of all timbered ground. Work shall commence forthwith

Reynolds specified that all timber must be "sound and straight red spruce, green or dry, and completely barked." For his part, he agreed to pay:

- *80 cents each for pieces 17 ft. 2 inches long.*
- *70 cents each for pieces 14 ft. long.*
- *3 cents per linear foot for pieces 9 inches in diameter at the small end.*
- *25 cents and 40 cents each for lagging 6 inches in diameter, 17 ft. 2 inches or 14 ft. long respectively.*
- *Ten cents for ties.*

and be continuous, with not less than two shifts after getting under cover with the tunnel. The tunnel shall be driven not less than sixty (60) feet in each month from the start and not less than one hundred and fifty (150) feet in each month after the installation of the air drill plant.

II. That the said A.E. Reynolds, party of the first part, hereby contracts and agrees, for and in consideration of the covenants and agreements hereinbefore set forth to be kept and performed by said second parties, to pay for said work, so completed, as follows, to wit: For the first one hundred (100) feet at the rate of six dollars ($6) per foot. For the next two hundred and fifty feet (250) at the rate of eight dollars ($8) per foot. And for the remainder of said tunnel, from said point three hundred and fifty (350) feet from the mouth up to and across the said Vermont vein at the rate of nine dollars ($9) per foot. Payment will be made on the 15th of each month for work completed during the previous month, fifteen percent being reserved until the completion of the contract, this reserve to be forfeited if the contract is not fully carried out as agreed. Timbers, ties, car, rails and their appurtenances will be furnished by said first party. A compressor plant and one air drill, air pipe with its fittings and air drills will be furnished by first party as soon as practicable, after which they must be used exclusively. The compressor plant will be set in place by first party, after which it must be operated at the expense of second parties who shall be responsible for its maintenance in good condition, ordinary wear and tear excepted. Pipe for ventilation will be furnished by first party, should it become necessary, second parties to put it in place and maintain it. A building for a blacksmith shop at the mouth of the tunnel will be furnished by first party as soon as practicable.

III. It is mutually agreed that when each of the payments is made as hereinbefore provided for, the said parties of the second part shall furnish to said party of the first part a receipt in full from each miner and laborer employed by them on said tunnel work, thereby releasing said party of the first part from any liability for the wages of such miners and workmen. Time checks necessarily issued by said second parties in favor of discharged men will be paid by said first party and the amount thereof be deducted from the payments of the payday next following. IN WITNESS WHEREOF the said parties have hereunto set their hands and seals the day and year first above written.

Payments were to be made on the 15th day of each month for all timbers delivered and accepted during the previous month. Delivery was to begin immediately. Reynolds had sole discretion in determining whether the timbers were acceptable, and failure to deliver acceptable timbers as promptly as requested was sufficient grounds for contract termination.

All signs pointed to a prolonged financial commitment to the project. Wage rates aside, Reynolds' willingness to invest in an oversized tunnel, dimensional lumber, and a surface plant that included a steam boiler, compressed air equipment, blacksmith shop, powder-house, and lodging were clear indications he meant business. As important, he insisted his contractors take up their tasks in a timely and concerted manner. They did. Within a month and without the benefit of George Staples—not simply a tunnel-crew owner but also a working foreman—who was injured and unable to work, the tunnel progressed according to plan. Two months later, on April 13, 1899, the *Times* faithfully provided a status report:

Heart of the Matter. Steam boilers drove air compressors, drills, and perhaps pumps and ventilation systems that delivered life to hard rock mines. Their safe and reliable operation was an indispensable feature of a paying mine. *(Rand Drill Company)*

Lungs of Life. Utilization of pneumatic drills and other equipment rivaled electricity for the greatest benefits to mine safety and efficiency. *(Rand Drill Company)*

The big tunnel which is now being driven by A.E. Reynolds to cut the Ocean Wave and Vermont vein is now in 50 feet. As far as it has been driven it is said to be a fine piece of workmanship. Since Mr. Geo. Staples met with an accident the work has been carried on by Dan McLeod and Chas. Hix. A car load of rails will be taken to the mouth of the tunnel as soon as the Henson creek road is in a condition to haul them up.

Promising news, but there was more to the story. Technical troubles beset the crew almost immediately, and their compensation, calculated by feet driven rather than by a daily rate, was looking marginal at best. The first fifty feet of tunneling was through dirt consisting of unconsolidated boulders, cobble, and fines that required careful timbering. Excavation was relatively easy, but carpentry was tedious. Once into solid rock, hand-drilling and blasting, slow in the best of conditions, slowed even more. The tunnel crew complained the rock was not only uncommonly hard, it also broke in unhelpful ways. Probably more frustrating,

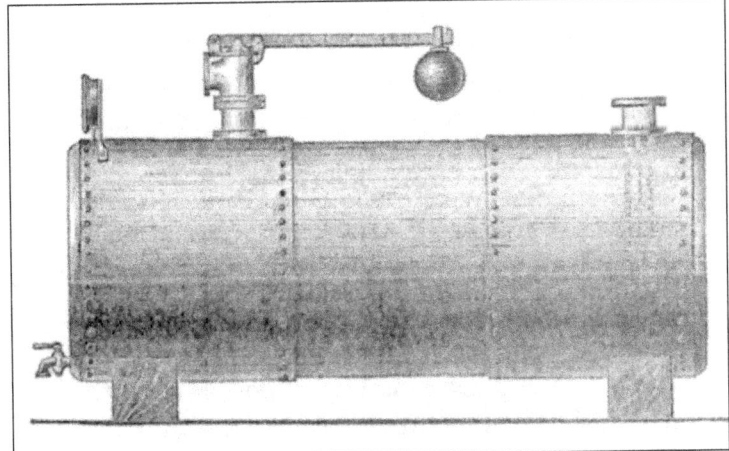

Unsung Hero. Little appreciated by the casual observer, the air receiver is a vital feature of any pressurized air system. It is a reservoir that dampens the negative effects of unavoidable variations in pressure generated by the air compressor. *(Rand Drill Company)*

Little Giant. The Rand Drill Company's "Little Giant" incorporated engineered design features that were a God-send to hard rock miners both in terms of their productivity, but also their health. *(Rand Drill Company)*

use of power tools awaited construction of structures to house a steam boiler and air compressor, both of which were slow in arriving. Nevertheless, a one-hundred-forty-seven foot (on average, a disappointing one ft. per day) milestone was reached in time for the 4th of July, but at great cost. Staples returned to work after the mandatory holiday, but partner McLeod had had enough.

In addition to tough going and its effect on compensation earned, the crew had quickly encountered a more life-threatening challenge. Barely into the mountain, breathable air was already a concern. Absent any means of ventilation, dead air and fumes from blasting hung stubbornly in the tunnel. Facing the loss of more of his miners, superintendent Abbott recommended to Reynolds that he increase the rate of pay from eight dollars to nine dollars per foot, and that he immediately invest in ventilation pipe. Reynolds agreed to nine dollars per foot, and wooden air pipe and barrels of asphalt to seal joints was soon procured in Creede.

Ventilating underground workings was a universal challenge. One of the central purposes of Reynolds Tunnel was passive ventilation of the historic and proposed workings of the Vermont and Ocean Wave from the lower tunnel through the upper workings and back to the surface through their upper adits. This would be accomplished by natural drafts induced by warm or cool air drawn into the rabbit warren of shafts, winzes, and tunnels at one elevation and expelled at a different temperature and barometric pressure at a different elevation. The direction of flow from higher to lower or vice-versa would change depending on the change in outside air temperature or pressure due to time of day or weather patterns or seasons. During the warm months of summer, heavier cool mine air would flow out of the Reynolds Tunnel adit, drawing fresh air down the shafts and winzes behind it. During colder months, the relatively warmer air of the mine would rise up the chimney-like shafts and winzes, drawing fresh outside air through the lower Reynolds Tunnel portal. Until this passive ventilation system of tunnels, shafts, and winzes was completed, mechanical means utilizing pipes and air compressors would have to be employed. Simple enough, cost of materials and labor aside, except for a source of power to drive the compressors.

Ventilation pipe was on the list of materials Reynolds was obligated to supply Staples and McLeod should they need it. Unexpected was the need to ventilate the tunnel so early into the project. In general, Abbott and Reynolds had two options. One, which already looked to be a dead-end, was rely on natural ventilation. This approach with minor variations was akin to doing nothing and trusting that tunnel dynamics would take care of the problem. Obviously less expensive, tunnel dynamics and long tunnels were incompatible. While miners were expected to wait until the toxic fumes and dust from blasting cleared the tunnel naturally, a slow process to be sure, or to re-enter the tunnel and resume work despite the foul air, both expectations had serious drawbacks. In addition to health effects, there was the matter of money. When miners were being paid by the foot, daily downtime was not their friend.

The second option was mechanical, expensive, but sooner or later inevitable. Wooden pipe was an option, tin pipe was better. In the spring of 1899 neither was in Reynolds' plan but he was realistic. Foul air or not, the 4th of July was reason enough to stop work and regroup. With Christmas Day as a possible exception, celebrating the 4th was one day every miner prized above all others. Not only was work set aside—no mine superintendent worthy of the title gave any thought to working on the 4th—from dawn to long into the night festivities, good food, and dancing was found everywhere. Lake City hosted the greatest variety, but five miles up Henson Canyon miners gathered in Snowden's Meadow to party and gossip and play baseball.

Somehow back at work on July 5th, both pleasant memories and the long awaited air compressor in service surrendered to more trouble at Reynolds Tunnel. The *Times* reported the disheartening news on July 6, 1899.

> *Work was temporarily suspended at the Reynolds Tunnel this week on account of the air compressor breaking down. Ten men have been employed in the driving of this tunnel and the work has been moving along nicely until this accident occurred. [Not really an "accident," but the consequence was the same.]*

With morale somewhat uplifted by an additional dollar per foot and the prospect of improved ventilation on the horizon, Staples' crew took the temporary loss of the compressor in stride and made good use of their downtime by addressing another common threat to their well-being. Large quantities of explosives were part of their stock-in-trade and its proper handling and storage usually paramount in their thinking. After considerable argument, one can be sure, a site near the tunnel portal was selected for the construction of a stout powder-house. The finished structure boasted eighteen inch thick stone walls, a two inch thick door, and an iron gable roof. It was stout enough to survive any external danger including stray bullets or a nearby wildfire. Interior dimensions of ten feet by ten feet accommodated enough explosives to outlast the most prolonged winter season.

Sadly for the workforce, loss of the compressor lingered and necessitated a return to hand-drilling. A return to hand-drilling meant a return to complaining about hard rock and unfair wages. Superintendent Abbott did not need exhortations from foreman Staples to get the point. The rock was the hardest he too had ever encountered, and hand-drilling was hardest when you saw a highly efficient power-drill lying idle at your feet for lack of power. Abbott also knew skilled labor was in short-supply. Not only was the district in the midst of recession, it also was in the midst of a smallpox epidemic. A prudent man would do what he could to keep his current workforce. Abbott and Reynolds were prudent men. They could not do anything about smallpox, but they could raise wages to ten dollars per foot.[4]

Despite an increase in pay, Abbott was not able to resolve ventilation problems, and morale remained a challenge. Pipe and asphalt had been procured in Creede, but finding a way to transport it to the site was another matter. His plan, once pipe and asphalt was on site, was to erect a tall vertical chimney-like structure connected to horizontal piping hung from the ceiling of the tunnel. He hoped that the difference in elevation would create a large enough temperature and pressure differential—mimicking the effect of connecting the upper workings with the lower adit—to naturally draw fresh air into the tunnel while flushing out fouled air. Into the mountain just one-hundred-forty-seven feet, Staples and Abbott had at least a thousand feet to go to intersect the Vermont vein. Every miner knew the problem would only get worse the farther they went. At some point dead air would make for dead miners, mentally incapacitated or sickened at best.

By the end of July 1899, J.J. Abbott was asking himself whatever happened to the joy and goodwill of the 4th. His compressor was still disabled, his ventilation pipe and asphalt were in Creede, and his workforce including George Staples was still disgruntled to the point of quitting. Earlier in the month Abbott sensed a need to consider terminating the contract with Staples on the basis that the rock was harder than anyone could have imagined and letting him rebid at $10 per foot. Or alternatively, voiding the contract in favor of a contract with Dan McCafferty who bid $10 originally and was better with air drills and self-financing his crew.

Apparently Staples not only had problems with his health, attitude, hard rock, bad air, and disgruntled miners, he also had problems paying his workforce in a timely manner. Abbott paid Staples fifteen days after the end of the month, as called for in his contract. As was the custom of the day, the workforce expected to be paid at the end of each week, meaning Staples needed a cash reserve or a line of credit to bridge the cashflow gaps between the first week and fifteen days after the end of each month. He had neither.

By August Abbott had had his fill of Staples and crew. Labor shortages or not, he asked Reynolds to send him $500 by the next mail to settle matters immediately with those he was going to release. He needed an additional $700 a week thereafter. There was no update on the disabled compressor, but part of its repair included the addition of a "receiver" (heavy-gauge tank) which would be located well into the tunnel and pressurized. This reservoir of high-pressure air would enable a more constant pressure than otherwise would be the case if the pneumatic drills were driven directly off the compressor. In a letter dated August 2, 1899, Superintendent Abbott updated Reynolds' Denver office manager, Charles F. McKenny:

> *"I expect to have to pay off Staples' men at once and it would probably be useless for me to ask Jordan [local bank President, no friend of Reynolds]*

for any overdraft or like consideration." On August 10th Abbott again wrote McKenny: "The new contract is let and work will begin as soon as the new air receiver and ventilating pipe can be put in place, which we hope will be by Saturday or Sunday. The section of pipe from Creede is just received and I presume the asphalt is now in." [5]

Word traveled quickly in Henson Canyon. Also on August 10th the *Times* published the news of management changes at the Reynolds Tunnel.

> *Work on the Vermont tunnel will be resumed today under the management of Dan McCafferty, who has taken the contract to complete the work. Mr. McCafferty informed us this morning that standard wages will be paid to all men employed and they will be required to work no longer than the men on the other mines of the camp. [8 hrs./day instead of 10 hrs./day]* [6]

Stating that the work day at the Vermont was the same as at other mines was significant. Throughout the mountain West the standard 10-hour shift was giving way under Western Federation of Miners labor union pressure to an 8-hour work day. Owner acceptance of this change was resisted as long as possible. It was customary to pay miners by the day, not the hour. (Not only did pressure to shorten the workday spell trouble, so too would calculating wages on an hourly versus daily basis which was on the horizon.) Abbott not only saw the necessity of raising daily wages, he saw the need to shorten the daily shift.

On August 24th superintendent Abbott, with contractor and foreman McCafferty in tow, prepared to resume work. After repeated delays, the new air receiver had arrived and was promptly installed. The compressor, steam plant, and air pipe also were good to go. Tunnel progress was all but assured except for one minor matter. On August 26th Abbott notified McKenny that their latest shipment of "powder," actually sticks of nitroglycerin, (the latest innovation in mining explosives offered by the Nitro Powder Company of Kingston, New York) was defective. Some of the sticks were deformed and seeping a noxious liquid. The boxes they were packed in were "oily." Abbott was convinced they were too dangerous to handle and complained to McKenny on August 30th:

> *Will Fuller sorted the boxes in the [railroad] car and he was sick for two days. The driver who took it up to the Ocean Wave tunnel [not yet established enough to be called the Reynolds Tunnel] hasn't got over it yet. The blacksmith helped unload and he was made sick by it, while I had the same experience just from handling a few sticks.* [7]

McKenny was Reynolds' trusted office manager for good reason. He was quick to question the Nitro Powder Company and E. Metzger, President of the company, was quick to explain. The oily condition of the boxes was due to paraffin wax, not nitroglycerin, which was used in packaging. Any yellowish discoloration noticed was due to naphthalene in the powder and any liquid was discolored that came in contact with it. The odor was the smell of nitro-naphthalene, the same compound that was found in moth balls. It was added to counteract poisonous gases when exploded. President Metzger acknowledged that it could cause headaches and nausea.[8]

WESTERN FEDERATION OF MINERS
(WFM)

Reynolds, like most mine owners, was staunchly opposed to unions of any kind. He considered them a band of "ruffians and murderers who sought the destruction of the private enterprise system and the substitution of socialism for capitalism." With considerable difficulty he managed to avoid operating any of his properties with a unionized workforce.[9]

Established in 1893, the WFM was a federation of local unions representing copper miners in Butte, Montana; silver and lead miners in Coeur D'Alene, Idaho; gold miners in Colorado; and hard rock miners in South Dakota and Utah. By 1901 the WFM was more or less a socialist party. Two years later it was considered the most militant labor organization in the country. Big Bill Haywood, an Idaho silver miner and union secretary who fled to the Soviet Union in 1921 to avoid a prison sentence, described the matter this way: how was it that the "mine owners did not find the gold, they did not mine the gold, they did not mill the gold, but by some weird alchemy all the gold belonged to them?"

The WFM went through a number of transformations. In 1916 it was named the International Union of Mine, Mill, and Smelter Workers, the Mine Mill for short. During President Roosevelt's New Deal it helped found the Congress of Industrial Organizations (CIO). In 1950, the CIO expelled the Mine Mill for refusing to remove its Communist leadership. In 1967 the Mine Mill merged with the Canadian Auto Workers, retaining the name Mine Mill Local 598.

The nation's working class had legitimate grievances and the WFM along with a multitude of other labor unions eventually were successful in remedying most of them. In A.E. Reynolds' world, there was no ground yielded to the WFM, but he did yield to the workforce when he saw no alternatives to their demands. During the banner-years of America's industrial revolution, in the era of robber-barons, Reynolds walked a tightrope between unbridled capitalism and anarchy. His approach to labor disputes—grant concessions sufficient to eliminate the need for a union—eventually gave way to including the workforce in the shareholder pool or leasing the property in question to them and collecting royalties based on their profits.[10]

Abbott was not impressed with Metzger's response and Reynolds backed his superintendent. In a telegram from Portland, Maine, A.E. instructed McKenny in no uncertain terms: "Powder must be made absolutely acceptable to Abbott or Metzger must refund and take it away."[11]

Metzger complied. Abbott received powder he liked the feel, smell, and looks of and McCafferty's men resumed drilling and blasting. By the first of October the tunnel was in 390 feet, having advanced 126 feet (four feet per day on average sounds a lot better than one foot during the previous month.) Abbott reported to Reynolds on October 3rd:

> *Every effort will be made by the contractor to equal or exceed 150 feet this month. He is a very hard worker himself and has picked a lot of Italians for drill men. The trouble is much more in getting the rock out of the way than in breaking the ground. I am satisfied that the mucking can be done to better advantage and hope to see that it is.*[12]

Oh, those pesky Italians. Abbott seems to have made good hiring decisions, but three miles down the road their brethren were about to shut down the Ute/ Ulay and prevent it reopening even at gunpoint. The matter, settled by the arrival of the Colorado militia and the Italian Counsel from Denver, led to the expulsion of many Italians from Hinsdale County. But these troubles were down the road. Abbott's Italians seemed unaffected, a valued sub-class if you will. Besides that, Abbott had other vexing problems. Not a week after his harmonious report to Reynolds on his tunnel progress, he struck another sour note. On October 10th he wrote:

> *When I went up to the Ocean Wave tunnel yesterday, I found McCafferty worn out and discouraged. He said he could not carry his contract any further. About the first of the month the tunnel passed into a tough, hard cross-grained formation that would neither drill nor break well. Instead of 14 holes for a round it has been requiring 21 and 23 and the last time it took 100 lbs. of powder instead of fifty.*[13]

There was more bad news. He advised Reynolds that McCafferty was working fifteen hours a day, paying himself half-wages, and "crowding his men to the limit." And still they have only made twenty-three feet in seven days. Moreover, their "pony compressor" was no longer up to the task. They needed a larger one, and A.E. needed to increase their pay yet again.[14]

Before Reynolds responded (there is no record that he did), Abbott took matters into his own hands. He launched a new round of requests. In an October 13th letter to McKenny he signaled optimism with his instructions to order a more potent explosive to combat the hard rock. He asked for 40% Gelatin, a

POWDER [15]

Powder, originally meaning "black powder," remained the common term for more powerful explosives developed throughout the nineteenth-century. The evolution of powder available to Western hard-rock miners is explained in exquisite detail by Eric Twitty in *Blown to Bits in the Mine*.

Western miners began replacing black powder with dynamite in the late 1860s. During the 1870s miners could choose between continued use of black powder or "straight dynamite." During the 1880s and 1890s explosives manufacturers also offered gelatin, extra dynamite, extra gelatin, ammonium nitrate, and non-nitro-glycerine dynamites. While they produced less poisonous gases and accounted for fewer accidents, miners were slow to adopt their use. Undeniable and eventually persuasive, they all were far more powerful than their black powder predecessors.

The big four powder companies were DuPont de Nemours & Company, Hercules Powder Company, Atlas Powder Company, and the Austin Powder Company. DuPont prospered greatly supplying Lincoln's civil war army with explosives. The Giant Powder Company came on the scene in 1868 with a game changer called dynamite. By the end of the century it was the miner's first choice. The term "dynamite" also was universal, applying to nearly all high explosives regardless of their distinguishing characteristics. *Straight dynamite* was a putty-like blend of nitro-glycerine and a combustible absorbent wrapped in a waxed cartridge. Nicknamed "Giant Powder," also the name of its manufacturer, its popularity was unmatched for many years. Generally speaking, the percentage of nitroglycerine—30%, 40%, and so forth—determined its strength relative to *straight dynamite*.

What made explosives "high" was the ability to explode without combustion with or without confinement. High explosives "detonated," thereby transforming their solid ingredients into a large volume of expanding gases and a sudden shock of energy, the combined effects of both shattering the hardest of rocks.

No discussion of dynamite and nitroglycerine is complete without mention of Alfred Nobel. Alfred invented neither compound. That accomplishment should be credited to Ascanio Sobrero, an 1846 University of Torino chemistry professor, who concluded his discovery was too dangerous to manufacture. Alfred Nobel thought otherwise. By the mid-1860s he had developed a relatively safe product for mining and military applications called "Nobel's Blasting Oil." After numerous unintended detonations, many of them cataclysmic, Nobel abandoned liquid nitroglycerine in 1867 and patented "dynamite." In league with American interests, he also licensed his technology to the Giant Powder Company. As usual, other companies with competing products soon followed, some safer, some not so much.

In 1888 Alfred read his own obituary—actually it was his brother Ludvig who had died—titled "The Merchant of Death is Dead." Horrified about his legacy, he included in his will the establishment in 1901 of the Nobel Peace Prizes awarded to individuals "who have conferred the greatest benefit to humankind."

large quantity of it, 14,000 lbs. of 1.25 inch diameter sticks in standard eight-inch lengths. At their present rate of progress, this order amounted to a full rail-car that would last until May 1st. McKenny scarcely had time to comply when Abbott, believing that he had convinced McCafferty that better ground lie just ahead, asked McKenny to order an additional 10,000 lbs. of "machine powder" to last him until September 1st.

Better ground did not lie just ahead. Barely six days after Abbott thought the tunnel was back on schedule, he wired McKenny an urgent appeal:

Can you let me have $500 on account of the Ocean Wave M&R CO.? I am likely to be forced to take summary action up there and pay some men off in a hurry. Yours in haste, J.J. Abbott. [16]

Merchant of Death. Credited with perfecting and commercializing "dynamite" that made weapons of war far more deadly, Alfred Nobel hoped he would be remembered for instituting annual Nobel Peace Prizes. (Wikipedia)

On October 26th, Abbott thanked McKenny for sending the requested $500, but that did not put to rest more unsettling news. The compressor had broken down again. Abbott lamented, "the compressor is so old and runs at so high a rate of speed that this is likely to occur at any time. I hope to find (it) running again this morning." [17]

Happily, Abbott's dire forecast did not materialize that morning. He found the compressor running. And apparently it continued to run at least intermittently well into November. But Abbott's truce with McCafferty and crew did not run well into November. On November 6th Abbott informed Reynolds that the tunnel was in five hundred feet and (oh, by the way) that his brother was replacing McCafferty. Abbott explained on November 9th, probably in response to a McKenny or Reynolds' inquiry.

I effected a settlement and full release with McCafferty, but only with considerable difficulty, as he had been drinking and was obstinate, unreasonable and abusive. Whiskey (and the mental and moral demoralization caused by it) is largely responsible for his failure to accomplish what was expected of him. (Abbott added that the workers remained loyal to him, but he was not optimistic about their equipment.)

Only one thing worries me and stands in the way of crowding the tunnel as it ought to be crowded. The compressor is altogether inadequate when we are in hard rock. Everything else is first class and well arranged. Another pony compressor, set beside the present one, would remedy this and soon save its cost. I watched ours for a long time yesterday when it was almost jumping off its foundation under 200 revolutions a minute, and yet the pressure could not be raised above 55 lbs. of air. [18]

Reynolds procrastinated. He already had invested more in his tunnel than he had envisioned and no doubt was looking to avoid further expenses if at all possible. More to the point, investments elsewhere were disappointing and he was strapped for cash. This would become a recurring problem that dogged the king's reign the balance of his life. Abbott's next report did not improve Reynolds' balance sheet nor his mood. On November 15th Abbott wrote:

I have been up to the Ocean Wave [Reynolds] tunnel in the snow storm today. It has advanced about 29 feet in the last 10 days, 15 of that being 8 feet wide for a siding, which we now need. This is the best progress we have ever made in that very hard rock, due allowance being made for the piece of extras width. We are getting all we can out of the compressor. It is in excellent condition in every particular, but breaks down at some point every few days on account of the high pressure at which we are compelled to drive it. In the hardest rock, we can maintain only from 50 to 55 pounds of air and then it takes from an hour to an hour and a half to put in a deep hole. We have a picked lot of men in every particular, each one of them trying his best to make the work go ahead. I never expect to see a better lot of the same, of any nationality. (Note here an uncommon compliment directed at "his" Italians.) [19]

Improved workforce morale was noteworthy. Despite unreliable equipment and "glassy, silicious stuff" passing itself off as rock, and despite willingly ignoring the "eight-hour rule," on November 23rd Abbott reported:

At the Ocean Wave [Reynolds] tunnel the rock gets worse rather than better. When the air runs down to 50 (psi) they have to stop the drill until the pressure gets back to something they can use. The men are working nine and ten hours without a grumble and my brother 15 to 18. We are getting the best results possible under the circumstances. [20]

A week later Abbott was even more encouraged. The tunnel was in 583 feet, advancing eighty-eight feet in twenty-six days (an average three feet per day) since

"McCafferty was let out." Fifteen feet of that tunnel was double wide to make room for a siding, thus Abbott calculated his boys should be credited with 95.5 feet in twenty-six days (an average 3.7 ft. per day). By comparison, McCafferty's crew made ninety-one feet in the preceding thirty days (seven-tenths of a foot less was apparently a significance difference). Abbott also attributed better results to a change in how work was performed which he predicted would deliver one-hundred-ten feet of tunnel in the next thirty days. The new approach shot the face of the tunnel no later than 3 A.M. His brother and two trammers would get up at 2:30 A.M. and have everything shoveled out ready for the machine men to resume drilling at 7 A.M. As an afterthought, Abbott further complimented his crew:

> *A large amount of extra work has been got out of the men during the past twenty days, in the way of trimming up the tunnel, straightening out and grading track & c. [because] McCafferty kept flattening his track until the inner end was down in the water more than 8 inches below grade. Now we have a fine track and a tunnel I am not at all ashamed of. I wish you could see it and all its appurtenances.* [21]

On balance, from Abbott's point of view, 1899 ended better than he thought it would when he relieved McCafferty in November. His workforce under supervision of his brother was performing heroically. As Christmas approached it seemed likely Reynolds would authorize purchase of another pony compressor, and despite overrunning his budget, thus far there was no blow-back from the front office. Confirming the tumultuous month of November, an overrun of $1,750 was eye-popping in light of the total cost of $5,410 ($3,696 labor) for the entire year. If for no other reason than this, Abbott must have sensed deep within his soul that this cost overrun was going to be a problem.[22]

"Ending well" could not be said for the county and state at large, a source of much trouble beyond Reynolds' control that nevertheless greatly burdened his plan. Despite the long-awaited arrival of D&RG rail service and its beneficial effects on ore shipments, the *Denver Times* reporting from Lake City painted a darker back-story that was not apparent in its choice of words. Curiously, the correspondent described the narrowly avoided bloodshed surrounding the Ute/Ulay strike and armed insurrection simply as "Italian troubles," and characterized the year's mining disappointments as normal "drawbacks." Not even deadly plague seemed cause for concern. But understating these developments and the resulting hardships on the local economy did not escape those most effected. J.J. Abbott was troubled but silent. So was A.E. Reynolds. Perhaps encouraged by the afterglow of Christmas, the December 31, 1899, *Denver Times* did its part to brush aside concerns that could dampen enthusiasm for the new year:

We are to be congratulated on this gain [ore shipments], too, for we have had drawbacks in plenty. In early spring we were in shape for an enormous output when the memorable smelter strike (our local boosters neglected sharing this with their readers) came upon us. Again we were just recovering when we were called to settle the Italian troubles, at which time the state militia was called here. And, lastly, and late in the fall, too, our county was almost at a standstill on account of an epidemic of smallpox which rage here. Surely we had our share and more, too, of the drawbacks that are liable to confront any mining camp. [23]

As usual, the new year did bring new optimism, and Reynolds' tunnel project was no exception. Work resumed after the Christmas break. The *Lake City Times* dutifully reported on January 25th that "a new double compound air compressor is received here and this morning was taken up to the Vermont." On February 1st the *Times* published one of its best examples of boosterism, partly as was the custom in the guise of a New Year's summary of past and future accomplishments, partly in response to "backcapping,"—malicious criticism from competing communities like Ouray. Also *as usual*, Reynolds Tunnel could be counted on as an inspirational role model for other Henson Canyon mines.

Immigrant Troubles. Downward pressures on wages and job opportunities were not limited to San Juan miners or Italians in particular. The late 1800s and early 1900s witnessed numerous protests, some violent, and numerous political campaigns featuring them. Henson Canyon was not spared, A.E. Reynolds Vermont Group and Tunnel was. *(Library of Congress)*

Don't advertise our faults, but our virtues. With all of our backcapping Hinsdale is coming to the front. Just keep still and our virtues will advertise themselves. There are few men even in our county who realize the amount of mining that is carried on here, or realize what the class of mining done now means to Hinsdale county Take the larger enterprises such as the Reynolds Vermont tunnel... What do they mean? It is hard to grasp the possibilities. For when tunnels like those reach their destination they will open worlds unknown to this mining section at such depth as has yet never been attained. They will make new mines—not new in one respect, for their surface workings have shown rich ore and have shipped large quantities—but this will open new zones that will mean mills and hundreds of men employed. [24]

Yes, "boosterism at its best," you say. But that said, such reporting—oft repeated—had an element of reality attached to it, and fell in line with much recurring evidence that fueled expectations for decades that Reynolds' tunnel would lead to great treasure.

On March 15th the *Times* editor revisited the subject of the Reynolds Tunnel by reporting on what must have seemed like an important milestone to more than just J.J. Abbott. "At the Vermont tunnel the excavation and foundation for the new double compound air compressor has been completed and the compressor put in place" was newsworthy. If nothing else, it signaled that serious new investment in infrastructure continued. A week later the editor again returned to the Vermont, sparing no detail:

There has been little said of late about the Reynolds enterprise on Henson Creek—the Vermont tunnel. For all that, work has been progressing continually, and so far as an outsider can judge, satisfactorily. This enterprise means so much to Hinsdale County that one feels better every time he thinks of it. To begin with, it is well known that when A.E. Reynolds makes a mining venture it is no idle undertaking. He mines on a larger scale than any man in Colorado, and works his mines to make them pay. That this property has a better showing right now than the famous Virginius had when Mr. Reynolds took hold of it years ago, is a statement which is backed up by mining men familiar with both properties. The Virginius is the mine that made Ouray, and the starting of the Vermont tunnel is believed to mark the beginning of a new era of prosperity, such as Lake City has never enjoyed before.

This property consists of a group of claims, the principal ones being the Ocean Wave, Wave of the Ocean and Vermont. All these have been large shippers of high grade ore in the past. They have been worked from time to time by lessors and have lain idle as long as they were worked, waiting for the right party to come along. He came. He has secured ground showing up the vein a distance of 7,000 feet, and the tunnel is being run to cut this vein in the middle.

The tunnel starts near the Capitol City road and is now in about 900 feet. A Times *man stopped at this place one day this week, and through the courtesy of J. W. [actually J.J.] Abbott, who is in charge, was shown into the tunnel. Just how much further it is expected to run to strike the vein could not be learned, as the management is very reticent about giving out information. Miners pronounce this the finest piece of mining in Hinsdale county. It is large and roomy, well timbered at the start, well ventilated, the track is on a positive grade and as straight as a Burlington road. The tunnel is being driven with two machines, running two shifts. Near the mouth of the tunnel is a building containing the air compressor, boiler, blacksmith shop and carpenter shop. The powder house is worthy of note, as there are few its equal to be found in the state.*

The power used for running the drills is a cross compound air compressor, set on a perfect foundation. Everything done about the place is of the highest and best order of mining. There is a little creek running by the building which may be utilized for milling purposes, and there is an ideal mill site at the mouth of the tunnel. All the dumps of these various claims contain a large amount of good concentrating ore, the accumulation of all the years of their working, and it is presumed they will be worked over whenever a mill is built. There are at present 15 or 16 men working, but when the ore is reached and work spreads out, the force may be expected to number 200 men or more. [25]

Two hundred men or more working Reynolds' vision was visionary indeed. March of 1900 ended with fifteen men working. March also ended with three avalanches that would close the county wagon road between the Vermont Group and town for months. Mines up and down Henson Creek volunteered men to shovel and blast a way through, but normal wagon traffic was not restored until June. Accustomed to long winters and frequent snow slides, this season was one of the worse. Even so, Abbott's crew was well-prepared and worked through it all. By mid-June Abbott was able to report to Reynolds that the tunnel was in twelve hundred feet. Reynolds' goal had been achieved, albeit late and at far greater expense than planned. Of more interest, Abbott also reported:

We struck a small, barren vein which appears to be significant only as marking the line of contact between the peculiar rock we have had so long and true porphyry.

The Vermont shaft, which was sunk for 200 feet at a point only 115 or 120 ft. west of where we now are, went down all the way in a big vein and at the bottom that vein was bigger than ever with some mineral and wider than the shaft. [26]

PORPHYRY AND VUGS

Porphyry refers to an igneous rock of coarse-grained crystals found in quartz, often purple-red in color. Associated ore deposits are often rich in copper, molybdenum, gold, and silver. The material is extremely hard. Reaching the end of it and transition zone into a more workable material would be a moment of great joy for Reynolds Tunnel miners.

A vug, a small cavity usually lined with crystals, often contained rich ores or the promise of them. In the case of the Vermont Group, they often resulted in varying degrees of stoping. In every case vugs were also reason for joy.

Abbott's understanding of the proximity and depth of the Vermont shaft may be somewhat mistaken, but the significance of his observation cannot be overemphasized. Prior to suspension of development of the upper workings under English syndicate leases executed in the late 1880s and early 1890s, plans to sink a shaft five hundred feet along a promising vein was pursued, but to what depth must have been unknown to Abbott. [Also apparently unconfirmed, drifts planned every sixty feet off of this shaft could have been started.] Whatever the depth, the bottom of the shaft was much closer to where Abbott stood, a discovery that would be made in due course. Also discovered in due course, the shaft had been sunk five hundred feet measured from the Level No. 3 portal to the bottom of which was only fifty feet or so above where Abbott stood. More significant still, the fact that the vein improved with depth was yet another clue the odds of unearthing high-grade treasure improved with depth.

In the short term, the solution to their recurring ventilation issues was at hand. Moreover, by Abbott's estimation, the face of Reynolds Tunnel was only twenty-five to thirty feet from the Ocean Wave/Vermont vein worked from above, less than a week's work away based on current experience. He also misjudged this, but not by much. During the prior week his shifts averaged five feet per day with rock breaking "better than ever before." Drilling was better, too. Twelve rounds broke sixty feet of tunnel.

Reynolds was not impressed. He was in a financial bind. Most likely in a foul mood, he bypassed his customary local business associates and traveled to New York in search of financial relief. In the meantime he instructed Abbott to stop work. On the cusp of victory, Abbott was deflated but not defeated. In a Western Union telegram dated July 1, 1900, delivered to Reynolds at New York City's Waldorf Hotel, he wrote: "Just opening Vermont vein scattering ore small amount high grade remarkable improvement past ten feet hope you will reconsider."[27]

Likely a surprise even to Abbott, Reynolds did reconsider, albeit with a reduced budget, but not before Abbott lost some of his workforce including his blacksmith who also was his machinist. Both skills were absolutely critical to operations. The primary responsibility of the machinist was operating and maintaining finicky compressors, pneumatic drills, and the boiler-generated steam plant that drove the compressors. The blacksmith also sharpened drill bits daily and fabricated parts. Office Manager McKenny sent Abbott $2,200, which no doubt was owed the miners (including the blacksmith/machinist) for weeks of work. Abbott redeemed some of his men including his blacksmith/machinist who could have been easily recruited by other mines. Less than a week after Reynolds' change of heart, tunnel work resumed [a certain testimony to Abbott's leadership and his crew's expectation that they were too close to victory to abandon the quest now.]

On July 9th Abbott reported to A.E., "We got started on Friday, running only one drill and otherwise reducing the force as much as possible." Work accomplished was improving turning by widening the tunnel where the main tunnel branched off to the west to undercut the Vermont, and to the east to undercut the Ocean Wave. Trimming the corners made for a more gradual turning radius for track and cars. Two rounds were shot in the west breast where Abbott reported they were back into hard rock; one round was shot in the east breast where the rock was not quite as hard. His only regret was not having "60% powder." From Abbott's accounts it is not difficult to discern lingering apprehension. Cashflow issues could continue manifesting in delayed wage payments, and marginal successes in the mine could continue hanging over the project like the noxious nitroglycerin fumes. [28]

By mid-July Abbott's reports to Reynolds occurred every few days instead of once a week or more. Reynolds had Abbott on a tight budget and a short leash. Equally plausible was Abbott getting excited about not only reaching the point where he could upraise to the five-hundred foot shaft and the old Vermont workings, he also was uncovering pay-dirt on the Vermont vein. On July 14th Abbott advised Reynolds that there was no tunnel work during the past three days due to putting in "switch and track, a slow and tedious job." He also reported encountering a promising quartz vein in the breast of the east (Ocean Wave) drift, and in the breast of the west (Vermont) drift a vug a foot wide and three to four feet long. Abbott wrote,

(I)n this (vug) appears a mass of black stuff which drains in from above and which is claimed to be in this vein, a certain proof of the proximity of gray copper ore. The vein as it now appears in both directions is strong and promising in appearance. There is a good gouge, lots of iron and oxidized stuff with a little galena. [29]

Gray copper ore was something to get excited about. Regardless of some-times being somewhat of a misnomer—it could contain copper but be black—it also could contain as much as 18% silver in place of copper. On July 19th Abbott, knowing that a competitive spirit was a common miner trait, resorted to compe-tition as a tried and true way of incentivizing progress. He reported to Reynolds that he had pitted a "white crew" against an "Italian crew." The "white crew" had driven the west drift thirty feet on the Vermont vein measuring just less than five feet wide. The Italians had driven the east drift twenty-four feet on a five foot width of the Ocean Wave vein. On July 24th Abbott reported that the competi-tors were each making three to four feet a day and were running out of powder. Inclined to order a car load of explosives, Abbott hesitated doing so until he discussed the matter with Reynolds. The cost of a car load aside, Reynolds' con-tract with E.B. Hendrie regarding the lease with option to purchase the Vermont properties was about to expire. Tunnel progress was way behind schedule and way over budget. What would Reynolds decide? Renegotiating his lease/pur-chase agreement with Hendrie was not a foregone conclusion.

Reynolds had invested a great deal in his tunnel, not least of which was reputation and pride. He was cautiously optimistic that investing a little more would produce the results he envisioned. He had experienced these moments of decision on the Virginius' Revenue Tunnel. At the same time, he knew enough about mining to know cutting losses may be painful but often wise. Consciously or not, the Reynolds Tunnel was special to him. At his age, it was probably abun-dantly clear that of all the many claims in his elephant corral of properties, this tunnel was his last best chance to make a mine. If he persuaded Hendrie to grant him contractual relief, he could continue the quest. On August 4th Abbott was dispatched to Estes Park, Colorado to negotiate a new contract with Hendrie.

In Estes Park Abbott explained to Hendrie in great detail that the tunnel was delayed by many months "by extraordinary hardness and toughness of the rock," and that "the present showing (of the Vermont vein) would not justify a cash price to exceed $5,000 for the whole group of claims." Hendrie was a reasonable man, but not that reasonable. When all was said and done, Abbott reported to Reynolds the details of a successful negotiation. On August 4, 1900, Abbott wrote:

> I said to Mr. Hendrie: "I shall tell Mr. Reynolds that you agree to the ex-tension of our option for one year (to February 1, 1902), and that a reduction of the purchase price from $31,500.00 to $20,000 is satisfactory to you. That with reference to the said reduction of price you feel it incumbent to consult a lady partner, for which you will require about four weeks, as she is now in Italy, and that you will state to her that the said reduction of purchase price to $20,000.00 is satisfactory to you." To this he distinctly assented. I then said that upon this understanding I would ask you to continue the work. [30]

REYNOLDS' ELEPHANT CORRAL

No doubt before but as early as the California gold rush, "going out to see the elephant" was a popular term used to describe searching out the unexpected. Will Bagley explains the term well in *With Golden Visions Bright Before Them*.[31] Bagley tells of twenty-six year old William Stinson hired to lead a party of Forty-Niners across the plains. In addition to his scouting skills, according to Bagley, Stinson also was a marketer, promising his wards "a sight of all the elephants on the route, in other words, of all the interesting objects on our journey." As the rush to California gained steam along the 1850 banks of the Missouri River, Bagley writes that an 1850 anonymous journalist reported on the "wagon-art" he observed. Painted on nearly every canvas top were the names of owners, various devices and mottoes, "quaint, odd, and appropriate:"

> *"Gold or a Grave," "Lucky Trip or Long Absence," "Never Say Die," and "Root Hog or Die" (perhaps intended to evoke fond images among hog farmers.) Covers sported images of 'a sprawling eagle, a huge elephant, a tall giraffe, a rampant lion, a stately ox….*

The origin of "to see the elephant" can be traced at least to April 13, 1796, when sea captain John Crowinshield brought the first elephant to America. Will Bagley writes:

> *Hachaliah Bailey made a fortune exhibiting a series of elephants, beginning in 1815 with the exceptionally talented Old Bet, who met a violent end when a New England farmer shot her for defiling the Sabbath. The saying appeared as early as 1834, and an 1872 compendium of Americanisms explained that it meant "to have seen all and to know everything…." Once elephants began appearing in circus parades in the late 1830s, the phrase spread like wildfire.*
>
> *Different people saw the elephant in different ways at different times. During the Civil War, it described a soldier's first experience with the savagery of combat…. David L. Bigler noted, for gold seekers, the phrase captured the romance that drew them west.*

Elephant Corral. Jargon for a frontier mercantile— In Reynolds' case, an extensive portfolio of mining properties—often including a livery stable and stockyard to outfit treasure-seekers with all manner of provisions needed to go "out to see the elephant." (*J. Harrison Mills*, Harper's Weekly)

The deal was done. Abbott resumed work. In his August 8th report to Reynolds and McKenny he happily stated,

> *We are in 95 feet in the East (Ocean Wave) drift and 75 feet in the West (Vermont) drift. The former continues much softer than the latter, but the west drift is now improving in that particular. There has just appeared a little fine grained galena in the west drift, not enough for any use but perhaps a good indication of something better after a time.* [32]

Work continued through August and possibly into September. Then, probably with some foreboding but no warning, another dreaded "Stop Work" order arrived. Abbott's miners were sent home and Reynolds turned his attentions elsewhere, never stated but likely to the Commodore properties in Creede or the May Day in Hesperus. Abbott was transferred back across the range to the Ouray district, probably to oversee further efforts to revitalize the Revenue Tunnel mines which were not generating the amount of dividends Reynolds was accustomed to in years past. Lacking the prospect of near-term dividends from his Henson Canyon project, it could wait. Toward this end, in a November 12th letter to Reynolds, Abbott reported on winterization measures at the Reynolds Tunnel. On December 11th, Abbott also filed an annual report to the Colorado Bureau of Mines covering calendar year 1900, providing a sharp snapshot of the matter. Addressing work beginning in January and ending in September, no ore was mined, no mill installed. Underground development totaled 1,500 feet of tunnel, and old workings abandoned equaled 4,000 feet.[33]

For Reynolds, record-keeping was a science with a set of laws and principles that could never be violated. But in the case of the September 1900 work stoppage on the Reynolds Tunnel the record book is blank. True, his finances were in dire straits, his history of late payments made that clear. Without first-class ore in sight and facing typical cost increases throughout the winter months, cashflow was sure to be a concern. His renegotiated lease/purchase agreement with Hendrie bought time and flexibility he needed to juggle obligations on other state-wide mining properties, but did that really matter in the long run? Apparently so.

Again, with no documented reason why, work on the Reynolds Tunnel resumed in June. On June 11, 1901, Abbott reported to Reynolds for the first time since the previous September. As usual, he was uncovering promising clues to the envisioned treasure. As usual, it probably was just a short distance ahead.

> *"As you are already advised, we have cut another vein in the Ocean Wave Tunnel."* He describes it as six inches to eight inches wide on the east side of the main tunnel and eighteen inches wide on the west side. *"The total distance run since we started is now about twenty-nine feet, and the two veins are about eighty feet apart."* [34]

For reasons unstated, Reynolds and Abbott extended the main tunnel farther north, beyond the twelve hundred foot mark where they abandoned Abbott's competition on the eastward drift towards the Ocean Wave and the westward drift towards the Vermont. When work was suspended in September each of these drifts were in about one-hundred-fifty feet. Twenty-nine feet north in the main tunnel beyond the intersection with these drifts they broke into "a streak of talc which shows black, decomposed stuff which may contain values." Reynolds' new superintendent replacing Abbott, Foster by name, hired since the shutdown, thought they had uncovered gray copper. Wisely consulted, Abbott thought otherwise.[35]

Apparently Reynolds thought otherwise, as well. Work extending the main tunnel northward was suspended. In fact, work in all directions was suspended, exactly when is not known, but perhaps as early as April and probably for the same reasons as usual. Prior to this shutdown the level of progress was below the threshold that required routine Abbott reporting. The consequence was dire but not necessarily eternal. The tunnels and surface plant would be put into safe-shutdown mode and placed under the watchful eye of Joseph Donnell, a seasoned Henson Canyon miner now at an age when "watching" was work enough. Exactly when the watchman came onboard is not known, but on July 1, 1902, Abbott had to remind Reynolds that he had not been paid since May. On July 19, 1902, this time with reverential respect rarely required by their lengthy relationship, Abbott again approached the king:

> *Dear Sir: You have evidently overlooked my request for $50.00 to pay Joseph Donnell for services as watchman last month. I know Mr. Donnell is much in need of this money for his family expense, and hope you will kindly send it by return mail. Yours very truly, J.J. Abbott.* [36]

With Abbott's diplomatic reminder that Mr. Donnell was owed backpay, we are shown how jarring the ride could be on Reynolds' cashflow rollercoaster. The valleys were getting deeper and broader and the peaks lower and sharper. But the Colorado mining king was not easily discouraged. His vision of a last best chance for redemption was worth at least $20,000 more. In February 1902, probably at the last possible moment, he had exercised his Vermont Group purchase option with E.B. Hendrie. His plans for his Vermont/Ocean Wave tunnel would live to see another day. How surprising was it that he could have difficulty paying watchman wages of $50 per month at the same time he could exercise a $20,000 purchase option? Not surprising to anyone who knew the king. Nor would it be surprising that uncovering treasure would require more than an ace-in-the hole, it would require a lot more of someone else's money, or their labor in lieu thereof.

Notes—Chapter Ten: Ace-in-the-Hole

[1] Guthrie, Woody, *Hard Travelin*.

[2] *Lake City Times*, February 16, 1899.

[3] (Chapters 9-12 rely heavily on documents archived in *Reynolds Collection* Manuscript [MSS 1220], located in the History Colorado Library, Denver, Colorado. Along with historic newspaper accounts, these primary sources provide invaluable insight into this epic quest.)

[4] July 16 - August 10, 1899, MSS 1220, Box 10, FF 713-716.

[5] August 30, 1899, MSS 1220, Box 10, FF 717.

[6] (Labor unrest over a long list of grievances was spreading throughout the San Juans. Nationwide, the unionization movement was entering its twentieth century golden age.)

[7] August 30, 1899, MSS 1220, Box 10, FF 717.

[8] August 26, 1899, MSS 1220, Box 10, FF 717.

[9] Scamehorn, Lee, *Albert Eugene Reynolds, Colorado's Mining King*, pg. 23.

[10] *Wikipedia*, "Western Federation of Miners (WFM)," and "Bill Haywood."

[11] September 7, 1899, MSS1220, Box 10, FF 718.

[12] October 3, 1899, MSS 1220, Box 10, FF 719.

[13] October 10, 1899, MSS 1220, Box 10, FF 719.

[14] Ibid.

[15] Twitty, Eric, *Blown to Bits in the Mine*, pgs. 1-34; *Wikipedia*, "Nobel Prize."

[16] October 23, 1899, MSS 1220, Box 10, FF 720.

[17] October 26, 1899, MSS 1220, Box 10, FF 720.

[18] November 9, 1899, MSS 1220, Box 10, FF 722.

[19] November 15, 1899, MSS 1220, Box 10, FF 722.

[20] November 23, 1899, MSS 1220, Box 10, FF 722.

[21] December 3, 1899, MSS 1220, Box 10, FF 723.

[22] December 4, 1899, MSS 1220, Box 10, FF 723.

[23] *Denver Times*, December 31, 1899.

[24] *Lake City Times*, February 1, 1900.

[25] *Lake City Times*, March 22, 1900.

[26] June 14, 1900, MSS 1220, Box 10, FF 731.

[27] July 1, 1900, MSS 1220, Box 10, FF 732.

[28] July 9, 1900, MSS 1220, Box 10, FF 732.

[29] July 14, 1900, MSS 1220, Box 10, FF 732.

[30] August 4, 1900, MSS 1220, Box 10, FF 735.

[31] Bagley, Will, *With Golden Visions Bright Before Them*, pgs. 31-32; 263.

[32] August 8, 1900, MSS 1220, Box 10, FF 735.

[33] Colorado Bureau of Mines [DMG] Report, December 11, 1900.

[34] June 11, 1901, MSS 1220, Box 10, FF 752.

[35] Ibid.

[36] July 19, 1902, MSS 1220, Box 11, FF 770.

CHAPTER 11

Cousin Harry

"Things ain't what they used to be and never were."
— Will Rogers —

If Henson Canyon burros had been as blessed with speech as Balaam's ass, they surely would have echoed Will Roger's sentiment. If A.E. Reynolds had entrusted his Vermont Group tunnel project to Cousin Harry in 1899 instead of 1914, his ace-in-the-hole might have spared him much time and trouble.

The faithful burro, at one time esteemed above even the beloved horse and certainly the obstinate mule, by the beginning of the twentieth-century probably sensed its usefulness at the Vermont and Ocean Wave lodes was in jeopardy. Before wagon roads, long before rail service and trucks, the burro's formed up in trains to pack all manner of supplies into the mountains, and sacks of all manner of ores back to the closest wagon road or railhead. What prospector or frontier parson could deny their surefooted service navigating broken trails in search of hidden treasure or lost souls? But even then they could be praised one day and berated the next. In the world A.E. Reynolds' envisioned, they would scarcely be remembered.

In 1899 burro duty at the Vermont and Ocean Wave lodes was still essential. From the earliest days access to both lodes depended on burros, so much so that the neighboring claim and mill site were patented under the name "Burro Cabin" and partly used as an irrigated pasture. His Virginius/Revenue Tunnel had begun with burros but ended with electric "mules." By 1899 A.E. Reynolds expected all of his mines would operate without burros. When completed, his Vermont Group tunnel would enable muck to be transported in mine cars out the portal from the mine's lowest levels to the dump, or hand-sorted ore to be transported in similar fashion and transferred to heavy freight wagons plying the county road to the railhead, all without the aid of burros. No longer would burros be needed to carry sacked ore down a broken trail from the upper workings. During the prime construction season of 1902 the completion of the Vermont Group tunnel was in doubt. The fate of burros was not.

In mid-1902, after nearly three years of overcoming disappointing and costly challenges, Reynolds' tunnel was within the proverbial "arms-length" of its objective. Over twelve hundred feet into the mountain, clearly under the upper workings of the Vermont, well along the ore vein Reynolds' "boys" had hoped to find that which would lead to the Ocean Wave, still the "stop work" order had come up from Denver. A.E. Reynolds' vast mining kingdom and indeed the West fell under the twin curse of a global precious-metals depression and a dearth of new bonanzas. Overextended as usual, no one felt this more directly than

BURROS[1]

Of course burros could be challenging. While crossing deep streams, according to George Darley, unless their ears were tied, burros would drown. Tying up their ears, they could be pulled across without danger. After a rope was tied to the burro's neck, it was pushed into the stream. The men on the opposite bank would pull. The burro may go under repeatedly, but it would be landed in good shape. As soon as its ears were untied, "his voice is loosened and breaks forth in trumpet tones of rejoicing, loud enough to be heard far and near."

This maneuver was never attempted with a mule. In fact, confusing the nature of burros and mules was common but a serious mistake. In *On the Backs of Burros* we learn that the personalities of the two could not

Balaam's "Burro." Balaam's love-hate relationship with his beast of burden was not shared by San Juans pilgrims — for the most part they were valued as indispensable as well as congenial companions. (*Wikipedia — Rembrandt's "Balaam and the Ass"*)

be more different. A burro responded to a kind word. A mule was unimpressed by any word. A burro was fearless on the most precipitous of trails. A mule would balk and might never advance. A burro would strive to carry the heaviest of loads. A mule would kneel down and await relief. In a dark tunnel a burro would resign itself to do its silent best to get itself and the loaded ore car back into daylight. A mule would pull ore cars for feed and settle scores later. While a mule could carry or pull heavier loads than a burro, their advantage did not compensate for their attitude. Simply put, burros were likeable and mules were not.

Reynolds unless it was the faithful burro. Lovable as they could be, and despite the fact they were inexpensive to keep even in the worst of times, nevertheless they often were turned loose in the wild or the streets of Lake City to fend for themselves.

The causes of the silver and gold decline were beyond even the most arrogant politicians in the United States Congress to remedy. High-grade reserves were largely depleted, or had successfully evaded discovery. Large enterprises either stopped paying dividends (thus investors stopped investing) or turned over operations to lessors who neither paid dividends nor paid themselves more often than not. Every phase of mining lower-grade ores witnessed cost increases—not even more cost-effective rail service could offset this trend. Amidst this sea of troubles, A.E. Reynolds had been forced to turn to others for the funds he needed to stay afloat. His reputation for fair dealing and his long list of successes had aided him greatly in this endeavor. Failure to achieve production goals at the Vermont Group not so much.

Reynolds' flush years of the 1880s that had sustained him through the 1890s was fueled by sweeping the table with the Virginius and the Revenue Tunnel. Double-digit returns from the Commodore silver mine in Creede also contributed its fair share. While prospects at Summitville, Lake City, Aspen, and elsewhere titillated Reynolds' fancy, many others in his elephant corral underperformed at great expense in the process. Still the king believed from deep within his soul that there was at least one more Virginius or Commodore awaiting his Midas touch. While his faith in the Vermont Group was being sorely tested, it was not abandoned.

Revenue Tunnel. Probably taken in the mid-1880s, this photo documents development prior to the introduction of electric "mules." The number of ore cars to keep up with production required mule- or horse-power. Burros would not do. (*History Colorado-Denver, Colorado*)

For a time his May Day gold mine near Hesperus, and the Frank Hough silver mine on Engineer Mountain above Lake City looked like they were better bets, but it was not to be. For every six cents invested, the May Day produced a dollar's worth of gold, but the reserves were quickly exhausted. At the Frank Hough, a fire that destroyed the surface plant, and the collapse of the main shaft were costly, demoralizing, and ended any promise of large returns there. Along with the arrival of 1914 spring, in the absence of a more promising alternative, a renewed interest in his mothballed Vermont Group tunnel returned to its prominent place on A.E.s to-do list.

With that a new era was birthed. Historic Vermont and Ocean Wave workings in Henson Canyon again looked like his best bet. After all, the costly infrastructure probably remained in good condition (it was not), and what was important by his reckoning was the quantity of silver ore he was convinced still remained (it probably did), not the quantity thus far removed (which was more than impressive). What he lacked was another Hubbell Reed or J.J. Abbott. Oh yes, what he also lacked was someone else's money.

Harry Van Horn filled both needs. Like most others in his day, he was a self-taught mining "engineer," Unlike most others, he had $25,000 to invest. Better yet, he was a close relative—his mother and A.E.'s mother were sisters, he and A.E. were cousins—and as a trusted employee he had previously served Reynolds as superintendent at Creede's Commodore Mine. His compensation at the Vermont Group would be a combination of "mill returns" from shipped ore and $25,000 worth of company stock. How could he have known that two years later his reward would be $759 on an investment of $34,000? [2]

After slumbering for more than a decade, the Vermont and Ocean Wave properties were awakened by a man with fresh interest and serious money. Harry bought into Reynolds' treasure hunt with the same experienced judgment his cousin possessed, no pig-in-a-poke, for sure. In mid-April, Harry visited Henson Canyon and performed his due diligence. The high-pressure compressor, troublesome in the best of times, was in bad shape and according to Harry perhaps beyond repair. But the remainder of the surface plant looked serviceable. Harry wrote from Creede:

> *As soon as we receive word that the tools etc. have been shipped so that we will have something to work with, I will go over there with about four men and make a start at the job. (Harry recruited five trusted employees: W.H. Kennedy, J.D. Bush, Andy [Alfred] Johnson, Gus Farnum, and John York.)* [3]

A month later, on May 12, 1914, Van Horn sent A.E. a pencil-written letter describing the damage twelve or thirteen years of mountain weathering could do to an unattended surface plant. Switching topics, Harry wrote that everything was moved up to the mine and they had a cabin in livable condition (considering it was spring). A new compressor was on order. He requested five sheets of eight foot and five sheets of ten-foot corrugated iron for roofs. Another cabin mentioned was probably the Ocean Wave boarding house. Both structures were a short walk to the Reynolds Tunnel portal and powder-house, a not much farther walk in the opposite direction to the Ocean Wave portals. Portals to the historic upper Vermont workings were a steep climb up nearby El Paso Gulch. Harry wrapped up his report by declaring that opening the tunnel would be a small job. [4]

On May 16th Van Horn advised Reynolds on a variety of insightful topics. The existing compressor foundation should accommodate the new compressor. There was no plan involving burros. Horses were the ticket but there was no stable for horses—do not send any until after June 1st. They needed coal, explosives either 1-1/8 or 1¼ inch diameter, and maybe ore cars. "Someone stated here that they believed the cars that were here were taken over to the Golden Fleece. We will know in a few days if there are any here." [5]

By the start of summer 1914 at least the lack of ore cars no longer plagued them. Later reports included mention of one horse. (Nothing further is known concerning a stable.) Van Horn's expeditionary force began to step off the pages of frontline reports to the home office. Excitement in the air was palpable. Kennedy was in charge when Van Horn was away. On June 17th he requested parts, lubricants, and an operator's manual for the compressor. He reported that Bush was laying track in the breast of the Ocean Wave drift, meaning the east crosscut where work on Reynolds Tunnel ended in 1902. Johnson and Farnum were working on the "upper drift" (location unstated and unclear, but it is likely that the work suspended in 1902 included a raise and drift following the vein to a higher elevation). John York (destined to become foreman and de facto superintendent) was working on the bunkhouse. Gus and Harry were about done in the engine room and were about to test steam and air lines. [6]

On August 11, 1914, Van Horn's report to the front office was music albeit slightly discordant to Charles McKenny's ears despite memories of the sour notes J.J. Abbott reported more than a decade earlier. Given that they were now able to drill, blast, and muck; they clearly had track, ore cars, and horse issues under control. Hoped for outcomes were another matter.

> At the beginning of work under the present arrangement, the drift on the Ocean Wave side was in 145 ft. from the intersection (1200 ft. from the adit) of the tunnel, and the Vermont side was in 115 feet. At the close of work yesterday evening the Ocean Wave side was in 215 feet and the Vermont side 135 feet, making 70 feet of work done on the Ocean Wave vein, and 20 feet on the Vermont, a total of 90 feet. In addition to several obstacles we have had to overcome, the ground does not seem to break well, and we have not made as good headway as I had hoped for. [7]

Not a passive man, Van Horn made adjustments. He wrote the Denver Rock Drill Company and requested they send him a "first-class drill man." Why? Because he had sent *his* "drill man" to the house over "whiskey trouble." On a sweet note, Kennedy was promoted to foreman. On November 11, 1914, Harry had better news. Coal, 29,700 pounds of "blacksmith coal," was delivered from Durango. The Ocean Wave drift was in 290 feet and being worked. The Vermont drift was in 170 feet "but not working it presently." The raise that would connect the Reynolds Tunnel to the upper Vermont workings, a connection that would provide ventilation, *was* being worked.

> *We are driving (the Ocean Wave drift) alternatively with the [Vermont] raise. The raise is up 63 feet from the track. During the past month we did some extra work shooting out for a switch, which we now have in place. The breast on the Ocean Wave is still very tight, and the ore seam is small. The raise shows considerable quartz of low values; it breaks good, but requires considerable time for timbering.*[8]

Harry's November update is the last available report until April of the following year. There is no way of knowing if winter conditions, labor unrest, or funding were at play. By the same token, how much underground development work may have been accomplished and how long work was suspended between November 1914 and April 1915 also was not documented. If Reynolds' funds had been in play, this would not have been the case. But someone else's money was at risk and a gap in documentation was the case. What is a plausible explanation relates to Harry's concern that the upraise being driven in hopes of opening the upper workings of the Vermont was probably in the wrong location. Conserving limited funds until he had an accurate underground survey probably was the rest of the story. We know that arranging for that took until April 15th, and that for this service he called upon another trusted Creede associate, W.O. Gish, who did not disappoint. In a letter to Reynolds dated April 22, 1915, Van Horn wrote:

> *The survey, which we have just completed, shows that the bottom of the shaft (abandoned several decades earlier when the upper workings of the Vermont were active) is fifty feet back in the footwall of the raise, and in order to make connections we will have to drive a drift straight back in the footwall fifty feet. We are plenty high enough with the raise, in fact, have gone a few feet farther than necessary.*
> *The pitch of the vein the shaft is on is 71 degrees, and the pitch of the vein the raise is on is 62 degrees. These two veins seem to get farther apart going in a westerly direction, but as the veins in this country are rather wavey, they may come closer to each other farther in. We now are of the opinion that the streak of ore, or vein nearest to the breast of the tunnel, is the Vermont Vein,*

and is the one the shaft is sunk on, and that the shaft was sunk at right angles with the vein. [9]

Instead of rejoicing with Van Horn over pinpointing the long-lost shaft, Reynolds focused on the fifty feet of wasted effort. Apparently he could not help himself. It was not his money, or all his money at least, but it was his nature and his mine. Its well-being depended in large measure on Van Horn's financial well-being. Unhappy with the cost, he *was* comforted by the consequences. Given the circumstances, tunneling a quarter-mile to intersect superintendent Stockder's 1887 five-foot square shaft fifty or sixty feet somewhere overhead was no small feat.

Miscalculating by fifty feet the intersection of the historic upper workings of the Vermont with the Reynolds Tunnel by way of Stockder's shaft would have been granted more grace by most investors. In fact, the natural ventilation it would provide would be critical to continued operations the farther into the mountain Van Horn drove the Reynolds Tunnel and its Vermont and Ocean Wave crosscuts. The uncovering of good ore in the Ocean Wave drift provided an added degree of encouragement, but good air pulled through Stockder's shaft would be a gift that kept on giving. The gift remained a clue, but now they knew where to look for it. Van Horn's detailed report further assured Reynolds they were on the right track and he had the right man at the helm.

> *We now have a very strong vein, the vein matter being fully three feet wide, and being composed mostly of quartz, and lately the whole thing has been improving in appearance with every round.*
>
> *My plan for driving the cross-cut (back to Stockder's Vermont shaft) is to work alternatively, one day in the breast of the Ocean Wave, and the next in the cross-cut, and have the trammer remove the muck, giving them a clean breast to set up in every morning, and I believe we will make better headway than we would to give a contract to drive the cross-cut, owing to the fact that we are limited in our boiler capacity, and it seems to me that by working it as I have suggested, that by the end of May we should have the cross-cut completed and an equal amount of work done in the heading of the Ocean Wave drift.*
>
> *The fact that there is still fifty feet of practically dead work to be done before we get air, proved to be very discouraging to the boys here, but they have all manfully agreed to use their best endeavors to expedite the work; the showing in the Ocean Wave has helped to cheer and encourage them, and they feel that in the end they will be repaid for all their hard work. Very truly yours, Harry Van Horn.* [10]

A month later, fresh off a visit with superintendent Van Horn, the *Silver World* editor reported more good news.

The latest survey at the Ocean Wave tunnel by W.O. Gish has proven two or three interesting facts surmised heretofore. It is now known that the vein along which the tunnel west of the crosscut as run is not the one on which the Vermont workings are situated, at the point where the upraise was made the two veins being about 60 ft. apart. It is therefore figured that it will require a crosscut of the 60 ft. to connect the upraise with the Vermont shaft. It is now quite clearly established that the crosscut intersects three veins which appear to be converging to a common junction eastward towards the Ocean Wave ground. As this present tunnel east from the crosscut is now in 408 ft. Supt. Harry Van Horn believes the intersection of the veins are likely to be encountered within 200 to 300 ft. at farthest (sic). Establishing the character and connections of the three veins in question will undoubtably be one of the most important developments in exploitation with the Ocean Wave crosscut. [11]

The vertical distance between the Reynolds Tunnel and the uppermost portal of the historic Vermont was 500 feet, confirming that in fact Stockder sank the shaft nearly that distance before work ceased decades earlier. (Confirming this accomplishment also suggested that other features of his plan—driving tunnels westward off the shaft every hundred feet—also was accomplished.) On June 13, 1915, proper alignment and depth of Stockder's shaft and Van Horn's upraise and drift were achieved. Gish was proven correct. With excitement leaping from the page, Van Horn wrote Reynolds good news and tidings of great joy.

At last we have accomplished what we have been striving for during the past few months, for to-day we broke into the old shaft and now fresh air is going through the tunnel, which is a great relief to us all. We got it almost to the foot where the survey showed it should be, and we cut it square. We were fortunate that we were not any lower, for the shaft was filled with dirt right up to about the level where we broke into it. we were not troubled with water at all; we started the round yesterday, and one of the drills holed through, and the water come out with considerable force, so we let it run all night, and this morning it was practically drained. [12]

The blessings natural ventilation afforded could not be overstated. Reynolds was still grumpy over the cost of overshooting Stockder's shaft, but pleased he did not have to pony up more funds to improve air quality. No longer did the trammer and drill man have to wait sometimes a day or more for the toxic fumes and dust from blasting to diminish enough to return to the breast to muck out the rock and resume drilling. No longer did the boys need to be as concerned that they were going to encounter dead air elsewhere in the mine. While there were limits to natural ventilation, once established the effects could always be enhanced by driving additional winzes or shafts in strategic locations. Reynolds' knockoff of his showcase Revenue Tunnel had achieved three of its four intended goals. Ventilation, drainage, and haulage were in the bank. Only pay-dirt remained.

As for "pay-dirt," certainly not simply for the thrill of the hunt, the Ocean Wave vein and historic workings remained the priority. An open Vermont shaft accessing five levels and probably 5,000 feet of Vermont drifts, stopes, winzes, and shafts must have been tempting, but not tempting enough. The Vermont would not be pursued beyond reaching the old shaft, at least not until their curiosity regarding the Ocean Wave had been satisfied or Reynolds changed his mind. Perhaps a quick walkthrough revealed that there were not rich stopes or piles of high-assay ore left behind when the last crew packed it in. Why pursuit of new ore was not a goal was never explained, but a likely reason had its roots in Ingham's geology lessons and Reynolds' convictions concerning which direction and at what depth rich ore reserves resided. Reynolds also respected the great success the Italians had demonstrated in the Ocean Wave's Dago Tunnel. What he could not be sure of until his crew got on that vein was whether Sam Jack's Italians had depleted the reserves.

For the time being, at least, Reynolds and Cousin Harry were more confident the geological clues before them pointed toward finding high-grade ore in the Ocean Wave. Vermont reserves—remaining in the upper workings, but more importantly at greater depths—were just that, reserves. Satisfied with fresh air flowing through the Vermont drift, Harry had more funds to chase Ocean Wave ore. Tunneling eastward toward the Ocean Wave, as of June 13, 1915, he reported:

> *The breast of the Ocean Wave is in 447 feet. It has been hard and tight for the past couple of weeks, but has the appearance of getting a little softer again. The vein matter is only a few inches wide now, but if it does as it has done before, it is liable to widen again with the next round of shots.* [13]

Good news for sure, but Van Horn was wary of trouble ahead. Four-hundred forty-seven feet into the Ocean Wave drift was beginning to pose new ventilation issues. The natural path of the airflow tended to bypass it, instead moving from the upper Vermont portals (five hundred feet overhead) 1200 ft. to (or from) the Reynolds Tunnel portal opening onto the county road. Air ducts and bulkheads were going to be needed to encourage airflow farther into the Ocean Wave drift until an upraise broke through to the old Ocean Wave upper workings, also five hundred feet overhead.

Insufficient cashflow was also trouble. Van Horn was doing his part, but his $25,000 cash investment was going fast. He recruited a subscriber who contributed "sweat equity"—work in exchange for a share of future profits assuming there would be any. Helpful as that would be, the boys needed cash. For decades the first stop in that sort of quest was the king himself, but not in 1915. In 1915 A.E. Reynolds had cashflow trouble of his own and also needed cash.

A subscriber was a reasonable second choice, better still if the subscriber was a son-in-law with well-endowed friends. Daughter Anna's husband Brad was the obvious choice. Following a brief visit to Denver, Harry wrote:

> *I have obtained another subscriber to the development fund, who is to pay for his interest in labor, and I wish you would say to Brad that I am depending on him to secure one or two cash subscribers, as we talked before I left, for now that we have got some ventilation in the mine, we want to go after the ore.* [14]

"Brad" was Bradish Morse. Recently married to Anna, he was a partner in the highly successful Morse Brothers Machinery and Supply Company of Denver. He also was assuming an increasingly important role in both the Reynolds and Morse family's business affairs. The Morse Brothers specialized in recycling mine, mill, railroad and industrial equipment. Brad was a prosperous businessman in his own right and well connected in Denver society. How successful he could be in attracting investors remained to be seen. In years to come Brad would become the *de facto* executor of the A.E. Reynolds estate and manager of Anna's inheritance largely encumbered by elephant corral leases and debts.

While Harry awaited an infusion of cash, he focused efforts on following the Ocean Wave vein eastward with the ultimate objective of driving an upraise into Sam Jack's 4th level Dago Tunnel. On July 19th he reported to Denver that the Ocean Wave breast was in five hundred feet. In a cash-strapped mine, feet per day was important but quality and quantity of vein material was more important. Harry was well-aware of the difference.

> *The vein matter is between two and three feet wide now. There is a good hanging wall; the breast is very dry, the vein matter does not seem to have any values in it, however it is looking more encouraging than it has at any time.* [15]

And cash was more important still. Van Horn reported that all bills were paid through August 1st, but thereafter he needed $700-750 per month to operate. He asked for Brad to raise $2,000. Almost as an afterthought, he added that the compressor was failing. He would order new "rings" from Morse Brothers, but that would be a temporary fix. On July 25, 1915, Cousin Harry wrote A.E.:

> *It is now just one week since I made the change by having one man work night shift to get out the dirt; the compressor runs two hours after the day shift goes off, and before the night man goes on, and I believe we are going to make it work all right. During the last seven days we have made 22 feet, and the ground will average as tough and hard as any we expect to have. The vein matter is still about two feet wide; it is rather soft quartz filled with iron; there seems to be no moisture, everything dry. The breast of the drift is now in 522 feet from the tunnel.* [16]

The "tunnel," of course, meaning the Reynolds Tunnel [which had yet to mimic the glorious outcomes of the Virginius' Revenue Tunnel on the far side of the mountain] was itself "in twelve-hundred feet" from daylight and fresh air. There was no mention of funds, but that was more likely an indication Van Horn understood his cousin's situation and knew better to broach the topic than an indication that a large sum of money was about to be deposited in the company's local bank account. Somehow work continued, in part due to the crew continuing to work without pay. By mid-August the Ocean Wave drift was in over 640 feet. On October 25th it was in 822 feet. Perhaps sensing cousin A.E.'s impatience with extensive tunneling and negligible vein material of any worth, Cousin Harry found a high note and ventured an upbeat opinion. You can imagine how often Reynolds had been down this road.

> For the last ten feet we have had a little streak of very good looking material. Some of it looks as though it might carry a considerable grey copper, and some of it seems to be more lead and zinc. I have divided it into two grades and sent a sample of each to Brad to have them assayed, as I am anxious to learn the value of the different ores, so that in case we should have enough to save, we can sort it intelligently.
>
> From the appearances and indications in the breast, I should judge that we are about through the pinch, and this streak of ore we have seems to be the tail end or feather edge of something ahead, as it is better and wider in the top than in the bottom.
>
> I found the boys all very enthusiastic over the showing, and they all feel confident now that we will eventually have a mine. [17]

With winter upon them, Reynolds was ready to make changes. On November 13, 1915, he reported to his "partners," and in so doing informed Van Horn and crew what their future was going to look like. In a letter "To the Subscribers to the Funds for Opening the Ocean Wave Mine," A.E. penned a six page proposition grounded in his assessment that they were looking at ten years of marketable ore but needed more capital and a mill. Still, further development of the Vermont was nowhere in his thinking, still believing that geology favored developing the Ocean Wave. Of course the case for this conclusion was not iron-clad, witnessed by subsequent actions that kept the Vermont a viable option. To parrot G. Thomas Ingham's thinking, the Vermont and Ocean Wave drifts were equally encouraging or discouraging. In other words, "keep digging dirt and find out for yourself."

Reynolds presented his case which amounted to a new deal. He explained that funds to date yielded eighteen months effort without paydirt. The project was nearly out of cash. There were clues pointing to marketable ore just a few hundred feet ahead, but more capital was needed to recover it. He advised that subscribers had the option to purchase the mine, continue with the current agreement, or he would help them structure a new arrangement. His advice was: 1) build a fifty tons/day mill [most likely he was envisioning a basic "mine-mouth mill"] next summer costing probably $15,000; 2) continue developing the vein this winter; 3) given that ore was heavy, what went into the dump was worth one half to fully as much as that shipped to a smelter. An on-site mill would solve this problem; and 4) the vein was about one thousand feet upwards. Probably at the point where they were now, it was one thousand feet to daylight, five-hundred feet to get under the old workings, something over five hundred feet with more or less ore the entire distance up to the surface.[18]

Without saying so exactly, Reynolds wanted out, or at least to hedge. In either case, he was but one pace ahead of bankruptcy and clearly looking for someone else's money. For the subscribers, most of whom were also working the mine, their investment was emotional as much as financial. Along with superintendent Van Horn, tempted to carry on under a new deal with Reynolds, they continued driving the Ocean Wave drift while they mulled over his proposition. Yes, they knew they were working at risk, but they had been miners long enough to know two things: mining law ensured they would be paid (assuming there was money which thus far there had been little to none) the day they were sent home, and the forthcoming Christmas break was always downtime they could count on anyway. In addition, there were two other unstated but obvious factors influencing their practical considerations. One, they were unaccustomed to failing in their obligations and were loath to accept defeat. Two, as smitten as any treasure-seeker could be, they began each day eager to decipher the last clue and uncover the next one. Their options were clear. They could quit

Mine-Mouth Mill. Available in a wide variety of designs, the cost of even the simple device pictured here often outweighed its usefulness in separating "paydirt" from "plain dirt." *(Library of Congress)*

IMMIGRANT ROOTS RUN DEEP

John E. York was tall, of medium build, with blue eyes and light brown hair. He was strong, healthy, of good moral character, and a diligent worker accustomed to giving his employer more than a full day's labor. His family heritage was typical of immigrant journeys from distant lands to the American West. York family experiences shaped John's character. John's character exemplified the character of "Young America." It also exemplified the character of a class of immigrants that accepted sacrifice as fair exchange for freedom and opportunity.

York's people emigrated from England in 1724 and settled in the Quaker Pipe Creek Settlement, Maryland Colony. Jeremiah age twenty-three and Sarah age twenty-four were the first Yorks in America. Jeremiah was born in 1701 in Yorkshire. Sarah Seymour was born in 1700 in Olney Buckinghamshire. They married in 1724 in Yorkshire. Faced with religious persecution and a life of serfdom, the newlyweds walked nine days from dawn to dark to board the *Intrepid*, chartered by fellow-believers for safe passage to Baltimore. Whatever Jeremiah's family name was when he walked up the weathered gang-plank to the *Intrepid* main deck, the young man and woman from Yorkshire made their marks next to the word "York" scripted carefully into the ship's musty logbook by the First Mate. "From Yorkshire" to the First Mate's way of thinking, was reason enough to log them in as "Yorks." So it was then, so it is to this day. There was no point in disputing the matter. They were onboard and about to leave behind a certain lifetime of poverty and oppression. With deep spiritual convictions to encourage them, Jeremiah and Sarah anxiously looked over the bow to the uncertain but expected opportunities of America.

Frontier hardships did not discourage Jeremiah and Sarah from filling their quiver with eleven sons and one daughter. Henry York, the middle son, was born August 6, 1732, in Pipe Creek Settlement. He married a second time on January 15, 1789, in Randolph, North Carolina. Margaret Lenderman was not yet fifteen at her wedding to fifty-seven year old Henry. She birthed seven sons and six daughters to Henry. Leonard was born January 18, 1804, in nearby Wilkes, North Carolina, married his cousin Susannah Catherine Lenderman on May 10, 1826, in Evansville, Indiana, and died in Schuyler, Missouri, a healthy one-hundred year old. Henry Mario was their first-born, delivered at the family farm with the assistance of the community mid-wife on March 29, 1828. Henry married Elizabeth Ann Ward on March 6, 1849, in Evansville, Indiana.

The prospect of cheap land in what soon became Davis County, Iowa, lured Henry and Elizabeth still farther west. Cheap land was not to be found, but the land they worked on shares somehow supported their family of twelve. The York line was hardy, prolific, and mobile. John Elmer, second oldest among the twelve, was born June 17, 1868, on the family farm. [19]

or work for pay—getting paid in either case was not certain—or they could work for a share of future ore sales, also not certain. They had at least to the New Year to decide.

John E. York, foreman and their nominal spokesman, endowed with vision as well as pluck, did not need that much time. He recognized probably as surely as did Reynolds that the Ocean Wave and Vermont Group was Reynolds' last best chance to make a mine, and now the mining king was handing that responsibility over to a handful of the king's minions. How often in a lifetime did that happen? Looking a gift horse in the mouth was never wise, but a wary glance was usually a good idea. Along with calculated risks also usually came ample rewards. York was not only an experienced machinist, a jack-of-all-trades really, he was an optimist and a risk-taker. And he was a team player.

John E. York was born into not only a deeply religious Quaker family, but one with uncompromising patriotism and self-sacrifice. John's father, Henry Mario York, along with Henry's four brothers, volunteered early in the Civil War to fight for the Union. Henry, George, Levi and Anderson were all wounded. Francis was killed. First and the youngest of the five to enlist was George. On

August 31, 1861, at the age of twenty-six, he joined Company A, 3rd Iowa Cavalry, as a Private, advanced to Corporal 8th Class a year later. George lost his left arm to cannon fire during the Battle of Shiloh and received a disability discharge on February 14, 1863. News of George's fate prompted brothers Henry and Francis to join the Iowa volunteers together. On August 9, 1862, at age thirty-five, Henry enlisted as Sergeant 2nd Class in Company B, 30th Iowa Infantry. Francis, age thirty-two, enlisted alongside Henry as a Corporal 8th Class, also in Company B, 30th Infantry.

Five months later, on January 11, 1863, at the Battle of Arkansas Post, Henry was so severely wounded that he was not able to be mustered out of service for sixteen months, until April 29, 1864. In the midst of his lengthy

Patriot Too. John E. York, true to family tradition and his servant's heart, took off a day without pay to sign up for service in World War I. *(Library of Congress)*

recovery, on March 2, 1863, he was promoted to Sergeant 3rd Class. On May 19, 1863, Francis was mortally wounded during the Battle of Vicksburg, and died three days later. Levi, at age twenty, enlisted next, followed a year later by Anderson, just sixteen at the time. Because of his age and the service and sacrifice of his brothers, he was turned down by one Iowa regiment after another. Frustrated but not deterred, Anderson walked into neighboring Missouri and signed up with Company H, Missouri Infantry.

Imagine the nature of discussions around the York dinner table. Growing up working the family farm, surely John often heard accounts of the voyage to America and life, heroism, and sacrifice during the colonial era and during the Civil War. His family legacy must have come to mind when years later his turn to enlist arrived. (In 1918, at the age of fifty, he responded to President Wilson's call for World War I volunteers. Despite being well beyond the age to serve, he understated his age and enlisted anyway. Before his number was called, World War I ended.)

Family farm life was hard and John had to carry his share of the burden from an early age. Charles, his brother two years senior, supervised his chores. It was Charles who helped John with his lessons when he was old enough to attend school. Charles was a bright student and enjoyed learning. Like so many other Iowans, for reasons unstated he also was attracted to the Western frontier. Also like so many others, he soon learned mining was not his calling. Instead, he accepted a teaching position in Creede, Colorado. Better suited to the classroom, he also was better suited to Iowa. He returned to Davis County to study the law.

John also was bright, but soon showed more interest in working with his hands than working with books. When there was equipment on the farm or nearby Ottumwa in need of repair, the job naturally fell to John. Charles liked books and John preferred blisters, nevertheless a close bond formed between the two brothers that lasted throughout their lives. Like Charles, John heard the call of the San Juans and traced his brother's steps to Creede, but not before marrying Betsy.

At age twenty, John married Betsy York on October 17, 1888, in Webster, Iowa. They took up housekeeping in Lancaster, Missouri, just a short coach ride from the York family farm. Nine years later Betsy was dead and John, childless, was traveling by rail and coach to Creede to spend a little time adjusting to Betsy's loss with his beloved brother Charles at his side. Once in Colorado, John never left. Opportunities abounded in the San Juans for anyone with mechanical abilities and a zeal for work. John possessed both. In fact, John was gifted with talents that could have qualified him as a mine mechanic or engineer, self-taught of course. Attracted to mining, he gained practical experience in Creede's Commodore Mine—A.E. Reynolds' Commodore Mine—under the watchful eye of Harry Van Horn. When operations at the Commodore ceased, York worked as a "stationary engineer" at the Bonanza Mine near Saguache, and in 1914 arrived in Lake City as part of Van Horn's expeditionary crew.

We can imagine what motivated John to leave his family behind in Iowa, live a solitary existence, and spend the balance of his life working one mine after another, often alone for months on end. Grief strickened, his brother Charles' invitation to join him in Creede was surely seen as a Godsend and encouragement befitting a faithful Quaker. More certain, working in the Commodore Mine for superintendent Van Horn was a divine appointment, one that repeatedly blessed him until it killed him.

York and Van Horn had gotten along well together in Creede. Working for Harry at the Commodore was a rich learning experience. From Harry's perspective, men like York were worth investing in. When Harry's call came to join him in Henson Canyon, York did not need to know the details. Driving a tunnel intended to rival the Virginius' Revenue Tunnel supervised by Friend Harry had justified his move to Lake City. Now eighteen months into the effort John found himself on the cusp of an even greater adventure.

On December 2, 1915, three weeks after Reynolds informed York and the other subscribers of their options for carrying on the work, York wrote superintendent Van Horn:

> *Friend Harry, — your letter enclosing Mr. Reynolds proposition received and all of the boys have read it except Bush and he will read it tomorrow. Johnson, Anders, and Hegner think it all right and for myself I think it a very good proposition and as reasonable as we could ask. I think Bush will agree to it. With a small mill (fifty tons/day) such as Mr. Reynolds has suggested, there is no question in my mind that this mine can (now) be made a good producer.*
>
> *Alfred, Fred and Bush are going to take a layoff for two weeks. I think about 17th. We will get along the best we can while they are away; Roland can help me in the mine and Gus can look after the outside. I think we can get in three rounds every four days. The time for last month is York, 30 shifts, Johnson, 30 shifts, Anders, 30 shifts, Hegner, 30 shifts, Bush, 20 shifts, and Roland 30 shifts. Very truly, J.E. York.*
>
> *[In a hand-written postscript York writes, "Bush has read and says he is agreed. So we are all agreed my* Lord.*"] [20]*

Reynolds' "New Deal," a new era, was about to begin. First came the customary end-of-year shutdown. Van Horn and all but York and Roland Ewart "went out" to Denver and Creede for the holidays. Ewart's family lived in Lake City. York remained at the mine to begin a raise in the Ocean Wave drift off the main tunnel. On January 6, 1916, the *Silver World* editor reported that "the big four of the Vermont crew who went to Denver and Creede to spend the Christmas holidays, Messrs. Bush, Johnson, Hegner and Anders, returned Tuesday night and have gone back to the mine for the long winter shift." [21]

With subscriber funding and Van Horn and York leadership, tunneling resumed in January 1916. In March the *Lake City Times* reported that "the Ocean Wave Mine forces were increased this week by the addition of Levi Carman to the payroll. This is one of the most encouraging signs of the coming activity on Henson Creek." [22]

Really? One miner, one mine? The editor's bold claim was sad testimony to the overall economic condition of the region which was not lost on Cousin Harry. On March 19th he was moved to write A.E., no longer in a position to insist on timely reporting. After apologizing for not writing sooner, and providing a diversionary weather report—no train out of Lake City since the last day of February due to heavy snows—Harry got down to business. He also was mindful to mention tantalizing fresh clues.

> *When I arrived here nearly two weeks ago the vein was tight and hard, but the very next day it began to get wider and softer. On the 2nd of March a little ore came in, and the vein continued to widen with every round of shots, until it was fully six feet wide. What ore there was went to the footwall, there is about four inches of very good looking ore, but the footwall is now turning out so fast that we could not take it all, and for the last two or three days have been following the hanging and leaving the rest, thinking that perhaps it will turn back in again a little farther ahead; if not, a little later we will come back and shoot into the foot as we are desirous of making room for a switch anyway.*
>
> *A few days ago the showing looked very encouraging indeed, but the breast is not looking so good today; I should judge the vein at the breast is fully ten feet wide now. Water ran from one hole quite freely yesterday, but not so much today. During the week we have saved out of what little ore we had, between two and three tons of a very good looking product. The breast of the drift is now in approximately 1060 feet.* [23]

Van Horn ended his letter with a request that Brad order more rails and stating that he was awaiting an assay report on ore sent a couple of weeks earlier. Unexplainedly, three months later Van Horn appeared to end his involvement with the project. Maybe the results of the assay were poor, we do not know. What we do know is that in a June 20, 1916, letter to "Officers and Directors of the Ocean Wave Mining & Reduction Company," he stated that he was not going to exercise his option to buy the company for $100,000. Instead, he would allocate his 25,000 shares (all that he had to show for his initial $25,000 cash investment) to his partners. Where he was located when he wrote this was not stated but most likely it was not Henson Canyon. We learn this from an unexpected source. In July, F.S. Williams penned a note to Van Horn advising him that he was owed $629.25. Williams operated a coal, hay, and grain hauling business. He apparently tried to collect in person for hauling coal without success, further advising

Van Horn that there was no one at the "Ocean Wave Camp ... as the men have about all gone away." [24]

An unpaid creditor was nothing unusual in Western mining circles, certainly not in this phase of A.E. Reynolds' mining legacy. Surprisingly, neither did this sort of bad behavior seem to discourage investors in Reynolds' projects. Contrary to Williams' observation that there was no one at the "Ocean Wave Camp," steady work for some portion of the summer by John York and his skeleton crew was evident by the additional footage in the Ocean Wave drift. Likewise, the presence of Rowland Ewart, sometimes cook, sometimes miner, sometimes watchman, and his family also suggested otherwise. [25]

Evidence of ongoing work at the Vermont/Ocean Wave surfaced in other forms. On September 8, 1916, Reynolds dispatched a "circular letter to stockholders of the Ocean Wave Mining & Reduction Co. advising that further investment would yield "a good mine." His three-page letter summarized the project well:

1) In the fall of 1899 with investor funds he created the company; 2) Reynolds Tunnel was driven 1200 feet to cut the Vermont-Ocean Wave vein. Work was discontinued in 1901 "owing to the fact that the money expended was in excess of the capital provided, and the property has laid idle for a term of years;" 3) "In April 1914 I made a contract with Mr. Harry Van Horn to expend $25,000... this work has been completed, and the work has been continued;" 4) In total Van Horn has spent between $34,000 and $35,000, "and the excess above the $25,000 is now due;" 5) "I [Reynolds] am trying to raise another $150,000 to pay debts and continue;" 6) Original estimate of length

Close Quarters. View of Rowland Ewart's Vermont kitchen. Wife Kate is standing to his right, identity of the others unknown. *(Courtesy of Bill & Inez Ewart)*

of the Ocean Wave drift to reach rich ore is 1500 feet. Current length of the drift is 1200 feet. The vein is 500 feet above the drift. The crew has ore for the past 250 feet and propose tunneling another 800–1000 feet since they "have ore in the face of the work at present." [26]

Further light had been shed on work progress and lack thereof in the absence of adequate funding. Unstated, still more encouraging clues argued for continuing the hunt, and for sustaining his belief that the Vermont and Ocean Wave properties remained his best chance to regain his fortune and preserve his reputation. As for John York and crew, they seemed to share Reynolds' vision despite discouraging signs. They had contributed hard cash and hard labor in return for nothing more than a promise of profits from future ore sales, always a doubtful proposition. Closely related, bills went unpaid and trusting suppliers and Lake City merchants had allowed debts to mount to troubling heights. When A.E. wrote his update, the project was idle and the boys had retreated to familiar Creede and Lake City haunts. A.E. was not dissuaded. What was another setback was but a temporary challenge. At times like this, A.E. was accustomed to enlisting support from trusted associates and family. On October 7, 1916, A.E. reached out to Cousin Harry.

In preparing to go ahead with the work on the Ocean Wave Mining Company's property, which has up to this time been developed chiefly by yourself and associates under a working agreement, it is necessary to dispose of more stock for the purpose of carrying on said work. [27]

"Preparing to go ahead with the work…" Was he serious? Yes, he was. The Reynolds Tunnel should pay as handsomely as his Revenue Tunnel had paid. He believed that. Doing so was just taking longer (a lot longer) than expected. In all sincerity, innocence, or naivety (you decide), A.E. proposed that the current investors buy additional shares for $0.50/share to complete another 500 feet of drift. Not doubting for a moment that Cousin Harry would respond favorably, he continued:

The situation presents itself to me about as follows: That you have carried on this work now until it has been determined that this vein is mineralized to the depth of this tunnel, and presumably to an indefinite depth below, and that you are just now approaching the part of the vein which is mineralized and that all of the ground which contained mineral in the old workings above is still ahead of you and will mostly fall within the next 500 feet. [28]

A.E. further proposed paying $11.00 a running foot for 500 feet. The crew would provide "ammunition and power," the company would provide rails, power pipe, and "if it becomes necessary, ventilating pipe and fan, the same to be placed by you… the drift to be kept the full size of the one you have heretofore run (a comfortable five foot wide by eight feet high) and to be run on a proper and uniform grade for economical working (meaning slight downhill slope to lessen effort required to move heavy ore cars.)" [29]

Reynolds could not help himself. His tried and true business model which had worked so well in decades past was again in play. And not unexpectedly, he could not let go of this project. He had appreciated for some time that it was his best chance to redeem his reputation and rebuild his fortune. It also may have begun to dawn on him that it also was his last chance—he was getting old and feeling it. Ever the optimist and shrewd gambler, he believed that the geology that G. Thomas Ingham and Ovando Hollister taught pointed to vast reserves before them. If for no other reason than pride, and of course a shortage of personal funds, he also was confident he could deftly side-track disappointments of the past and once again make a strong case for someone else's money. He did not have to wait long to find out if his instincts were still keen. Cousin Harry responded from Creede within the week.

> *I have taken up the matter contained in your letter in regard to the Ocean Wave mine, with the boys here, with the following results. J.F. Wilson agrees to take additional $500 of stock at $0.50 per share; J. E. York is in for $250; Alfred Johnson is in for $125. D.H. McCullock, J.D. Bush and G. J. Hegner are out. York and Johnson are eager to start work on a contract or daily pay basis. Lee Carmen who is employed there earlier will make one crew "to get started."*
>
> *It will take two men three or four days to clean up the tunnel, lay track and pipe, and place a small dam in the creek to hold water for the boiler, and I have planned for York and Johnson to leave here on the 22nd reaching the mine on the 25th and get everything ready for operation the 1st of November. [Why the tunnel needed cleaned up is never explained—perhaps they did no mucking after the last round of charges of the summer campaign, maybe there were "cave-ins."]* [30]

Surely Harry's failure to commit to purchasing additional shares in the project did not escape Reynolds' attention, but there is no record of his reaction and it did not seem to matter. As savvy as Reynolds was, he may have come to terms with the notion some time earlier that reliance on Cousin Harry's patience and goodwill had run its course. The boys' commitments, on the other hand, although a far cry from Reynolds' estimate to complete another five hundred feet of the Ocean Wave drift, was a positive sign regarding not only financing but especially labor. Their commitment was helpful, no question about that—but at the same time, more money would be needed. True to form, Reynolds was confident he could leverage his vast holdings for finances. He also was confident he could hedge his bet knowing where to find more.

On balance, Reynolds' last best chance to make a mine was back on track. With or without Cousin Harry, John York and the boys would do, and sufficient funding would be available when needed. From A.E.'s Denver office perspective, ever the overcomer, the Vermont/Ocean Wave treasure hunt looked more promising than ever.

Notes—Chapter Eleven: Cousin Harry

[1] Darley, George M., *Pioneering in the San Juan*, pg. 65. Also: Smith, P. David and Lyn Bezek, *On the Backs of Burros.*

[2] Scamehorn, Lee, *Albert Eugene Reynolds*, pgs. 176-179. The Ocean Wave Mining and Reduction Company was organized to manage funds and sell stock. Reynolds' cousin is mistakenly named Frank Van Horn. According to archival material, his name is Harry Van Horn.

[3] April 19, 1914, Reynolds Collection, History Colorado Library, MSS 1220, Box 16, FF 1199.

[4] May 12, 1914, MSS 1220, Box 16, FF 1202.

[5] May 16, 1914, MSS 1220, Box 16, FF 1202.

[6] June 17, 1914, MSS 1220, Box 16, FF 1205.

[7] August 11, 1914, MSS 1220, Box 17, FF 1211.

[8] November 11, 1914, MSS 1220, Box 17, FF 1219.

[9] April 22, 1915, MSS 1220, Box 17, FF 1235.

[10] Ibid.

[11] *Silver World*, May 13, 1915.

[12] June 13, 1915, MSS 1220, Box 17, FF 1240.

[13] Ibid.

[14] Ibid.

[15] July 19, 1915, MSS 1220, Box 17, FF 1244.

[16] July 25, 1915, MSS 1220, Box 17, FF 1245.

[17] October 25, 1915, MSS 1220, Box 17, FF 1253.

[18] November 13, 1915, MSS 1220, Box 17, FF 1255.

[19] U.S. Census Bureau; York family online postings.

[20] December 2, 1915, MSS 1220, Box 17, FF 1258.

[21] *Silver World*, January 6, 1916.

[22] *Lake City Times*, March 2, 1916.

[23] March 9, 1916, MSS 1220, Box 17, FF 1271.

[24] July 1916, MSS 1220, Box 17, FF 1285.

[25] *Lake City Times*, September 14, 1916, reprinted in *Silver World*, September 22, 2006.

[26] September 8, 1916, MSS 1220, Box 18, FF 1293.

[27] October 7, 1916, MSS 1220, Box 18, FF 1297.

[28] Ibid.

[29] Ibid.

[30] October 13, 1916, MSS 1220, Box 18, FF 1297.

Bibliography

Bagley, Will, *Overland West* Series, Vol. I, "So Rugged and Mountainous," University of Oklahoma Press, Norman, OK, 2010.

Bagley, Will, *Overland West* Series, Vol. II, "With Golden Visions Bright Before Them," University of Oklahoma Press, Norman, OK, 2012.

Baker, Steven G, *Juan Rivera's Colorado, 1765: The First Spaniards Among the Ute and Paiute Indians on the Trails to Teguayo*, Western Reflections Publishing Company, Lake City, CO, 2015.

Bancroft, Hubert Howe, *History of Colorado*, Western Reflections Publishing Company, Lake City, CO, 2008.

Barry, John M., *The Great Influenza*, Penguin Books, London, England, 2005.

Becker, Cynthia S. and P. David Smith, *The Life & Times of Lafayette Head*, Western Reflections Publishing Company, Lake City, CO, 2019.

Brown, Robert L., *An Empire of Silver*, Caxton Printers, Ltd. Caldwell, ID, 1968.

Bruns, Robert J. *The First We Know: Pioneer History of the San Juans*, unpublished manuscript first cited in Nossaman, Vol. I., pg. 37. San Juans County Historical Society Archival Collections, Silverton, CO.

Burchard, H.C., *1880 Report of the Director of the Mint*.

Burke, Marril Lee, *Ghosts of the Lake Fork Region*, Western Reflections Publishing Company, Lake City, CO, 2009.

Carey, Alex, *Memories, Scenes and Humorous High Lights of Lake City*, unpublished handwritten notes. (Courtesy of Grant Houston, *Silver World*, May 7, 2014.)

"Central City—Black Hawk Historic District," December 14, 2019, Colorado Encyclopedia, (https://coloradoencyclopedia.org/article/central-city).

"Central City, Colorado—Boom & Bust," *Legends of America*, (https://www.legendsofamerica.com/co-centralcity/).

Chamberlin, Rollin T., "Memorial to William Frank Eugene Gurley," *Proceedings Volume of the Geological Society of America, Annual Report for 1943*, April 1944.

Colorado Mining Directories, History Colorado, Denver, Colorado.

Corbett, Thomas B., *The Legislative Manual of the State of Colorado*, Denver Times Publishing House and Bindery, First Edition, Denver, CO., 1877.

Creede Candle, February 14, 1920.

Curry, Thomas Sherrod III, *"San Juans Scenery the Result of Successive Eruptions, Erosion,"* *Silver Thread Scenic & Historic Byway*, Summer, 2007.

Darley, George M., *Pioneering in the San Juans*, Fleming H. Revell Company, 1899. (Community Presbyterian Church of Lake City, CO, reprint, 1986).

Ellis, Richard N., "The Spanish," *The Western San Juans Mountains*, Rob Blair, ed., University Press of Colorado, Niwot, Colorado, 1996.

Everhart, William C., ed., *The Mining Frontier*, U.S. Department of the Interior, National Park Service, Region Four, San Francisco, CA, 1959.

Fossett, Frank, Colorado, *Its Gold and Silver Mines, Tourist's Guide to the Rocky Mountains*, C.G. Crawford, Printer and Stationer, New York, 1879.

Frajola, R., "Transcontinental Pony Express: April 1860 to October 1861," May 2006. (https://rfrajola.com/pony/page1_1.htm.).

Gehling, Richard, *The Pikes Peak Gold Rush* Online: (https://sites.google.com/site/pikespeakgoldrush/a,) 2009.

Genealogy Trails History Group, "Jefferson County, Colorado, Genealogy and History." (https://genealogytrails.com/colo/jefferson/).

Gibbons, Rev. J. J., *In the San Juans, 1898 Sketches*, Calumet Book & Engraving Co., Chicago, IL, 1898 (St. Patrick's Parish, Telluride, CO, 1972).

Gurley, Albert E., *The History and Genealogy of the Gurley Family*, Willimantic, CT.

Hall, Frank, *History of the State of Colorado*, Vols. II and IV., Western Reflections Publishing Company, Lake City, Colorado, reprint of The Blakely Printing Company, Chicago, IL, 1895.

Henderson, Charles W., *Mining in Colorado: A History of Discovery*, USGS Professional Paper 138, Washington, D.C. GPO, 1926.

History Colorado, Stephen H. Hart Research Center, *Reynolds Collection*, Manuscript (MSS) 1220, Denver, CO [numerous citations].

Hollister, Ovando James, *The Mines of Colorado*, Promontory Press, New York, 1974. (Original: Samuel Bowles & Company, Springfield, MA,1867).

Ingham, G. Thomas, *Digging Gold Among the Rockies*, Western Reflections Publishing Company, Lake City, CO, 2008.

Irving, John Duer and Howland Bancroft, *Geology and Ore Deposits Near Lake City, CO*, USGS Bulletin 478, GPO Washington, D.C. 1911.

Lake City Phonograph, Lake City, CO (numerous citations).

Lake City Silver World, Lake City, CO (numerous citations).

Lake City Times, Lake City, CO (numerous citations).

L.A. Vinton & Co., *Resources & Mineral Wealth of Hinsdale County, Colorado*, Lake City, CO 1895.

Lipman, Peter W., Thomas A. Steven, Robert G. Luedke, and Wilbur S. Burbank, "Revised Volcanic History of the San Juan, Uncompahgre, Silverton, and Lake City Calderas in the Western San Juan Mountains, Colorado, *Journal of Research of the U.S. Geological Survey*, November-December 1973, Volume 1, Number 6, U.S. Department of the Interior, Washington, D.C.

Morse, Milo and Fay Bielser, *A Brief History of Mining in Hinsdale County*, B&B Printers, Gunnison, CO, 2000.

Nossaman, Allen, *Many More Mountains*, Vol. 1, Sundance Books, Durango, CO, 2006.

O'Rourke, Paul M., *Frontier in Transition: A History of Southwestern Colorado*, U.S. Bureau of Land Management, No. 10, Colorado State Office, Denver, CO, 1980.

Ouray *Plaindealer*, February 22, 2013.

Paul, Rodman W., *The Far West and the Great Plains in Transition 1859-1900*, Harper & Row, New York, 1988.

Paul, Rodman W., *Mining Frontiers of the Far West 1848-1880*, Holt, Rinehart and Winston, New York, 1963.

Paulson, Don, Curator, Ouray County Historical Society, Ouray County *Plaindealer*, February 22, 2013.

Pettit, Jan, *Utes, The Mountain People*, "Introduction by Eddie Box," Johnson Books, Boulder, CO, 1990.

Pioneers of the San Juans Country, Vols. I-III, Sarah Platt Decker Chapter, D.A.R., Durango, Colorado, The Out West Printing and Stationary Company, Colorado Springs, CO, 1942.

Poxson, Ben, *A Reminiscence*, Chronicles Publishing Company, San Francisco, CA, 1988.

Rand Drill Company, *Illustrated Catalog*, Rand Drill Company, New York, NY, 1886.

Reck, Jamie and Kevin Alexander, Ph.D., *Henson Creek Watershed Analysis*, United States Environmental Protection Agency, Denver, CO, 2007.

Reynolds Collection (MSS 1220), History Colorado Library, Denver, CO.

Rickard, T. A., *Across the San Juans Mountains*, Bear Creek Publishing Company, Ouray, CO, 1980.

Sagstetter. Elizabeth M. and William E., *The Mining Camps Speak*, Benchmark Publishing of Colorado, Denver, CO, 1998.

Scamehorn, Lee, *Albert Eugene Reynolds, Colorado's Mining King*, University of Oklahoma Press, Norman, OK, 1995.

Smith, Duane A., *San Juans Gold: A Mining Engineer's Adventures, 1879-1881*, Western Reflections Publishing Company, Montrose, CO, 2002.

Smith, Duane A., *Song of the Hammer and Drill*, University Press of Colorado, Boulder, CO, 2000.

Smith, Duane A., *The Trail of Gold and Silver*, University Press of Colorado, Boulder, CO, 2009.

Smith, P. David, *Mountains of Silver*, Western Reflections Publishing Company, Montrose, CO, 2004.

Smith, P. David, *The Story of Lake City*, Western Reflections Publishing Company, Lake City, CO, 2016.

Sprague, Marshall, *The Great Gates*, Little, Brown & Company (Canada) Limited, Toronto, 1964.

Steele, Joe M, *Guide to Lake City Geology*, B&B Printers, Gunnison, CO, 2002.

Steven. T.A., P.W. Lipman, F.S. Fisher, C.L. Bieniewski, and H.C. Meeves, *Mineral Resources of Study Areas Continuous to the Uncompahgre Primitive Area, San Juans Mountains, Southwestern Colorado*, USGS Bulletin 1391-E, GPO, Washington, D.C., 1977.

Stone, Wilbur Fisk, ed., *History of Colorado*, Vol. II, S.J. Clarke Publishing Co, Chicago, IL, 1918.

Tucker, E.F., *Otto Mears and the San Juans*, Western Reflections Publishing Company, Montrose, CO, 2003.

Twitty, Eric, *Basins of Silver*, Western Reflections Publishing Company, Lake City, CO, 2008.

Twitty, Eric, *Blown to Bits in the Mine*, Western Reflections Publishing Company, Lake City, CO, 2001.

Twitty, Eric, *Inventory of Select Historic Sites, Hinsdale County, Colorado*, Hinsdale County Commission, 2009. (Unpublished manuscript on-file in Hinsdale County Administrator's office.)

Twitty, Eric, *Riches to Rust*, Western Reflections Publishing Company, Montrose, CO, 2002.

U.S. Department of the Interior, National Park Service, National Register of Historic Places.

Vandenbusche, Duane and Grant Houston, *Images of America, Lake City*, Arcadia Publishing, Charleston, SC, 2019.

Wagner. Sandra with Pete and Lindsey Leavell, *4UR Ranch, A History*, The History Press, Charleston, SC, 2020.

Wikipedia (numerous citations).

Wills, Thomas, "A Short History of Hotchkiss, Colorado, https://gregstratman.com/A-Short-History-of-Hotchkiss-Colorado.

Wright, Carolyn and Clarence, *Tiny Hinsdale of the Silvery San Juans*, Big Mountain Press, 1964.

Index